Costume Society of America Series

Also in the Costume Society of America Series

As Seen in Vogue: A Century of American Fashion in Advertising
DANIEL DELIS HILL

A Separate Sphere: Dressmakers in Cincinnati's Golden Age
CYNTHIA AMNÉUS

Historic Fashion Calendar Series
EDITED BY SALLY QUEEN

Costume in the Performing Arts, 2007
Western Wear, 2006
Shoes, 2005
Wedding Dress, 2004
Underwear, 2003
Embellishment, 2002

Clothing and Textile Collections
in the United States

  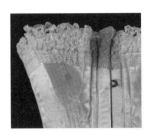

CLOTHING and TEXTILE COLLECTIONS
in the UNITED STATES

A CSA Guide

Edited by Sally Queen and Vicki L. Berger

Texas Tech University Press

This book is typeset in Adobe Garamond. The paper used in this book meets the minimum requirements of ANSI/NISO Z39.48-1992 (R1997).∞

Printed in the United States of America

06 07 08 09 10 11 12 13 14 / 9 8 7 6 5 4 3 2 1
SB

Texas Tech University Press
Box 41037
Lubbock, Texas 79409-1037 USA
800.832.4042
ttup@ttu.edu
www.ttup.ttu.edu

Library of Congress Cataloging-in-Publication Data

Clothing and textile collections in the United States : A CSA Guide / edited by Sally Queen and Vicki L. Berger.

   p. cm. — (Costume Society of America series)
   Summary: "This Costume Society of America guide to clothing and textile collections in the United States lists 2,604 collections whose holdings include general clothing, costumes, uniforms, accessories, banners, flags, quilts. Entries include extended descriptions of holdings for more than 800 collections and black and white photographs for 245 collections"—Provided by publisher.

   Includes bibliographical references and index.
   ISBN-13: 978-0-89672-572-0 (pbk. : alk. paper)
   ISBN-10: 0-89672-572-3 (pbk. : alk. paper) 1. Clothing and dress—Collectors and collecting—United States—Directories. 2. Fashion—Collectors and collecting—United States—Directories. 3. Costume museums—United States—Directories. 4. Textile museums—United States—Directories. I. Queen, Sally. II. Berger, Vicki L. III. Costume Society of America. IV. Series.
   GT605.C56 2005
   391'0075—dc22   2005030999

CREDITS, FRONT COVER

Top row, left to right

Detail, inaugural ball gown for First Lady Dorothy Macaulay Martin, 1985. Courtesy of North Carolina Museum of History.

Detail, chasuble, circa 1700–1710. Courtesy of Legion of Honor, Fine Arts Museums of San Francisco.

Woman's brooch, blue enamel leaf, circa 1840–1860. Courtesy of National Museum of American History, Smithsonian Institution, Behring Center.

Detail, jacket of William C. "Buffalo Bill" Cody, circa 1890s. Courtesy of Buffalo Bill Museum and Grave.

Detail, evening dress from Charles James, 1956. Courtesy of Cincinnati Art Museum.

Middle row, left to right

Cap, white linen, 19th century. Courtesy of Louisiana State Museum.

Woman's boot, circa 1900. Courtesy of Indiana University, Elizabeth Sage Historic Costume Collection.

Detail, pieced star and flag quilt, 1861–1865, made by Martha A. Moore Baker. Courtesy of Connecticut Historical Society Museum.

Detail, shot silk striped and brocaded open robe gown and blue silk petticoat, 1780–1785, Courtesy of Kent State University Museum.

Detail, Hunkpapa Lakota eagle-feather headdress with quillwork, 1884–1885, worn by Chief Rain In The Face. Standing Rock Reservation, North Dakota. Photograph by Walter Larrimore. Courtesy of National Museum of the American Indian, Smithsonian Institution.

Bottom row, left to right

Detail, Confederate Marine uniform, circa 1862. Courtesy of Atlanta History Center, Military Collection.

Detail, lace from Seenock Lace Company, date unknown. Courtesy of Slater Mill Historic Site.

Detail, flag, circa 1790, hand-woven and hand-sewn. Courtesy of Beaufort Historical Association.

Detail, gown bodice, circa 1857, striped silk taffeta. Courtesy of Valentine Richmond History Center.

Detail, folk costume, early- to mid-nineteenth century. Courtesy of Vesterheim Norwegian-American Museum.

BACK COVER

Top row, left to right

Detail, quilt, circa 1888. Courtesy of International Quilt Study Center, James Collection.

Detail, livery uniform, circa 1895–1920. Courtesy of Staatsburgh State Historic Site.

Detail, young girl's cotton dress, circa 1840. Courtesy of Travellers Rest Plantation and Museum.

Detail, costume for an adolescent from Scheherazade, 1910. Courtesy of Wadsworth Atheneum Museum of Art.

Shoes of Harry S. Truman, 1949. Courtesy of Harry S. Truman National Historic Site.

Bottom row, left to right

Detail, Robe á la Française, English, circa 1750. Courtesy of Metropolitan Museum of Art, Costume Institute.

Detail, figured coverlet, mid-nineteenth century. Courtesy of American Textile History Museum.

Detail, man's waistcoat woven to shape, 1745–1760. Courtesy of Historic Deerfield.

Detail, Thunderbird Chilkat robe woven by Dorica Jackson, 1976, made of mountain goat wool with red cedar bark, 1976. Courtesy of Sitka National Historical Park.

Detail, Baltimore album quilt, 1852, attributed to Mary Simon from Baltimore, Maryland. Courtesy of the Maryland Historical Society

SPINE

Beaded tennis shoes by Teri Greeves, 1999. Courtesy of the Heard Museum.

A WORD TO THE READER

THE COSTUME SOCIETY OF AMERICA (CSA) is pleased to welcome you to the rich world of clothing and textile collections in the United States. Our field guide is part of the CSA series published by Texas Tech University Press. The society is an association of diverse members—curators, conservators, educators, designers, collectors, costume historians, and enthusiasts—who share a common passion. Perhaps you share that passion and are fascinated by exhibits of clothing and costumes, uniforms, accessories such as shoes or jewelry, flags, quilts, and coverlets. Our field guide will lead you to these treasures that our members know about and are excited to share with you.

How did these treasures come to be preserved, studied, and exhibited in the collections listed here? The answer is in any number of ways but surprisingly often from America's own attics and closets. During the twentieth century, many people could more easily afford to replace old items with the latest trends yet could not bring themselves to discard these objects, which went into trunks, boxes, or sacks for storing and thereby survived to reflect more than the material culture of their eras. Some went into museums and historical societies; others to private collectors or small house museums. Many others remain in homes within the family. Owners of such heirlooms, seeking to preserve them, stand also to benefit from the combined expertise represented in this guide.

While the community of U.S. collections is strong in twentieth-century objects, there is also a wealth of American and international objects from the eighteenth and nineteenth centuries, or even earlier. They continue to be preserved and valued for many reasons, some for their historical significance and the stories they tell. Others are saved purely for their art.

This field guide seeks to make known and solidify the community of collections open to the public. Identifying that community has taken many years, starting with the efforts of Elizabeth Ann Coleman and Suman Shenoi to gather information about U.S. and international collections. Sally Queen and Vicki Berger continue the earlier work through America's Closets—a visionary, multipurpose database project to record, track, and share information from collections across the Americas. This first publication from that project focuses on collections within the United States.

Immense resources are needed to support a project and publication of this scope. The Sun-shine Lady Foundation, headed by Doris Buffett, and the Costume Society of America saw the need and graciously lent their support. Sally Queen and Associates put together a dedicated and passionate team who sustain this project and whose efforts produced this book. Their work continues to need the support of others who share their passion.

The Costume Society of America is proud to support this mission. We ask that as you use this guide, you join us in supporting the community of collections that stands to benefit from networking with each other in the common interests of preservation and study. It is through such exchange that other valuable collections may come to light and be included in the next edition.

ROSALYN M. LESTER
President, Costume Society of America
Professor Emeritus, Radford University,
2006

ACKNOWLEDGMENTS

PROJECT THIS SIZE is the work of many people who performed tasks, big and small. The accumulation of the small tasks built a better and more accurate field guide.

We wish to thank the many individuals and organizations who provided moral and financial support. Our advisory team of Alicia Annas, Claudia Kidwell, Harold Mailand, and Rosalyn Lester offered sound advice and valuable direction. The Costume Society of America's leadership team of Donna Locke, Patricia Cunningham, Loreen Finkelstein, and Cornelia Powell guided the process. Kaye Boyer and Kim Righi from the CSA staff helped with technical and procedural matters. Our thanks to Elizabeth Ann Coleman and Suman Shenoi for their 1980s international data gathering and to John Monahan, who retrieved the electronic files for reference materials. Phyllis Specht, CSA series editor, was our biggest cheerleader and counselor from the beginning to the end. Judith Keeling, Kathy Dennis, and the team at Texas Tech University Press supported the concept and pushed to make this title a part of the CSA series. Also at Texas Tech, Barbara Werden and Matt Crawford made the data lively with their graphic design and maps.

A dedicated team worked on the project for over two years: Martha Davis, database developer; Michelle Jankowiak, data entry and verification; and the Arizona team of Roger Berger and Sarah Nucci. Collection data verifiers included Mary Fry, Claudia Kidwell, and Joe Nucci. Thank you to our state editors who helped us find, verify, and contact the collections in their areas: Karen Augusta, Anne Bissionette, Barbara Broudo, Sarah Chupka, Carol D'Angelo, Joyce Donley, Joy Emery, Jane Farrell-Beck, Jennifer Feik, Shelly Foote, Lynn Gorges, Martha Grimm, Janet Hasson, Jan Hiester, Patricia Hunt-Hurst, Claudia Kidwell, Margo Krager, Donna Locke, Jan Loverin, Faye Lovvorn, JoEllen Maack, Harold Mailand, David Newell, Sharon Nucci, Rachel Pannabecker, Wayne Phillips, Julianne Trautmann, Kristen Stalling, and Cindy Stewart.

A special thanks is due Lou Ivey for her careful, detailed, and determined editing of the final document.

Our heartfelt thanks goes to the more than eight hundred curators and collection managers who took the time to tell us about the clothing and textile holdings in their collections and the hundreds of museums and historic sites that shared their images for this guide.

We thank the Costume Society of America, the Sunshine Lady Foundation, and America's Closets for their financial support in the data gathering and publication. Their endorsement of the project and subject importance was a huge boost.

Mostly we thank our husbands, Bruce and Roger, for their patience and support in this huge endeavor.

INTRODUCTION

NO EXPRESSIONS in any culture are more personal than its clothing and textiles. Documenting everything from function to aesthetics, mores to spirituality, occupation to status and personal taste, they embody social narratives—living histories so to speak. Worn and passed down, cut and recut within and over generations, their construction lines (both present and past) map the very bodies of those who wore them. They speak not only of those who caused them to be made up but also those who developed the technology and who processed fibers or developed fabrics and finishes. Their stories belong also to those who designed patterns, prints, or embellishments; and no less to those who did the weaving, printing, cutting, or fashioning. Together clothing and textiles enable us to piece histories, large and small, of individuals and families, regions and nations, economics and economies, labor and class, and not least the ever-fascinating preoccupation with adornment in all its forms.

Community and Purpose

This guide is a product of America's Closets, an ongoing project to identify and promote clothing and textile collections at institutions open to the public. Few institutions are devoted solely to such collections. For that reason many interested individuals may be unaware of valuable holdings at art, history, science, children's, tribal, and military museums, as well as colleges, universities, historical societies, and historic houses. To date, America's Closets has identified in the United States 2,604 collections that preserve clothing, costumes, uniforms, accessories, textiles, flags, and quilts among their permanent collections.

We hope what follows makes the discovery process easier; facilitates exchange among curators, conservators, researchers, educators, students, designers, collectors, and all other interested groups and individuals; and encourages institutions not listed here to make their presence known to America's Closets in the online database at www.americasclosets.com. Most importantly, we hope this guide encourages you to visit and support these collections and institutions.

The *Official Museum Directory*, published annually by the American Association of Museums and National Register Publishing, lists in the 2005 directory over 8,300 museums divided into thirteen types: aquariums, arboretums/botanical gardens, art museums, children's museums, general museums, historic sites/houses, history museums, natural history museums, nature centers, planetariums, science museums/technology centers, specialized museums (circus, fire-fighting, scouting, and many others), and zoos. According to the *Official Museum Directory* the listings are a concise introduction to "our country's diverse community of museums" (p. A2).

This diversity, combined with our own museum visits and teaching experiences, inspired us during the process of collecting information on clothing and textile collections for the field guide. We learned from our respondents that museums may be supported by federal, state, county, city, or tribal governments; by private sources; or by a combination of these. We met dedicated volunteers who manage small historical societies with no paid staff. We also met museum professionals whose institutions

have hundreds of employees. We heard about straightforward governance structures (one board, one institution) as well as complex ones (one governance board, multiple branch museums, each with its own board, guild, and other support groups).

Our conversations support the theory that clothing and textile collections are not pigeonholed in any one type of museum. In fact, what appears to be more important than "type" of museum in locating specific collections is the museum's mission statement. The mission statement drives the collecting policy and plan, which guide curators and acquisition committees in deciding what clothing and textile artifacts to collect. The collection descriptions submitted by our respondents reflect the museums' missions. In many cases, the mission statement is included in the museum's website and will be a beacon to finding a specific collection.

Collections in this guide include smaller ones such as the Historic Hamill House in Georgetown, Colorado, with only seventy items of clothing, accessories, and textiles. Though modest in size, this collection helps illustrate the material culture of gold- and silver-rush Colorado history on a most human scale. Among the larger collections, the Philadelphia Museum of Art holds more than 20,000 objects documenting the art of dress, design, and high fashion past and present.

Make no mistake. This guide is by no means exhaustive. This edition includes only those collections we were able to identify through March 2005. A stepping-off point for further discovery, it lists contact information for 2,604 institutions that make their holdings available to the public through display, special events, programming, exhibitions, websites, or by appointment.

All of the listings have basic contact information. More than eight hundred include detailed information about the range and focus of their collections and access information. By raising the visibility of these U.S. collections and their international treasures of objects, we hope to facilitate visitation and support, study and exchange. So use this guide to meet your needs—to donate your grandfather's World War I uniform, to plan a tour or vacation, or to research and network. However you use it will further our common mission to educate and preserve.

How to Use This Guide

Information in this guide is in two forms: basic contact information and basic contact information plus collection details. Basic contact information was compiled from many public sources. Each institution received a survey asking for more detailed information on the clothing, accessories, uniforms, costumes, general textiles, quilts, and flags in their holdings. The detailed collection information comes from the surveys completed by more than eight hundred curators and collection managers. A few select institutions provided images, so you could see their objects from the comfort of your home or office and be inspired to plan a visit to their next exhibition or a behind-the-scenes look into the "closets."

Updates and revisions—new institution name, new contact person, or detailed collection information and changes—can be submitted at www.americascloset.com.

THE LISTINGS

The information is organized by state. Each chapter begins with a state map with cities marked where collections exist. If a city has more than one institution with collections, it is marked with the number of collections. For example, Indianapolis has eight institutions and is listed as "Indianapolis (8)." The population key helps you know the size of the city—if a small town supports more than one collection, applaud their commitment! Metropolitan areas such as New York City, Chicago, and Los Angeles contain large numbers of collections and cover a large traveling area often with many city names. Additional information is included for these large metropolitan areas. The regional

insert for each map shows neighboring states for planning purposes. The maps are not intended to provide specific directions, so consult other resources for directions and traveling times.

After each state map, cities are listed alphabetically with the institutions listed alphabetically in each city. Some institutions have multiple collections, and each is listed separately if the curator chose to differentiate.

Basic contact information includes name of institution, street address, city, state, zip, phone number, and website address. For example:

Birmingham Museum of Art
2000 8th Avenue North
Birmingham, AL 35203
Tel: 205-254-2566 Fax: 205-254-2710
www.artsbma.org

Detailed information includes the following:

Hours: Days of the week and hours when institution is open to the public. Hours do change, so call ahead or check the institution's website for the latest information. If you want to see specific clothing or textiles, call ahead for an appointment (see Helpful Hints).

Contact: Person who is responsible for access to the collection and collection details. It could be the curator (paid or volunteer), collections manager, or director at a small site where the staff and volunteers wear many hats.

Institution type: Collections are found in a variety of institutions open to the public, including art museums; history museums; historical societies; historic houses; theater museums; or specific collections in federal, state, county, city, or university institutions. Often there are several designations to help you know the type of collection and funding agency.

Collection type: Categories are clothing, accessories, uniforms, costumes, general textiles, quilts, and flags.

Clothing is defined broadly as objects that were worn by people, with general categories of underwear, main wear, and outerwear. Wearable art is included in this category.

Accessories, including hats, gloves, jewelry, purses, pocketbooks, scarves, socks and stockings, belts, and bags, are defined as what was carried or added to clothing for function or decoration. Military accessories are generally called accoutrements.

Uniforms are defined as military and civilian clothing worn specifically for visual job distinction. The largest category is military uniforms and accoutrements.

Costumes are defined as fanciful clothing and ensembles for performance wear, fancy dress, and specific events such as Halloween. Previous to 1950, *costume* was the broad term for all clothing and accessories; however, in the last half of the twentieth century, the definition has evolved from the broader meaning to the more specific. We use it here in the more specific sense.

General textiles is a broad category used to refer to any flat textile, including yard goods and household textiles such as tablecloths, sheets, wall hangings, and rugs. Textiles include unwoven fibers, wool batts, and silkworm cocoons to show the beginnings of cloth and clothing. Textile collections also include fiber art, tapestries, samplers, quilts, and flags.

Quilts and flags are specific objects in the general textile category. The location of these specific objects are of great interest to our readers, and we list them separately for easy access. The quilt category includes quilts for bed coverings and wall art, coverlets, and bedspreads. Flags are flat textiles designed to show affiliation and allegiance.

Description: At the beginning of each description is a date range for objects in the collection, giving a general idea for research and exhibitions. After the date range is a general description of the clothing and textiles provided by the collection contact person. More information might be available on the institution's website.

$:Institutions may charge for exhibitions and study time to underwrite the costs involved for staff and materials. If the listing does not have the dollar sign, watch for a donation basket usually found at the entrance and show your support with a generous contribution.

✍: Indicates the collections where you may make an appointment to look at items in the collection not on exhibit.

THE MAPS

Please note that owing to constraints of format the projections for these maps differ slightly in width and height from the more frequently used Mercater projection and that each state map shows only the cities in which collections are located. Nonetheless they should provide the reader with a clear representation of the following:

- Where cities or towns with collections are in relation to each other
- The relative sizes of the cities or towns in which the collections reside
- Where the major interstates fall

This information should prove to be a valuable trip-planning tool and will provide insight to such things as what amenities might be available in a particular collection's hometown. In addition the regional insets are there to encourage readers to consider collections of interest in nearby states as well as to show the regional divisions of the Costume Society of America, which offers to its members and to the general public a significant resource in networking and in clothing and textile expertise.

Helpful Hints for Behind-the-Scenes Visits

Clothing and textile enthusiasts may wish to expand a self-guided tour of exhibits into a behind-the-scenes appointment to examine artifacts and their documentation. Reasons for such an appointment are as varied as the special interests of the visitors. Family reunion participants might want to visit Uncle Bill's World War I military uniform or Aunt Susie's wedding dress. A designer, dressmaker, or tailor might want to examine and sketch the construction details and techniques of garments or accessories, for example, a 1930s bias-cut gown or a pair of shoes. A researcher might want to study a collection of quilts belonging to a specific family or geographical region. A genealogist might want to see clothing and accessories of a newly found relative.

Advance planning will prepare the way for a more detailed visit. Begin your preparations by mining this field guide for possible museums and historic sites that fit your project. Early on, visit the website of the targeted museum. In addition to standard information such as the physical address and a locator map, you may find a section that describes the artifact collection and references to the clothing and textile holdings. Website visitors may find artifact records, including accession number, several fields of documentation information, and photographs. To win the hearts of the clothing and textile stewards, complete this preliminary research before making contact with the museum.

Look for the staff roster to locate the curator of clothing and textiles or the collections manager. It is the curator's job to provide patron services such as behind-the-scene visits. With your preliminary materials organized and your project goals or request clearly outlined, make contact! Our respondents indicated that two, three, or even four weeks' advance notice is required to prepare for your visit. Ask if the institution charges a fee for such appointments and if photography and sketches are allowed.

After the date is set, assemble the materials necessary to meet the goals of the visit. For the family reunion visit mentioned above, this might mean family genealogy information and a camera. Clothing and textile specialists might bring the following:

camera
laptop
writing tablet
pencils (no ink pens near artifacts, please)
sketch pad and/or graph paper
clean, white, cotton gloves
clean, white, cotton bed sheet to use as a
    table cover
tape measure
magnifying glass
thread counter
other materials related to specific research
    project

Ask the museum for an advance copy of policies, procedures, or guidelines that apply to patron visits.

On the day of the visit, stay in a flexible mode. You may be asked to check some of your belongings at a security office—this is for your protection and the security of the artifacts. You may be working at a table set up in a hallway or in a well-appointed laboratory. A staff member will probably be with you at all times. Photography may or may not be allowed. Hopefully, any museum constraints will be offset by the excitement of examining the Fortuny gown, the World War II military uniform, or the apron made from a feed sack.

After the visit, send a thank-you letter to your host and copy his or her superior. A cash donation, small or large, for acid-free tissue or boxes or other materials needed for the clothing and textile collection would be greatly appreciated by the staff.

The 2,604 institutions listed in this field guide have clothing and textile treasures waiting for you. Use the guide to find them!

Clothing and Textile Collections
in the United States

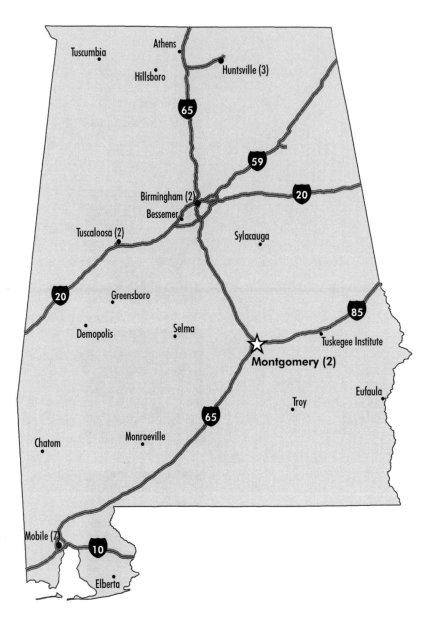

Tuscumbia

Athens

Hillsboro

Huntsville (3)

65

59

Birmingham (2)

20

Bessemer

Tuscaloosa (2)

Sylacauga

20

Greensboro

85

Selma

Demopolis

Tuskegee Institute

☆ Montgomery (2)

Eufaula

Troy

65

Monroeville

Chatom

Mobile (7)

10

Elberta

Population

- • 0 - 50,000
- • 50,001 - 100,000
- ● 100,001 - 250,000
- ● 250,001 - 500,000
- ● > 500,000
- ☆ State Capital

CSA Region VI Southeast

ALABAMA

Alabama Veterans Museum
100 Pryor Street
Athens, AL 35612
Tel: 256-771-7578
www.alabamaveteransmuseum.com

Bessemer Hall of History
1905 Alabama Avenue
Bessemer, AL 35020
Tel: 205-426-1633
www.bhamrails.info/bess_hall_hist.htm

Birmingham Civil Rights Institute
520 16th Street North
Birmingham, AL 35203
Tel: 866-328-9696
www.bcri.bham.al.us

Birmingham Museum of Art
2000 8th Avenue North
Birmingham, AL 35203
Tel: 205-254-2566 Fax: 205-254-2710
www.artsbma.org
Hours: Mon–Sat 11–5 pm, Sun 12–5 pm
Contact: Anne Forschler-Tarrasch
Institution type: Art museum, city museum
Collection type: Clothing, accessories, costumes,
general textiles, quilts
Description: 1750–present. Collection strengths
are late-nineteenth century and early-twentieth
century American costumes and quilts.

✍

Washington County Museum
403 Court Street
Chatom, AL 36518
Tel: 251-847-2201
www.alabamamuseums.org/w_wcm.htm

Bluff Hall Antebellum Home and Museum
405 North Commissioners Avenue
Demopolis, AL 36732-0159
Tel: 334-289-9644

Baldwin County Heritage Museum
25521 U.S. Highway 98
Elberta, AL 36530
Tel: 334-986-8375
www.alabamamuseums.org/b_bchm.htm

Shorter Mansion Museum
340 North Eufaula Avenue
Eufaula, AL 36027
Tel: 334-687-3793
www.eufaulapilgrimage.com

*Detail, crocheted bedspread by Florence Hobson
Morrison, circa 1950. Courtesy of Alabama Historical Commission: Magnolia Grove.*

Magnolia Grove-Historic House Museum

1002 Hobson Street
Greensboro, AL 36744
Tel: 334-624-8618
www.preserveala.org/magnoliagrove.html

Pond Spring, The Wheeler Plantation

12280 Alabama Highway 20
Hillsboro, AL 35643
Tel: 256-637-8513
www.wheelerplantation.org

Burritt on the Mountain

3101 Burritt Drive
Huntsville, AL 35801
Tel: 256-536-2882
www.burrittmuseum.com

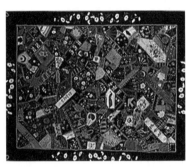

Crazy quilt by Susie Keziah Hobbs Fennell Henderson, 1887. Courtesy of Huntsville Museum of Art.

Huntsville Museum of Art

300 Church Street South
Huntsville, AL 35801
Tel: 256-535-4350 Fax: 256-532-1743
www.hsvmuseum.org
Hours: Mon–Sat 10–5 pm, Thu 10–8 pm, Sun 12–5 pm
Institution type: Art museum
Description: 1850–present
$ ✍🏻

The Veterans Memorial Museum

2060A Airport Road
Huntsville, AL 35801
Tel: 256-883-3737
www.memorialmuseum.org

Conde-Charlotte Museum House

104 Theatre Street
Mobile, AL 36602
Tel: 334-432-1722
www.alabamamuseums.org/c_ccmh.htm

Historic Mobile Preservation Society

350 Oakleigh Place
Mobile, AL 36604
Tel: 251-432-1281
www.historicmobile.org

Mobile Medical Museum

1504 Springhill Avenue
Mobile, AL 36616-1363
Tel: 251-434-5055

Mobile Museum of Art

4850 Museum Drive
Mobile, AL 36608
Tel: 251-208-5200
www.mobilemuseumofart.com

The Museum of Mobile

111 South Royal Street
Mobile, AL 36652
Tel: 251-208-7569 Fax: 251-208-7686
www.museumofmobile.com
Hours: Mon–Sat 9–5 pm, Sun 1–5 pm
Contact: Dave W. Morgan
Institution type: City museum
Collection type: Clothing, accessories, uniforms, costumes, quilts
Description: 1800–present. More than 60,000 total artifacts, including vintage clothing, quilts, silver, and Civil War and Mardi Gras memorabilia.
$ ✍🏻

Richards—DAR House

256 North Joachim Street
Mobile, AL 36603
Tel: 251-208-7320

USS Alabama Battleship Memorial Park

2703 Battleship Parkway
Mobile, AL 36601
Tel: 251-433-2703
www.ussalabama.com

Monroe County Heritage Museum
Old Monroe County Courthouse
Monroeville, AL 36461
Tel: 334-789-2781
www.tokillamockingbird.com

**Alabama Department of
Archives and History**
624 Washington Avenue
Montgomery, AL 36130-0100
Tel: 334-242-4361 Fax: 334-240-3433
www.archives.state.al.us
Hours: Mon–Fri 8:30–4:30 pm
Contact: Robert B. Bradley, Chief Curator
Institution type: History museum, state museum
Collection type: Clothing, accessories, uniforms,
    general textiles, quilts, flags
Description: 1800–present. Collection includes
    household textiles, bedding, civilian clothing,
    military uniforms, flags, and textile working
    tools.
✍

First White House of the Confederacy
644 Washington Avenue
Montgomery, AL 36102-1861
Tel: 334-242-1861

Sturdivant Hall
713 Mabry Street
Selma, AL 36702-1205
Tel: 334-872-5626
www.sturdivanthall.com

**Isabel Anderson Comer Museum
and Arts Center**
711 North Broadway
Sylacauga, AL 35150
Tel: 256-245-4016
www.comermuseum.freeservers.com

Pioneer Museum of Alabama
248 U.S. Highway 231 North
Troy, AL 36081
Tel: 334-566-3597
www.pioneer-museum.org

Paul W. Bryant Museum
300 Bryant Drive
Tuscaloosa, AL 35487
Tel: 205-348-4668
www.bryantmuseum.ua.edu

University of Alabama
Department of Clothing and Textiles
Mary Harman Bryant Building
Tuscaloosa, AL 35487
Tel: 205-348-6396
Hours: By appointment
✍

Alabama Music Hall of Fame
617 Highway 72 West
Tuscumbia, AL 35674
Tel: 256-381-4417
www.alamhof.org

Tuskegee Institute National Historic Site
1212 Old Montgomery Road
Tuskegee Institute, AL 36087-0010
Tel: 334-727-3200
www.nps.gov/tuin

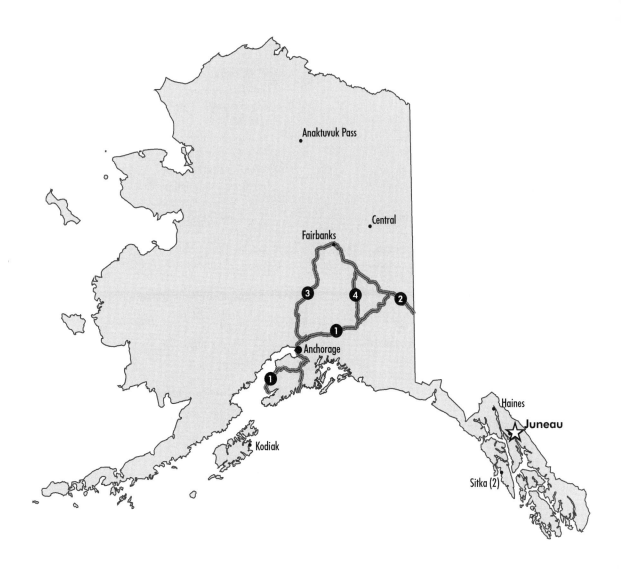

Anaktuvuk Pass

Central

Fairbanks

3   **4**   **2**

1

Anchorage

1

Haines

Juneau

Kodiak

Sitka (2)

Population

● 0 - 50,000

● 50,001 - 100,000

● 100,001 - 250,000

● 250,001 - 500,000

● > 500,000

☆ State Capital

CSA Region V Western

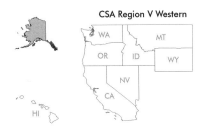

WA

MT

OR   ID   WY

NV

CA

HI

ALASKA

Simon Paneak Memorial Museum
341 Mekiana Road
Anaktuvuk Pass, AK 99721
Tel: 907-661-3413 Fax: 907-661-3414
www.north-slope.org/nsb/55.htm
Hours: Mon–Fri 8:30–5 pm
Contact: Grant Spearman
Institution type: County museum
Collection type: Clothing, accessories
Description: 1961–present. Collection includes a
variety of caribou skin clothing, boots, socks,
mittens, pants, and parkas.
$ ✍

Alaska Aviation Museum
4721 Aircraft Drive
Anchorage, AK 99502
Tel: 907-248-5325
www.alaskaairmuseum.com

Circle Historical Museum
128 Mile Steese Highway
Central, AK 99730
Tel: 907-520-1893

University of Alaska Museum of the North
907 Yukon Drive
Fairbanks, AK 99775
Tel: 907-474-7505 Fax: 907-474-5469
www.uaf.edu/museum
Hours: Mon–Sun, hours vary by season and day

Contact: Molly Lee, Curator and Collections
Manager
Institution type: Art museum, history museum,
university collection
Collection type: Clothing, accessories, uniforms,
costumes, general textiles, flags
Description: 1850–present. The Ethnology Collection contains objects made and used by
Alaska Natives and people from the circum-
polar north from the 1890s to the present,
including clothing, beadwork, ivory carvings,
masks, dolls, basketry, and gear used in subsis-
tence activities. The History Collection has
objects of Western manufacture, including
clothing, goods, folk art, tools, Russian American material, and other memorabilia.
$ ✍

Alaska Indian Arts
Historic Building #13
Haines, AK 99827
Tel: 907-766-2160
www.alaskaindianarts.com/home.html

Alaska State Museum
395 Whittier Street
Juneau, AK 99801
Tel: 907-465-2901
www.museums.state.ak.us
Hours: Mon–Sun 8:30–5:30 pm (Summer);
Mon–Sun 10–4 pm (Winter)
Contact: Curator of Collections

Institution type: History museum, state museum

Collection type: Clothing, accessories, general textiles

Description: 1850–1960. The collection was established on June 6, 1900, when an act of Congress created the Historical Library and Museum for the Territory of Alaska to collect and exhibit objects from the territory. Clothing and accessory items include a medallion presented to Alexander Baranov by Catherine the Great, a tri-corner hat, a brocaded caftan from the 1840s, and material related to Russian exploration.

$ ✑

Baranov Museum

101 Marine Way
Kodiak, AK 99615
Tel: 907-486-5920
www.baranov.us

Nepcetaq (stick or cling to the face) shaman's mask, nineteenth century. Courtesy of Sheldon Jackson Museum

Sheldon Jackson Museum

104 College Drive
Sitka, AK 99835
Tel: 907-747-8981 Fax: 907-747-3004
www.museums.state.ak.us

Hours: Sun–Sat 9–5 pm (Summer); Tue–Sat 10–4 pm (Winter)

Contact: Rosemary Carlton, Curator of Collections

Institution type: State museum

Collection type: Clothing, accessories, general textiles

Description: 1850–1960. Alaska ethnographic

materials made through early twentieth century—tools, equipment, ceremonial regalia, and objects of Alaskan Native culture. Of note is the Eskimo Mask Collection.

$ ✑

Thunderbird Chilkat robe woven by Dorica Jackson, 1976. Courtesy of Sitka National Historical Park.

Sitka National Historical Park

103 Monastery Street
Sitka, AK 99835
Tel: 907-747-0141 Fax: 907-747-0149
www.nps.gov/sitk

Hours: Mon–Sun 8–5 pm

Contact: Sue Thorsen

Institution type: History museum, historic house, federal museum, state museum

Collection type: Clothing, accessories, uniforms, costumes, general textiles, flags

Description: 1850–present. The Russian Orthodox collection includes vestments, altar cloths, and banners. The Tlingit collection includes chilkat robes, beaded robes, appliqué robes, beaded bibs, and shirts.

$ ✑

ARIZONA

Bisbee Mining and Historical Museum
5 Copper Queen Plaza
Bisbee, AZ 85603
Tel: 520-432-7071
www.bisbeemuseum.org

Fort Verde State Historic Park
125 East Holloman
Camp Verde, AZ 86322
Tel: 928-567-3275 Fax: 928-567-4036
www.pr.state.az.us/parks/parkhtml/fortverde.html
Hours: Mon–Sun 8–5 pm
Contact: Nora E. Graf
Institution type: State museum
Collection type: Clothing, accessories, uniforms, general textiles, quilts
Description: 1850–1899. Military uniforms 1860–1880 are the primary focus. Also includes civilian clothing and other items including lacework and quilts.
$ ✍

Cave Creek Museum
6140 East Skyline Drive
Cave Creek, AZ 85327
Tel: 480-488-2764 Fax: 480-595-0838
www.cavecreekmuseum.org
Hours: Wed–Sun 1–4:30 pm
Contact: Collection Manager
Institution type: History museum
Collection type: Clothing, accessories, costumes, general textiles, flags

Description: 1850–present. Oldest object is an 1860 antebellum dress.
$ ✍

Chandler Museum
178 East Commonwealth Avenue
Chandler, AZ 85244
Tel: 480-782-2717 Fax: 480-782-2765
www.chandlermuseum.org
Hours: Tue–Sun 11–4 pm
Contact: Jan Dell, Museum Coordinator
Institution type: History museum
Collection type: Clothing, uniforms, general textiles
Description: 1900–present. Small textile collection of clothing includes dresses from the 1940s to the 1960s, 1920s wedding dresses, and World War II military uniforms.
✍

Slaughter Ranch Museum
6153 Geronimo Trail
Douglas, AZ 85607
Tel: 520-558-2474

The Amerind Foundation
2100 North Amerind Road
Dragoon, AZ 85609
Tel: 520-586-3666
www.amerind.org

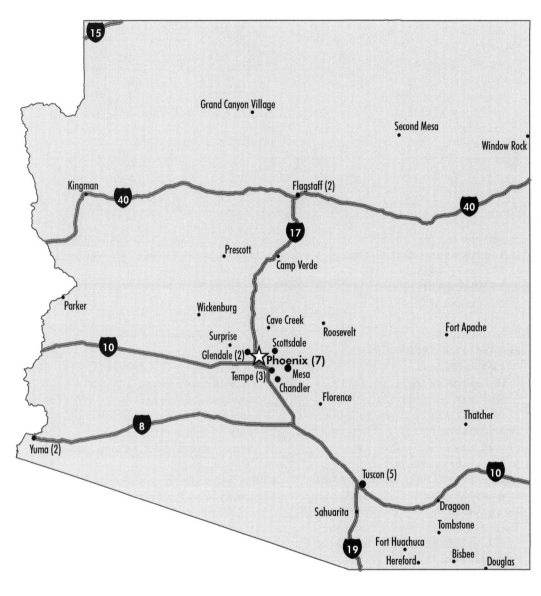

Grand Canyon Village

Second Mesa

Window Rock

Kingman

Flagstaff (2)

40

40

17

Prescott

Camp Verde

Parker

Wickenburg

Cave Creek

Fort Apache

Surprise

Roosevelt

10

Scottsdale

Glendale (2)

Phoenix (7)

Tempe (3)

Mesa

Chandler

Florence

8

Thatcher

Yuma (2)

Tuscon (5)

Dragoon

Sahuarita

Tombstone

10

19

Fort Huachuca

Bisbee

Hereford

Douglas

Population

- • 0 - 50,000
- • 50,001 - 100,000
- ● 100,001 - 250,000
- ● 250,001 - 500,000
- ● > 500,000
- ☆ State Capital

CSA Region VII Southwest

UT | CO | KS
NM | OK
TX

Arizona Historical Society, Flagstaff

2340 North Fort Valley Road
Flagstaff, AZ 86001
Tel: 928-774-6272 Fax: 928-774-1596
www.arizonahistoricalsociety.org
Hours: Mon–Sat 9–5 pm
Contact: Susan Wilcox
Institution type: History museum, historic house, state museum
Collection type: Clothing, accessories, uniforms, costumes, general textiles, quilts
Description: 1850–1960. Items made or used in Northern Arizona: uniforms and costumes, late 1880s–1950s; many hats of all time periods; and some quilts, 1890–1930s.
$ ✍

Museum of Northern Arizona

3101 North Fort Valley Road
Flagstaff, AZ 86001
Tel: 928-774-5213
www.musnaz.org

Pinal County Historical Society and Museum

715 South Main Street
Florence, AZ 85232
Tel: 520-868-4382

Apache Cultural Center and Museum

State Route 73 and Indian Route 46
Fort Apache, AZ 85926
Tel: 928-338-4625
www.wmat.nsn.us
Hours: Mon–Fri 8–5 pm
$ ✍

Fort Huachuca Historical Museum

Boyd and Grierson Street, Bldg. 41401
Fort Huachuca, AZ 85613
Tel: 520-533-3898
http://huachuca-www.army.mil/
history/museum.htm

The Bead Museum

LIESE COLLECTION
5754 West Glenn Drive
Glendale, AZ 85301
Tel: 623-931-2737 Fax: 623-930-8561
www.thebeadmuseum.com
Hours: Mon–Sat 10–5 pm, Sun 11–4 pm

Seed beaded leather apron from Zimbabwe and South Africa, circa 1920. Courtesy of The Bead Museum.

Contact: Karen Karn, Collections Manager
Institution type: History museum, art museum
Collection type: Accessories, general textiles
Description: Pre-1700–present. Several hundred examples of bead jewelry, a few beaded parts of costumes, examples of beaded cloth, and beaded lace. Pieces from around the world dating from 1600 to present, with most items from 1850 to the present.
$ ✍

Historic Sahuaro Ranch

9802 North 59th Avenue
Glendale, AZ 85311
Tel: 623-930-4200 Fax: 623-939-0250
www.sahuaroranch.org
Hours: Wed–Fri 10–2 pm, Sat 10–4 pm, Sun 12–4 pm
Contact: Carole DeCosmo
Institution type: History museum, historic house
Collection type: Clothing, accessories, general textiles, quilts
Description: 1860–1960. Small collection suitable to Arizona historic house. A few clothing items and accessories, earliest dated around 1886. One silk crazy quilt and several pieced everyday quilts common to farm life.
$ ✍

Grand Canyon National Park Museum Collection

Center and Albright Maintenance Area, South Rim
Grand Canyon Village, AZ 86023
Tel: 928-638-7769
www.nps.gov/grca

Coronado National Memorial

4101 East Montezuma Canyon Road
Hereford, AZ 85615
Tel: 520-366-5515
www.nps.gov/coro

Mohave Museum of History and Arts

400 West Beale
Kingman, AZ 86401
Tel: 928-753-3195
www.ctaz.com/~mocohist/museum/index.htm

Mesa Southwest Museum

53 North MacDonald
Mesa, AZ 85201
Tel: 480-644-2230
www.mesasouthwestmuseum.com

Colorado River Indian Tribes Museum

Route 1, Box 23-B
Parker, AZ 85344
Tel: 928-669-9211
www.itcaonline.com/tribes_colriver.html

Arizona Capitol Museum

1700 West Washington Street
Phoenix, AZ 85007
Tel: 602-542-4675 Fax: 602-542-4690
www.lib.az.us/museum
Hours: Mon–Fri 8–5 pm
Contact: Collections Manager
Institution type: History museum, state museum
Collection type: Clothing, accessories, uniforms, costumes, general textiles, flags
Description: 1900–present. An eclectic mix of clothing and textile materials interspersed throughout all the collections.

✑🖂

Hall of Flame Museum of Firefighting

6101 East Van Buren
Phoenix, AZ 85008
Tel: 602-275-3473
www.hallofflame.org

Heard Museum

2301 North Central Avenue
Phoenix, AZ 85004
Tel: 602-252-8840 Fax: 602-252-9757
www.heard.org
Hours: Mon–Sun 9:30–5 pm
Contact: Diana Pardue

Beaded tennis shoes by Teri Greeves, 1999. Courtesy of the Heard Museum.

Institution type: Art museum, history museum
Collection type: Clothing, accessories, costumes, general textiles
Description: 1850–present. More than 1,000 Navajo and Pueblo textiles, Native American clothing from North and Central America, and more than 300 examples of Guatemalan clothing.

$ 🖂

Delphos dress and jacket by Mariano Fortuny, circa 1920s. Courtesy of Phoenix Art Museum.

Phoenix Art Museum

FASHION DESIGN COLLECTION
1625 North Central Avenue
Phoenix, AZ 85004
Tel: 602-257-2119 Fax: 602-253-8662
www.phxart.org

Hours: Tue–Sun 10–5 pm, Thu 10–9 pm
Contact: Dennita Sewell
Institution type: Art museum
Collection type: Clothing, accessories, uniforms
Description: 1700–present. Phoenix Art Museum's Fashion Design Department was founded in 1966. Notable for its broad range and depth, the permanent collection has more than 5,000 objects of men's, women's, and children's dress and accessories. Three exhibits annually in the Fashion Design Gallery.

$ ✍

Phoenix Museum of History

105 North 5th Street
Phoenix, AZ 85004
Tel: 602-253-2734 Fax: 602-253-2348
www.pmoh.org
Hours: Tue–Sat 10–5 pm
Contact: Katherine H. Child
Institution type: History museum
Collection type: Clothing, accessories, uniforms
Description: 1850–1960. Late-1800s to early-1900s dresses and undergarments and World War I and World War II uniforms.

$ ✍

Pioneer Arizona Living History Village

3901 West Pioneer Road
Phoenix, AZ 85086
Tel: 623-465-1052
www.pioneer-arizona.com

Pueblo Grande Museum

4619 East Washington Street
Phoenix, AZ 85034
Tel: 602-495-0901
http://phoenix.gov/PARKS/pueblo.html
Hours: Mon–Sat 9–5 pm, Sun 12–5 pm
Contact: H. Young
Institution type: City museum
Collection type: General textiles
Description: 1850–present. Small collection of Navajo textiles from northeastern Arizona, hand-woven in a variety of styles from 1850 through the late twentieth century.

$ ✍

Sharlot Hall Museum

415 West Gurley Street
Prescott, AZ 86301
Tel: 928-445-3122 Fax: 928-776-9053
www.sharlot.org
Hours: Mon–Sat 10–4 pm (Oct–Mar); Mon–Sat 10–5 pm, Sun 10–2 pm (Apr–Sep)
Contact: Mick Woodcock, Sandra Lynch
Institution type: History museum, historic house, state museum
Collection type: Clothing, accessories
Description: 1850–present. Men's, women's, and children's clothing from 1860s to present, and a small amount of Native American material. Geographic scope of collection is mostly Arizona.

✍

Tonto National Monument

Highway 188
Roosevelt, AZ 85545
Tel: 928-467-2241
www.nps.gov/tont

Titan Missile Museum

1580 West Duval Mine Road
Sahaurita, AZ 85614
Tel: 520-625-7736
Hours: Mon–Sun 9–5 pm
Contact: James Stemm, Assistant Curator
Institution type: History museum
Collection type: Clothing, accessories, uniforms, flags
Description: 1900–present. Uniforms, helmets, patches, and insignia relating to early missile site.

$ ✍

Sylvia Plotkin Judaica Museum

10460 North 56th Street
Scottsdale, AZ 85253
Tel: 480-951-0323
www.spjm.org

Hopi Cultural Center

Route 264
Second Mesa, AZ 86043
Tel: 928-734-6650

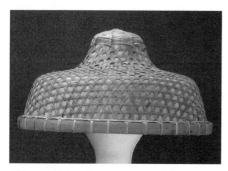

Chinese coolie hat of woven straw, twentieth century. Courtesy of West Valley Art Museum.

West Valley Art Museum

ETHNIC DRESS COLLECTION

17420 North Avenue of the Arts

Surprise, AZ 85374

Tel: 623-972-0635 Fax: 623-972-0456

www.wvam.org

Hours: Tue–Sun 10–4 pm

Contact: Lori Tolzer

Institution type: Art museum

Collection type: Clothing, accessories, general textiles

Description: 1850–present. Collection includes 4,000 artifacts. Categories consist of ethnic dress, international costume, and international textiles, along with paintings, prints, drawings, and sculpture. The main focus of the ethnic dress and international costume collection is the Asian countries, South America, and Africa, with other examples from around the globe. The textile collection focuses mainly on African countries.

$ ✍

Square dance dress, circa 1950. Courtesy of Arizona Historical Society Museum at Papago Park.

Arizona Historical Society Museum at Papago Park

1300 North College Avenue

Tempe, AZ 85281

Tel: 480-929-0292 Fax: 480-967-5450

www.arizonahistoricalsociety.org

Hours: Tue–Sat 10–4 pm, Sun 12–4 pm

Contact: David Tatum, Chief Curator

Institution type: History museum, state museum

Collection type: Clothing, accessories, uniforms, costumes, quilts

Description: 1850–present. Representing Arizona's territorial period through the twentieth century, the collection includes men's and women's formal, business, recreational, military, professional sports, casual wear, and local TV production costumes. Approximately 350 pieces of clothing plus accessories.

$ ✍

Arizona State University Museum of Anthropology

ASU, Anthropology Building, Room 240

Tempe, AZ 85287-2402

Tel: 480-965-6224

www.asu.edu/museums

Hours: Mon–Fri 11–3 pm

$ ✍

Tempe Historical Museum

809 East Southern Avenue

Tempe, AZ 85282

Tel: 480-350-5100 Fax: 480-350-5150

www.tempe.gov/museum

Graham County Historical Society

3430 West Highway 70

Thatcher, AZ 85546

Tel: 928-348-0470

www.rootsweb.com/~azgraham/museum.html

Tombstone Courthouse State Historic Park

219 Toughnut Street

Tombstone, AZ 85638

Tel: 520-457-3311

www.azstateparks.com

Arizona Historical Society, Tucson
949 East 2nd Street
Tucson, AZ 85719
Tel: 520-628-5774 Fax: 520-629-8966
www.arizonahistoricalsociety.org
Hours: Mon–Sat 10–4 pm
Contact: Laraine Daly Jones
Institution type: History museum, historic house, state museum
Collection type: Clothing, accessories, uniforms, general textiles, quilts
Description: Pre-1700–1960. More than 5,000 pieces interpreting the history of Arizona and northern Mexico, from the Spanish arrival in 1540 through 1960. Strengths include women's clothing 1875–1950, with the Cele Peterson Collection emphasizing the mid-twentieth century. U.S. military uniforms and accoutrements 1846–1916, including rare Topographical Engineers and Mounted Rifles uniforms, 100 quilts, 10 silk Mantones de Manila, and 50 Navajo rugs. A technical library and research archive with more than 1 million photographic images complement the costume collection.
$ ✍

Arizona State Museum
CORDRY MEXICAN INDIAN COSTUME COLLECTION
1013 East University Boulevard
Tucson, AZ 85721
Tel: 520-621-6302 Fax: 520-621-2976
www.statemuseum.arizona.edu
Hours: Mon–Sat 10–5 pm, Sun 12–5 pm
Contact: Diane Dittemore
Institution type: State museum
Collection type: Clothing, accessories, costumes
Description: 1850–present. Artifacts focus on Southwestern archaeology and ethnology. Costumes include several hundred Plains dresses, vests, moccasins, leggings, and pipe bags. Collection also includes Apache, Navajo, South American, Filipino, Chinese, and Mexican traditional clothing, numbering around 100. Objects date from 1890 through the 1960s.
$ ✍

Pima Air and Space Museum
6000 East Valencia Road
Tucson, AZ 85706

Tel: 520-574-0462 Fax: 520-574-9238
www.pimaair.org
Hours: Mon–Sun 9–5 pm
Contact: James Stemm, Assistant Curator
Institution type: History museum
Collection type: Clothing, accessories, uniforms, flags
Description: 1900–present. Uniforms, helmets, uniform accessories, patches, and insignia.
$ ✍

Tucson Museum of Art and Historic Block
140 North Main Avenue
Tucson, AZ 85701
Tel: 520-624-2333
www.tucsonarts.com

Western Archeological and Conservation Center, National Park Service
255 North Commerce Park Loop
Tucson, AZ 85745
Tel: 520-670-6501 Fax: 520-670-6525
Hours: Mon–Fri 8–4 pm
Contact: Curator, Museum Collections Repository
Institution type: History museum, federal museum
Collection type: Clothing, accessories, general textiles, quilts
Description: Pre-1700–present. Prehistoric and historic items from collections of national parks and monuments of the Southwest United States. The main prehistoric collection is from Canyon de Chelly National Monument. The main historic collection is from Faraway Ranch, Chiricahua National Monument.
✍

Desert Caballeros Western Museum
21 North Frontier Street
Wickenburg, AZ 85390
Tel: 928-684-2272
www.westernmuseum.org

Navajo Nation Museum
Highway 264 and Post Office Loop Road
Window Rock, AZ 86515
Tel: 928-871-7941

Arizona Historical Society, Yuma

240 Madison Avenue

Yuma, AZ 85364

Tel: 928-782-1841 Fax: 928-783-0680

www.arizonahistoricalsociety.org

Hours: Tue–Sat 10–4 pm

Contact: Carol Brooks

Institution type: History museum, historic house, state museum

Collection type: Clothing, accessories, uniforms, costumes

Description: 1800–1960. Clothing from 1800s to 1940s and military and railroad uniforms in a range of sizes and conditions.

$ ✍

Yuma Territorial Prison State Historic Park

1 Prison Hill Road

Yuma, AZ 85364

Tel: 928-783-4771

www.pr.state.az.us

Old Independence Regional Museum

380 South 9th Street

Batesville, AR 72501

Tel: 870-793-2121 Fax: 870-793-2101

www.oirm.org

Hours: Tue–Sat 9–4:30 pm, Sun 1:30–4 pm

Contact: Twyla Wright

Institution type: History museum

Collection type: Clothing, accessories, uniforms, general textiles

Description: 1850–present. Museum houses a small collection with an assortment of clothing and textile objects from North Arkansas, including a man's waistcoat; a nurse's uniform; women's hats, purses, gloves, shoes, and clothing; baby clothes; and military uniforms.

$

Heritage Center Museum

403 Public Square

Berryville, AR 72616

Tel: 870-423-6312

Prairie County Museum

2009 West Main Street

Des Arc, AR 72040

Tel: 875-256-3711

Desha County Museum

Highway 54

Dumas, AR 71639

Tel: 870-382-4222

Gay Nineties Button and Doll Museum

338 Onyx Cave Lane

Eureka Springs, AR 72632

Tel: 479-253-9321

University of Arkansas Collections

Biomass 125, 1 University of Arkansas

Fayetteville, AR 72701

Tel: 479-575-3456 Fax: 479-575-7464

www.uark.edu/~arsc/collections

Hours: By appointment

Contact: Mary Suter

Institution type: University collection

Collection type: Clothing, quilts, flags

Description: 1850–present. Collection includes Arkansas associated quilts from the 1880s to the present and clothing and costumes from the late 1800s to the late 1900s.

Fort Smith Museum of History

320 Rogers Avenue

Fort Smith, AR 72901

Tel: 479-783-7841

www.fortsmithmuseum.com

Arkansas Post Museum

5530 Highway 165 South

Gillett, AR 72055

Tel: 870-548-2634 Fax: 870-548-3003

www.arkansasstateparks.com/parks/park.asp?id=45

Hours: Mon–Sat 8–5 pm, Sun 1–5 pm

Contact: Thomas E. (Pete) Jordon, Director

Institution type: State museum

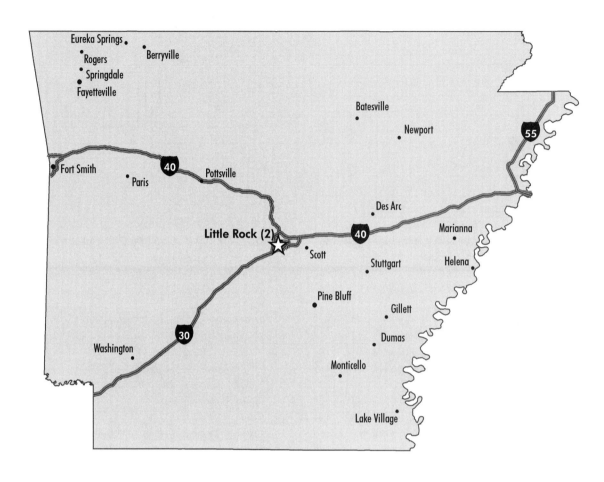

Eureka Springs
Rogers
Springdale
Fayetteville
Berryville

Batesville
Newport

55

Fort Smith
Paris
40
Pottsville

Des Arc

40

Marianna

Little Rock (2)
Scott
Stuttgart
Helena

Pine Bluff
Gillett

30
Dumas

Washington
Monticello

Lake Village

Population

• 0 - 50,000

• 50,001 - 100,000

● 100,001 - 250,000

● 250,001 - 500,000

● > 500,000

☆ State Capital

CSA Region VI Southeast

Collection type: Clothing, uniforms, quilts

Description: 1850–1960. Collection contains clothing, including military uniforms, and quilts from the time of the Civil War to the early twentieth century.

$ 🖊

Phillips County Library and Museum Association

623 Pecan Street
Helena, AR 72342
Tel: 870-338-7790

Hours: Tue–Sat 10–4 pm
Contact: Danielle Burch
Institution type: County museum, city museum
Collection type: Clothing, accessories, uniforms, general textiles
Description: 1800–1960. The museum holds a large collection of women's clothing dating from 1830s through the present and a small collection of men's clothing, including uniforms from World War I and World War II to the present.

🖊

Museum of Chicot County Arkansas

614 Cokley Street
Lake Village, AR 71653
Tel: 870-265-2868

Historic Arkansas Museum

200 East 3rd Street
Little Rock, AR 72201
Tel: 501-324-9351 Fax: 501-324-9345
www.arkansashistory.com

Hours: Mon–Sat 9–5 pm, Sun 1–5 pm
Contact: Bill Worthen, Swannee Bennett, or Patricia Grant
Institution type: Art museum, history museum, historic house, state museum
Collection type: Clothing, accessories, uniforms, general textiles, quilts, flags
Description: Pre-1700–1960. Collection contains 200 Arkansas-made quilts, 1840–1940; clothing from 1830 to the 1940s, including headgear and footwear; jewelry; and Civil War uniforms as part of the overall holdings that include an extensive collection of decorative arts.

🖊

Gown, Hillary Clinton's inaugural dress, 1979. Courtesy of Old State House Museum

Old State House Museum

300 West Markham
Little Rock, AR 72201
Tel: 501-324-8637 Fax: 501-324-9688
www.oldstatehouse.com

Hours: Mon–Sat 9–5 pm, Sun 1–5 pm
Contact: Jo Ellen Maack
Institution type: History museum, state museum
Collection type: Clothing, accessories, costumes, quilts, flags
Description: 1850–present. Begun in 1942, the First Ladies' gowns collection is one of the largest in the country, with objects dating from 1889 to the present. The collection also contains more than 100 quilts made by black Arkansans from the 1890s to the present and Arkansas Civil War battle flags from Arkansas regiments, including the 3rd Confederate Infantry flag that flew over eight Arkansas companies and two Mississippi companies.

$ 🖊

Marianna-Lee County Museum Association

67 West Main Street
Mariannna, AR 72360
Tel: 870-295-2469

Drew County Historical Museum

404 South Main
Monticello, AR 71655
Tel: 870-367-7446

Jacksonport State Park

205 Avenue Street
Newport, AR 72112
Tel: 870-523-2143 Fax: 870-523-4620
www.arkansasstateparks.com/parks/park.asp?id=17
Hours: Tue–Sat 8–5 pm, Sun 1–5 pm
Contact: Donna Bentley
Institution type: History museum, historic house,
state museum
Collection type: Clothing, accessories, uniforms,
general textiles, quilts, flags
Description: Pre-1700–present. Clothing, flags,
uniforms from the Civil War to Vietnam,
shoes, quilts, and other objects such as saddles
and china.
$ 🖊

Logan County Museum

202 North Vine Street
Paris, AR 72855
Tel: 479-963-3936

Pine Bluff and Jefferson County Historical Museum

201 East 4th Street
Pine Bluff, AR 71601
Tel: 870-541-5402

Potts Inn Museum

Town Square
Pottsville, AR 72801
Tel: 501-968-1877

Rogers Historical Museum

322 South 2nd Street
Rogers, AR 72756
Tel: 479-621-1154 Fax: 479-621-1155
www.rogersarkansas.com/museum
Hours: Tue–Sat 10–4 pm
Institution type: History museum, historic house,
city museum
🖊

Traveling dress of Mary Van Winkle Steele, circa 1870. Courtesy of Rogers Historical Museum.

Plantation Agriculture Museum

4815 Highway 161
Scott, AR 72142
Tel: 501-961-1409
www.arkansasstateparks.com/parks/park.asp?id=44
Hours: Tue–Sat 8–5 pm, Sun 1–5 pm
Contact: Randy Noah
Institution type: History museum, state museum
Collection type: General textiles, quilts
Description: 1900–1960. Primarily an agricultural
collection with a number of hand tools, culti-
vation implements, cotton gins, mule har-
nesses, and related artifacts as well as quilts and
textiles of the twentieth century.
$ 🖊

Shiloh Museum of Ozark History

118 West Johnson Avenue
Springdale, AR 74764
Tel: 479-750-8165 Fax: 479-750-8693
www.springdaleark.org/shiloh
Hours: Mon–Sat 10–5 pm
Contact: Carolyn Reno, Collections Manager
Institution type: History museum, city museum
Collection type: Clothing, accessories, uniforms,
costumes, general textiles, flags

Description: 1850–present. Clothing and textiles from northwest Arkansas and the Arkansas Ozarks, primarily from the late 1800s through the 1900s, and is part of a larger general collection of historic artifacts.

Museum of the Arkansas Grand Prairie

921 East 4th Street
Stuttgart, AR 72160
Tel: 870-673-7001
Hours: Tue–Fri 8–4 pm, Sat 10–4 pm
Contact: Pat Peacock
Institution type: City museum
Collection type: Clothing, accessories, uniforms, general textiles
Description: 1850–1960.

Old Washington Historic State Park

U.S. 278
Washington, AR 71862
Tel: 870-983-2684 Fax: 870-983-2736
www.oldwashingtonstatepark.com
Hours: Mon–Sun 8–5 pm
Contact: Glenda Friend
Institution type: Historic house, state museum
Collection type: Clothing, accessories, uniforms, general textiles
Description: 1850–1960. Washington was a major stopping point on the Southwest Trail—one of eight major trails that pioneers traveled on their way to Texas and the Great Southwest. Old Washington has thirty original buildings and looks like the town in the mid-nineteenth century. The clothing and textile collection contains primarily women's garments and accessories from the mid-nineteenth century through the twentieth century.

Fall River Mills

Eureka

Redding (2)

Quincy

Downieville

Oroville

Nevada City

Willits

Mendocino

Yuba City

Ukiah (2)

Lakeport

Auburn

Woodland

Placerville

South Lake Tahoe

Calistoga

Davis

Yountville

Sacramento (3)

Sonoma (3)

Vacaville

Lodi

San Andreas

Bridgeport

Columbia

Stockton

Sonora

Greater San Francisco Area (22)

Atwater

Merced

Oakhurst (2)

Santa Cruz

Gilroy

Los Banos

Watsonville

Hollister

Fresno (3)

Pacific Grove

San Juan Bautista

Carmel

Monterey (2)

Hanford

Porterville (2)

King City

Earlimart

San Simeon

Ridgecrest

Atascadero

Bakersfield

San Luis Obispo (2)

Santa Maria

Mission Hills

Lancaster

Lompoc

Santa Ynez

Solvang

Goleta

Fillmore

Newhall

Apple Valley

Santa Barbara (2)

Ojai

Simi Valley

Redlands

Carpinteria

Port

Ventura (2)

Hueneme

Greater Los Angeles Area (41)

Hemet

Temecula

Oceanside

Vista

Julian

San Diego (7)

Coronado

Population

• 0 - 50,000

• 50,001 - 100,000

• 100,001 - 250,000

● 250,001 - 500,000

● >500,000

☆ State Capital

▲ Greater Metropolitan Area

CSA Region V Western

AK

WA

MT

OR

ID

WY

NV

HI

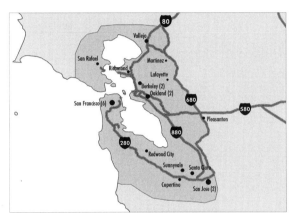

Greater San Francisco Metropolitan Area (22)

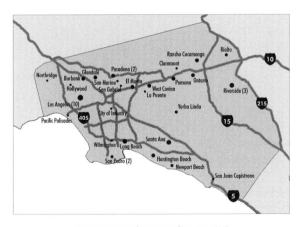

Greater Los Angeles Metropolitan Area (41)

Victor Valley Museum and Art Gallery

11873 Apple Valley Road
Apple Valley, CA 92308
Tel: 270-240-2111
www.vvmuseum.com
Hours: Wed–Sat 10–4 pm, Sun 1–4 pm
$ 🖎

Atascadero Historical Society Museum

6500 Palma Avenue
Atascadero, CA 93422
Tel: 805-466-8341

Castle Air Museum

5050 Santa Fe Drive
Atwater, CA 95301
Tel: 209-723-2178
www.elite.net/castle-air

Placer County Department of Museums

KAISER COLLECTION

101 Maple Street
Auburn, CA 95603
Tel: 530-889-6500 Fax: 530-889-6510
www.placer.ca.gov/museum
Hours: Tue–Sun 11–4 pm
Contact: Curator of Collections
Institution type: History museum, historic house,
county museum
Collection type: Clothing
Description: 1850–1899. Clothing worn by the
Nichols family in Dutch Flat, California,
around 1880–1900. A wedding ensemble worn
by Sarah Olive (Wilson) Nichols is the high-
light.

✍

Kern County Museum

TEXTILE COLLECTION

3801 Chester Avenue
Bakersfield, CA 93301
Tel: 661-852-5000 Fax: 661-322-6415
www.kcmuseum.org
Hours: Mon–Sat 10–5 pm, Sun 12–5 pm
Contact: Jeff Nickell
Institution type: History museum, county
museum
Collection type: Clothing, accessories, uniforms,
costumes, general textiles, flags
Description: 1850–1960. The museum is located
on approximately fourteen acres of land in
Bakersfield, California, and includes more than
fifty historic structures. The textile collection
contains more than 250,000 textiles, photographs, vehicles, implements, and other artifacts representative of Kern County's unique
history.

$ ✍

Judah L. Magnes Museum

2911 Russell Street
Berkeley, CA 94705
Tel: 510-549-6950
www.magnes.org

**Phoebe Apperson Hearst Museum
of Anthropology**

103 Kroeber Hall, University of California
Berkeley, CA 94720-3712
Tel: 510-642-3682
http://hearstmuseum.berkeley.edu

Bodie State Historic Park

Highway 395
Bridgeport, CA 93517
Tel: 760-647-6445
www.parks.ca.gov/?page_id=509

**Theodore Theodosus Museum and
Research Center**

6122 Orangethorpe Avenue Suite 109
Buena Park, CA 90620
Tel: 714-522-1112
Hours: By appointment
Contact: Ted Theodosus Gonzales
Collection type: Clothing, accessories, uniforms,
costumes, general textiles, quilts, flags
Description: 1750–present. California-style
clothing and textiles of all kinds and types, costumes from screen and stage, and Knott Family
and Wrigley Family clothing and others found
in California. This is a private collection with
plans for permanent facility for exhibitions,
study, and educational space. Objects are currently exhibited at local museums and historical properties.

$ ✍

Woodbury University

FASHION STUDY COLLECTION

Fashion Design Department, School of
Architecture and Design
7500 Glenoaks Boulevard
Burbank, CA 91510-7846
Tel: 818-767-0888x239 Fax: 818-504-9320
www.woodbury.edu
Hours: Vary
Contact: Louise Coffey-Webb
Institution type: University collection
Collection type: Clothing, accessories, costumes,
general textiles
Description: 1760–present. Study collection for
undergraduate students. Areas emphasize con-
struction and design elements for fashion and
textiles that support classes in world textiles,
millinery, shoemaking, and costume design as

Costume Academy Award winner for Brothers Grimm, *1962. Courtesy of Woodbury University.*

well as fashion design and marketing. Collection includes clothing, textiles, and fashion archives. Themed displays are changed each semester.

Sharpsteen Museum

1311 Washington Street
Calistoga, CA 94515
Tel: 707-942-5911
www.sharpsteen-museum.org
Hours: Mon–Fri 11–4 pm
Contact: Mary Elizabeth Compton
Institution type: History museum, historic house, city museum
Collection type: Clothing, accessories, uniforms, general textiles, flags
Description: 1850–1914. Objects pertaining to the Upper Napa Valley, Franz Valley, and Knights Valley local history.

Mission San Carlos Borromeo Del Rio Carmelo

3080 Rio Road
Carmel, CA 93923
Tel: 831-624-3600
www.carmelmission.org

Carpinteria Valley Historical Society and Museum of History

956 Maple Avenue
Carpinteria, CA 93013
Tel: 805-684-3112

Workman and Temple Family Homestead Museum

15415 East Don Julian Road
City of Industry, CA 91745-1029
Tel: 626-968-8492 Fax: 626-968-2048
www.homesteadmuseum.org
Hours: Wed–Sun 1–5 pm
Contact: Paul R. Spitzzeri
Institution type: Historic house, city museum
Collection type: Clothing, accessories, general textiles
Description: 1850–1960. Clothing, accessories, and everyday textiles from 1830 to 1930 but mainly centers on materials from the 1920s.

Petterson Museum of Intercultural Art

730 Plymouth Road
Claremont, CA 91711
Tel: 909-399-5544 Fax: 909-399-5508
www.pilgrimplace.org/asp/Site/OurServices/
PettersonMuseum/view.asp
Hours: Fri–Sun 2–4 pm, and by appointment
Contact: Carol Bowdoin Gil
Institution type: Art museum, history museum
Collection type: Clothing, accessories, costumes, general textiles
Description: Pre-1700–present. Artifacts and folk art of many cultures and is especially strong in Chinese costume and textile. Collection also includes Mexican and Guatemalan costume and textiles, art pieces and everyday functional pieces, and many handmade dolls in ethnic dress.

Columbia State Historic Park

22708 Broadway
Columbia, CA 95310
Tel: 209-532-0150
www.parks.ca.gov/default.asp?page_id=552

Museum of History and Art

1100 Orange Avenue
Coronado, CA 92118
Tel: 619-435-7242
www.coronadohistory.org/gallery.html

Cupertino Historical Museum

10185 North Stelling Road
Cupertino, CA 95014
Tel: 408-973-1495

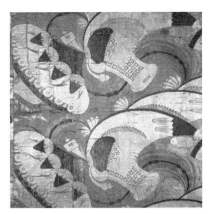

Bizarre silk textile, circa 1705. Courtesy of Design Collection, University of California–Davis.

University of California–Davis, Department of Environmental Design

1 Shields Avenue
Davis, CA 95616
Tel: 530-752-3623 Fax: 530-752-1392
www.ucdavis.edu
Hours: Mon–Thu 9–5 pm
Contact: Adele Zhang
Institution type: University collection
Collection type: Clothing, accessories, uniforms, costumes, general textiles
Description: Pre-1700–present. Historical and ethnographic textiles and costumes dating from the sixteenth century to the present; pieces from Europe and the Americas; and items from the Middle East, India, Indonesia, Asia, and Africa. Significant artifacts include "bizarre" silks; an early-twentieth-century embroidered and appliquéd wool and silk wall hanging from Rasht, Iran; and wearable art.

Downieville Museum

330 Main Street
Downieville, CA 95936
Tel: 530-289-3423

Colonel Allensworth State Historic Park

Star Route 1
Earlimart, CA 93219
Tel: 661-849-3433
www.parks.ca.gov/default.asp?page_id=583

El Monte Historical Society Museum

3150 North Tyler Avenue
El Monte, CA 91731
Tel: 626-444-3813

Clarke Historical Museum

240 East E Street
Eureka, CA 95501
Tel: 707-443-1947
www.clarkemuseum.org
Hours: Tue–Sat 11–4 pm
Contact: Pam Service
Institution type: History museum
Collection type: Clothing, accessories, uniforms, costumes, general textiles, flags
Description: 1850–present. Textiles relating to Humboldt County history.

Fort Crook Historical Museum

Fort Crook Avenue and Highway 299
Fall River Mills, CA 96028
Tel: 530-336-5110
www.geocities.com/ftcrook

Fillmore Historical Museum

350 Main Street
Fillmore, CA 93016
Tel: 805-524-0948

Fresno Metropolitan Museum

1515 Van Ness Avenue
Fresno, CA 93721
Tel: 559-441-1444 Fax: 559-441-8607
www.fresnomet.org

Kearney Mansion Museum

7160 West Kearney Boulevard
Fresno, CA 93706
Tel: 559-441-0862
www.valleyhistory.org/
    KearneyMansionMuseum.html

Meux Home Museum

1007 R Street
Fresno, CA 93721
Tel: 209-233-8007

City of Gilroy Museum

195 5th Street
Gilroy, CA 95020
Tel: 408-848-0470
www.ci.gilroy.ca.us/comserv/rec_museum.html

Casa Adobe de San Rafael

1330 Dorothy Drive
Glendale, CA 91206
Tel: 818-548-2000

Museum of Goleta Valley History

304 North Los Carneros Road
Goleta, CA 93117
Tel: 805-964-4407
www.goletahistory.org

Hanford Carnegie Museum

109 East 8th Street
Hanford, CA 93239
Tel: 209-584-1367

Hemet Museum

100 State Street
Hemet, CA 92346
Tel: 909-929-4409
www.hemetmuseum.org

San Benito County Historical Society Museum

498 5th Street
Hollister, CA 95024
Tel: 831-635-0335
www.sbchistoricalsociety.org

Hollywood Heritage Museum

2100 Highland Avenue
Hollywood, CA 90068
Tel: 323-874-2276

Huntington Beach International Surfing Museum

411 Olive Avenue
Huntington Beach, CA 92648
Tel: 714-960-3483
www.surfingmuseum.org

Julian Pioneer Museum

2811 Washington Street
Julian, CA 92036
Tel: 706-765-0227

Monterey County Agricultural and Rural Life Museum

1160 Broadway
King City, CA 93939
Tel: 831-385-8020
www.mcarlm.org

La Puente Valley Historical Society

15900 East Main Street
La Puente, CA 91744
Tel: 626-369-7220

Dress purchased from estate of Mrs. John D. Rockefeller, circa 1890. Courtesy of Patti Parks McClain Museum of Vintage Fashion.

Patti Parks McClain Museum of Vintage Fashion

CENTURY COLLECTION
1712 Chapparal Lane
Lafayette, CA 94549
Tel: 925-280-1890
Hours: 11–3 pm weekdays by appointment
Institution type: History museum
Collection type: Clothing, accessories
Description: Pre-1700–present. All aspects of clothing from the seventeenth century to the twentieth century for men, women, and children.

$ ✍

Lake County Historic Courthouse Museum

255 North Main Street
Lakeport, CA 95453
Tel: 707-263-4555
www.lakecounty.com/things/museums.html

Lancaster Museum and Art Gallery

44801 West Sierra Highway
Lancaster, CA 93534
Tel: 661-723-6250

San Joaquin County Historical Society and Museum

11793 North Micke Grove Road
Lodi, CA 95240
Tel: 209-331-2055
www.sanjoaquinhistory.org/about.htm

Lompoc Valley Historical Society

200 South H Street
Lompoc, CA 93436
Tel: 805-736-3888

Rancho Los Cerritos Historic Site

4600 Virginia Road
Long Beach, CA 90807
Tel: 562-570-1755
www.rancholoscerritos.org

Osage dress, late 1800s. Courtesy of Autry National Center, Museum of the American West.

Autry National Center, Museum of the American West

700 Western Heritage Way
Los Angeles, CA 90027
Tel: 323-667-2000
www.autrynationalcenter.org/index_gp.php
Hours: Tue–Sun 10–5 pm, Thu 10–8 pm
Contact: Carolyn Bruckner
Institution type: Art museum, history museum
Collection type: Clothing, accessories, costumes, general textiles
Description: 1850–present. Autry National Center explores the experiences and perceptions of the diverse peoples of the American West and includes the Museum of the American West and the Southwest Museum. Museum of the American West has more than 4,500 costumes, clothing, textiles, and accessories; costumes designed for the American cowboy entertainers such as Gene Autry and their costumes created by Rodeo Ben, Nathan

Turk, and Nudie Cohn; clothing and accessories of everyday cowboys; and clothing and accessories of Native Americans. Portions of the collection are online.

$ ✍

Autry National Center, Southwest Museum of the American Indian

234 Museum Drive
Los Angeles, CA 90065
Tel: 323-221-2164
www.autrynationalcenter.org/index_mw.php

California African American Museum

600 State Drive
Los Angeles, CA 90037
Tel: 212-744-7432 Fax: 213-744-2050
www.caamuseum.org
Hours: Wed–Sat 10–4 pm
Contact: Drew Talley
Institution type: Art museum, history museum, state museum
Collection type: Clothing, accessories, costumes, general textiles, quilts
Description: 1900–present. Eclectic collection of textiles and costumes related to Americans of African descent and the continent of Africa, including kente cloth, quilts, a tuxedo jacket of "Big" Joe Turner, and a Poro secret society costume.

$ ✍

Fashion Institute of Design and Merchandising (FIDM) Museum

919 South Grand Avenue
Los Angeles, CA 90015
Tel: 213-624-1200x3367 Fax: 213-624-7617
www.fashionmuseum.org
Hours: Mon–Fri 9–6 pm
Contact: Kevin Jones
Institution type: University museum
Collection type: Clothing, accessories, costumes, general textiles
Description: 1750–present. Collection includes12,000 costumes, accessories, and textiles from the late-eighteenth century through the present day, including film and theater costumes. Designer holdings include Chanel, Yves Saint Laurent, Dior, and Lacroix. The institute permanently houses the Rudi Gernreich Archive, the Hollywood Costume Collection from the City of Los Angeles Department of

Detail, Rudi Gernreich, mini dress, 1968. Courtesy of Fashion Institute of Design and Merchandising Museum.

Recreation and Parks, and the Annette Green Fragrance Collection. A 2,000-piece study collection is available for hands-on research.

Japanese American National Museum

369 East 1st Street
Los Angeles, CA 90012
Tel: 213-625-0414
www.janm.org

Woman's mantua, stomacher, and petticoat, circa 1700. Courtesy of Los Angeles County Museum of Art.

Los Angeles County Museum of Art

COSTUME AND TEXTILES
5905 Wilshire Boulevard
Los Angeles, CA 90036
Tel: 323-857-6081 Fax: 323-857-6218
www.lacma.org
Hours: Mon, Tue, Thu 12–8 pm, Fri 12–9 pm, Sat–Sun 11–8 pm

Contact: Sharon Takeda, Senior Curator and Department Head
Institution type: County museum, art museum
Collection type: Clothing, general textiles
Description: Pre-1700–present. Encyclopedic collection of more than 25,000 items spanning more than 2,000 years, with an almost equal balance of costumes and textiles.

$

Los Angeles Museum of the Holocaust

6006 Wilshire Boulevard
Los Angeles, CA 90036
Tel: 323-761-8170
www.lamuseumoftheholocaust.org

Los Angeles Police Department Museum

6045 York Boulevard
Los Angeles, CA 90042
Tel: 323-344-9445
www.laphs.com

UCLA Fowler Museum of Cultural History

University of California Los Angeles
Los Angeles, CA 90024
Tel: 310-206-7005
www.fmch.ucla.edu
Hours: Wed–Sun 12–5 pm, Thu 12–8 pm
Contact: Curator
Institution type: University museum
Collection type: Clothing, accessories, costumes, general textiles
Description: Pre-1700–present. Comprehensive collections of ethnographic and archeological textiles from Africa, Central and South America, Asia, and parts of Europe and the Middle East. Collection contains over 15,000 objects of textiles and related costumes, including accessories such as hats, shoes, belts, and bags.

Ralph Milliken Museum

Merced County Park, U.S. Highway 152
Los Banos, CA 93635
Tel: 209-826-5505

John Muir National Historic Site

4202 Alhambra Avenue
Martinez, CA 94553
Tel: 925-228-8860
www.nps.gov/jomu

Kelly House Museum

Main at Lansing
Mendocino, CA 95460
Tel: 707-937-5791
www.mendocinohistory.org

Merced County Courthouse Museum

21st and N Streets
Merced, CA 95340
Tel: 209-723-2401
www.mercedmuseum.org

San Fernando Valley Historical Society

10940 Sepulveda Boulevard
Mission Hills, CA 91345
Tel: 818-365-7810

Maritime Museum and History Center of Monterey

5 Custom House Plaza
Monterey, CA 93940
Tel: 831-375-2553
www.montereyhistory.org/maritime_museum.htm

Robert Lewis Stevenson House

530 Houston Street
Monterey, CA 93940
Tel: 925-631-4379
www.mchsmuseum.com/stevensonhouse.html

Nevada County Historical Society

214 Church Street
Nevada City, CA 95959
Tel: 530-265-5468

William S. Hart County Park and Museum

24151 San Fernando Road
Newhall, CA 91321
Tel: 661-254-4584
www.hart-friends.org

Newport Sports Museum

100 Newport Center Drive
Newport Beach, CA 92660
Tel: 949-721-9333

California State University, Northridge

HISTORIC TEXTILE AND APPAREL
COLLECTION
18111 Nordhoff Street
Northridge, CA 91330-8308
www.csun.edu
Hours: Accessible to students only
Contact: Nancy J. Owens
Institution type: University collection
Collection type: Clothing, accessories, uniforms, costumes, general textiles
Description: 1850–present. Teaching collection for students. The oldest items are from the 1880s, mostly of American origin. Majority of items are from the 1950s and 1960s and represent middle-class and upper-middle-class clothing.

Fresno Flats Historical Park

49777 Road 427
Oakhurst, CA 93644
Tel: 559-683-6570
www.fresnoflatsmuseum.org

King Vintage Museum

49269 Golden Oak Drive #208
Oakhurst, CA 93644
Tel: 559-683-1993

The Camron-Stanford House

1418 Lakeside Drive
Oakland, CA 94612
Tel: 510-444-1876

Levi's decorated by Peggy Moulton, 1974. Courtesy of Oakland Museum of California.

Oakland Museum of California

COSTUME AND TEXTILE COLLECTION
1000 Oak Street
Oakland, CA 94607
Tel: 510-238-3842 Fax: 510-238-6579
www.museumca.org
Hours: Wed–Sat 10–5 pm, Sun 12–5 pm, 1st Friday 10–9 pm

Contact: Inez Brooks-Myers
Institution type: Art museum, history museum
Collection type: Clothing, accessories, uniforms, costumes, general textiles
Description: 1700–present. Collection includes wearable art, shoes, and fans. Collection focus is on California. Strengths include hippie style and counterculture, 1960–1970.

✍

Mission San Luis Rey Museum
4050 Mission Avenue
Oceanside, CA 92057
Tel: 760-757-3651
www.sanluisrey.org

Ojai Valley Historical Society and Museum
130 West Ojai
Ojai, CA 93023
Tel: 805-660-1390

Museum of History and Art, Ontario
225 South Euclid Avenue
Ontario, CA 91762
Tel: 909-983-3198

Butte County Pioneer Museum and Lott Home Museum
1735 Montgomery Street
Oroville, CA 95965
Tel: 530-538-2937
www.cityoforoville.org/pioneermuseum.html
Hours: Fri–Sun 12–3 pm
Institution type: History museum, historic house, city museum
CHINESE TEMPLE
Contact: David Dewey
Collection type: Clothing, general textiles, flags
Description: 1800–1914. Chinese tapestries and other items used in the temple and the nearby theater and garments from China and the Western world displayed on mannequins comparing and contrasting the two during the 1900s.
LOTT HOME MUSEUM
Hours: Fri, Sun, Mon 11:30–3:30 pm
Contact: David Dewey
Collection type: Clothing, uniforms, general textiles, quilts
Description: 1850–1960. Clothing from the 1850s to the 1940s, family quilts, and handwork for table coverings.

PIONEER MEMORIAL MUSEUM
Hours: Fri–Sun 12–4 pm
Contact: David Dewey
Collection type: Clothing, accessories, uniforms, general textiles, quilts
Description: 1850–1914. Objects of the pioneer days of California (1849–1890) and items up to the mid-1930s, featuring clothing, handwork, and other textiles in use by the pioneers.

$

The Stowitts Museum and Library
591 Lighthouse Avenue
Pacific Grove, CA 93950
Tel: 831-655-4488
www.stowitts.org

Will Rogers State Historic Park
1501 Will Rogers State Park Road
Pacific Palisades, CA 90272
Tel: 310-454-8212

Pacific Asia Museum
46 North Los Robles Avenue
Pasadena, CA 91101
Tel: 626-449-2742
www.pacificasiamuseum.org

Pasadena Museum of History
470 West Walnut Street
Pasadena, CA 91103
Tel: 626-577-1660
www.pasadenahistory.org

Petaluma Adobe State Historic Park
3325 Adobe Road
Petaluma, CA 94954
Tel: 707-762-4871
www.parks.ca.gov/default.asp?page_id=474

El Dorado County Historical Museum
104 Placerville Drive
Placerville, CA 95667
Tel: 530-621-5865
www.co.el-dorado.ca.us/museum

Amador-Livermore Valley Historical Society Museum
603 Main Street
Pleasanton, CA 94566
Tel: 925-462-2766

Historical Society of Pomona Valley

1460 East Holt Boulevard, #78
Pomona, CA 91767
Tel: 909-623-2198

Hours: Sun 2–5 pm, or by appointment
Contact: Kathryn Herrman
Institution type: Historic house
Collection type: Clothing, accessories, general textiles, quilts
Description: 1800–1960. Domestic and agricultural objects, 1830–1920. Emphasis is on California, but collection also contains artifacts from around the United States.

$ ✍

Civil Engineer Corps and Seabee Museum

1000 23rd Avenue
Port Hueneme, CA 93043
Tel: 805-982-5165

Porterville Historical Museum

257 North D Street
Porterville, CA 93257
Tel: 559-784-2053

Zalud House

393 North Hockett Street
Porterville, CA 93257
Tel: 559-782-7548

Hours: Wed–Sat 10–4 pm, Sun 2–4 pm
Contact: Lynn Shell
Institution type: City museum
Collection type: Clothing, accessories
Description: 1915–1960

$ ✍

Plumas County Museum

500 Jackson Street
Quincy, CA 95971
Tel: 530-283-6320

John Rains House

8810 Hemlock Avenue
Rancho Cucamonga, CA 91730
Tel: 909-989-4970
www.co.san-bernardina.ca.us/museum/
branches/rains.htm

Shasta College Museum and Research Center

11555 Old Oregon Trail
Redding, CA 96003
Tel: 530-225-4669

Turtle Bay Exploration Park

HISTORY COLLECTION

840 Auditorium Drive
Redding, CA 96099-2360
Tel: 530-243-8850 Fax: 520-243-8929
www.turtlebay.org

Hours: Wed–Mon 9–5 pm (Winter); Mon–Sun 9–5 pm (Summer)
Contact: Robyn Peterson, Senior Director of Programs and Exhibit
Institution type: Art museum, history museum
Collection type: Clothing, accessories, uniforms, costumes, general textiles, flags
Description: 1850–present. Eclectic collection ranging from formal wear to commemorative shirts, many household textiles, and a large collection of mid-twentieth-century women's wear, shoes, hats, and purses.

$ ✍

Kimberly Crest House

1325 Prospect Drive
Redlands, CA 92373
Tel: 909-792-2111
www.kimberlycrest.org

San Mateo County Historical Association and Museum

777 Hamilton Street
Redwood City, CA 94063
Tel: 650-299-0104
www.sanmateocountyhistory.com

Rialto Historical Society

201–205 North Riverside Avenue
Rialto, CA 92376
Tel: 909-875-1750

Richmond Museum of History

400 Nevin Avenue
Richmond, CA 94802
Tel: 510-235-7387

Maturango Museum of the Indian Wells Valley

100 East Las Flores
Ridgecrest, CA 93555
Tel: 760-375-6900
www.maturango.org

Hours: Mon–Sun 10–5 pm
Contact: Elizabeth Babcock
Institution type: Art museum, history museum

Collection type: Clothing, accessories, uniforms

Description: 1900–present. Small collection of representative clothing from the homesteading, mining, and modern eras.

$ ✍

March Field Air Museum

22550 Van Buren Boulevard
Riverside, CA 92518
Tel: 909-697-6600
www.marchfield.org

Mission Inn Foundation and Museum

3696 Main Street
Riverside, CA 92501
Tel: 909-781-8241

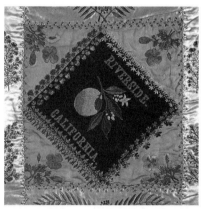

Detail, Riverside citrus heritage quilt, circa 1896. Courtesy of Riverside Municipal Museum.

Riverside Municipal Museum

3580 Mission Inn Avenue
Riverside, CA 92507
Tel: 951-826-5273 Fax: 951-369-4970
www.riversideca.gov/museum/rmm/rmm1.html

Hours: Tue–Fri 9–5 pm, Sat–Sun 11–5 pm

Contact: Brenda Buller Focht

Institution type: City museum

Collection type: Clothing, accessories, general textiles, quilts

Description: 1800–present. 2,500 objects, including women's, men's, and children's clothing, Chinese and Japanese clothing, quilts, coverlets, and embroidered blankets.

✍

California Military Museum

1119 Second Street
Sacramento, CA 95814

Tel: 916-442-2883
www.militarymuseum.org

California State Indian Museum

2618 K Street
Sacramento, CA 95816
Tel: 916-324-8043

Crocker Art Museum

216 O Street
Sacramento, CA 95814
Tel: 916-264-5423 Fax: 916-264-7372
www.crockerartmuseum.org

Hours: Tue–Sun 10–5 pm, Thu 10–9 pm

Contact: Collections manager

Institution type: Art museum, city museum

Collection type: Clothing, accessories, costumes, general textiles

Description: 1800–1960

$ ✍

Calaveras County Museum and Archives

30 North Main Street
San Andreas, CA 95249
Tel: 209-754-3910

Vintage uniform, twentieth century. Courtesy of Marine Corps Recruit Depot Command Museum.

Marine Corps Recruit Depot Museum

1600 Henderson Avenue, Building 26
Suite 212
San Diego, CA 92140-5000
Tel: 619-524-6719 Fax: 619-524-0076
www.mcrdshistory.com/comm_museum.htm

Hours: Mon–Fri 8–4 pm

Contact: Barbara S. McCurtis

Institution type: History museum

Collection type: Clothing, accessories, uniforms, general textiles, flags

Description: 1915–present. Uniforms, weapons, equipment, photographs, and battlefield pickups representative of U.S. Marine Corps history.

Mingei International Museum

1439 El Prado
San Diego, CA 92101
Tel: 619-239-0003
www.mingei.org

San Diego Aerospace Museum

2001 Pan American Plaza, Balboa Park
San Diego, CA 92101
Tel: 619-234-8291x10
www.aerospacemuseum.org

San Diego Hall of Champions Sports Museum

2131 Pan American Plaza, Balboa Park
San Diego, CA 92101
Tel: 619-234-2544
www.sdhoc.com

Boy's three-piece suit, circa 1862. Courtesy of San Diego Historical Society.

San Diego Historical Society

COSTUMES AND TEXTILES
COLLECTION

1649 El Prado, Suite 3, Casa de Balboa
Building, Balboa Park
San Diego, CA 92101
Tel: 619-232-6203x121 Fax: 619-232-6297
www.sandiegohistory.org
Hours: Mon–Sun 10–4:30 pm
Contact: Curator of collections
Institution type: History museum, historic house

Collection type: Clothing, accessories, uniforms, costumes, general textiles, quilts, flags
Description: 1760–present. More than 7,000 pieces of costumes, accessories, and textiles that illustrate the history of dress in America, with specific attention to pieces with San Diego connections. Collection includes clothing for men, women, and children; fashion accessories such as shoes, handbags, and jewelry; quilts and coverlets; and military uniforms.

$

San Diego Museum of Man

1350 El Prado, Balboa Park
San Diego, CA 92101
Tel: 619-239-2001
www.museumofman.org

San Diego State University

ALICIA ANNAS HISTORICAL
COLLECTION

Department of Theater, 5500 Campanile Drive
San Diego, CA 92182-7601
Tel: 619-594-1242 Fax: 619-594-7431
http://theatre.sdsu.edu
Hours: Mon–Fri 9–6 pm
Contact: Holly Durbin, Curator of Collections
Institution type: University collection
Collection type: Clothing, accessories, uniforms, costumes, general textiles, quilts, flags
Description: 1900–present. Historical Collection has 800 women's garments with strengths in 1900–1940. Classroom Study Collection has 200 women's garments, 1950–1990, for studying construction techniques and design elements. Also holds a women's lingerie collection, 1920–1960, and a women's shoe and handbag collection featuring items from 1940 to 1960.

$

California Historical Society

678 Mission Street
San Francisco, CA 94105
Tel: 415-357-1848
www.calhist.org
Hours: By appointment
Contact: Kevin Jones, Curator at Fashion Institute of Design and Merchandising Museum
Institution type: History museum, state museum
Collection type: Clothing, accessories, uniforms, costumes, general textiles

Description: 1800–present. California Historical Society collection is currently housed at Fashion Institute of Design and Merchandising Museum in Los Angeles.

Chinese Cultural Center of San Francisco

750 Kearny Street, 3rd Floor
San Francisco, CA 94108
Tel: 415-986-1822
www.c-c-c.org

Chasuble, circa 1700–1710. Courtesy of Legion of Honor, Fine Arts Museums of San Francisco.

California Palace of the Legion of Honor, Fine Arts Museums of San Francisco

THE CAROLINE AND H. MCCOY JONES DEPARTMENT OF TEXTILE ARTS

1000 34th Avenue and Clement Street
San Francisco, CA 94121
Tel: 415-750-7609 Fax: 415-750-7692
www.thinker.org
Hours: Tue–Sat 9:30–5 pm
Contact: Diane Mott
Institution type: Art museum, city museum
Collection type: Clothing, accessories, costumes, general textiles
Description: Pre-1700–present. Exhibits feature selections from the museums' European holdings—tapestries, ecclesiastical vestments and furnishings, fashion and costume, and ancient Mediterranean textiles.

$ 🖎

de Young Museum, Fine Arts Museums of San Francisco

THE CAROLINE AND H. MCCOY JONES DEPARTMENT OF TEXTILE ARTS

Japanese ceremonial robe kaparamip, *circa 1912–1926. Courtesy of deYoung, Fine Arts Museums of San Francisco.*

50 Hagiwara Tea Garden Drive
San Francisco, CA 94115
Tel: 415-750-7609 Fax: 415-750-7692
www.thinker.org
Hours: Tue–Sun 9:30–5 pm
Contact: Diane Mott
Institution type: Art museum, city museum
Collection type: Clothing, accessories, costumes, general textiles
Description: Pre-1700–present. The de Young Museum and the California Palace of the Legion of Honor are sister institutions administered by the Fine Arts Museums of San Francisco. The 12,000 objects in the Department of Textiles and Costumes are housed at the de Young. Collection includes fashionable dress from the eighteenth century to the present with an emphasis on post–World War II couture. Collection also includes European tapestries, Near East and central Asian carpets, Anatolian kilims, and Uzbek embroideries.

$ 🖎

The Mexican Museum

Fort Mason Center, Building D
San Francisco, CA 94123
Tel: 415-202-9700
www.mexicanmuseum.org

San Gabriel Mission Museum

428 South Mission Drive
San Gabriel, CA 91776
Tel: 626-457-3048
www.sangabrielmission.org/mission_giftshop
_and_museum.htm

History San Jose
1650 Senter Avenue
San Jose, CA 95112
Tel: 408-287-2290
www.historysanjose.org

San Jose Museum of Quilts and Textiles
110 Paseo de San Antonio
San Jose, CA 95112
Tel: 408-971-0232x10
www.sjquiltmuseum.org

San Juan Bautista State Historic Park
19 Franklin Street
San Juan Bautista, CA 95045
Tel: 831-623-4881

Mission San Juan Capistrano Museum
31522 Camino Capistrano
San Juan Capistrano, CA 92693
Tel: 949-234-1300x320
www.missionsjc.com

Mission San Luis Obispo De Tolosa
751 Palm Street
San Luis Obispo, CA 93401
Tel: 805-543-6850
www.missionsanluisobispo.org

San Luis Obispo County Historical Museum
696 Monterrey Street
San Luis Obispo, CA 93401
Tel: 805-543-0638
www.slochs.org

The Huntington Library, Art Collections, and Botanical Gardens
1151 Oxford Road
San Marino, CA 91108
Tel: 626-405-2100
www.huntington.org
Hours: Tue–Sun 10:30–4:30 pm (Summer);
Tue–Sun 12–4:30 pm (Winter)
Institution type: Art museum, historic house
$ ✍

Fort MacArthur Museum
3601 South Gaffey Street
San Pedro, CA 90731
Tel: 310-548-2631
www.ftmac.org

Los Angeles Maritime Museum
Berth 84, foot of 6th Street
San Pedro, CA 90731
Tel: 310-548-7618
www.lamaritimemuseum.org

Marin History Museum
1125 B Street
San Rafael, CA 94901
Tel: 415-454-8538
www.marinhistory.org

Hearst Castle
750 Hearst Castle Road
San Simeon, CA 93452
Tel: 805-927-2020
www.hearstcastle.com

The Bowers Museum of Cultural Art
2002 North Main Street
Santa Ana, CA 92706
Tel: 714-567-3600
www.bowers.org

Santa Barbara Historical Museum
136 East De la Guerra Street
Santa Barbara, CA 93101
Tel: 805-966-1601
www.santabarbaramuseum.com

Santa Barbara Museum of Art
1130 State Street
Santa Barbara, CA 93101
Tel: 805-963-4364
www.sbmuseart.org

De Saisset Museum
VESTMENT COLLECTION
Santa Clara University, 500 El Camino Real
Santa Clara, CA 95053
Tel: 408-554-4528 Fax: 408-554-7840
www.scu.edu/desaisset
Hours: Tue–Sun 11–4 pm
Contact: Jean MacDougall
Institution type: Art museum, history museum,
university museum

Collection type: Clothing, accessories, general textiles

Description: Pre-1700–1960. Ecclesiastical garments and liturgical accessories from Mission Santa Clara from the seventeenth century to 1920. One third of the collection is French or Spanish from 1650 to 1800. Half of the vestments were sewn in Mexico from silk brocade or damask imported from China and the Philippines. A portion of the vestments were likely sent from Mexico to California along with the founding Franciscan padres in the 1770s. Collection also includes eighteenth- and nineteenth-century funeral vestments thought to have been sewn by the Native Americans living at Mission Santa Clara.

Museum of Art and History

705 Front Street
Santa Cruz, CA 95064
Tel: 831-459-3606
www.santacruzmah.org

Santa Maria Historical Society Museum

616 South Broadway
Santa Maria, CA 93454
Tel: 805-922-3130

Santa Ynez Valley Historical Society

3596 Sagunto Street
Santa Ynez, CA 93460
Tel: 805-688-7889

Ronald Reagan Presidential Library and Museum

40 Presidential Drive
Simi Valley, CA 93065
Tel: 800-998-6741
www.reagan.utexas.edu

Elverhoj Museum

1624 Elverhoj Way
Solvang, CA 93463
Tel: 805-686-1211
www.elverhoj.org

California State Parks

363 3rd Street West
Sonoma, CA 95476
Hours: Vary by site and season

Institution type: Historic house, state museum
$ ✍️

CHARMIAN LONDON CLOTHING AND TEXTILE COLLECTION
Contact: Carol A. Dodge
Collection type: Clothing, accessories, general textiles
Description: 1900–1960. Collection includes custom and individualized women's clothing and accessories, circa 1910–1940.

Oriental silk robe of Charmian London, circa 1920. Courtesy of California State Parks.

FISCHER-HANLON HOUSE CLOTHING AND TEXTILE COLLECTION
Contact: Carol A. Dodge
Collection type: Clothing, accessories, quilts
Description: 1850–1960. Collection includes mostly women's clothing, circa 1880s–1930s, some children's garments, 3 men's items, and some quilts.

Depot Park Museum

270 1st Street
Sonoma, CA 95476
Tel: 707-938-1762
www.vom.com/~depot

Sonoma State Historic Park

VALLEJO FAMILY COLLECTION
20 East Spain Street
Sonoma, CA 95476
Tel: 707-938-1519
Hours: Mon–Sun 10–5 pm
Contact: Carol A. Dodge, Museum Curator
Institution type: History museum, historic house
Collection type: Clothing, accessories, uniforms
Description: 1850–1899. Original clothing and accessories belonging to the family of Mariano Guadalupe Vallejo, Mexican commandant of the northern frontier of Alta California. Items date from 1834 to late 1800s.
$ ✍️

Tuolumne County Museum and History Center

158 West Bradford Avenue
Sonora, CA 95370
Tel: 209-532-1317
www.tchistory.org/museum.html
Hours: Mon–Sun 10–4:30 pm
Contact: Collection manager
Institution type: History museum, county museum
Collection type: Clothing, accessories, uniforms, general textiles, flags
Description: 1850–present. Clothing and textile collection reflects items used in Tuolumne County from 1850 to the present.

South Lake Tahoe Historical Society and Museum

3058 Lake Tahoe Boulevard
South Lake Tahoe, CA 96156
Tel: 530-541-5458

The Haggin Museum

1201 North Pershing Avenue
Stockton, CA 95203
Tel: 209-540-6311
www.hagginmuseum.org

The Lace Museum

552 South Murphy Avenue
Sunnyvale, CA 94086
Tel: 408-730-4695
www.thelacemuseum.org

Temecula Valley Museum

28314 Mercedes Street
Temecula, CA 92590
Tel: 909-694-6452
www.cityoftemecula.org/cityhall/commserv/museum/index.htm

Grace Hudson Museum

431 South Main Street
Ukiah, CA 95482
Tel: 707-467-2836
www.gracehudsonmuseum.org

Held-Poage Memorial Home and Research Library

603 West Perkins Street
Ukiah, CA 95482
Tel: 707-462-6969

Vacaville Museum

213 Buck Avenue
Vacaville, CA 95688
Tel: 707-447-4513
www.vacavillemuseum.org

Vallejo Naval and Historical Museum

TEXTILE COLLECTION
734 Marin Street
Vallejo, CA 94590
Tel: 707-643-0077 Fax: 707-643-2443
www.vallejomuseum.org
Hours: Tue–Sat 10–4:30 pm
Contact: James Kern, Executive Director
Institution type: History museum
Collection type: Clothing, accessories, uniforms, flags
Description: 1850–present. Men's and women's clothing circa 1850 to the present, a large collection of U.S. Navy uniforms and accessories, ships' flags, and Helen Marchand vest collection of wearable art.

$

San Buenaventura Mission Museum

225 East Main Street
Ventura, CA 93001
Tel: 805-643-4318 Fax: 805-643-7831
www.sanbuenaventuramission.org
Hours: Mon–Fri 10–5 pm, Sat 9–5 pm, Sun 10–4 pm
Contact: Curator of collections
Institution type: History museum
Collection type: Clothing
Description: 1700–1899. Collection includes clergy apparel—chasubles and cassocks.

$

Ventura County Museum of History and Art

CLOTHING AND TEXTILE COLLECTION
100 East Main Street
Ventura, CA 93001
Tel: 805-653-0323 Fax: 805-653-5267
www.venturamuseum.org
Hours: Tue–Sun 10–5 pm
Contact: Kathy Henri, Collections Manager
Institution type: Art museum, history museum, county museum
Collection type: Clothing, accessories, uniforms, costumes, general textiles, flags
Description: 1800–present. Objects from the early

Spanish and Mexican residents of the area as well as general American clothing from the 1860s to the 1980s. Distinctive artifacts include a circa 1910 dress printed with the text of a local newspaper and a pair of circa 1820 Spanish *calzoneras* (trousers).

$ ✍

Vista Historical Museum

651A East Vista Way
Vista, CA 92085-1032
Tel: 760-630-0444

Pajaro Valley Historical Association

332 East Beach Street
Watsonville, CA 95076
Tel: 831-722-0305

Hurst Ranch Historical Foundation

1227 South Orange Avenue
West Covina, CA 91791
Tel: 626-814-8465
www.hurstranch.com

Mendocino County Museum

400 East Commercial Street
Willits, CA 95490
Tel: 707-459-2736
www.co.mendocino.ca.us/museum

Banning Residence Museum

401 East M Street
Wilmington, CA 90744
Tel: 310-548-7777
www.banningmuseum.org

Drum Barracks Civil War Museum

1052 Banning Boulevard
Wilmington, CA 90744
Tel: 310-548-7509
www.drumbarracks.org

Yolo County Historical Museum

512 Gibson Road
Woodland, CA 95695
Tel: 530-666-1045
http://yolo.net/vme/ychm

Richard Nixon Library and Birthplace

18001 Yorba Linda Boulevard
Yorba Linda, CA 92886
Tel: 714-993-5075 Fax: 714-528-0544
www.nixonlibrary.org

Photograph of First Lady Patricia Nixon in gown designed by Adele Simpson, 1972. Gown in permanent collection of Richard Nixon Library. Photograph courtesy of the Nixon Presidential Staff, NARA.

Hours: Mon–Sun 10–5 pm
Contact: Olivia Anastasiadis
Institution type: History museum, historic house
Collection type: Clothing, accessories, uniforms, costumes, general textiles, flags
Description: 1850–present. Personal clothing from President Richard Nixon, First Lady Pat Nixon, and their daughters, Tricia and Julie, as well as textile artifacts from the president's mother, Hannah Nixon. Many of Mrs. Nixon's evening gowns were designed by famous designers such as Adele Simpson, Ferdinand Sarmi, Harvey Berin, Philip Hulitar, Molly Parnis, and Priscilla of Boston.

$ ✍

Napa Valley Museum

55 Presidents Circle
Yountville, CA 94599
Tel: 707-944-0500
www.napavalleymuseum.org

Community Memorial Museum of Sutter County

1333 Butte House Road
Yuba City, CA 95993
Tel: 530-822-7141
www.syix.com/museum

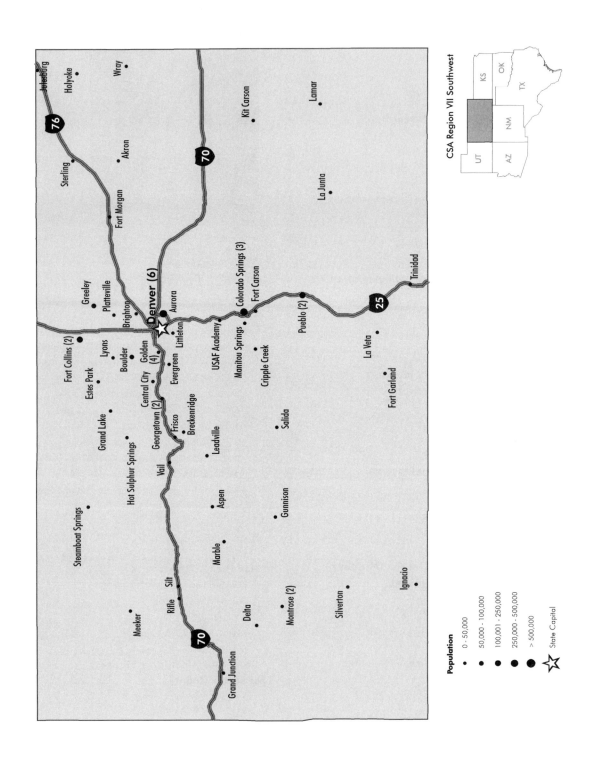

Population

· 0 - 50,000
• 50,000 - 100,000
● 100,001 - 250,000
● 250,000 - 500,000
● > 500,000
☆ State Capital

CSA Region VII Southwest

UT | KS
AZ | NM | OK
    | TX

COLORADO

Washington County Museum
34445 Highway 63
Akron, CO 80720
Tel: 970-345-6446

Aspen Historical Society
620 West Bleeker Street
Aspen, CO 81611
Tel: 970-925-3721
www.aspenhistory.org

Aurora History Museum
15001 East Alameda Parkway
Aurora, CO 80012
Tel: 303-739-6660
www.aurora-museum.org

Boulder History Museum
PHYLLIS PLEHATY COSTUME
COLLECTION
1206 Euclid
Boulder, CO 80302
Tel: 303-449-3464 Fax: 303-938-8322
www.boulderhistorymuseum.org
Hours: Tue–Fri 10–4 pm, Sat 12–4 pm
Contact: Laura Lee, Collections Manager
Institution type: History museum
Collection type: Clothing, accessories
Description: 1850–present. Majority of the collec-
tion is from the late 1880s to the1920s and is
focused around the people of Boulder County,
Colorado. Predominately women's clothing.
$ ✍

Summit Historical Society
309 North Main Street
Breckenridge, CO 80424
Tel: 970-453-9022
www.summithistorical.org

Adams Museum
9601 Henderson Road
Brighton, CO 80601
Tel: 303-659-7103

Gilpin History Museum
228 East High Street
Central City, CO 80427
Tel: 303-582-5283
www.coloradomuseums.org/gilpin.htm

Colorado Springs Pioneer Museum
215 South Tejon
Colorado Springs, CO 80903
Tel: 719-385-5990
www.cspm.org

**Pro Rodeo Hall of Fame and Museum
of the American Cowboy**
101 Pro Rodeo Drive
Colorado Springs, CO 80919
Tel: 719-528-4761
www.prorodeo.com/hof/visitor.htm

**World Figure Skating Museum
and Hall of Fame**
20 1st Street
Colorado Springs, CO 80906

Tel: 719-635-5200

www.worldskatingmuseum.org

The Old Homestead House Museum

353 East Myers Avenue

Cripple Creek, CO 80813

Tel: 719-689-3090 Fax: 719-689-2461

www.cripple-creek.co.us/homestead.htm

Hours: Mon–Sun 11–5 pm (May–Oct)

Contact: Director

Institution type: History museum, historic house

Collection type: Clothing, accessories

Description: 1850–1914. Built as a parlor house in 1896 in the Red Light District of the World's Greatest Gold Camp, Cripple Creek, Colorado, it was the finest and most expensive house during the district's gold rush era (1893–1916). Many original items include crystal chandeliers, parlor furniture, piano, and furnishings for the five bedrooms. Collection includes licenses, receipts, directories, and clothing items that would have been worn by the women in the bordello.

$

Delta County Museum

251 Meeker Street

Delta, CO 81416

Tel: 970-874-8721

Black American West Museum and Heritage Center

3091 California Street

Denver, CO 80205

Tel: 303-292-2566

www.blackamericanwest.org

Byers-Evans House

1310 Bannock Street

Denver, CO 80204

Tel: 303-866-2303

Hours: Vary by day and by season

Institution type: State museum

Colorado Historical Society

1300 Broadway

Denver, CO 80203

Tel: 303-866-3682 Fax: 303-866-4464

www.coloradohistory.org

Hours: Mon–Sat 10–4:30 pm, Sun 12–4:30 pm

Contact: Curator of Material Culture

Wedding dress, two-piece, blue wool flannel, 1901. Courtesy of Colorado Historical Society.

Institution type: History museum, historic house, state museum

Collection type: Clothing, accessories, uniforms, general textiles, quilts, flags

Description: Pre-1700–present. General historic collection reflects the population of Colorado and the western region. Strengths include late-nineteenth-century holdings; American Indian holdings, especially Plains Indians and Puebloan cultures; and military holdings, especially relating to the U.S. Army, 10th Mountain Division. Also includes a general range of quilts, flags, and household textiles.

$

Denver Art Museum

100 West 14th Avenue Parkway

Denver, CO 80204

Tel: 720-865-5000

www.denverartmuseum.org

Molly Brown House Museum

1340 Pennsylvania Street

Denver, CO 80203

Tel: 303-832-4092 Fax: 303-832-2340

http://mollybrown.org

Hours: Tue–Sat 10–3:30 pm, Sun 12–3:30 pm

Contact: Kerri Atter or Monica Dean

Institution type: Historic house

Collection type: Clothing, accessories, costumes, general textiles, flags

Description: 1850–1960. Collection includes clothing and accessories primarily from the years of Molly Brown's lifetime, 1867–1932.

$

Wedding dress, circa 1880s. Courtesy of Molly Brown House.

Museo de Las Americas
861 Santa Fe Drive
Denver, CO 80204
Tel: 303-571-4401
www.museo.org

Estes Park Area Historical Museum
200 Fourth Street
Estes Park, CO 80517
Tel: 970-586-6256
www.estes.on-line.com/epmuseum

Hiwan Homestead Museum
4208 South Timbervale Drive
Evergreen, CO 80439
Tel: 303-674-6262
www.jchscolorado.org/museum.html

Third Armored Cavalry Museum
Building 2160
Fort Carson, CO 80913
Tel: 719-526-1368
www.3acr.com

Avery House Historic District
108 North Meldrum
Fort Collins, CO 80521
Tel: 970-221-0533
www.poudrelandmarks.com
Hours: Wed, Sun 1–3 pm
Contact: Martha Spark, Costume Committee Chair
Institution type: Historic house
Collection type: Clothing, accessories, costumes, general textiles

Description: 1850–1914. Major emphasis is on the Victorian era, 1837–1901, and Edwardian era, 1901–1911. Women's, men's, and children's costumes and accessories representative of the Colorado region during this time.
$

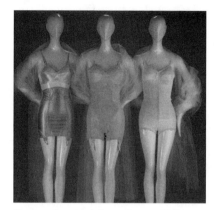

Bras, corselet, and girdles, underwear, 1940-1960s. Courtesy of Historic Costume Collection at Colorado State University.

Colorado State University
314 Gifford
Fort Collins, CO 80523-1574
Tel: 970-491-1983 Fax: 970-491-4376
www.cahs.colostate.edu/dm
Hours: Mon–Fri 9–5 pm (Aug–May)
Contact: Linda Carlson
Institution type: University collection
Collection type: Clothing, accessories, uniforms, costumes, general textiles
Description: 1850–present. Research and study collection of mainly nineteenth- and twentieth-century Western dress, including accessories. Special holdings include the Ruth Payne Hellmann Lace Collection; the Maxson Asian Textiles Collection, made up of over 300 kimono; and designer garments from Mr. Blackwell, Arnold Scaasi, Calvin Klein, Carolina Herrera, and James Galanos.

Fort Collins Museum
200 Mathews
Fort Collins, CO 80524
Tel: 970-221-6738
www.fcgov.com/museum

Fort Garland Museum

29477 Highway 159
Fort Garland, CO 81133
Tel: 303-866-2303
www.coloradohistory.org/hist_sites/ft_garland/
    ft_garland.htm
Hours: Vary by day and by season
Institution type: State museum

Fort Morgan Museum

414 Main City Park
Fort Morgan, CO 80701
Tel: 970-867-6331
www.ftmorganmus.org

Frisco Historical Society

120 Main Street
Frisco, CO 80443
Tel: 970-668-3428

Historic Hamill House Museum

305 Argentine Street
Georgetown, CO 80444
Tel: 303-569-2840 Fax: 303-569-2111
www.historicgeorgetown.org
Hours: Mon–Sun 10–4 pm (Jun–Dec)
Contact: Curator of collections
Institution type: Historic house
Collection type: Clothing, accessories, costumes
Description: 1850–1960. The costumes range in
    date from 1860 to 1940 and are typical for a
    mid-nineteenth-century historic house.
$ ✍

Hotel De Paris Museum

409 6th Avenue
Georgetown, CO 80444
Tel: 303-569-2311
www.hoteldeparismuseum.org

Buffalo Bill Museum and Grave

987½ Lookout Mountain Road
Golden, CO 80401
Tel: 303-526-0744 Fax: 303-526-0197
www.buffalobill.org
Hours: Mon–Sun 9–5 pm (Jun–Oct); Tue–Sun
    9–4 pm (Nov–May)
Contact: Shelley L. Howe
Institution type: History museum, city museum
Collection type: Clothing, accessories, uniforms,
    costumes, general textiles, flags

Jacket of William F. "Buffalo Bill" Cody, circa 1890s. Courtesy of Buffalo Bill Museum and Grave.

Description: 1800–present. Artifacts and personal
    items from the life and times of William F.
    "Buffalo Bill" Cody, including Native Amer-
    ican and frontier clothing, show posters and
    programs, photographs, fine art and furniture,
    antique firearms, and various memorabilia
    from the Wild West Show such as original
    tack, saddles, and clothing.
$ ✍

Friends of the Astor House Museum and Clear Creek History Park

GOLDEN LANDMARKS COLLECTION
822 12th Street
Golden, CO 80401
Tel: 303-278-3557 Fax: 303-278-8916
www.astorhousemuseum.org
Hours: Tue–Sat 10–4:30 pm
Contact: Mark Dodge
Institution type: History museum, historic house,
    city museum
Collection type: Clothing, general textiles
Description: 1850–1899. Clothing items from the
    late nineteenth century, collected from the
    Golden and central Colorado area. Includes
    mostly children's and women's clothing.
$ ✍

Golden Pioneer Museum

923 10th Street
Golden, CO 80401
Tel: 303-278-7151
www.goldenpioneermuseum.com

Rocky Mountain Quilt Museum

1111 Washington Avenue
Golden, CO 80401

Tel: 303-277-0377 Fax: 303-215-1636
www.rmqm.org

Hours: Mon–Sun 10–4 pm

Contact: Martha Spark, Collections Manager

Institution type: History museum, art museum

Collection type: Quilts

Description: 1800–present. Quilts from the Rocky Mountain region and across America. Examples from major quilting styles, starting in the early 1800s and continuing through to the twenty-first century. Major collections are from Eugenia Mitchell in 1990 (100 quilts) and Art Quilts in 2004 (60 quilts).

$ ✍

Museum of Western Colorado

462 Ute Avenue
Grand Junction, CO 81501
Tel: 970-242-0971
www.wcmuseum.org

Grand Lake Area Historical Society

Lake Avenue at Pitkin Street
Grand Lake, CO 80447
Tel: 970-887-1210

Snakeskin Flapper Dress, 1925. Courtesy of City of Greeley Museums.

City of Greeley Museums

919 7th Street
Greeley, CO 80631
Tel: 970-350-9220 Fax: 970-350-9570
www.greeleymuseums.com

Hours: Vary by site and by season

Contact: Erin Quinn, Collections Coordinator

Institution type: History museum, historic house, city museum

Collection type: Clothing, accessories, uniforms, costumes, general textiles, quilts

Description: 1850–present. Textile collection includes approximately 8,000 artifacts. Approximately 5,000 of these objects are clothing, footwear, headwear, and accessories. Remainder are household textiles such as bedding, table linens, and curtains. Emphasis is on items that were either used or made by people from northeastern Colorado. Heavy concentration is in women's clothing, especially dresses of all time periods, as well as baby clothing and table linens.

$ ✍

Gunnison County Pioneer and Historical Society

South Adams Street and Highway 50
Gunnison, CO 81230
Tel: 970-641-4530

Phillips County Museum

109 South Campbell Avenue
Holyoke, CO 80734
Tel: 970-854-2129

Grand County Museum

110 East Byers
Hot Sulphur Springs, CO 80451
Tel: 970-725-3939
www.grandcountymuseum.com

Southern Ute Indian Cultural Center

Highway 172 North
Ignacio, CO 81137
Tel: 970-563-9583
www.southernutemuseum.org

Fort Sedgwick Historical Society

114 East 1st Street
Julesburg, CO 80737
Tel: 970-474-2061
www.kci.net/~history

Hours: Mon–Sat 10–4 pm, Sun 1–4 pm (Memorial Day–Labor Day)

Contact: Collections manager

Institution type: History museum

Collection type: Clothing, accessories, uniforms, costumes, general textiles, flags

Description: 1850–present. The Fort Sedgwick Historical Society maintains two museums, Depot Museum and Fort Sedgwick Museum, which contain clothing and textiles of local interest.

$ ✍

Kit Carson Historical Society
300 Park Street
Kit Carson, CO 80825
Tel: 719-962-3306
Hours: Mon–Sun 9–5 pm (Memorial Day–Labor Day)
Contact: President
Institution type: History museum
Collection type: Clothing, uniforms, general textiles, quilts
Description: 1850–1960. Men's, women's, and children's clothing items from the late 1800s through the early 1900s. Other items include quilts, World War I and World War II uniforms, some VFW clothing and caps, and leather and buffalo hide items.

$ ✍

Koshare Indian Museum
115 West 18th
La Junta, CO 81050
Tel: 719-384-4411 Fax: 719-384-8836
www.koshare.org
Hours: Mon–Sun 10–5 pm, Mon and Wed 10–9 pm
Contact: Tina Wilcox
Institution type: History museum
Collection type: Clothing, accessories, costumes

$ ✍

Fort Francisco Museum
306 Main Street
La Veta, CO 81055
Tel: 719-742-5501

Big Timbers Museum
7515 U.S. Highway 50
Lamar, CO 81052
Tel: 719-336-2472

Heritage Museum and Gallery
102 East 9th Street
Leadville, CO 80461
Tel: 719-486-1878

Littleton Historical Museum
6028 South Gallup
Littleton, CO 80120
Tel: 303-795-3950
www.littletongov.org/museum

Lyons Redstone Museum
340 High Street
Lyons, CO 80540
Tel: 303-823-6692

Miramount Castle Museum
9 Capitol Hill Avenue
Manitou Springs, CO 80829
Tel: 719-685-1011

Marble Historical Society
412 West Main Street
Marble, CO 81623
Tel: 970-963-1710

White River Museum
565 Park Street
Meeker, CO 81641
Tel: 970-878-9982

Montrose County Historical Museum
Main and Rio Grande Streets
Montrose, CO 81402
Tel: 970-249-6135

Ute Indian Museum
17523 Chipeta Drive
Montrose, CO 81401
Tel: 970-249-3098

Fort Vasquez Museum
13412 U.S. Highway 85
Platteville, CO 80651
Tel: 970-785-2832
www.coloradohistory.org

El Pueblo Museum
301 North Union
Pueblo, CO 81003
Tel: 719-583-0453
www.coloradohistory.org

Rosemount Museum
419 West 14th Street
Pueblo, CO 81003
Tel: 719-545-5290
http://rosemount.org

Rifle Creek Museum

337 East Avenue
Rifle, CO 81650
Tel: 970-625-4862

Salida Museum

406½ West Rainbow Boulevard
Salida, CO 81201
Tel: 719-539-4602

Silt Historical Society

8th and Orchard
Silt, CO 81652
Tel: 970-876-2668

San Juan County Historical Society Museum

Courthouse Square
Silverton, CO 81433
Tel: 970-387-5838

Cowboy and working outfit, circa 1900. Courtesy of Tread of Pioneers Museum.

Tread of Pioneers Museum

800 Oak Street
Steamboat Springs, CO 80477
Tel: 970-879-2214 Fax: 970-879-6109
Hours: Tue–Sat 11–5 pm
Contact: Candice Lombardo
Institution type: History museum, historic house
Collection type: Clothing, accessories, general textiles
Description: 1850–present. Hundreds of vintage skis, ski accessories, and fashions. Extensive Native American artifact collection includes baskets, rugs, blankets, pottery, and beadwork. Other items include hundreds of pioneer and rural Victorian artifacts, including clothing and other textiles; western and ranching implements; and photographs of early western people and everyday activities of the West.
$ ✍

Overland Trail Museum

Junction I-75 and Highway 6
Sterling, CO 80751
Tel: 970-522-3895
www.sterlingcolo.com

A. R. Mitchell Memorial Museum and Gallery

150 East Main Street
Trindad, CO 81082
Tel: 719-846-4224

U.S. Air Force Academy Museum

2346 Academy Drive
USAF Academy, CO 80840
Tel: 719-632-USAF

Colorado Ski Museum and Hall of Fame

231 South Frontage Road East
Vail, CO 81657
Tel: 970-467-1876
www.skimuseum.net

Wray Museum

205 East 3rd Street
Wray, CO 80758
Tel: 970-332-5063

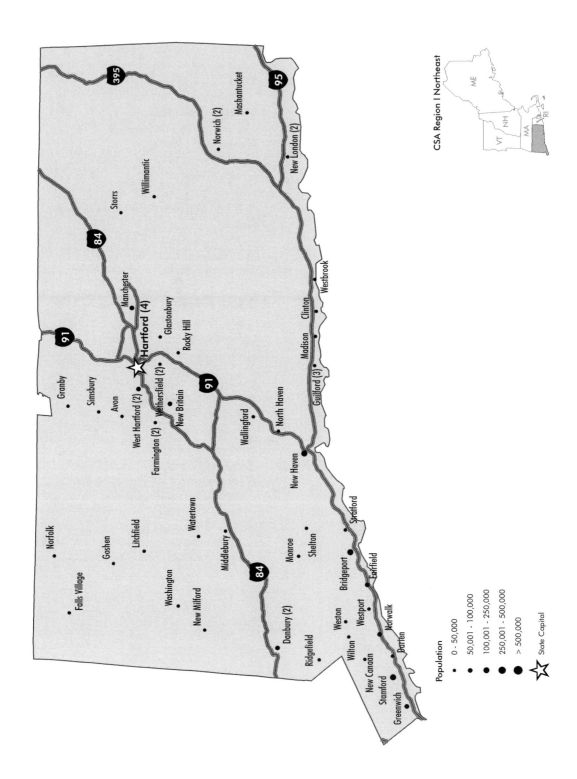

CSA Region I Northeast

Population
. 0 - 50,000
• 50,001 - 100,000
● 100,001 - 250,000
⬤ 250,001 - 500,000
⬤ > 500,000
☆ State Capital

CONNECTICUT

Avon Historical Society

184 Waterville Road
Avon, CT 06001
Tel: 860-678-7621
www.vintageaviation.net/ahs/
avonhistoricalsociety.htm

Hours: Sun 2–4 pm (Jun–Sep), and by appointment
Contact: Nora Howard
Institution type: History museum, historic house
Collection type: Clothing, accessories, uniforms
Description: 1800–1960. Twentieth-century military uniforms, dresses from 1830 to the 1930s, undergarments, and children's nineteenth-century clothing. Items pertain to the Avon area and central Connecticut.

The Barnum Museum

820 Main Street
Bridgeport, CT 06604
Tel: 203-331-1104 Fax: 203-331-0079
www.barnum-museum.org

Hours: Tue–Sat 10–4:30 pm, Sun 12–4:30 pm
Contact: Kathleen Maher
Institution type: History museum
Collection type: Clothing, accessories, costumes
Description: 1800–1899. Started by PT Barnum in 1893 as a museum for the study of history and sciences, the museum holds 10,000 specimens of natural science objects, ethnographic and anthropological materials, and eighteenth- and nineteenth-century domestic and military materials. 1,500 objects of Bridgeport families, including costumes, books, accessories, letters, photographs, and toys. Broadsides, costumes, and promotional objects and souvenirs showcase Barnum's enterprises and performers, notably Tom Thumb and Jenny Lind.

$

Stanton House

63 East Main Street
Clinton, CT 06413
Tel: 203-669-2132

Danbury Museum and Historical Society

43 Main Street
Danbury, CT 06810
Tel: 203-743-5200
www.danburyhistorical.org

Military Museum of Southern New England

125 Park Avenue
Danbury, CT 06810
Tel: 203-790-9277 Fax: 203-790-0420
www.usmilitarymuseum.org

Hours: Tue–Sat 10–5 pm, Sun 12–5 pm
Contact: Curator of collections
Institution type: History museum
Collection type: Clothing, accessories, uniforms
Description: 1915–present. Collection includes World War I to modern military uniforms.

$

Darien Historical Society

45 Old Kings Highway North
Darien, CT 06820
Tel: 203-655-9233
http://historical.darien.org
Hours: Tue, Fri 9–2 pm, Wed–Thu 9–4 pm
Contact: Babs White
Institution type: History museum
Collection type: Clothing, accessories, costumes, general textiles
Description: 1850–1960. More than 1,500 costume items, men's, women's, and children's, including accessories and paisley shawls.

$ ✍

Wedding gown and corset, 1897. Courtesy of Fairfield Historical Society.

Fairfield Historical Society

636 Old Post Road
Fairfield, CT 06824
Tel: 203-259-1598 Fax: 203-255-2716
www.fairfieldhistoricalsociety.org
Hours: Tue–Sat 10–4:30 pm, Sun 1–4:30 pm
Contact: Adrienne Saint-Pierre
Institution type: History museum
Collection type: Clothing, accessories, uniforms, costumes, general textiles, quilts, flags
Description: 1700–present. Men's, women's, and children's clothing and accessories worn or used in Fairfield from 1730 to the present. The menswear collection houses a number of outstanding early-nineteenth-century examples. Women's clothing is strong in nineteenth and twentieth century with a few examples of eighteenth-century garments and accessories.

$ ✍

Canaan Historical Society

44 Railroad Street
Falls Village, CT 06031
Tel: 860-824-7235

Hill-Stead Museum

ALFRED ATMOR POPE COLLECTION
35 Mountain Road
Farmington, CT 06032
Tel: 860-677-4787 Fax: 860-677-0174
www.hillstead.org
Hours: Tue–Sun 10–5 pm (May–Oct); Tue–Sun 11–4 pm (Nov–Apr)
Contact: Cynthia Cormier
Institution type: Historic house
Collection type: Clothing, accessories, costumes, general textiles
Description: 1750–1960. Collection includes 25 costumes, primarily dresses worn by Theodate Pope Riddle during her lifetime (1868–1946); 1 man's suit; 2 Japanese Hapi coats; 11 hats and bonnets, including Riddle's grandmother's Quaker bonnet; table, bed, and bath linens, including several Japanese silk cloths, mats, and runners; and 24 oriental rugs from the mid-eighteenth century to the early twentieth century.

$ ✍

Stanley-Whitman House, Farmington

37 High Street
Farmington, CT 06032
Tel: 860-677-9222
www.stanleywhitman.org

Historical Society of Glastonbury

1944 Main Street
Glastonbury, CT 06033
Tel: 860-633-6890

Goshen Historical Society

21 Old Middle Road
Goshen, CT 06756
Tel: 860-491-9610
www.goshenhistoricalsociety.org

Salmon Brook Historical Society

208 Salmon Brook Street
Granby, CT 06035
Tel: 860-653-9713
www.salmonbrookhistorical.org

Hours: Sun 2–4 pm (Jun–Oct)
Contact: Jean Potetz
Institution type: History museum, historic house
Collection type: Clothing, accessories, uniforms, costumes, general textiles, quilts, flags
Description: 1800–1960. Clothing and quilts mostly from the nineteenth and twentieth centuries.

$ ✍

Bruce Museum of Arts and Science

1 Museum Drive
Greenwich, CT 06830
Tel: 203-869-0376 Fax: 203-869-0963
www.brucemuseum.org
Hours: Tue–Sat 10–5 pm, Sun 1–5 pm
Institution type: Art museum
$ ✍

Henry Whitfield State Historical Museum

248 Old Whitfield Street
Guilford, CT 06437
Tel: 203-453-2457
www.chc.state.ct.us/whitfieldhouse.htm

The Hyland House

84 Boston Street
Guilford, CT 06437
Tel: 203-453-9477
www.hylandhouse.com

The Thomas Griswold House and Museum

171 Boston Street
Guilford, CT 06437
Tel: 203-453-3176
www.guilfordkeepingsociety.com

Connecticut Historical Society Museum

1 Elizabeth Street
Hartford, CT 06105
Tel: 860-236-5621
www.chs.org
Hours: Galleries: Tue–Sun 12–5 pm; Library: 10–5 pm Tue–Sat; Museum study collections: Mon–Fri 9–5 pm by appointment
Contact: Curator of collections
Institution type: History museum
Collection type: Clothing, accessories, uniforms, general textiles, quilts, flags
Description: 1700–present. Representative spec-

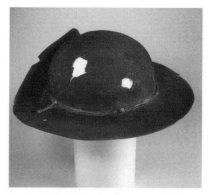

Revolutionary War round hat, felted wool, shot through by a musket ball that killed Phineas Meigs, 1782. Courtesy of Connecticut Historical Society Museum.

trum of costumes and accessories made or worn in Connecticut with strengths in middle- and working-class garments and men's and women's wear, 1875–1910. Uniforms from the Revolutionary War to the present. More than half of the collection can be linked to the makers or owners, often with related artifacts and archival materials. Textile holdings are notable for quilts, silk and crewel embroideries, bed rugs, and hand-woven linens.

$ ✍

Harriet Beecher Stowe Center

77 Forest Street
Hartford, CT 06105
Tel: 860-522-9258 Fax: 860-522-9259
www.stowecenter.org
Hours: Tue–Sat 9:30–4:30 pm, Sun 12–4:30 pm
Contact: Dawn C. Adiletta
Institution type: History museum, historic house
Collection type: Clothing, accessories, general textiles
Description: 1760–1960. Material relating to extended Beecher-Stowe families and nineteenth-century residents of Nook Farm in Hartford, Connecticut.

$ ✍

Mark Twain House

351 Farmington Avenue
Hartford, CT 06105-4498
Tel: 860-247-0998x10
www.marktwainhouse.org

Dress, Charles James, 1964. Courtesy of Wadsworth Atheneum Museum of Art.

Man's dressing gown, circa 1840. Courtesy of Litchfield History Museum.

Wadsworth Atheneum Museum of Art

600 Main Street
Hartford, CT 06103-2990
Tel: 860-278-2670
www.wadsworthatheneum.org
Hours: Wed–Fri 11–5 pm, Sat–Sun 10–5 pm
Contact: Curator of collections
Institution type: Art museum
Collection type: Accessories, costumes, general textiles
Description: Pre-1700–present. Eighteenth- to twenty-first-century women's fashionable dress textiles from Coptic to contemporary, including fiber art. Collection also includes Ballets Russes' costumes and costume designs.
$ 🖎

Litchfield History Museum

7 South Street
Litchfield, CT 06759
Tel: 860-567-4501 Fax: 860-567-3565
www.litchfieldhistoricalsociety.org
Hours: Tue–Sat 1–5 pm, Sun 1–5 pm (mid Apr–Nov); Research library: 10–4 pm (year-round)
Contact: Jeannie A. Ingram
Institution type: History museum
Collection type: Clothing, accessories, uniforms, costumes, general textiles, quilts, flags
Description: 1760–present. Strengths include nineteenth-century women's formal dresses, skirts, blouse, underwear, and outerwear; nine-teenth- and twentieth-century uniforms, particularly Red Cross uniforms; eighteenth-century women's costumes; nineteenth- and twentieth-century quilts and woven bed coverings; children's clothing from the nineteenth and twentieth centuries; eighteenth- and nineteenth-century women's shoes; and 500 examples of lace and other flat textiles.
$ 🖎

Madison Historical Society

853 Boston Post Road
Madison, CT 06443
Tel: 203-245-4567

Old Manchester Museum

126 Cedar Street
Manchester, CT 06040
Tel: 860-647-9983
www.manchesterhistory.org

Mashantucket Pequot Museum and Research Center

110 Pequot Trail
Mashantucket, CT 06338
Tel: 860-396-6800
www.pequotmuseum.org
Hours: Mon–Sun 9–5 pm
$ 🖎

Middlesex County Historical Society

151 Main Street
Middlebury, CT 06457
Tel: 860-346-0746
www.middlesexhistory.org

Monroe Historical Society

433 Barnhill Road
Monroe, CT 06468
Tel: 203-261-1383
www.monroehistoricsociety.org

New Britain Youth Museum

30 High Street
New Britain, CT 06051
Tel: 860-225-3020 Fax: 860-229-4982
Hours: Tue–Fri 1–5 pm, Sat 10–4 pm
Contact: Curator of collections
Institution type: History museum
Collection type: Clothing, accessories, uniforms, costumes, general textiles
Description: 1850–present. Small collection houses miscellaneous costumes, international dolls, and mid-twentieth-century European costumes and textiles.

New Canaan Historical Society

13 Oenoke Ridge
New Canaan, CT 06840
Tel: 203-966-1776 Fax: 203-972-5917
www.nchistory.org
Hours: Tue–Sat 9:30–4 pm
Contact: Deborah Bede
Institution type: History museum, historic house
Collection type: Clothing, accessories, uniforms, costumes, general textiles, flags
Description: Pre-1700–present. Objects connected to New Canaan history with exceptional depth and breadth. The majority of the collection is women's dress, including exceptional linen dress from circa 1780, an eighteenth-century woman's worked bodice of checked linen, early-nineteenth-century dresses, and dresses from 1910 to 1920, including unusual 1920s day dresses. Men's wear includes a seventeenth-century man's sleeved waistcoat. Collection also features formal and everyday wear and military uniforms from the late nineteenth century through the twentieth century, Kashmir and paisley shawls, hat and shoes, fans and bags, and personal grooming items.

Knights of Columbus Museum

1 State Street
New Haven, CT 06511
Tel: 203-865-0400 Fax: 203-865-0351
www.kofc.org/about/museum/index.cfm

New London County Historical Society

11 Blinman Street
New London, CT 06320
Tel: 860-443-1209

U.S. Coast Guard Museum

15 Mohegan Avenue
New London, CT 06320-4195
Tel: 860-444-8511
www.uscg.mil/hq/g-cp/museum/
MuseumIndex.htm

The New Milford Historical Society

6 Aspetuck Avenue
New Milford, CT 06776-0359
Tel: 860-354-3069
www.nmhistorical.org

Norfolk Historical Museum

13 Village Green
Norfolk, CT 06058
Tel: 860-542-5761

North Haven Historical Society

27 Broadway
North Haven, CT 06473
Tel: 203-239-3288
Hours: Tue, Thu 1–4:30 pm (Sep–Jun)
Contact: Gloria Furnival
Institution type: History museum, historic house
Collection type: Clothing, accessories
Description: 1760–present. Collection is limited to clothing and accessories worn in North Haven mostly from the 1800s. The historical society hosts an annual costume display and lecture.

Lockwood-Mathews Mansion Museum

295 West Avenue
Norwalk, CT 06850
Tel: 203-838-9799
www.lockwoodmathews.org

Faith Trumball Chapter Daughters of the American Revolution Museum
42 Rockwell Street
Norwich, CT 06360
Tel: 860-887-8737

The Slater Memorial Museum–Norwich Free Academy
108 Crescent Street
Norwich, CT 06360
Tel: 860-887-2506 Fax: 860-885-0379
www.norwichfreeacademy.com/slater_museum

Keeler Tavern Museum
132 Main Street
Ridgefield, CT 06877
Tel: 203-438-5485
www.keelertavernmuseum.org

Academy Hall Museum of the Rocky Hill Historical Society
785 Old Main Street
Rocky Hill, CT 06067
Tel: 860-563-6704
www.rockyhillhistory.org

Shelton Historical Society
70 Ripton Road
Shelton, CT 06484
Tel: 203-925-1803 Fax: 203-926-9567
www.sheltonhistoricalsociety.org
Hours: Tue–Thu 10–2 pm
Contact: Deborah Rossi, Curator
Institution type: History museum, historic house
Collection type: Clothing, accessories, uniforms, costumes, general textiles, flags
Description: 1700–present. Local collection reflects the rural and industrial past of Shelton. Highlights include a pair of 1830s black satin dancing slippers, a woman's work dress from the latter half of the nineteenth century with significant patching and alterations, dresses made in Shelton in the 1950s and 1960s, and prom dresses from the 1980s.
$ ✍️

Simsbury Historical Society
800 Hopmeadow Street
Simsbury, CT 06070
Tel: 860-658-2500
www.simsburyhistory.org

Stamford Historical Society
1508 High Ridge Road
Stamford, CT 06903
Tel: 203-322-1565
www.cslib.org/stamford

Mansfield Historical Society Museum
954 Storrs Road
Storrs, CT 06268
Tel: 860-429-6575
www.mansfield-history.org

The Stratford Historical Society and Catherine R. Mitchell Museum
967 Academy Hill
Stratford, CT 06615
Tel: 203-378-0630
www.stratfordhistoricalsociety.com

Wallingford Historical Society
180 South Main Street
Wallingford, CT 06492
Tel: 203-294-1996

Gunn Memorial Library and Museum
5 Wykeham Road
Washington, CT 06793
Tel: 860-868-7756
www.gunnlibrary.org

Watertown Historical Society
22 DeForest Street
Watertown, CT 06795-2522
Tel: 860-274-1050
www.watertown-ct.org/Historical_Soc/
Hist_Soc_.htm

Museum of American Political Life
University of Hartford
200 Bloomfield Avenue
West Hartford, CT 06117
Tel: 860-768-4090

Noah Webster House and West Hartford Historical Society
227 South Main Street
West Hartford, CT 06107
Tel: 860-521-5362
http://noahwebsterhouse.org

Military Historians, Headquarters and Museum

North Main Street
Westbrook, CT 06498
Tel: 860-399-9460

The Coley Homestead and Barn Museum

104 Weston Road
Weston, CT 06883
Tel: 203-226-1804

Shoes and stockings, 1938. Courtesy of Westport Historical Society.

Westport Historical Society

25 Avery Place
Westport, CT 06880
Tel: 203-222-1424
www.westporthistory.org
Hours: Mon–Fri 10–4 pm, Sat 12–3 pm
Contact: Andrea Maritzer Fine, Museum Shop Manager and Photographer
Institution type: History museum
Collection type: Clothing, accessories, uniforms, costumes, general textiles
Description: 1850–present. 1,300 items donated by Westporters, primarily women's, men's, and children's clothing and accessories representing the lifestyles of the actors, writers, musicians, artists, and others who have called Westport their home since the turn of the twentieth century.

$ ✐

The Wethersfield Historical Society

150 Main Street
Wethersfield, CT 06109
Tel: 860-529-7656
www.wethhist.org

Webb-Deane-Stevens Museum

211 Main Street
Wethersfield, CT 06109
Tel: 860-529-0612 Fax: 860-571-8636
www.webb-deane-stevens.org
Hours: Wed–Mon 10–4 pm (May–Oct); Sat–Sun 10–4 pm (Nov–Apr)
Contact: Donna Baron, Curator
Institution type: History museum, historic house
Collection type: Clothing, accessories, uniforms, costumes, general textiles, flags
Description: 1700–1960. Costume collection supports the mission of interpreting the colonial period and its influence in the lower Connecticut River Valley. Collection includes provenanced eighteenth-century women's gowns, shoes, and accessories, men's clothing and hats, and women's and children's clothing from circa 1820 to 1925 with many of the artifacts donated by the original owners' descendants and detailed provenances of manufacture or use in Connecticut.

$ ✐

Windham Textile and History Museum

157 Union-Main Street
Williamantic, CT 06226
Tel: 203-456-2178
www.millmuseum.org

Wilton Historical Museums

224 Danbury Road
Wilton, CT 06897
Tel: 203-762-7257

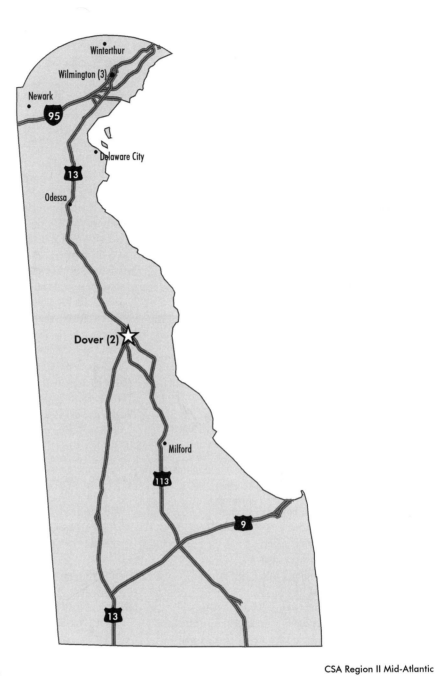

Winterthur

Wilmington (3)

Newark

95

13

Delaware City

Odessa

Dover (2)

Milford

113

9

13

Population

- 0 - 50,000
- 50,001 - 100,000
- 100,001 - 250,000
- 250,001 - 500,000
- \> 500,000

☆ State Capital

CSA Region II Mid-Atlantic

NY

PA

NJ

MD

DELAWARE

Fort Delaware Society
108 Old Reedy Point Bridge Road
Delaware City, DE 19706
Tel: 302-834-1630
www.del.net/org/fort

Delaware State Museums
102 South State Street
Dover, DE 19901
Tel: 302-739-5316
www.destatemuseums.org

Delaware State University
1200 North DuPont Highway
Dover, DE 19001
Tel: 302-857-6466

Milford Historical Society
501 NW Front Street
Milford, DE 19963
Tel: 302-422-4222

University of Delaware
201 Allison Annex, University of Delaware
Newark, DE 19716
Tel: 302-831-8545

Historic Houses of Odessa, Delaware
109 Main Street
Odessa, DE 19730
Tel: 302-378-4069

Hagley Museum and Library
298 Buck Road East
Wilmington, DE 19807
Tel: 302-658-2400 Fax: 302-658-6716
www.hagley.lib.de.us
Hours: Mon–Sun 9:30–4:30 pm
Contact: Debra Hughes, Curator of Collections
and Exhibits
Institution type: History museum, historic house
Collection type: Clothing, accessories, general tex-
tiles, flags
Description: 1800–present.
$ ✍

Historical Society of Delaware
505 Market Street
Wilmington, DE 19801
Tel: 302-655-7161
www.hsd.org

Rockwood Museum
610 Shipley Road
Wilmington, DE 19809
Tel: 302-761-4340
www.rockwood.org

Winterthur Museum
Route 52 Kennett Pike
Winterthur, DE 19735
Tel: 302-888-4600
www.winterthur.org
Hours: Tue–Sun 10–5 pm
Contact: Linda Eaton

Dress, Quaker dress worn by Elizabeth Richardson Hodgson (1812–1867). Courtesy of Winterthur Museum and Gardens.

Institution type: History museum, art museum, historic house

Collection type: Clothing, accessories, costumes, general textiles, quilts

Description: Pre-1700–1899. World-renowned collection of textiles and a small, growing collection of clothing and accessories of approximately 800 objects. Wide variety of objects from eighteenth-century dresses to Colonial Revival fancy dress, from dolls to lace, from pockets to pocketbooks. Of particular interest is a group of provenanced Quaker clothing.

$ ✍

DISTRICT OF COLUMBIA

U.S. Army Center of Military History, Museum Division
NATIONAL MUSEUM (NMUSA)
  COLLECTION
ARMY ART COLLECTION
103 3rd Avenue
Fort McNair, DC 20319-5058
Tel: 202-761-5373 Fax: 202-761-5444
www.army.mil/cmh-pg
Hours: By appointment while building is under
  construction
Contact: Steve McGeorge, Chief, Collections
  Branch
Institution type: Art museum, history museum,
  federal museum
Collection type: Accessories, uniforms, flags
Description: 1760–present. U.S. Army uniforms,
  accoutrements, equipment, and accessories
  from the eighteenth century to the present.
  Especially strong in early- to mid-nineteenth-
  century materials and nineteenth-century
  colors.

American Red Cross
1730 E Street NW
Washington, DC 20006
Tel: 202-639-3300 Fax: 202-628-1362
www.redcross.org/museum/exhibits/exhibits.asp
Hours: Mon–Fri 8:30–4 pm, and selected week-
  ends
Contact: Curator of collections
Institution type: Art museum, history museum

Collection type: Clothing, accessories, uniforms,
  general textiles, quilts, flags
Description: 1850–present. Established in 1919.
  A small part of the collection encompasses
  large-item textiles such as uniforms
  (1914–present), flags (1864–present), quilts
  (1918–present), and accessories
  (1864–present). Selected textile items are used
  as elements in exhibitions on a rotating basis.

Arthur M. Sackler Gallery
1050 Independence Avenue SW
Washington, DC 20560
Tel: 202-357-4880
www.si.edu/asia

Black Fashion Museum
2007 Vermont Avenue NW
Washington, DC 20004
Tel: 202-667-0744
www.bfmdc.org
Hours: By appointment only
Contact: Director
Institution type: Art museum, history museum
Collection type: Clothing, accessories, costumes
Description: 1850–present. Museum's mission is
  to identify, acknowledge, and spotlight the
  achievements and contributions of people of
  the African diaspora to the fashion industry
  past, present and future. Exhibits include
  authentic slave dresses and the clothes of Ms.
  Rosa Parks. Continuing exhibitions spotlight

Washington (20)

Fort McNair

Population

- 0 - 50,000
- 50,001 - 100,000
- 100,001 - 250,000
- 250,001 - 500,000
- > 500,000

 State Capital

CSA Region II Mid-Atlantic

the pioneering work of Lois K. Alexander-Lane, founder of the Black Fashion Museum and Harlem Institute of Fashion.

$

Boy's three-piece suit, 1785. Courtesy of DAR Museum.

DAR Museum

1776 D Street NW
Washington, DC 20006
Tel: 202-879-3241 Fax: 202-628-0820
www.dar.org/museum
Hours: Mon–Fri 9:30–4 pm, Sat 9–5 pm
Contact: Alden O'Brien
Institution type: History museum
Collection type: Clothing, accessories, costumes, general textiles, quilts, flags
Description: 1700–1914. Representative collection of American civilian clothing, largely women's and children's. Collection includes approximately 120 women's main garments; shawls, purses, and more than 100 shoes; selection of corsets, 1768–1890; embroidered cotton collars, shawls, and kerchiefs, 1750–1900; jewelry, including a good selection of mourning jewelry and hair jewelry; and men's waistcoats, 1740–1850.

✍

Dumbarton House

2715 Que Street NW
Washington, DC 20007
Tel: 202-337-2288 Fax: 202-337-0348
www.dumbartonhouse.org
Hours: Tue–Sat 10–2:00 pm
Contact: Brian J. Lang
Institution type: Historic house

Regimental coat of Lt. Eli Dagworthy, 44th Regiment of Foot, 1767-1775. Courtesy of Dumbarton House, National Society of Colonial Dames.

Collection type: Clothing, accessories, uniforms, costumes, general textiles, quilts
Description: 1760–1849. Textile collection features late-eighteenth- to early-nineteenth-century clothing, jewelry, and accessories, quilts and coverlets, and uniforms. Important objects include a green lampas and gilt thread coat belonging to Thomas Sixth Lord Fairfax; a British 44th Regiment of Foot uniform; Washington family jewelry and clothing, including a quilted carriage cloak owned by Eliza Parke Custis Law (1797–1821); waistcoats; and clothing with a Joseph Nourse (1754–1841) family provenance.

$

Dumbarton Oaks

BYZANTINE COLLECTION
PRE-COLUMBIAN COLLECTION
HOUSE COLLECTION
1703 32nd Street NW
Washington, DC 20007
Tel: 202-339-6414
www.doaks.org
Hours: Tue–Sun 2-5 pm
Contact: Curator of collection
Institution type: Art museum, university collection
Collection type: General textiles
Description: Pre-1700–1850. The Byzantine Collection includes approximately 250 late antique, Byzantine, and Islamic textiles; the Pre-Columbian Collection includes 35 textiles; and the House Collection includes 4 fifteenth- and sixteenth-century tapestries.

✍

Evening dress by Madeleine et Madeleine for Marjorie Merriweather Post, 1921. Courtesy of Hillwood Museum and Gardens.

Hillwood Museum and Gardens

4155 Linnean Avenue NW
Washington, DC 20008
Tel: 202-686-8500 Fax: 202-966-7846
www.hillwoodmuseum.org
Hours: Tue–Sat 10–5 pm, reservations required
Contact: Howard Kurtz
Institution type: Historic house
Collection type: Clothing, accessories, uniforms, costumes, general textiles
Description: Pre-1700–present. Russian, liturgical, and lace objects, and clothing and accessories worn by Mrs. Marjorie Merriweather Post and her family, including fancy dress costumes from 1923 to 1929.

$ 🖐🗔

House of the Temple

1733 16th Street NW
Washington, DC 20009
Tel: 202-232-3579
www.srmason-sj.org/library.htm

International Spy Museum

800 F Street NW
Washington, DC 20004
Tel: 202-393-7798
www.spymuseum.org

National Air and Space Museum

6th Street and Independence Avenue SW
Washington, DC 20560
Tel: 202-357-1552
www.nasm.si.edu

National Museum of African Art

950 Independence Avenue SW
Washington, DC 20560
Tel: 202-357-4600x277
www.nmafa.si.edu

Woman's brooch, blue enamel leaf, circa 1840–1860. Courtesy of National Museum of American History, Behring Center, Smithsonian Institution.

National Museum of American History, Smithsonian Institution, Behring Center

14th and Constitution Avenue NW
Washington, DC 20013-7012
Tel: 202-357-2700
www.americanhistory.si.edu
Hours: Mon–Sun 10–5:30 pm
Institution type: Federal museum
🖐🗔
DIVISION OF HOME AND COMMUNITY LIFE, COSTUME COLLECTION
Contact: Bonnie Lilienfeld
Collection type: Clothing, accessories, costumes
Description: Pre-1700–present. More than 30,000 garments and accessories representing the changing appearance of Americans from the eighteenth century until the present day. Collection illustrates the social, cultural, technical, and economic influences affecting dress made or worn in America. It features men's, women's, and children's garments and accessories that are worn or carried; fashion prints, photographs, and original illustrations and posters; and

objects related to personal grooming and to clothing manufacturing and the selling of clothing.

DIVISION OF HOME AND COMMUNITY LIFE, DOMESTIC LIFE COLLECTION

Contact: Bonnie Lilienfeld

Collection type: Costumes, general textiles

Description: 1760–present. Costume holdings include a few post–World War II children's Halloween costumes. Doll holdings include several hundred dolls from the late eighteenth century to the present. The majority are dolls used for play. There are also character dolls, fashion dolls, and collector dolls. Textile holdings include approximately 75 miscellaneous curtains, draperies, trimmings, and valances.

DIVISION OF HOME AND COMMUNITY LIFE, TEXTILES COLLECTION

Contact: Bonnie Lilienfeld

Collection type: Clothing, costumes, general textiles, quilts

Description: Pre-1700–present. Collection illustrates the history of the American textile industry from the seventeenth through the twenty-first century. Collection includes fibers, yarns, and fabrics as well as textile machinery made in America and foreign countries. Collection also includes quilts, coverlets, samplers, spinning wheels, and sewing machines. The collection's strongest period is nineteenth-century American textiles and features a large collection of textile machinery patent models.

DIVISION OF MEDICINE AND SCIENCE

Contact: Roger Sherman or Ann Seeger

Collection type: Clothing, accessories

Description: 1900–present. Physics collection has a few articles of clothing, including a jumpsuit worn by Emilio Segre and academic hoods worn by Edwin McMillan. Biological sciences collection has laboratory coats, some associated with specific scientists, T-shirts with slogans for Earth Day or for various causes, and goggles.

DIVISION OF MILITARY AND DIPLOMATIC COLLECTION

Contact: Margaret Vining

Collection type: Clothing, accessories, uniforms

Description: 1700–present. Uniforms and accoutrements from the eighteenth century through the twenty-first century. Collection also features a child's 1944 military uniform made in the style of the army uniform his uncle wore during World War II; children's "sailor suits"; clothing design influenced by a military uniform; and a wedding dress and lingerie made from World War II parachutes.

Ann Miller costume, circa 1970. Courtesy of National Museum of American History, Behring Center, Smithsonian Institution.

DIVISION OF MUSIC, SPORTS, AND ENTERTAINMENT

Contact: Dwight Bowers, Ellen Hughes, or Jane Rogers

Collection type: Clothing, accessories, uniforms, costumes

Description: 1850–present. Popular culture collection includes music, television, theater, and other entertainment objects, as well as sports and leisure clothing, uniforms, and accessories.

DIVISION OF POLITICS AND REFORM

Contact: Larry Bird, Lisa Kathleen Grady, or Harry Rubenstein

Collection type: Clothing, accessories, costumes, general textiles, flags

Description: 1700–present. Topical political and national history collection includes clothing and textiles that represent people and events, including clothing worn by First Ladies while not in office at the White House; clothing worn to political events; diplomatic uniforms; gowns worn to the White House; gowns worn by diplomats' wives; and reform and aesthetic movement garments.

National Museum of American Jewish Military History

1811 R Street NW
Washington, DC 20009
Tel: 202-265-6280
www.nmajmh.org

Hours: Mon–Fri 9–5 pm
Institution type: History museum

National Museum of Natural History, Smithsonian Institution

10th Street and Constitution NW
Washington, DC 20560
Tel: 202-357-1300
www.nmnh.si.edu

Hunkpapa Lakota eagle-feather headdress, 1884–1885. Courtesy of National Museum of the American Indian, Smithsonian Institution.

National Museum of the American Indian, Smithsonian Institution

4th Street and Independence Avenue SW
Washington, DC 20560
Tel: 202-633-1000
www.americanindian.si.edu
Hours: Mon–Sun 10–5:30 pm
Contact: Public Relations Office
Institution type: Federal museum
Collection type: Clothing, accessories
Description: Pre-1700–present. Items from 10,000 BC to the present. Clothing and accessories and numerous other types of items relating to Native Americans from both North and South America are displayed in ongoing exhibits. The resource center on the third floor serves as a limited onsite research area with a small closed stack library open daily during regular hours.

The Navy Museum

805 Kidder Breese Street SE
Washington, DC 20374
Tel: 202-433-6897
www.history.navy.mil

The Textile Museum

2320 S Street NW
Washington, DC 20008
Tel: 202-667-0441 Fax: 202-483-0994
www.textilemuseum.org
Hours: Mon–Sat 10–5 pm, Sun 1–5 pm
Contact: Rachel Shabica, Registrar
Institution type: Art museum
Collection type: General textiles
Description: Pre-1700–present. Founded in 1925 with a collection of 275 rugs and 60 related textiles from the traditions of non-Western cultures. Holdings now represent the full spectrum of non-Western textile arts with more than 17,000 objects spanning 5,000 years, from 3,000 BCE to the present.

Detail, dress, 1894. Courtesy of Tudor Place.

Tudor Place Historic House and Garden

1644 31st Street NW
Washington, DC 20004
Tel: 202-965-0400x103 Fax: 202-965-0164
www.tudorplace.org
Hours: Tue–Sat 10–4 pm, Sun 12–4 pm
Contact: Melinda Linderer
Institution type: Historic house
Collection type: Clothing, accessories, uniforms, costumes, general textiles, flags

Description: 1700–present. Broad collection of historic textiles amassed over a 178-year period (1805–1983) by members of the Peter family. Highlights include costumes and accessories once owned by Martha Washington, the grandmother of Martha Peter.

$

United States Holocaust Memorial Museum

100 Raoul Wallenberg Place SW
Washington, DC 20024
Tel: 202-488-0400
www.ushmm.org
Hours: Mon–Sun 10–5:30 pm
Contact: Chief curator
Institution type: Federal museum

Collection type: Clothing, accessories, uniforms, costumes, general textiles, flags
Description: 1915–1960. More than 10,000 objects that document and illustrate the history of the Holocaust (1939–1945) and the period immediately before and after it took place. Textiles include uniforms, costumes, clothing, badges, armbands, flags, banners, and domestic items.

Woodrow Wilson House

2340 S Street NW
Washington, DC 20008
Tel: 202-387-4062x14
www.woodrowwilsonhouse.org

Pensacola
Valparaiso
10
Fernandina Beach
Tallahassee (5)
75
St. Augustine
Cross Creek
Ocala
Daytona Beach (2)
Port Orange
Cedar Key
Tavares   Eustis
Mount Dora   Sanford
Orlando   Maitland
Winter Park
New Port Richey
Polk City
Tarpon Springs
Clearwater   Lakeland
Tampa
St. Petersburg   Lake Wales
95
Ellenton
Sarasota   Stuart
Clewiston
Lake Worth (2)
Fort Myers   Boca Raton
Delray Beach (2)
Deerfield Beach
Fort Lauderdale (4)
Miami Beach
Miami (3)   (2)
Coral Gables   Coconut
Grove
Key West

Population

- 0 - 50,000
- 50,001 - 100,000
- 100,001 - 250,000
- 250,001 - 500,000
- > 500,000

 State Capital

CSA Region VI Southeast

KY   WV   VA
AR   TN   NC
MS   LA   GA   SC
LA

Boca Raton Historical Society

71 North Federal Highway
Boca Raton, FL 33432
Tel: 561-395-6766
www.bocahistory.org

Cedar Key Historical Society Museum

2nd Street at Highway 24
Cedar Key, FL 32625
Tel: 352-543-5549

Ah-Tah-Thi-Ki Museum

HC-61, Box 21-A
Clewiston, FL 33440
Tel: 863-902-1115
www.seminoletribe.com/museum

The Barnacle State Park

3485 Main Highway
Coconut Grove, FL 33133
Tel: 305-442-6866 Fax: 305-442-6872
www.floridastateparks.org/thebarnacle/default.cfm
Hours: Fri–Mon 9–4 pm
Contact: Susannah Worth
Institution type: Historic house
Collection type: Clothing, accessories, costumes, general textiles, quilts
Description: 1850–1960. Men's, women's, and children's clothes, 1890–1933; household textiles; and 20 oriental rugs. Highlights include man's three-piece bast fiber suit; handbags made of local materials (palmetto and sisal); early pennants from the Biscayne Yacht Club; Mr. and Mrs. Munroe's matching dressing

Straw bag, circa 1890–1939, thought to have been made in Coconut Grove. Courtesy of The Barnacle State Park.

gowns circa 1900 and his straw fedora; canvas leggings for walking in the tall grass; early-twentieth-century swimsuits (including an Annette Kellerman suit); a pair of Eskimo wood snow goggles; an undated sampler; 150 paper patterns for embroidery; and 4 quilts.
$ ✍

Lowe Art Museum, University of Miami

1301 Stanford Drive
Coral Gables, FL 33124-6310
Tel: 305-284-5423 Fax: 305-284-2024
www.lowemuseum.org
Hours: Tue–Wed, Thu 12–7 pm, Fri–Sat 10–5 pm, Sun 12–5 pm
Institution type: Art museum, university collection
$ ✍

Cotton Cloth of Igbo people, twentieth century. Courtesy of Lowe Museum of Art.

ALFRED I. BARTON COLLECTION OF SOUTHWEST NATIVE AMERICAN ART

Contact: Kara Schneiderman, Registrar

Collection type: Clothing, accessories, general textiles

Description: 1850–present. 422 textiles, baskets, and other utilitarian objects, including rare examples of the Navajo, Pueblo, and Rio Grande weaving traditions. Costumes and textiles from the northwest coast of the United States and Canada, the Plains/Plateau areas, and Southeast/Woodlands areas.

AFRICAN TEXTILES

Contact: Kara Schneiderman, Registrar

Collection type: Clothing, accessories, costumes, general textiles

Description: Pre-1700, 1915–present. 720 objects representing the various sub-Saharan cultures of West Africa, including costumes, textiles, and textile manufacturing objects such as printing blocks.

ANCIENT AMERICAN ART

Contact: Kara Schneiderman, Registrar

Collection type: General textiles

Description: Pre-1700. Textiles and textile fragments from ancient Peru, primarily Chancay, Chimu, and Huari cultures, with some Inca and Moche examples.

$ ✍

GUATEMALAN TEXTILES

Contact: Kara Schneiderman, Registrar

Collection type: Clothing, accessories, costumes, general textiles

Description: 1900–present. Established in 1958 with a core of 50 textiles collected in the early twentieth century by the leading Harvard anthropologist Samuel K. Lothrop. In an exchange with the Columbia Museum of Art, South Carolina, the collection numbers 457 examples and complements the Lowe's textile holdings in North American Native textile material and Pre-Columbian holdings. Collecting continues in this area, adding primarily mid- to late-twentieth-century costumes and textiles from Guatemala.

$ ✍

Marjorie Kinnan Rawlings Historic State Park

18700 South County Road 325
Cross Creek, FL 32640
Tel: 352-466-3672
www.floridastateparks.org/
    marjoriekinnanrawlings/default.cfm

Halifax Historical Museum

252 South Beach Street
Daytona Beach, FL 32114
Tel: 904-255-6976
www.halifaxhistorical.org

The Museum of Arts and Sciences and Center for Florida History

1040 Museum Boulevard
Daytona Beach, FL 32114
Tel: 386-255-0285
www.moas.org

Deerfield Beach Historical Society

380 East Hillsboro Boulevard
Deerfield Beach, FL 33443
Tel: 954-429-0378

The Morikami Museum and Japanese Gardens

4000 Morikami Park Road
Delray Beach, FL 33446
Tel: 561-495-0233
www.morikami.org

Museum of Lifestyle and Fashion History

322 NE 2nd Avenue/Pineapple Grove Way
Delray Beach, FL 33444
Tel: 561-243-2662
www.mlfhmuseum.org

**The Judah P. Benjamin Confederate
Memorial at Gamble Plantation
Historic Site**

3708 Patten Avenue
Ellenton, FL 34222
Tel: 941-723-4536
www.abfla.com/parks/GamblePlantation/
  gambleplantation.html

**Eustis Historical Museum and
Preservation Society**

536 North Bay Street
Eustis, FL 32726
Tel: 352-483-0046
www.eustis.org/launch/attractions/Historic.htm

Amelia Island Museum of History

233 South 3rd Street
Fernandina Beach, FL 32034
Tel: 904-261-7378
www.ameliaislandmuseumofhistory.org

International Swimming Hall of Fame

1 Hall of Fame Drive
Fort Lauderdale, FL 33316
Tel: 954-462-6536
www.ishof.org/museum.htm

Museum of Art

1 East Las Olas Boulevard
Fort Lauderdale, FL 33301
Tel: 954-525-5500
www.moafl.org

Old Fort Lauderdale Village and Museum

219 SW 2nd Avenue
Fort Lauderdale, FL 33301
Tel: 954-463-4431
www.oldfortlauderdale.org
Hours: Tue–Fri 11–5 pm, Sat–Sun 12–5 pm
Contact: Curator of collections
Institution type: History museum, historic house
Collection type: Clothing, accessories
Description: 1900–present
$ ✍

Stranahan House

335 SE 6th Avenue
Fort Lauderdale, FL 33301
Tel: 954-524-4736
www.stranahanhouse.com

Southwest Florida Museum of History

2300 Peck Street
Fort Myers, FL 33901
Tel: 239-332-5955
www.cityftmyers.com/attractions/historical.aspx

Key West Museum of Art and History

281 Front Street
Key West, FL 33040
Tel: 305-295-6616
www.kwahs.com

Polk Museum of Art

800 East Palmetto Street
Lakeland, FL 33801
Tel: 863-688-7743
www.polkmuseumofart.org

**Lake Wales Depot Museum and
Cultural Center**

325 South Scenic Highway
Lake Wales, FL 33853
Tel: 863-678-4209
www.cityoflakewales.com/depot

Museum of the City of Lake Worth

414 Lake Avenue
Lake Worth, FL 33460
Tel: 561-586-1700

**National Museum of Polo and
Hall of Fame**

9011 Lake Worth Road
Lake Worth, FL 33467
Tel: 561-969-3210
www.polomuseum.com

Maitland Historical Museums

820 Lake Lily Drive
Maitland, FL 32751
Tel: 407-644-2451
www.maitlandhistory.org/cms

Historical Museum of Southern Florida

101 West Flagler Street
Miami, FL 33130
Tel: 305-375-1492
www.historical-museum.org

Latin American Art Museum

2206 SW 8th Street
Miami, FL 33135
Tel: 305-644-1127

Vizcaya Museum and Gardens

3251 South Miami Avenue
Miami, FL 33129
Tel: 305-250-9133 Fax: 305-285-2004
www.vizcayamuseum.org
Hours: Mon–Sun 9:30–5:30 pm
Institution type: Historic house, county museum
$ ✍

Bass Museum of Art

2121 Park Avenue
Miami Beach, FL 33139
Tel: 305-673-7530
www.bassmuseum.org

Miss Sea Shell on the Sea Shore, circa 1910. Courtesy of Jewish Museum of Florida.

Jewish Museum of Florida

301 Washington Avenue
Miami Beach, FL 33139
Tel: 305-672-5044 Fax: 305-672-5933
www.jewishmuseum.com
Hours: Tue–Sun 10–5 pm
Contact: Ira Newman
Institution type: History museum, historic house
Collection type: Clothing, accessories, uniforms, costumes, general textiles, flags
Description: 1760–present. Material evidence of Jewish life in Florida since 1763, when Jews were first allowed.
$ ✍

West Pasco Historical Society Museum and Library

6431 Circle Boulevard
New Port Richey, FL 34652
Tel: 727-847-0680

Appleton Museum of Art

4333 NE Silver Springs Boulevard
Ocala, FL 34470
Tel: 352-236-7100
www.appletonmuseum.org

Orange County Regional History Center

65 East Central Boulevard
Orlando, FL 32801
Tel: 497-836-8587
www.thehistorycenter.org
Hours: Mon–Sun 10–5 pm
Contact: Wanda Edwards
Institution type: County museum
Collection type: Clothing, accessories, uniforms, general textiles
Description: 1850–1960. Clothing, uniforms, and textiles collected by residents of central Florida, mostly World War I and World War II uniforms.
$ ✍

West Florida Historic Preservation

T. T. WENTWORTH JR. COLLECTION
120 Church Street
Pensacola, FL 32502
Tel: 850-595-5985 Fax: 850-595-5989
www.historicpensacola.org
Hours: Mon–Fri 10–4 pm
Contact: Lynne Robertson
Institution type: History museum, historic house, state museum, university collection
Collection type: Clothing, accessories, uniforms, costumes, general textiles, flags
Description: 1800–present
$ ✍

American Water Ski Educational Foundation

1251 Holy Cow Road
Polk City, FL 33868
Tel: 863-324-2472
www.waterskihalloffame.com

Hungarian Folk-Art Museum

546 Ruth Street
Port Orange, FL 32127
Tel: 904-767-4292

Sanford Museum

520 East 1st Street
Sanford, FL 32771
Tel: 407-302-1000
www.ci.sanford.fl.us/cf03.html

John and Mable Ringling Circus Museum

5401 Bay Shore Road
Sarasota, FL 34243
Tel: 941-359-5700
www.ringling.org/circus_museum.asp

Lightner Museum

75 King Street
St. Augustine, FL 32084
Tel: 904-824-2874
www.lightnermuseum.org

Florida Holocaust Museum

55 5th Street South
St. Petersburg, FL 33701
Tel: 727-820-0100
www.flholocaustmuseum.org

Elliott Museum

825 NE Ocean Boulevard
Stuart, FL 34996
Tel: 772-225-1961
www.elliottmuseumfl.org

Florida State University

THE KILLINGER COLLECTION AND
COSTUMES OF HANYA HOLM
Department of Dance, 210 Montgomery Hall
Tallahassee, FL 32306
Tel: 850-644-1023
Hours: By appointment
Contact: Tricia Young
Institution type: University collection
Collection type: Clothing, accessories, costumes,
general textiles
Description: 1900–1959. Costumes from master-
works of early-twentieth-century modern
dance. The Killinger Collection includes cos-
tumes of Denishawn and Ted Shawn and His

*Bird head piece and body
suit, costume by Hanya
Holm, circa 1940. Cour-
tesy of Florida State University Department of
Dance.*

Men Dancers numbering 400 items. Costumes
of Hanya Holm number 600 items.

Florida State University

Department of Textiles and Consumer Sciences
Tallahassee, FL 32306
Tel: 850-644-2498
www.chs.fsu.edu/tcs

*Dresses, 1920s.
Courtesy of Florida
State University
Department of
Textiles and Con-
sumer Sciences.*

Hours: Mon–Fri 8–5 pm

Contact: Jose Blanco

Institution type: University collection

Collection type: Clothing, accessories, general textiles

Description: 1800–present. More than 5,000 clothing items ranging from the early 1800s to the 1980s, mostly related to Florida history. Holdings include magazines, textiles, and the Carter Collection of Pre-Columbian Peruvian Textiles.

Mission San Luis

2021 Mission Road

Tallahassee, FL 32304

Tel: 850-575-5641

http://dhr.dos.state.fl.us/archaeology/sanluis

Lily Pulitzer dresses, circa 1970. Courtesy Museum of Florida History.

Museum of Florida History

500 South Bronough Street

Tallahassee, FL 32399

Tel: 850-245-6400 Fax: 850-245-6433

www.museumoffloridahistory.com

Hours: Mon–Fri 9–4:30 pm, Sat 10–4:30 pm, Sun 12–4:30 pm

Contact: Kieran Orr, Registrar

Institution type: History museum, historic house, state museum

Collection type: Clothing, accessories, uniforms, costumes, general textiles, flags

Description: 1850–present. General historical collection emphasizes documentation to a particular Florida individual, community, or theme.

Tallahassee Museum of History and Natural Science

3945 Museum Drive

Tallahassee, FL 32310-6325

Tel: 850-575-8684 Fax: 850-574-8243

www.tallahasseemuseum.org

Hours: Mon–Sat 9–5 pm, Sun 12:30–5 pm

Contact: Linda Deaton

Institution type: History museum, historic house

Collection type: Clothing, accessories, uniforms, general textiles, flags

Description: 1850–present. Mid-nineteenth-century items, mostly women's garments and accessories.

Ybor City Museum State Park

1818 9th Avenue East

Tampa, FL 33605

Tel: 813-247-6323

www.ybormuseum.org

Tarpon Springs Cultural Center

101 South Pinellas Avenue

Tarpon Springs, FL 34689

Tel: 727-942-5605

Lake County Historical Museum

317 West Main Street

Tavares, FL 32778

Tel: 352-343-9600

Heritage Museum of Northwest Florida

115 Westview Avenue

Valparaiso, FL 32580

Tel: 850-678-2615

www.heritage-museum.org

Charles Hosmer Morse Museum of American Art

445 North Park Avenue

Winter Park, FL 32789

Tel: 407-645-5311 Fax: 407-647-1284

www.morsemuseum.org

Hours: Mon–Fri 9:30–4 pm, Sat–Sun 12–4 pm

Contact: Curator of collections

Institution type: Art museum

Collection type: Clothing, accessories, costumes, general textiles

Description: 1850–present. Items from three generations of one family. Items are from the Chicago, New York, and Orlando areas.

$ ✍

GEORGIA

Thronateeska Heritage Foundation
100 Roosevelt Avenue
Albany, GA 31701
Tel: 229-432-6955
www.heritagecenter.org

University of Georgia
HISTORIC COSTUME AND TEXTILES
COLLECTION
Dawson Hall
Athens, GA 30602
Tel: 706-542-4853 Fax: 706-542-4890
www.uga.edu/fcs
Hours: Mon–Fri 9–5 pm
Contact: Patricia Hunt-Hurst
Institution type: University collection
Collection type: Clothing, accessories, uniforms,
costumes, general textiles
Description: 1800–present. Women's clothing,
accessories, and wedding dresses. American
designers represented are McCardell, Trigere,
Bill Blass, Geoffery Beene, and Anne Fogarty.
Collection also features a Chanel coat, Reboux
hat, and YSL jacket. Other highlights include a
few ethnographic items, including a peasant
tunic from pre-1940s China, a North African
kaftan, and sari fabric.

Atlanta History Center
130 West Paces Ferry Road
Atlanta, GA 30305-1366
Tel: 404-814-4000 Fax: 404-814-2041
www.atlantahistorycenter.com

*Dress from Gone with the Girdle: Freedom, Restraint, and
Power in Women's Dress exhibit, circa 1850. Courtesy of
Atlanta History Center.*

*Confederate
marine uniform,
circa 1862. Cour-
tesy of Atlanta His-
tory Center,
Military Collec-
tion.*

Hours: Mon–Sat 10–5:30 pm, Sun 12–5:30 pm
Institution type: History museum, historic house
$ 🖅

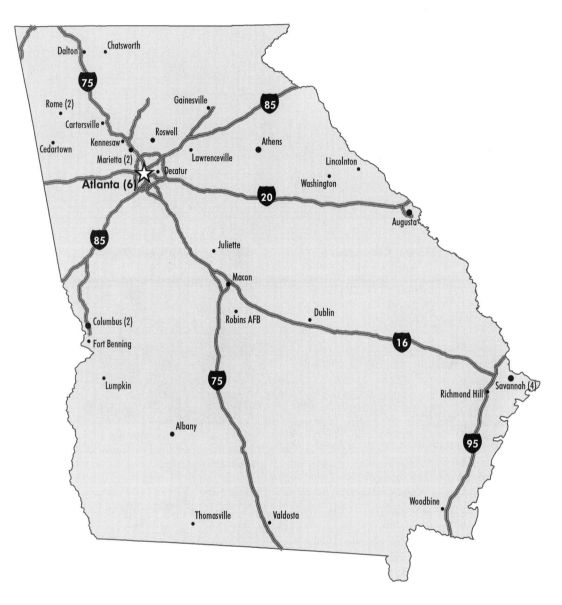

Chatsworth
Dalton
75
Rome (2)
Cartersville
Cedartown
Kennesaw
Marietta (2)
Atlanta (6)
Decatur
Roswell
Gainesville
85
Lawrenceville
Athens
Lincolnton
Washington
20
Augusta
85
Juliette
Macon
Columbus (2)
Robins AFB
Dublin
Fort Benning
16
Lumpkin
Richmond Hill
Savannah (4)
75
Albany
95
Thomasville
Valdosta
Woodbine

Population

- ●   0 - 50,000
- ●   50,001 - 100,000
- ●   100,001 - 250,000
- ●   250,001 - 500,000
- ●   > 500,000
- ☆   State Capital

CSA Region VI Southeast

TEXTILES AND SOCIAL HISTORY

Contact: Susan Neill

Collection type: Clothing, accessories, costumes, general textiles, quilts

Description: 1800–present. More than 10,000 civilian costumes, accessories, flat textiles, and other personal objects that represent Atlanta within the context of Georgia and the Southeast. Collection features men's, women's, and children's clothing and personal accessories such as hats, shoes, handbags, jewelry, spectacles, and luggage. Domestic textiles include quilts, coverlets, bedspreads, rugs, table linens, flags, and banners. Collection also includes textile production and care equipment such as spinning wheels, looms, washing machines, and irons.

DUBOSE CIVIL WAR COLLECTION

Collection type: Uniforms, general textiles, flags

Description: 1800–present. More than 5,000 objects, including numerous uniforms. The DuBose Civil War Collection along with the Thomas Swift Dickey Civil War Ordnance Collection and collections on loan from the United Daughters of the Confederacy and the Old Guard of the Gate City Guard make this Civil War military collection one of the top five in the United States. Also includes more than 2,000 items from other military periods.

Delta Air Transport Heritage Museum

DELTA AIR LINES CORPORATE ARCHIVES

1050 Delta Boulevard, Building B, Department 914

Atlanta, GA 30354

Tel: 404-714-2731

www.deltamuseum.org

Hours: Mon–Sun 9–5 pm

Contact: Marie Force

Institution type: History museum

Collection type: Accessories, uniforms

Description: 1915–present. Employee uniforms from Delta Air Lines from 1934 to the present and uniforms from airlines affiliated with Delta, including Chicago and Southern Air Lines (1930s–1953), Northeast Airlines (1930s–1972), Western Airlines (1930s–1987), and Pan Am (1980s–1991). Features flight attendant uniforms and accessories as well as pilot, maintenance, reservations, and airport service uniforms.

Fernbank Museum of Natural History

767 Clifton Road NE

Atlanta, GA 30314

Tel: 404-929-6300

www.fernbank.edu/museum

Georgia Capitol Museum

431 Capitol Street

Atlanta, GA 30334

Tel: 404-651-6996

www.sos.state.ga.us/museum/default.htm

The Salvation Army Southern Historical Center

1032 Metropolitan Parkway SW

Atlanta, GA 30310

Tel: 404-752-7578 Fax: 404-753-1932

www.salvationarmysouth.org/museum

Hours: Mon–Fri 9–12 and 1–4 pm

Contact: Michael Nagy

Institution type: History museum, university collection

Collection type: Accessories, uniforms, flags

Description: 1915–present. Salvation Army uniforms, primarily from the United States and some from overseas missions, generally 1930s to present. Salvation Army flags, primarily from the Southern United States.

Spelman College Museum of Fine Art

350 Spelman Lane SW

Atlanta, GA 30314

Tel: 404-861-3643

www.spelman.edu/museum/index.shtml

Augusta Richmond County Museum

560 Reynolds Street

Augusta, GA 30901

Tel: 706-722-8454

www.augustamuseum.org

Rose Lawn Museum

224 West Cherokee Avenue

Cartersville, GA 30120

Tel: 770-387-5162

www.roselawnmuseum.com

The Polk County Historical Society

205 North College Street

Cedartown, GA 30125

Tel: 770-749-0073

Chief Vann House State Historic Site

WALKING IN TWO WORLDS

52A Highway and 225 North
Chatsworth, GA 30705
Tel: 706-695-2598 Fax: 706-517-4255
http://home.alltel.net/vannhouse
Hours: Tue–Sat 9–5 pm, Sun 2–5:30 pm
Contact: Julia Autry
Institution type: History museum, historic house,
state museum
Collection type: Clothing, accessories
Description: 1800–1849
$ ✑

Port Columbus National Civil War Naval Center

1002 Victory Drive
Columbus, GA 31902
Tel: 706-324-7334
www.portcolumbus.org

The Columbus Museum

1251 Wynnton Road
Columbus, GA 31906
Tel: 706-649-0713
www.columbusmuseum.com

Whitfield Historical Society

701 Chattanooga Avenue
Dalton, GA 30720
Tel: 706-278-0217

DeKalb Historical Society Museum

101 East Court Square
Decatur, GA 30030
Tel: 404-373-1088
www.dekalbhistory.org

Dublin-Laurens Museum

311 Academy
Dublin, GA 31021
Tel: 912-272-9242

National Infantry Museum

396 Baltzell Avenue
Fort Benning, GA 31905-5593
Tel: 706-545-2958

Georgia Mountains History Museum of Brenau University

1 Centennial Circle
Gainesville, GA 30501
Tel: 770-536-0889
www.negahc.org/about/history.php

Jarrell Plantation Historic Site

711 Jarrell Plantation Road
Juliette, GA 31046
Tel: 478-986-5172 Fax: 478-986-5919
http://gastateparks.org/info/jarrell
Hours: Tue–Sat 9–5 pm, Sun 2–5:30 pm
Contact: Bretta Perkins, Interpretative Ranger
Institution type: State museum
Collection type: Clothing, accessories, uniforms,
quilts
Description: 1850–1960. More than 300 clothing
and related items that belonged to the Jarrell
family, mostly 1880–1950. Holdings also
include World War I uniforms; quilting, tat-
ting, crochet, and other craft supplies; shoes;
and household linens.
$ ✑

Kennesaw Mountain National Battlefield Park

900 Kennesaw Mountain Drive
Kennesaw, GA 30152
Tel: 770-427-4686

Gwinnett History Museum

455 South Perry Street SW
Lawrenceville, GA 30045
Tel: 770-822-5178 Fax: 770-237-5612
Hours: Mon–Thu 10–4 pm, Sat 12–5 pm
Institution type: History museum, county
museum
$ ✑

Elijah Clark Memorial Museum

2959 McCormick Highway
Lincolnton, GA 30817
Tel: 706-359-3458
http://gastateparks.org/info/elijah

Bedingfield Inn

Cotton Street on the Square
Lumpkin, GA 31815
Tel: 229-838-6419
www.bedingfieldinn.org

Georgia Music Hall of Fame

200 Martin Luther King Jr. Boulevard
Macon, GA 31201
Tel: 478-750-8555
www.gamusichall.com

Marietta Museum of History

1 Depot Street, Suite 200
Marietta, GA 30060
Tel: 770-528-0430
www.mariettahistory.org

The Root House Museum

145 Denmead Street
Marietta, GA 30060
Tel: 770-426-4982
www.cobblandmarks.com/roothouse.htm

Fort McAllister

3894 Fort McAllister Road
Richmond Hill, GA 31324
Tel: 912-727-2339
www.fortmcallister.org

Museum of Aviation Flight and Technology Center

1942 Heritage Boulevard
Robbins Air Force Base, GA 31098
Tel: 478-926-6870

Chieftains Museum

501 Riverside Parkway
Rome, GA 30161
Tel: 706-291-9494
www.chieftainsmuseum.org

Oak Hill and Martha Berry Museum

2277 Martha Berry Highway NW
Rome, GA 30149
Tel: 706-291-1883
www.berry.edu/oakhill

Roswell Historical Society and City of Roswell Research Library and Archives

950 Forrest Street
Roswell, GA 30075
Tel: 770-594-6405 Fax: 770-594-6402
www.roswellhs.org
Hours: Mon–Thu 1–4:30 pm
Contact: Elaine DeNiro, Archivist
Institution type: History museum

Yellow cotton dress with claret printed floral sprigs, circa 1830. Courtesy of Roswell Historical Society.

Collection type: Clothing, accessories, uniforms, general textiles, quilts, flags
Description: 1800–present. Clothing dating from the 1830s to the 1970s, mostly from the Roswell area. Emphasis is on women's clothing. Collection also features local quilts.

Archives Museum, Temple Mickve Israel

20 East Gordon Street
Savannah, GA 31401
Tel: 912-233-1547
www.mickveisrael.org

Davenport House Museum

324 East State Street
Savannah, GA 31401
Tel: 912-236-7938

Juliette Gordon Low Birthplace

10 East Oglethorpe Avenue
Savannah, GA 31401
Tel: 912-233-4501
www.girlscouts.org/birthplace

Savannah History Museum

303 Martin Luther King Jr. Boulevard
Savannah, GA 31401
Tel: 912-651-6850
www.chsgeorgia.org
Hours: Mon–Sun 8:30–5 pm
Contact: Lydia Moreton
Institution type: History museum
Collection type: Clothing, accessories, uniforms

Court dress, 1887. Courtesy of Savannah History Museum.

Description: 1800–present. Collection primarily includes women's and children's clothing.

$ ✍

Lapham-Patterson House
626 North Dawson Street
Thomasville, GA 31792
Tel: 912-225-4004

Lowndes County Historical Society and Museum
305 West Central Avenue
Valdosta, GA 31601
Tel: 229-247-4780
www.valdostamuseum.org

Washington Historical Museum
308 East Robert Toombs Avenue
Washington, GA 30673-2038
Tel: 706-678-2105
www.washingtonwilkes.org
Hours: Tue–Sat 10–5 pm, Sun 2–5 pm
Contact: Stephanie Macchia
Institution type: History museum, historic house, city museum
Collection type: Clothing, accessories, uniforms, costumes, general textiles
Description: Pre-1700–present. Holdings include rare Confederate artifacts, including butternut artillery pants, vests, jackets, flags, and weapons; collection of Southeast Indian artifacts; and period furnishings.

$ ✍

Woodbine International Fire Museum
110 Bedell Avenue
Woodbine, GA 31569-0058
Tel: 912-576-5351

Detail, dress of kapa cloth. Courtesy of Lyman Museum.

Lyman Museum

276 Haili Street
Hilo, HI 96720
Tel: 808-935-5021 Fax: 808-969-7685
www.lymanmuseum.org
Hours: Mon–Sat 9:30–4:30 pm
Contact: Curator
Institution type: History museum, historic house
Collection type: Clothing, accessories, uniforms, general textiles, quilts
Description: 1800–present. Hawaiian Kapa Moe, or sleeping blankets; Hawaiian and American quilts; and clothing, including missionary clothing, ethnic costumes, dresses, and some early sugar plantation work clothes.
$ ✍

Bishop Museum

1525 Bernice Street
Honolulu, HI 96817
Tel: 808-848-4144 Fax: 808-848-4114
www.bishopmuseum.org
Hours: Mon–Sun 9–5 pm
Contact: M. Drake
Institution type: Art museum, history museum, state museum
Collection type: Clothing, accessories, uniforms, costumes, general textiles, quilts, flags
Description: 1800–present. Clothing of immigrant groups to Hawaii, textiles, costumes, theater costumes, uniforms, quilts, and handwork.
$ ✍

Daughters of Hawaii

2913 Pali Highway
Honolulu, HI 96817
Tel: 808-595-3167 Fax: 808-595-4395
www.daughtersofhawaii.org
Hours: Mon–Sun 9–4 pm
Contact: Collections chairman
Institution type: Historic house
Collection type: Clothing, accessories, uniforms
Description: Pre-1700–1899. Clothing and textiles are housed at Queen Emma Summer Palace and Hulihee Palace.
$ ✍

Honolulu Academy of Arts

900 South Beretania Street
Honolulu, HI 96814
Tel: 808-532-8732
www.honoluluacademy.org
Hours: Tue–Sat 10–4:30 pm, Sun 1–5 pm
Contact: Sara Oka, Collection Manager

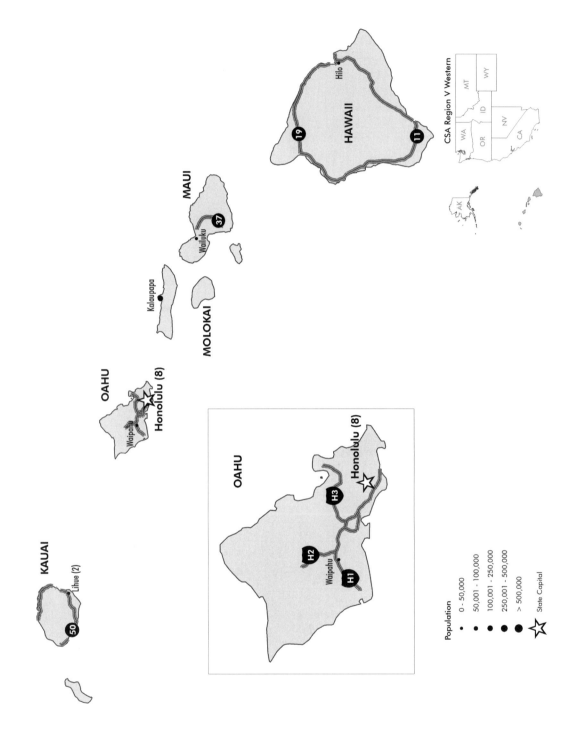

KAUAI

Lihue (2)

50

OAHU

Waipahu

Honolulu (8)

MOLOKAI

Kalaupapa

MAUI

Wailuku

37

HAWAII

Hilo

19

11

CSA Region V Western

WA

OR

ID

MT

WY

NV

CA

AK

OAHU

H3

Honolulu (8)

H2

Waipahu

H1

Population

· 0 - 50,000

· 50,001 - 100,000

● 100,001 - 250,000

● 250,001 - 500,000

● > 500,000

☆ State Capital

Institution type: Art museum

Collection type: Clothing, accessories, uniforms, costumes, general textiles, flags

Description: Pre-1700–present. Strengths are in Asian costumes and Southeast Asian textiles.

$ ✍

Iolani Palace

364 South King Street
Honolulu, HI 96804
Tel: 808-522-0822 Fax: 808-532-1051
www.iolanipalace.org

Hours: Tue–Sat 9–4 pm

Contact: Stuart Ching

Institution type: Historic house

Collection type: Clothing, accessories, uniforms, costumes, general textiles, flags

Description: 1850–99. Iolani Palace was the official residence of the Hawaiian Kingdom's last two monarchs—King Kalakaua, who built the palace in 1882, and his sister successor, Queen Lili`uokalani. In this national historic landmark, today's visitor can enjoy one of the most precise historic restorations to be found in America and learn much about Hawaiian history and heritage.

$ ✍

Japanese Cultural Center

2454 South Beretania Street
Honolulu, HI 96826
Tel: 808-945-7633 Fax: 808-944-1123
www.jcch.com

Hours: Mon–Sun 10–4 pm

Contact: Christy Takamune, Gallery Director

Institution type: History museum

Collection type: Clothing, accessories, uniforms, costumes, general textiles, quilts, flags

Description: 1850–present. Items brought by Japanese immigrants to Hawaii as well as those made in Hawaii by immigrants. Additional objects include items found throughout the Japanese American community.

$ ✍

Mission Houses Museum

553 South King Street
Honolulu, HI 96813
Tel: 808-531-0481
www.missionhouses.org

Admiral Perry silk winter kimono, 1854. Courtesy of University of Hawaii.

University of Hawaii

UNIVERSITY OF HAWAII COSTUME COLLECTION

2515 Campus Road
Honolulu, HI 96822
Tel: 808-956-2234 Fax: 808-956-2241
www2.ctahr.hawaii.edu/costume

Hours: By appointment

Contact: Carol D'Angelo

Institution type: University collection

Collection type: Clothing, accessories, costumes, general textiles

Description: 1800–present. Specializes in Asian, Hawaiian, Western, and ethnic garments and textiles. One of a kind collection of Hawaiian garments that trace the history of Hawaii.

✍

USS Arizona Memorial

1 Arizona Memorial Place
Honolulu, HI 96818
Tel: 808-422-2771 Fax: 808-483-8608
www.nps.gov/usar

Hours: Mon–Sun 7:30–5 pm

Contact: Marshall Owens

Institution type: History museum, federal museum

Collection type: Clothing, accessories, uniforms, flags

Description: 1915–1960. Materials relating to the history of the USS *Arizona*, the military presence in Hawaii, the December 7, 1941, attack, and the subsequent military history through the Battle of Midway.

✍

Kalaupapa National Historical Park

7 Paahi Street
Kalaupapa, HI 96742
Tel: 808-567-6802x42 Fax: 808-567-6729
www.nps.gov/kala
Hours: By appointment
Contact: Susan Buchel
Institution type: History museum, federal museum
Collection type: Clothing, accessories, general textiles
Description: Pre-1700–present. Items used by Hansen's Disease patients or those who cared for them while isolated at the Kalaupapa settlement.

Grove Farm Homestead

Grove Farm Plantation, Nawiliwili Road
Lihue, HI 96766
Tel: 808-345-3202 Fax: 808-245-7988
www.hawaiimuseums.org/mc/isKauai_grove.htm
Hours: Mon, Wed, Thu 10–1 pm
Collection type: Quilts
Institution type: Historic house
Description: 1850–1900. Collection is housed in restored Wilcox family home and features the Wilcox quilts made in Hawaii.

$

Kauai Museum Association

4428 Rice Street
Lihue, HI 96766
Tel: 808-245-6931 Fax: 808-245-6864
www.kauaimuseum.org
Hours: Mon–Fri 9–4 pm, Sat 10–4 pm
Contact: Margaret Lovett
Institution type: Art museum, history museum, historic house
Collection type: Clothing, quilts
Description: 1800–present. Collection includes Hawaiian quilts—a Hawaiian cultural art form.

$

Maui Historical Society-Bailey House Museum

2375A Main Street
Wailuku, HI 96793
Tel: 808-244-3326 Fax: 808-244-3920
www.mauimuseum.org
Hours: Mon–Sat 10–4 pm
Contact: Executive director
Institution type: Art museum, history museum, historic house
Collection type: Clothing, accessories, general textiles, quilts, flags
Description: 1800–1960. Examples of traditional Hawaiian kapa cloth, Hawaiian flag quilts, batiste dresses (1886–1915) and petticoats with handmade lace, dresses from the early 1800s, and hats made of lauhala and other natural materials.

$

Hawaii's Plantation Village

94-695 Waipahu Street
Waipahu, HI 96797
Tel: 808-677-0110 Fax: 808-676-6727
Hours: Mon–Fri 9–3 pm, Sat 10–3 pm
$

IDAHO

Idaho State Historical Museum

610 North Julia Davis Drive

Boise, ID 83702

Tel: 208-334-2120

www.idahohistory.net

Museum of North Idaho

115 NW Boulevard

Coeur d'Alene, ID 83816-0814

Tel: 208-664-3448

www.museumni.org

Hours: Seasonal

Contact: Dorothy Dahlgren

Institution type: History museum

Collection type: Clothing, accessories, uniforms, general textiles, quilts, flags

Description: 1850–present. Clothing and accessories from people who lived in North Idaho. Items include flags, some military uniforms, and small collection of quilts and bedding.

$ 🖐

The Historical Museum at St. Gertrude

HC3, Box 121

Cottonwood, ID 83522

Tel: 208-962-7123

www.historicalmuseumatstgertrude.com

Twin Falls County Museum

21337-A US Highway 30

Filer, ID 83328

Tel: 208-736-4675

Blaine County Historical Museum

218 North Main Street

Hailey, ID 83333

Tel: 208-726-8405

www.bchistoricalmuseum.org

South Bannock County Historical Center

110 East Main Street

Lava Hot Springs, ID 83246

Tel: 208-776-5254 Fax: 208-776-5228

Hours: Mon–Sun 12–5 pm

Contact: Curator of collections

Institution type: History museum

Collection type: Clothing, accessories, uniforms, general textiles

Description: 1850–present. Clothing, artifacts, and photographs from the late 1880s; uniforms from World War I and World War II to Desert Storm; and over 6,000 photographs and family histories.

Nez Perce County Museum

0306 Third Street

Lewiston, ID 83501

Tel: 208-743-2535

www.npchistsoc.org

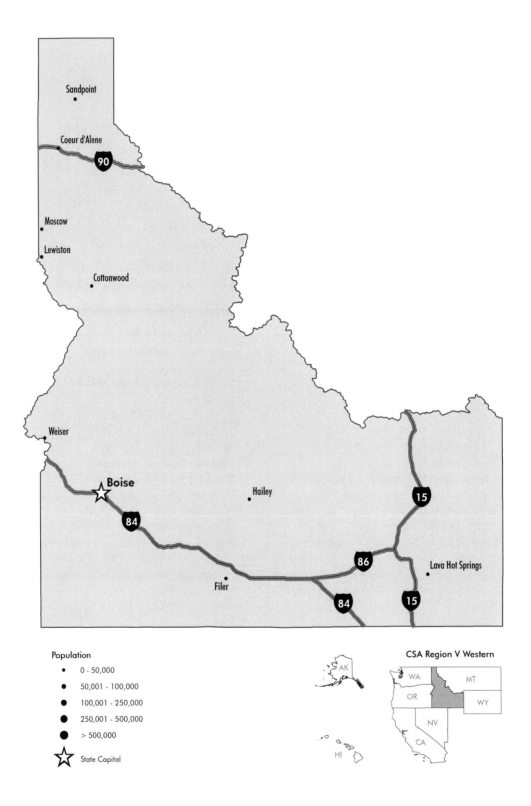

Sandpoint
•

Coeur d'Alene
•
90

Moscow
•

Lewiston
•

Cottonwood
•

Weiser
•

☆ **Boise**

84

Hailey
•

15

86

Lava Hot Springs
•

Filer
•

84

15

Population

• 0 - 50,000

• 50,001 - 100,000

● 100,001 - 250,000

● 250,001 - 500,000

● > 500,000

☆ State Capital

CSA Region V Western

AK

WA   MT
OR   ID   WY
NV
CA
HI

University of Idaho, Leila Old Historical Costume Collection

Niccolls Building, Margaret Ritchie School of
    Family and Consumer Sciences
Moscow, ID 83844-33183
Tel: 208-885-6545 Fax: 208-885-5751
www.agls.uidaho.edu/fcs

Bonner County Historical Museum

611 South Ella Avenue
Sandpoint, ID 83864
Tel: 208-263-2344
www.bonnercountyhistory.org

Snake River Heritage Center

2295 Paddock Avenue
Weiser, ID 83672
Tel: 208-549-0205

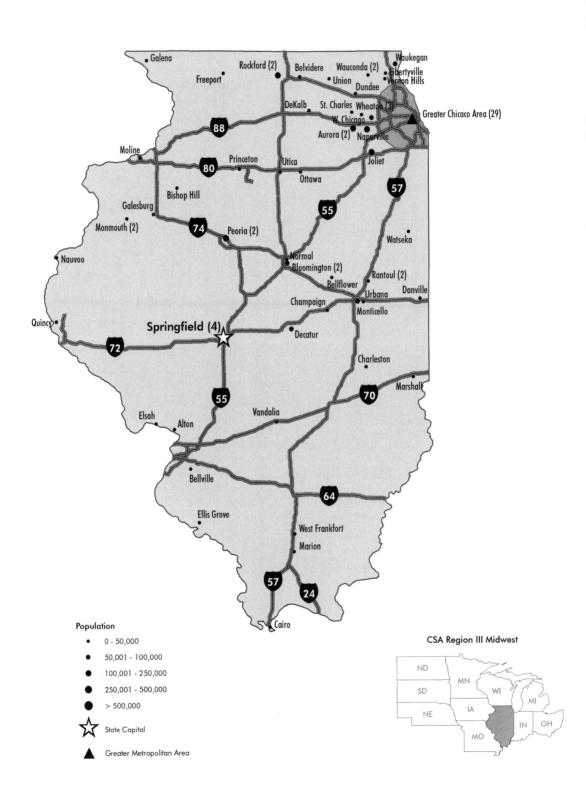

Population

- 0 - 50,000
- 50,001 - 100,000
- 100,001 - 250,000
- 250,001 - 500,000
- > 500,000
- ☆ State Capital
- ▲ Greater Metropolitan Area

CSA Region III Midwest

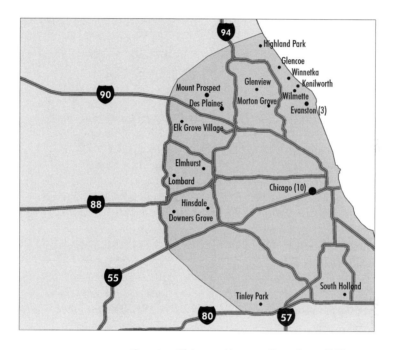

Greater Chicago Metropolitan Area (29)

Alton Museum of History and Art
2809 College Avenue
Alton, IL 62002
Tel: 618-462-2763

Aurora Historical Society
Cedar and Oak Streets
Aurora, IL 60506
Tel: 630-906-0650
www.aurorahistoricalsociety.org

Schingoethe Center for Native American Cultures
1400 Marseillaise Place
Aurora, IL 60506
Tel: 630-844-5656
www.aurora.edu/museum

St. Clair County Historical Society
701 East Washington Street
Belleville, IL 62220
Tel: 618-234-0600

Bellflower Historical and Genealogical Society

407 West Center Street
Bellflower, IL 61724
Tel: 309-722-3757

Boone County Historical Museum

311 Whitney Boulevard
Belvidere, IL 61008
Tel: 815-544-8391
www.boonecountyhistoricalmuseum.org

Bishop Hill Heritage Museum

Steeple Building, 103 North Bishop Hill Street
Bishop Hill, IL 61419
Tel: 309-927-3899
www.bishophill.com

David Davis Mansion

1000 East Monroe Drive
Bloomington, IL 61701
Tel: 309-828-1084 Fax: 309-828-3493
www.daviddavismansion.org
Hours: Wed–Sun 9–4 pm
Contact: Jeff Soulsberg
Institution type: History museum, historic house, state museum
Collection type: Clothing, general textiles
Description: 1850–1960. Family clothing and household textiles, 1872–1940.

✍🏻

McLean County Museum of History

200 North Main
Bloomington, IL 61701
Tel: 309-827-0428 Fax: 309-827-0100
www.mchistory.org
Hours: Mon–Sat 10–5 pm, Tue 10–9 pm, Sun 1–5 pm (Sep–May)
Institution type: County museum
$ ✍🏻

Magnolia Manor

2700 Washington Avenue
Cairo, IL 62914
Tel: 618-734-0201

Champaign County Historical Museum

102 East University Avenue
Champaign, IL 61820
Tel: 217-356-1010
www.champaignmuseum.org

Eastern Illinois University

MARY JOSEPHINE BOOTH CLOTHING COLLECTION

600 Lincoln
Charleston, IL 61920-3099
Tel: 217-581-6995 Fax: 217-581-6090
www.eiu.edu
Hours: By appointment
Contact: Jean Dilworth
Institution type: University museum
Collection type: Clothing, accessories
Description: 1915–1960. Dresses and hats from Mary Josephine Booth, who was librarian at Eastern Illinois University from the early 1900s to the 1950s. Other items include 1 copy of 1877, volume 9 of *Demorest's Magazine* and 1874–1882 editions and a brown silk walking suit.

✍🏻

Chicago Cultural Center

78 East Washington Street
Chicago, IL 60602
Tel: 312-744-6630

Chicago Historical Society

HOPE B. MCCORMICK COSTUME CENTER

1601 N. Clark Street
Chicago, IL 60614
Tel: 312-642-4600 Fax: 312-266-2077
www.chicagohistory.org
Hours: Research center: Tue, Thu–Sat 10–4:30 pm, Wed 1–4:30 pm
Contact: Collections manager
Institution type: History museum
Collection type: Clothing, accessories
Description: 1750–present. More than 50,000 items in the collection tell the story of Chicago history and its diverse citizens with objects and records related to the city. Collection is strong in late-nineteenth-century clothing of men, women, and children. Earliest pieces are suits worn by George Washington and John Adams and objects belonging to Abraham Lincoln and Mary Todd Lincoln. Designer collection ranges from Charles Worth and Paul Poiret to Issey Miyake and Yohji Yamamoto. Famous Chicagoans' clothing includes Michael Jordan's basketball uniforms, Mahalia Jackson's choir robe, and Jane Byrne's inaugural suit.

$ ✍🏻

Clarke House Museum

1827 South Indiana Avenue
Chicago, IL 60616
Tel: 312-745-0040

Hellenic Museum and Cultural Center

801 West Adams, 4th Floor
Chicago, IL 60601
Tel: 312-726-1234
www.hellenicmuseum.org

Oriental Institute Museum, University of Chicago

1155 East 58th Street
Chicago, IL 60637
Tel: 773-702-9520

Polish Museum of America

984 North Milwaukee Avenue
Chicago, IL 60622
Tel: 773-384-3352
www.prcua.org/pma

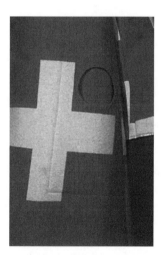

Coat, detail of Jean Charles de Castelbajac designed coat, 2000. Courtesy of the School of the Art Institute of Chicago.

The School of the Art Institute of Chicago

THE FASHION RESOURCE CENTER
37 South Wabash Avenue, Room 1016
Chicago, IL 60603
Tel: 312-899-1215 Fax: 312-263-0141
www.artic.edu/saic
Hours: Mon–Fri 9–4 pm, Sat 12–1 pm, and by appointment
Contact: Gillion Carrara, Director
Institution type: Art museum, university museum
Collection type: Clothing, accessories, general textiles

Description: 1961–present. Late-twentieth-century and twenty-first-century hands-on study collection of designer garments and accessories includes 300 garments and accessories for handling and examination. An expanding collection of over 200 runway presentations and interview videotapes include annual student fashion shows, ready-to-wear and couture presentations, fashion history, technical instruction, and menswear shows. Vintage magazines and rare books are housed with current fashion magazines.
$ 🖎

Spertus Museum, Spertus Institute of Jewish Studies

618 South Michigan Avenue, 3rd Floor
Chicago, IL 60605
Tel: 312-322-1747 Fax: 312-922-3934
www.spertus.edu
Hours: Sun–Wed 10–5 pm, Thu 10–7 pm, Fri 10–3 pm
Contact: Arielle Weininger
Institution type: Art museum, history museum, university museum
Collection type: Clothing, accessories, uniforms, costumes, general textiles, flags
Description: 1800–present
$ 🖎

Swedish American Museum Association of Chicago

3225 West Foster Avenue
Chicago, IL 60625
Tel: 773-538-5722
www.swedishamericanhist.org

Ukrainian National Museum, Library and Archive

721 North Oakley Boulevard
Chicago, IL 60612
Tel: 312-421-8020
www.ukrntlmuseum.org

Vermilion County Museum Society

116 North Gilbert Street
Danville, IL 61832-8405
Tel: 217-442-2922 Fax: 217-442-8405
www.vermilioncountymuseum.org
Hours: Tue–Sat 10–5 pm
Contact: Sue Richter

Institution type: History museum, historic house, county museum

Collection type: Clothing, accessories, general textiles

Description: 1800–present. Objects related to Vermilion County history.

$ ✍

Macon County Museum Complex

5580 North Fork Road
Decatur, IL 62521
Tel: 217-422-4919
www.maconhistory.org

Ellwood House Museum

509 North 1st Street
DeKalb, IL 60115
Tel: 815-756-4609 Fax: 815-756-4645
www.ellwoodhouse.org
Hours: Tue–Fri 1–3 pm, Sat–Sun 1–3 pm (Mar–Dec 15)
Contact: Fran Larson, Curator
Institution type: History museum, historic house
Collection type: Clothing, accessories
Description: 1850–1960. Mainly clothing from 1870 to 1920 but also items from 1850 to 1950. Mostly Midwestern items but also items from New York and Paris.

$ ✍

Des Plaines History Center

781 Pearson Street
Des Plaines, IL 60016
Tel: 847-391-5399 Fax: 847-297-4741
http://dpkhome.northstarnet.org/DPHS
Hours: Mon–Fri 9–4 pm, Sun 1–4 pm
Contact: Lynne Mickle, Curator of Collections
Institution type: History museum, historic house, city museum
Collection type: Clothing, accessories, uniforms, costumes
Description: 1850–present. More than 800 costume pieces dating from the mid-1800s to the present day, including outerwear, underwear, headwear, footwear, accessories, and personal gear. Approximately half relate to local history, such as wedding gowns, military uniforms, group or event related pieces, and items purchased at local businesses. Other items include large collection of catalogs from Sears, Montgomery Ward, and JCPenney from 1912 to 1994.

✍

The Downers Grove Park District Museum

831 Maple Avenue
Downers Grove, IL 60515
Tel: 630-963-1309
www.dgparks.org

Dundee Township Historical Society

426 Highland Ave.
East Dundee, IL 60118
Tel: 847-428-6996
http://dulhome.northstarnet.org/DTHS

Farmhouse Museum

399 Biesterfield Road
Elk Grove Village, IL 60007
Tel: 847-439-3994 Fax: 847-690-1442
www.elkgrove.org/heritage
Hours: Tue–Thu 9–12 pm, Fri 9–6 pm, 3rd Sun 1–4 pm (Sep–May); Tue–Thu 10–1 pm, Fri 9–6 pm, 3rd Sun 1–4 pm (Jun–Aug)
Institution type: History museum, historic house, city museum

$ ✍

Pierre Menard Home State Historic Site

4230 Kaskaskta Road
Ellis Grove, IL 62241
Tel: 618-859-3031

Elmhurst Historical Museum

120 East Park Avenue
Elmhurst, IL 60126
Tel: 630-833-1457 Fax: 630-833-1326
www.elmhurst.org/elmhurst/museum
Hours: Tue–Sun 1–5 pm
Contact: Marcia Lautanen-Raleigh, Curator
Institution type: City museum
Collection type: Clothing, accessories, uniforms, costumes, general textiles, quilts, flags
Description: 1760–present. Collection contains 231 dresses, including wedding dresses, 1800–1980; women's formal and utilitarian wear; 58 uniforms, including World War I, World War II, and Vietnam; army, navy, and air corps, as well as WASP and WAVE uniforms; 108 pairs of shoes; 180 hats and 40 bonnets; 100 purses; 29 quilts; doilies, table linens, and handkerchiefs; 61 flags; and men's clothing, 1840–present.

School of Nations Museum

1 Maybeck Place
Elsah, IL 62028
Tel: 618-374-5236

Christian Dior cocktail dress, circa 1950. Courtesy of Evanston Historical Society

Evanston Historical Society

GWEN SIMPSON COSTUME COLLECTION

225 Greenwood Street
Evanston, IL 60201
Tel: 847-475-3410
www.evanstonhistorical.org
Hours: Thu–Sun 1–5 pm
Contact: Janet C. Messmer
Institution type: History museum
Collection type: Clothing, accessories, uniforms, costumes, general textiles, flags
Description: 1800–present. Costume collection is particularly strong in women's garments 1850–1950. Collection is 90 percent women's clothing, 5 percent menswear, and 5 percent infants' and children's clothing.
$ ✍

Mitchell Museum of the American Indian

2600 Central Park Avenue
Evanston, IL 60201
Tel: 847-475-1030 Fax: 847-475-0911
www.mitchellmuseum.org
Hours: Tue–Sat 10–5 pm, Thu 10–8 pm, Sun 12–4 pm
Contact: Janice Klein

Institution type: History museum
Collection type: Clothing, accessories, general textiles
Description: 1850–present. Focus on the native peoples of North America from the Paleo-Indian period through the present day. The collection includes the material culture of the Woodland, Plains, Southwest, Northwest Coast, and Arctic regions.
$ ✍

The Willard House Museum

1730 Chicago Avenue
Evanston, IL 60201-4585
Tel: 847-864-1397

Freeport Arts Center

121 North Harlem Avenue
Freeport, IL 61032
Tel: 815-235-9755

Galena-Jo Daviess County Historical Society and Museum

211 South Bench Street
Galena, IL 61036
Tel: 815-777-9129 Fax: 815-777-9131
www.galenahistorymuseum.org
Hours: Mon–Sun 9–4:30 pm
Contact: Alice Toebaas
Institution type: History museum
Collection type: Clothing, accessories, uniforms, general textiles, quilts, flags
Description: 1800–1960. Substantial collection of dresses circa 1840 through 1950 and hats, undergarments, accessories, men's military uniforms, quilts, and coverlets.
$ ✍

Illinois Citizen Soldier Museum

1001 Michigan Avenue
Galesburg, IL 61401
Tel: 309-342-1181

Glencoe Historical Society

377 Park Avenue
Glencoe, IL 60022
Tel: 847-835-0040
www.glencoehistoricalsociety.org/home/index.shtml

Glenview Area Historical Society
1121 Waukegan Road
Glenview, IL 60025
Tel: 847-724-2235

Highland Park Historical Society
326 Central Avenue
Highland Park, IL 60035
Tel: 847-432-7090 Fax: 847-432-7307
www.highlandpark.org/historic
Hours: Tue–Fri 10–3 pm, Sat–Sun 2–4 pm
Contact: Melissa Fearn
Institution type: History museum, historic house,
   city museum
Collection type: Clothing, uniforms
Description: 1850–present. Clothing worn by
   Highland Park women since 1885 and men's
   clothing, primarily uniforms.

Hinsdale Historical Society
15 South Clay Street
Hinsdale, IL 60522
Tel: 630-789-2600
www.hinsdalehistory.org
Hours: Fri–Sat 10–2 pm; Archives: Wed 10–2 pm
Contact: Susan Olsson
Institution type: History museum, historic house
Collection type: Clothing, accessories, uniforms,
   general textiles
Description: 1850–1960. Men's, women's, and
   children's clothing dating from circa 1870 to
   the 1930s, with the bulk in women's clothing
   and accessories from the late 1880s to the
   1920s. Historical society includes an archive
   and a historic house museum built in 1873 and
   collects objects originating circa 1880 and
   Hinsdale specific items.

Joliet Area Historical Museum
204 North Ottawa Street
Joliet, IL 60432
Tel: 815-280-1500
www.jolietmuseum.org

Kenilworth Historical Society
415 Kenilworth Avenue
Kenilworth, IL 60043-1134
Tel: 847-251-2565
www.kenilworthhistory.org

Libertyville-Mundelein Historical Society
413 North Milwaukee Avenue
Libertyville, IL 60048
Tel: 847-362-2330

Lombard Historical Museum
23 West Maple
Lombard, IL 60148
Tel: 630-629-1885

Williamson County Historical Society
105 South Van Buren
Marion, IL 62959
Tel: 618-997-5863
www.thewchs.com

Clark County Museum
502 South 4th Street
Marshall, IL 62441
Tel: 217-826-6098

Rock Island County Historical Society
822 11th Avenue
Moline, IL 61265
Tel: 309-764-8590
www.richs.cc

Buchanan Center for the Arts
64 Public Square
Monmouth, IL 61462
Tel: 309-734-3033

Wyatt Earp Birthplace Home
406 South 3rd Street
Monmouth, IL 61462
Tel: 309-734-3181

Piatt County Museum
315 West Main
Monticello, IL 61856
Tel: 217-762-4731

**Morton Grove Historical Museum and
Haupt-Yehl House**
6240 Dempster Street
Morton Grove, IL 60053
Tel: 847-965-0203
www.mortongroveparks.com

Mount Prospect Historical Society
101 South Maple Street
Mount Prospect, IL 60056

Tel: 847-392-9006 Fax: 847-392-8995
www.mtphist.org

Hours: Mon–Fri 11–6 pm

Contact: Curator of collections

Institution type: History museum, historic house, city museum

Collection type: Clothing, accessories, uniforms, general textiles

Description: 1850–1950. Artifacts that relate to Mount Prospect, the development of the Midwest, and suburban growth. The 6,800 objects in the collection include textiles, farming equipment, household utensils, architectural details, art works, promotional material from Mount Prospect businesses, personal collections, and period furniture.

Naper Settlement
523 South Webster Street
Naperville, IL 60540
Tel: 630-420-6010
www.napersettlement.org

Historic Nauvoo—Museum of Church History and Art
JOSEPH SMITH HISTORIC SITE
149 Water Street
Nauvoo, IL 62354
Tel: 217-453-2246
www.historicnauvoo.org

Illinois State University
LOIS JETT HISTORIC COSTUME COLLECTION

Turner Hall 144, Department of Family and Consumer Sciences
Normal, IL 61790-5060
Tel: 309-438-2517 Fax: 309-438-5659

Hours: Mon–Fri 8–5 pm

Contact: Julianne Trautmann

Institution type: University collection

Collection type: Clothing, accessories

Description: 1850–present. Women's clothing and accessories, primarily from the twentieth-century Midwestern area of United States. University holds a limited men's and children's collection.

Ottawa Scouting Museum
1100 Canal Street
Ottawa, IL 61350
Tel: 815-431-9353

Lakeview Museum of Arts and Sciences
1125 West Lake Avenue
Peoria, IL 61614
Tel: 309-686-7000
www.lakeview-museum.org

Peoria Historical Society
611 SW Washington Street
Peoria, IL 61602
Tel: 309-674-1921
www.peoriahistoricalsociety.org

Bureau County Historical Society Museum
109 Park Avenue West
Princeton, IL 61356
Tel: 815-875-2184

Historical Society of Quincy and Adams County
425 South 12th Street
Quincy, IL 62301
Tel: 217-222-1835

Korean War Veterans National Museum and Library
1007 Pacesetter Drive
Rantoul, IL 61866
Tel: 217-893-4111
www.theforgottenvictory.org

Octave Chanute Aerospace Museum
1011 Pacesetter Drive
Rantoul, IL 61866
Tel: 217-893-1613
www.aeromuseum.org

Midway Village and Museum Center
6799 Guilford Road
Rockford, IL 61107
Tel: 815-397-9112 Fax: 815-397-9156

Hours: Mon–Fri 10–5 pm, Sat–Sun 12–5 pm (Jun–Aug); Thu–Fri 12–4 pm, Sat–Sun 12–5 pm (Apr–May, Sep–Oct)

Tinker Swiss Cottage Museum

411 Kent Street
Rockford, IL 61102
Tel: 815-964-2424 Fax: 815-964-2466
www.tinkercottage.com
Hours: Tue–Sun 1–4 pm
Contact: Donna Langford
Institution type: Historic house
Collection type: Clothing, accessories, general textiles
Description: 1800–1914. Items worn and used by the Tinker family dating from 1850 to 1915, including tapa cloth from the Sandwich Islands, where the Tinker family served as missionaries in the 1830s.
$ ✍

South Holland Historical Society

16250 Wausau Avenue
South Holland, IL 60473
Tel: 708-596-2722

Illinois Historic Preservation Agency and Historic Sites Division

313 South 6th Street
Springfield, IL 62701
Tel: 217-785-5056
www.illinois-history.gov
Hours: Vary by site
Contact: Collections manager
Institution type: State museum
Collection type: Clothing, accessories, uniforms, general textiles
Description: 1800–present. Includes the Abraham Lincoln Presidential Library.
✍

Illinois State Museum

502 South Spring Street
Springfield, IL 62706
Tel: 217-782-7387
www.museum.state.il.us

Museum of Funeral Customs

1440 Monument Avenue
Springfield, IL 62702
Tel: 217-544-3480 Fax: 217-544-3484
www.funeralmuseum.org
Hours: Tue–Sat 10–4 pm, Sun 1–4 pm
Contact: Jason Meyers
Institution type: History museum
Collection type: Clothing, accessories, general textiles

Mourning clothing, circa 1900. Courtesy of Museum of Funeral Customs.

Description: 1850–present. Mourning clothing, accessories, jewelry, burial clothing, casket veils, and textiles associated with funeral service. Collection includes American objects from the late nineteenth century through the twentieth century.
$ ✍

The Pearson Museum

Southern Illinois University School of Medicine
801 North Rutledge Street
Springfield, IL 62794
Tel: 217-545-8017
www.siumed.edu/medhum/pearson

St. Charles Heritage Center

215 East Main Street
St. Charles, IL 60174
Tel: 630-584-6967 Fax: 630-584-6007
www.siumed.edu/medhum/pearson
Hours: Tue–Sat 10–4 pm, Sun 12–4 pm
Contact: Julie Bunke
Institution type: History museum, historic house, city museum
Collection type: Clothing, general textiles
Description: 1850–1950. Late-nineteenth- and early-twentieth-century textiles.
$ ✍

Tinley Park Historical Society

6727 West 174th Street
Tinley Park, IL 60477
Tel: 708-429-4210

McHenry County Museum and Historical Society

6422 Main Street

Union, IL 60180

Tel: 815-923-2267

www.mchsonline.org

Hours: Tue–Fri, Sun 1–4 pm (May–Oct)

Contact: Grace Moline

Institution type: History museum

Collection type: Clothing, accessories, uniforms, costumes, general textiles, quilts

Description: 1800–present. Quilts and quilt tops ranging in date from early nineteenth century through the present, with emphasis on 1900 to 1940. Large collection of late-nineteenth-century to present women's clothing and accessories.

$ ✍

Spurlock Museum, University of Illinois at Urbana-Champaign

600 South Gregory Street

Urbana, IL 61801

Tel: 217-333-2360

www.spurlock.uiuc.edu

Hours: Tue 12–8 pm, Wed–Fri 9–5 pm, Sat 10–4 pm

Contact: Jennifer White, Registrar

Institution type: State museum

Collection type: Clothing, accessories, uniforms, general textiles, flags

Description: Pre-1700–present. World culture museum contains collections from around the world.

LaSalle County Historical Society Museum

Mill and Canal Streets

Utica, IL 61373

Tel: 815-667-4861

www.lasallecountymuseum.org

The Little Brick House

621 St. Clair

Vandalia, IL 62471

Tel: 618-283-2371

Cuneo Museum and Gardens

1350 North Milwaukee

Vernon Hills, IL 60061

Tel: 847-362-3042

Iroquois County Historical Society

103 West Cherry Street

Watseka, IL 60924

Tel: 815-432-2215 Fax: 815-432-2215

www.oldcourthousemuseum.org

Hours: Mon–Fri 10:30–4:30 pm, Sat 1–4 pm (Apr–Nov)

Contact: Members of Accession Committee

Institution type: History museum, historic house, county museum

Collection type: Clothing, accessories, uniforms, quilts

Description: 1850–present. County historical society contains items donated with connection to Iroquois County, including fashions of the eras, military uniforms, quilts, and accessories.

$ ✍

Lake County Discovery Museum

27277 Forest Preserve Road

Wauconda, IL 60084

Tel: 847-968-3400 Fax: 847-526-0024

www.lakecountydiscoverymuseum.org

Hours: Mon–Sat 11–4:30 pm, Sun 1–4 :30 pm

Contact: Katherine Hamilton-Smith

Institution type: History museum, county museum

Collection type: Clothing, accessories, uniforms, general textiles, quilts

Description: 1850–present. Quilts, dresses, hats, shoes, and military uniforms and related gear. Silks from the John High Collection include a large collection of woven silk pictures, sometimes called Stevengraphs, bookmarkers, and other woven silk items.

$ ✍

Wauconda Township Historical Society

711 North Main Street

Wauconda, IL 60084

Tel: 847-526-9303

Haines Museum, Waukegan Historical Society

1917 North Sheridan Road

Waukegan, IL 60087

Tel: 847-336-1859

West Chicago City Museum

132 Main Street

West Chicago, IL 60185

Tel: 630-231-3376

Frankfort Area Historical Museum

2000 East St. Louis Street
West Frankfort, IL 62896
Tel: 618-932-6159

DuPage County Historical Museum

102 East Wesley Street
Wheaton, IL 60187
Tel: 630-682-7343 Fax: 630-682-6549
www.dupageco.org/museum
Hours: Mon, Wed, Fri, Sat 10–4 pm, Sun 1–4 pm
Contact: Senior curator or curator
Institution type: History museum, county
museum
Collection type: Clothing, accessories, uniforms,
costumes, general textiles, quilts, flags
Description: 1760–present. Materials interpret
DuPage County, primarily 1830s to present.
Middle class, Midwestern, everyday, and spe-
cial occasion clothing and accessories. Specific
collections include Mildred Davison Textile
Notebooks, Lace Sample Notebooks, Colonial
Coverlet Guild of America collection of textiles
(111 coverlets, plus quilts and lace), and
CCGA archives. Other items include weaving
study group materials, weaving samples and
drafts, and mid-1800s Jacquard pattern cards.

$

*Enlisted man's
service coat,
1917–1919. Cour-
tesy of First Divi-
sion Museum at
Cantigny.*

The First Division Museum at Cantigny

1 South 151 Winfield Road
Wheaton, IL 60187
Tel: 630-260-8185 Fax: 630-630-9298
www.rrmtf.org/firstdivision
Hours: Tue–Sun 10–5 pm (Memorial Day–Labor
Day); Tue–Sun 10–4 pm, Fri–Sun 10–4 pm
(Feb)
Institution type: History museum

Wheaton History Center

606 North Main Street
Wheaton, IL 60187
Tel: 630-682-9472
www.wheaton.lib.il.us/whc

Wilmette Historical Museum

609 Ridge Road
Wilmette, IL 60091
Tel: 847-853-7666
www.wilmettehistory.org
Hours: Sun–Thu 1–4:30 pm
Contact: Jane Carlin Textor
Institution type: History museum, city museum
Collection type: Clothing, accessories, costumes,
quilts
Description: 1850–present. Garments owned and
worn by residents of Wilmette and the town of
Gross Point (now dissolved). The character of a
bustling suburb of Chicago in the nineteenth
century is readily seen in the craftsmanship and
quality of the costumes. Holdings include a
small collection of quilts and textiles.

Winnetka Historical Society

411 Linden
Winnetka, IL 60093
Tel: 847-501-6025
www.winnetkahistory.org

Hillforest Victorian House Museum

213 5th Street
Aurora, IN 47001
Tel: 812-926-0087 Fax: 812-926-1075
www.hillforest.org
Hours: Tue–Sun 9–5 pm (Apr–Dec)
Institution type: Historic house
$ ✍️

Museum at Prophetstown

3549 Prophetstown Trail
Battle Ground, IN 47920
Tel: 765-567-4700 Fax: 567-567-4736
www.prophetstown.org
Hours: Tue–Sat 1–4 pm (Winter); Mon–Sat 10–5
pm, Sun 1–5 pm (remaining year)
Contact: Becky Stuckey
Institution type: History museum
Collection type: Clothing, uniforms, general textiles, quilts
Description: 1900–1960. Original table linens,
bed coverings, and clothing circa 1920; damask
tablecloths and napkins, women's dress
clothing, and hats; World War I army uniform;
quilts and embroidered pillowcases; children's
clothing; undergarments; table runners; and
doilies. Many items are embellished with hand
needlework.
$ ✍️

Lawrence County Historical and Genealogical Society

931 15th Street
Bedford, IN 47421
Tel: 812-278-8575

Hours: Mon–Wed 9–4 pm, Thu 9–8 pm, Fri 9–4
pm, Sat 9–3 pm
Contact: Helen Burchard
Institution type: County museum
Collection type: Clothing, flags
Description: 1800–present
✍️

*Woman's boot, circa 1900. Courtesy of Indiana
University, Elizabeth Sage Historic Costume Collection.*

Indiana University

ELIZABETH SAGE HISTORIC COSTUME
COLLECTION
1021 East 3rd Street, MME 232
Bloomington, IN 47405-2201
Tel: 812-855-4627 Fax: 812-855-0362
www.indiana.edu/~amid/sage/sage.html
Hours: By appointment only
Contact: Kathleen Rowold

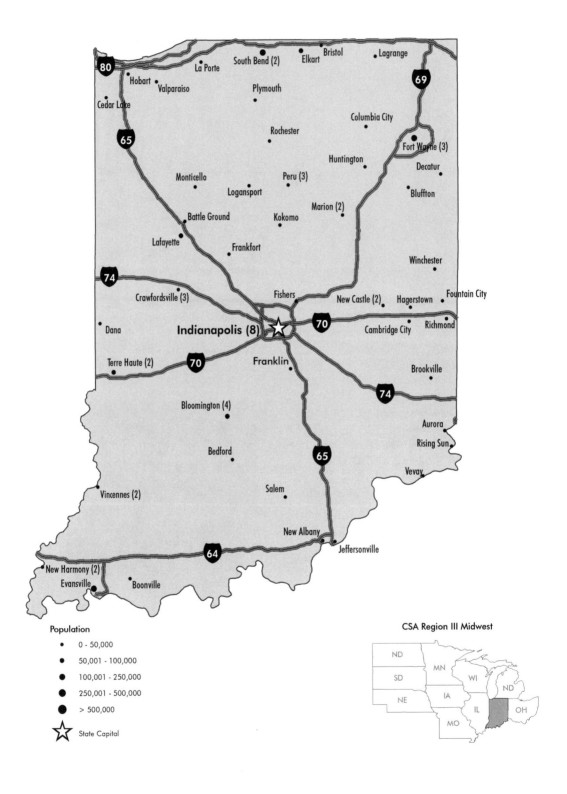

Bristol
Lagrange
South Bend (2) Elkart
La Porte
Hobart
Valparaiso
Plymouth
Cedar Lake
Columbia City
Rochester
Fort Wayne (3)
Huntington
Decatur
Monticello
Peru (3)
Bluffton
Logansport
Marion (2)
Battle Ground
Kokomo
Lafayette
Frankfort
Winchester
Fishers
Crawfordsville (3)
New Castle (2) Hagerstown Fountain City
Dana
Cambridge City Richmond
Indianapolis (8)
Terre Haute (2)
Franklin
Brookville
Bloomington (4)
Aurora
Bedford
Rising Sun
Vevay
Vincennes (2)
Salem
New Albany
Jeffersonville
New Harmony (2)
Evansville
Boonville

Population

- 0 - 50,000
- 50,001 - 100,000
- 100,001 - 250,000
- 250,001 - 500,000
- > 500,000
☆ State Capital

CSA Region III Midwest

ND
MN
SD
WI
ND
NE
IA
IL
OH
MO

Institution type: University collection

Collection type: Clothing, accessories, costumes, general textiles

Description: 1800–present. Women's, men's, and children's clothing and accessories from 1800 to the present, as well as fashion publications, prints, plates, videos, and home sewing patterns.

Mathers Museum of World Cultures

601 East 8th Street

Bloomington, IN 47408-3812

Tel: 812-855-6873 Fax: 812-855-0205

www.indiana.edu/~mathers

Hours: Tue–Fri 9–4:30 pm, Sat–Sun 1–4:30 pm

Institution type: University museum

GARMENTS COLLECTION

Contact: Ellen Sieber, Curator of Collections

Collection type: Clothing, accessories

Description: 1850–present. Everyday, special occasion, and ritual clothing and accessories from a very wide range of geographic locations and cultures. Particular collections include Mexican dance costumes, everyday wear from South American cultures, Plains Indian garments, and sub-Saharan African material.

TEXTILES COLLECTION

Contact: Ellen Sieber, Curator of Collections

Collection type: General textiles, quilts

Description: 1850–present. Range of materials from southern Indiana quilts to Tibetan thankas. Examples of the skill and variety in traditional textile work are Southeast Asian batik and ikat, Andean in-loom embroidery, African resist dying and embroidery, Sea Island Gullah quilts, Middle Eastern tapestry and carpet-weaving, Seminole patchwork, and Pueblo and Navajo upright and belt loom textiles.

Monroe County Historical Museum

202 East 6th Street

Bloomington, IN 47408

Tel: 812-332-2517

Wylie House Museum, Indiana University

317 East 2nd Street

Bloomington, IN 47401

Tel: 812-855-6224

www.indiana.edu/~libwylie

Hours: Tue–Sat 10–2 pm (Mar–Nov)

Institution type: Historic house, university museum

Wells County Historical Museum

420 West Market Street

Bluffton, IN 46714

Tel: 260-824-9956

www.wchs-museum.org

Warrick County Museum

217 South 1st Street

Boonville, IN 47601

Tel: 812-897-3100

Elkhart County Historical Museum

Rush Memorial Center

304 West Vistula Street

Bristol, IN 46507

Tel: 574-848-4322 Fax: 574-848-5703

Franklin County Seminary and Museum

5th and Mill Streets

Brookville, IN 47012

Tel: 765-647-5182

www.franklinchs.com

Huddleston Farmhouse Inn and Museum

838 National Road, Mount Auburn

Cambridge City, IN 47327

Tel: 765-478-3172

www.historiclandmarks.org/what/huddleston.html

Lake of the Red Cedars Museum

7803 Constitution Drive

Cedar Lake, IN 46303

Tel: 219-374-7562

Hours: Thu–Sun 1–4 pm (May–Oct)

Contact: Anne Zimmerman

Institution type: History museum, historic house

Collection type: Clothing, accessories, costumes, general textiles

Description: 1900–1960. Collection is housed in an old hotel with sixteen rooms set up in the lifestyle of the 1900s and the 1920s through the 1940s. One room is devoted entirely to clothing and accessories, with other clothing items displayed in the room settings.

$

Whitley County Historical Museum

108 West Jefferson Street
Columbia City, IN 46725
Tel: 260-244-6372
www.whitleynet.org/historical
Hours: Mon–Wed 8–2 pm
Contact: Susan Richey
Institution type: History museum, historic house,
county museum
Collection type: Clothing, accessories, uniforms,
costumes, general textiles, flags
Description: 1850–present
✍🗅

General Lew Wallace Study and Museum

Wallace Avenue at Pike Street
Crawfordsville, IN 47933-3777
Tel: 765-362-5769
www.ben-hur.com

The Lane Place

212 South Water Street
Crawfordsville, IN 47933
Tel: 765-362-3416

The Old Jail Museum

225 North Washington
Crawfordsville, IN 47933
Tel: 765-362-5222
www.crawfordsville.org/jail.html

Ernie Pyle State Historic Site

120 West Briarwood Avenue
Dana, IN 47847-0338
Tel: 765-665-3633 Fax: 765-665-9312

Adams County Historical Museum

420 West Monroe Street
Decatur, IN 46733
Tel: 260-724-2341

National New York Central
Railroad Museum

721 South Main Street
Elkhart, IN 46515
Tel: 574-294-3001
www.nycrrmuseum.org

Reitz Home Museum

224 SE 1st Street
Evansville, IN 47713
Tel: 812-426-1871
www.reitzhome.evansville.net

Conner Prairie

13400 Allisonville Road
Fishers, IN 46038
Tel: 317-776-6000
www.connerprairie.org

Fort Wayne Museum of Art

311 East Main Street
Fort Wayne, IN 46802
Tel: 260-422-6467
www.fwmoa.org

The History Center

ALLEN COUNTY HISTORICAL MUSEUM
COLLECTION
302 East Berry Street
Fort Wayne, IN 46802
Tel: 260-426-2882 Fax: 260-424-4419
www.fwhistorycenter.com
Hours: Tue–Fri 9–5 pm, Sat–Sun 12–5 pm
Contact: Walter Font
Institution type: History museum, historic house,
county museum, city museum
Collection type: Clothing, accessories, uniforms,
general textiles, quilts, flags
Description: 1700–present. Primarily women's
and children's clothing from the second quarter
of the nineteenth century to the first quarter of
the twentieth century. Collection includes
clothing, adornment, personal gear, bedding,
floor coverings, household accessories, window
coverings, tapestries, and samplers.
$ ✍🗅

The Lincoln Museum

200 East Berry Street
Fort Wayne, IN 46802
Tel: 260-455-2730 Fax: 260-455-6922
www.thelincolnmuseum.org

Levi Coffin House

113 U.S. 27 North
Fountain City, IN 47341
Tel: 765-847-2432

Clinton County Museum

301 East Clinton Street
Frankfort, IN 46041
Tel: 765-659-2030
www.cchsm.cjb.net

Johnson County Museum of History

THE JOHNSON COUNTY HISTORICAL
SOCIETY COLLECTIONS
135 North Main Street
Franklin, IN 46131
Tel: 317-736-4655 Fax: 317-736-5451
www.co.johnson.in.us/admin1/museum.html
Hours: Mon–Fri 9–4 pm, 2nd Sat 10–3 pm
Contact: Jill Hasprunar
Institution type: History museum, county
museum
Collection type: Clothing, accessories, uniforms,
costumes, general textiles, flags
Description: 1760–present
$ 🖎

Wilbur Wright Birthplace and Interpretative Center

1525 North County Road 750 East
Hagerstown, IN 47346
Tel: 765-332-2495 Fax: 765-332-2805
www.birthplace.com
Hours: Mon–Sat 10–5 pm, Sun 1–5 pm (Mar
15–Nov 15)

Hobart Historical Society Museum

706 East 4th Street
Hobart, IN 46342
Tel: 219-942-0970

Huntington County Historical Society Museum

315 Court Street
Huntington, IN 46750
Tel: 219-356-7264

The Children's Museum of Indianapolis

AMERICAN AND WORLD CULTURES
3000 North Meridian Street
Indianapolis, IN 46206
Tel: 317-334-4000 Fax: 317-920-2001
www.childrensmuseum.org
Hours: Mon–Sun 10–5 pm (Apr–Labor Day)
Contact: Andrea Hughes, American Culture; Jana
Bennett, World Cultures

Tatted baby's shoes and rattle, circa 1918. Courtesy of the Children's Museum of Indianapolis

Institution type: Art museum, history museum
Collection type: Clothing, accessories, uniforms,
costumes, general textiles, quilts, flags
Description: 1800–present. Two main categories
in the collection are costume (clothing and
accessories) and domestic pieces (household
furnishings and artistic works). Pieces are from
the early 1800s to the present and include
men's, women's, and children's clothing and
accessories. The domestic pieces collection contains artifacts mostly from the mid-nineteenth
century through the mid-twentieth century.
Strengths of the collection include many
women's dresses from the mid-nineteenth century to the mid-twentieth century and Halloween and play costumes.
$ 🖎

Eiteljorg Museum of American Indians and Western Art

500 West Washington Street
Indianapolis, IN 46204
Tel: 317-636-9378
www.eiteljorg.org

Indiana Medical History Museum

3045 West Vermont Street
Indianapolis, IN 46222
Tel: 317-635-7329 Fax: 317-635-7349
www.imhm.org

Indianapolis Museum of Art

4000 Michigan Road
Indianapolis, IN 46208
Tel: 317-923-1331 Fax: 317-926-8931
www.ima.art.org

Evening ensemble by Norman Norell, 1956. Courtesy of Indianapolis Museum of Art.

Boy's printed brown wool challis dress, circa 1867–1875. Courtesy of Indiana State Museum.

Hours: Tue–Wed, Fri–Sat 10–5 pm, Thu 10–8:30 pm, Sun 12–5 pm

Contact: Nicoo Imami-Paydar

Institution type: Art museum

Collection type: Clothing, accessories, costumes

Description: 1800–present. More than 6,000 pieces, including Asian, African, European, and American textiles, costumes, and accessories. One of the first American art museums to initiate a textile collection (1888). The fine arts collection features holdings in women's costumes and accessories of nineteenth- and twentieth-century Europe and America. Creations by designers Norman Norell, Bill Blass, and Halston—all natives of Indiana—are an area of special emphasis.

Indiana State Museum

650 West Washington Street
Indianapolis, IN 46204-2725
Tel: 317-232-1637
www.indianamuseum.org

Hours: Mon–Sat 9–5 pm, Sun 11–5 pm

Contact: Mary Jane Teeters-Eichacker

Institution type: History museum, state museum

Collection type: Clothing, accessories, uniforms, costumes, general textiles, quilts, flags

Description: 1750–present. Clothing and accessories for men, women, and children, including military uniforms, work clothing, and a large collection of Indiana Amish clothing. Earliest artifact is a 1760s English silk dress; the most recent are T-shirts from the 1990s. Majority of the collection is in women's clothing of the late

nineteenth century and early twentieth century. Holdings include collection of contemporary Indiana sports clothing; the Golden Troupe Collection of 1860–1890 stage costumes; over 150 examples of Indiana's coverlet weavers; over 2,000 needlework items; and 800 quilts.

Morris-Butler House Museum

1204 North Park Avenue
Indianapolis, IN 46202
Tel: 317-636-5409 Fax: 317-636-2630
www.historiclandmarks.org/what/morrisbutler

Hours: Wed–Sat 10–3:30 pm (Feb–mid-Dec)

Contact: Shannon Borbely

Institution type: History museum, historic house

Collection type: Clothing, accessories, costumes, general textiles

Description: 1850–1899

$ 🖎

President Benjamin Harrison Home Museum

1230 North Delaware Street
Indianapolis, IN 46202
Tel: 317-631-1888
www.pbhh.org

Hours: Mon–Sat 10–3:30 pm

Institution type: History museum, historic house

$ 🖎

CIVIL WAR UNIFORMS COLLECTION

Contact: Jennifer Capps

Collection type: Uniforms

Description: 1850–1899. Union uniform of Col.

(Left to right) Gown of Caroline Scott Harrison, gown of Mary Harrison McKee, and cape of Mary Harrison McKee, 1890s. Courtesy of President Benjamin Harrison Home.

John Hardin McHenry of Kentucky—navy blue wool, double-breasted with two rows of brass buttons, stand-up collar with hole from wound in Shiloh; navy blue wool Civil War jacket; and single-breasted man's jacket with buttons crested and Massachusetts on them.

FLAGS COLLECTION

Contact: Jennifer Capps

Collection type: Flags

Description: 1850–1960. Thirty-six-, thirty-eight-, forty-two-, forty-four-, and fifty-star flags. Highlights include flag hoisted from top of Allen home in Indianapolis to announce to neighborhood the election of Benjamin Harrison as president and 205"x102" American flag containing forty-four stars.

ORIGINAL HARRISON CLOTHING COLLECTION

Contact: Jennifer Capps

Collection type: Clothing, accessories

Description: 1850–1914. Dresses, gowns, stockings, shoes, hats, and personal items that belonged to First Lady Caroline Harrison and her daughter Mary Harrison McKee. Most date to their time in the White House (1889–1893).

TEXTILES COLLECTION

Contact: Jennifer Capps

Collection type: General textiles, quilts

Description: 1850–1914. Crazy quilts dating from the 1880s, with President Benjamin Harrison campaign ribbons or other items sewn into the quilts and signature quilts with period political figures' signatures. Other items include coverlet, Henry Overholt rugs, bedding, pillows, and other household linens.

Textile Arts Center

928 North Alabama Street
Indianapolis, IN 46202
Tel: 317-266-8398 Fax: 317-266-8399
www.textileconservation.com

Hours: By appointment

Contact: Harold F. Mailand

Institution type: Historic house

Collection type: Clothing, accessories, uniforms, costumes, general textiles, quilts, flags

Description: Pre-1700–present. Collection emphasizes textiles and costumes having a German-American-Indiana reference, circa 1837, and represents technological advances in weaving, manufacturing, and communication of "soft" goods. Progenitor cultures using natural fibers include China (silk), India (cotton), Europe (linen), and Old Turkish Empire (wool), Europe, North America, North Africa, and South America. Collection contains mostly common and festive clothing, coverlets, quilts, and embellished fabrics. Other items include hard goods that have been historically used for cleaning, ironing, and storing textiles and costumes.

$ 🖊

Howard Steamboat Museum and Mansion

1101 East Market Street
Jeffersonville, IN 47130
Tel: 812-283-3728 Fax: 812-283-6049
www.steamboatmuseum.org

Hours: Tue–Sat 10–4 pm, Sun 1–4 pm

Contact: Yvonne B. Knight

Institution type: History museum, historic house

Collection type: Clothing, accessories, uniforms, costumes, general textiles, flags

Description: 1800–1960. Small collection of dresses, undergarments, hats, shoes, hair ornaments, fans, and accessories owned by the family who built the mansion. Other items include 1819 sampler, "Little Lord Fauntleroy" suit, captain's jacket, beaver hat, World War II military uniforms, more than 6 flags (1898 and others), paintings on silk, and beaded purse.

$ 🖊

Howard County Historical Society Museum

1200 West Sycamore Street
Kokomo, IN 46901
Tel: 765-452-4314
www.howardcountymuseum.org
Hours: Tue–Sun 1–4 pm
Contact: Curator of collections
Institution type: County museum
Collection type: Clothing, accessories, uniforms, general textiles
Description: 1850–present.
$ ✍

La Porte County Historical Society Museum

809 State Street
La Porte, IN 46350
Tel: 219-326-6808
www.lapcohistsoc.org

Tippecanoe County Historical Association

909 South Street
Lafayette, IN 47901
Tel: 765-476-8411
www.tcha.mus.in.us

Machan Museum

405 South Poplar Street
Lagrange, IN 46761
Tel: 260-463-3232

Cass County Historical Society Museum

1004 East Market Street
Logansport, IN 46947
Tel: 574-753-3866

Marion Public Library Museum

600 South Washington Street
Marion, IN 46953
Tel: 765-668-2900
www.marion.lib.in.us

The Quilters Hall of Fame

926 South Washington Street
Marion, IN 46953
Tel: 765-664-9333
www.quiltershalloffame.org
Hours: Tue–Sat 10–4pm (Mar–Dec)
Contact: Ann Calland
Institution type: History museum, historic house
Collection type: Clothing, accessories, quilts

Description: 1851–1959. Clothing and accessories belonging to Marie D. Webster, a famous quilter, lecturer, and author of the early 1900s.
$ ✍

White County Historical Society Museum

101 South Bluff Street
Monticello, IN 47960
Tel: 574-583-3998

Culbertson Mansion State Historic Site

914 East Main Street
New Albany, IN 47150
Tel: 812-944-9600
www.in.gov/ism/HistoricSites

Henry County Historical Society

606 South 14th Street
New Castle, IN 47362
Tel: 765-529-4028

Indiana Basketball Hall of Fame

408 Trojan Lane
New Castle, IN 47362
Tel: 765-529-1891
www.hoopshall.com

New Harmony State Historic Site

419 Tavern
New Harmony, IN 47631
Tel: 812-682-3271
www.in.gov/ism/HistoricSites
Hours: Mon–Sun 9:30–5 pm
Institution type: History museum, state museum
$ ✍

Working Men's Institute

HARMONY SOCIETY TEXTILES
407 West Tavern Street
New Harmony, IN 47631
Tel: 812-682-4806 Fax: 812-682-4806
www.newharmonywmi.lib.in.us
Hours: Tue–Sat 10–4:30 pm, Sun 12–4 pm
Contact: Curator
Institution type: Art museum, history museum
Collection type: Clothing
Description: 1800–1849. Primarily woolens, cottons, and silks that were manufactured from 1814 to 1824 by the Harmony Society during their tenure at New Harmony, Indiana.
✍

Circus City Festival Museum

154 North Broadway
Peru, IN 46970
Tel: 765-472-3918

Grissom Air Museum

1000 West Hoosier Boulevard
Peru, IN 46970-3647
Tel: 765-689-8011
www.grissomairmuseum.com

Miami County Museum

51 North Broadway
Peru, IN 46970
Tel: 765-473-9183 Fax: 765-473-3880
www.miamicountymuseum.com
Hours: Tue–Sat 9–5 pm
Institution type: County museum
✍

Marshall County Historical Society and Museum

123 North Michigan Street
Plymouth, IN 46563
Tel: 574-936-2306 Fax: 574-936-9306
www.mchistoricalsociety.org
Hours: Tue–Fri 9–5 pm, Sat 10–4 pm
Institution type: History museum
✍

Wayne County Historical Museum

1150 North A Street
Richmond, IN 47374
Tel: 765-962-5756 Fax: 765-939-0909
www.waynet.org/nonprofit/historical_museum
.htm
Hours: Tue–Fri 10–4 pm, Sat–Sun 1–4 pm
(Mar–Dec)
Contact: Jan Livingston, Executive Director
Institution type: History museum
Collection type: Clothing, accessories, uniforms,
costumes, general textiles, quilts, flags
Description: 1760–present. Strengths are everyday
clothing and Quaker garments and accessories
circa 1820–1950. 80 quilts and 60 coverlets,
most of them regionally made. Also public
service and military uniforms, foreign costumes, shoes, and hats.
$ ✍

Ohio County Historical Society

212 South Walnut Street
Rising Sun, IN 47040
Tel: 812-438-4915 Fax: 812-438-4925
www.ohiocountyinmuseum.org
Hours: Mon–Tue, Thu–Fri 11–4 pm, Sat–Sun
1:30–4:30 pm
Contact: William J. Dichtl
Institution type: History museum, county
museum
Collection type: Quilts
Description: 1800–1960. Collection includes
Ohio County–made quilts and coverlets. Pat-
terns include Log Cabin, Fan, and Autograph.
Dates cover 1848 to 1937.
$ ✍

Fulton County Historical Society Museum

37 East 375 North
Rochester, IN 46975
Tel: 574-223-4436 Fax: 574-224-4436
www.icss.net/~fchs
Hours: Mon–Sat 9–5 pm
Contact: Peggy Van Meter or Lola Riddle
Institution type: History museum
Collection type: Clothing, accessories, uniforms,
costumes, general textiles, flags
Description: 1850–present. Clothing donated to
museum since 1870. Items include many hats,
purses, and other accessories, including shoes.
✍

Stevens Museum

307 East Market Street
Salem, IN 47167
Tel: 812-883-6495

College Football Hall of Fame

111 South St. Joseph Street
South Bend, IN 46601
Tel: 574-235-5711 Fax: 574-235-5700
www.collegefootball.org
Hours: Mon–Sun 10–5 pm
Contact: Kent Stephens
Institution type: History museum
Collection type: Clothing, accessories, uniforms
$ ✍

Northern Indiana Center for History
808 West Washington
South Bend, IN 46601
Tel: 574-235-9664 Fax: 574-235-9059
www.centerforhistory.org
Hours: Tue–Sat 10–5 pm, Sun 12–5 pm
Institution type: History museum, historic house
$ ✍

COPSHAHOLM HISTORIC HOUSE
COLLECTION
Contact: David Bainbridge
Collection type: Clothing, accessories, general textiles, quilts
Description: 1700–present. Men's and women's clothing belonging to the J. D. Oliver family; European church vestments; and quilts, lace, and linens.

PERMANENT COLLECTION
Contact: David Bainbridge
Collection type: Clothing, accessories, uniforms, costumes, general textiles, quilts, flags
Description: 1800–present. Local history collection from middle income and international societies includes items from the Studebaker and Oliver industrial families and the 1868 inaugural gown belonging to Mrs. Schyler Colfax when Colfax was elected to the vice presidency. Collection is national repository of the All American Girls Professional Baseball League.

Native American Museum
5170 East Poplar Street
Terre Haute, IN 47803
Tel: 812-877-6007

Vigo County Historical Museum
1411 South 6th Street
Terre Haute, IN 47802
Tel: 812-235-9717 Fax: 812-235-9717
http://web.indstate.edu/community/vchs/index
.php

**Historical Society Porter County
Old Jail Museum**
153 Franklin Street
Valparaiso, IN 46383
Tel: 219-465-3595

**Switzerland County Historical
Society Museum**
15 Tapps Ridge Road
Vevay, IN 47043
Tel: 812-427-3560

**George Rogers Clark National
Historical Park**
401 South 2nd Street
Vincennes, IN 47591
Tel: 812-882-1776x110 Fax: 812-882-7270
www.nps.gov/gero

**William Henry Harrison Mansion,
Grouseland**
3 West Scott Street
Vincennes, IN 47591
Tel: 812-882-2096

Randolph County Historical Museum
416 South Meridan
Winchester, IN 47394
Tel: 317-584-1334

IOWA

Amana Heritage Society
705 44th Avenue
Amana, IA 52203
Tel: 319-622-3567 Fax: 319-622-6481
www.amanaheritage.org
Hours: Mon–Sat 10–4, Sun 12-4
Contact: Jennifer Engelkemier
Institution type: History museum, historic house
Collection type: Clothing, accessories, uniforms, general textiles, quilts
Description: 1850–present. More than 3,000 pieces pertaining to the history of the Amana Colonies. Strengths include nineteenth- and twentieth-century textiles manufactured in Amana, Iowa, as well as handwork, including knit, crocheted, tatted, and quilted pieces and some items that Amana settlers brought with them from Germany.
$ ✍

Textile sack and doll in traditional dress, circa 1930s. Courtesy of Amana Heritage Society.

Detail, man's silk dress coat, circa 1725–1750. Courtesy of Iowa State University.

Iowa State University
Department of Apparel, Education Studies, and Hospitality Management
1058 LeBaron Hall
Ames, IA 50011
Tel: 515-294-4233 Fax: 515-294-6364
http://www.extension.iastate.edu/textiles/historic.html
Hours: By appointment
Contact: Susan Torntore
Institution type: University collection
Collection type: Clothing, costumes, general textiles
Description: Pre-1700–present. 7,500 items include textiles, circa AD 600 to present; Mid-western U.S. clothing; European and U.S. designer clothing; textiles and ethnic dress from Guatemala, China, Japan, Korea,

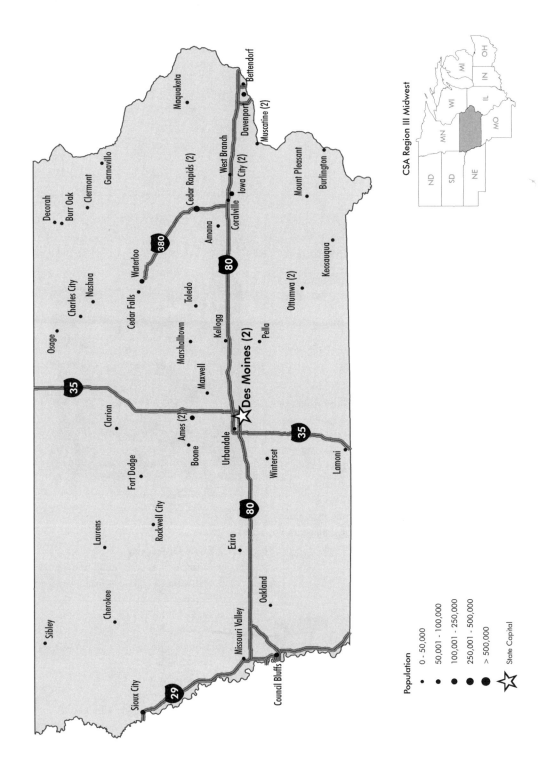

Population
· 0 - 50,000
• 50,001 - 100,000
● 100,001 - 250,000
● 250,001 - 500,000
● > 500,000
☆ State Capital

CSA Region III Midwest

Indonesia, India, Africa, and the United States; a few pre-Columbian Peruvian pieces; a few Roman-Egyptian fragments; and a few quilts. In 2007, the collection will move into a new facility on campus, the Center for Visual Learning in Textiles and Clothing, which will include a conservation lab, gallery, reference library, and online catalog.

The Octagon Center for the Arts

427 Douglas Avenue
Ames, IA 50010-6281
Tel: 515-232-5331
www.octagonarts.org

Family Museum of Arts and Science

2900 Learning Campus Drive
Bettendorf, IA 52722
Tel: 563-344-4106
www.familymuseum.org

Mamie Doud Eisenhower Birthplace Foundation

709 Carroll Street
Boone, IA 50036
Tel: 515-432-1896

Des Moines County Historical Society

1616 Dill Street
Burlington, IA 52601
Tel: 319-753-2449
Hours: Sat–Sun 1:30–4:30 pm (May–Oct) and by appointment
Contact: James Hunt or Debra Olson
Institution type: History museum, historic house
Collection type: Clothing, accessories, uniforms, general textiles, quilts, flags
Description: 1760–present. Three museums—The Apple Trees Museum, Phelps House Museum, and Hawkeye Log Cabin—share clothing and textiles collection dating from the late eighteenth century to the twentieth century, with emphasis on late Victorian and Edwardian garments. Collection includes military uniforms from the Civil War to the Vietnam War. Textiles include homespun sheets, coverlets, and crazy quilts.

Laura Ingalls Wilder Park and Museum

3603 236th Avenue
Burr Oak, IA 52101
Tel: 563-735-5916
www.lauraingallswilder.us

Cedar Falls Historical Society

308 West 3rd Street
Cedar Falls, IA 50613
Tel: 319-266-5149 Fax: 319-268-1812
www.cedarfallshistorical.org
Hours: Call for hours
Contact: Kelly Schott or Doris Schmitz
Institution type: History museum, historic house
Collection type: Clothing, accessories, uniforms, costumes, general textiles, quilts, flags
Description: 1800–present. Clothing collection is made up of all aspects of clothing with a few early items. Majority of items are from the early 1900s. Large variety of 1920s–1940s items; accessories, including hats, shawls, stockings, and shoes; and textiles, including quilts from 1880 to 1950, samplers, and blankets.

MOURNING COLLECTION
Contact: Kelly Schott
Collection type: Clothing, accessories
Description: 1850–1890. Primarily Midwestern mourning clothing of women and children of the last half of the nineteenth century, the collection includes 15 dresses, 32 bonnets, books, fans, jewelry, and ephemera associated with mourning and funerals.

Cedar Rapids Museum of Art

410 3rd Avenue SE
Cedar Rapids, IA 52401
Tel: 319-366-7503
www.crma.org

National Czech and Slovak Museum and Library

30 16th Avenue SW
Cedar Rapids, IA 52404
Tel: 319-362-8500 Fax: 319-363-2209
www.ncsml.org
Hours: Mon–Sun 9–4 pm
Contact: Edith Blanchard
Institution type: Art museum, history museum, historic house
Collection type: Clothing, accessories, uniforms, costumes, general textiles, flags

Costume, Kyjov region of Moravia, late nineteenth century. Courtesy of National Czech and Slovak Museum and Library.

Description: 1800–present. Collection represents Czech and Slovak culture, both Old and New Worlds, and is the largest collection of *kroje* (traditional folk costumes) outside of the Czech Republic. Kroje are made up of several elaborately decorated pieces, including vests, aprons, blouses, shirts, caps, headscarves, pants, and skirts. Most pieces are embroidered, beaded, or otherwise embellished. Other items include bedding, table linens, and flags used by Czechs and Slovaks and their American descendants.

$ 🖎

Floyd County Historical Museum

500 Gilbert Street
Charles City, IA 50616-2738
Tel: 641-228-1099
www.floydcountymuseum.org

Sanford Museum and Planetarium

VIRGINIA HERRICK QUILT BLOCK
COLLECTION

117 East Willow Street
Cherokee, IA 51012
Tel: 712-225-3922 Fax: 712-225-0446
http://mail.cherokee.k12.ia.us/~sanford
Hours: Mon–Fri 9–5 pm, Sat–Sun 12–5 pm
Contact: Linda A. Burkhart
Institution type: History museum
Collection type: Quilts
Description: 1900–1960. Virginia Herrick made

sampler blocks of over two hundred quilt patterns in addition to collecting over twelve volumes of information about patterns and quilt names.

🖎

4-H Schoolhouse Museum

302 South Main
Clarion, IA 50525
Tel: 515-532-2256

Man's vest, circa 1903. Courtesy of State of Iowa Historic Site Montauk.

State of Iowa Historic Site Montauk

26223 Harding Road
Clermont, IA 52135
Tel: 563-423-7173
www.iowahistory.org/sites/montauk/
montauk.html
Hours: Mon–Fri 8–4:30 pm
Contact: Nadine West
Institution type: Historic house, state museum
Collection type: Clothing, accessories, quilts
Description: 1850–1959. Clothing worn by Governor William Larrabee's wife, Anna Matilda, and daughters, Augusta, Julia, Anna, and Helen. Other items include accessories, some quilts, men's and children's items from the 1850s to 1959, and some items from Paris, New York, and Chicago.

🖎

Johnson County Historical Society

310 5th Street
Coralville, IA 52241
Tel: 319-351-5738
www.jchsiowa.org

Historic General Dodge House

605 3rd Street
Council Bluffs, IA 51503
Tel: 712-322-2406
www.councilbluffsiowa.com

Putnam Museum of History and Natural Science

1717 West 12th Street
Davenport, IA 52804
Tel: 563-324-1933
www.putnam.org

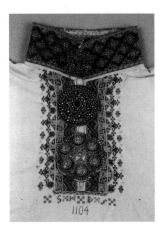

Folk costume from East Telemark, Norway, early- to mid-nineteenth century. Courtesy of Vesterheim Norwegian-American Museum.

Vesterheim Norwegian-American Museum

523 West Water Street
Decorah, IA 52101-0379
Tel: 563-382-9681 Fax: 563-382-8828
www.vesterheim.org
Hours: Mon–Sun 9–5 pm (May–Oct), Tue–Sun 10–4 pm (Nov–Apr)
Contact: Laurann Gilbertson, Textile Curator
Institution type: History museum
Collection type: Clothing, accessories, uniforms, costumes, general textiles
Description: 1760–present. Decorative and household textiles, clothing, and accessories brought from Norway by immigrants to America (20 percent of collection) and decorative and household textiles, clothing, and accessories that were made or used by Americans of Norwegian descent (80 percent of collection). Strengths include Norwegian folk dress and jewelry, Norwegian woven coverlets, American women's wear from 1890 to 1920, and World War II uniforms from the 99th Infantry Battalion.

$ 🖐

Salisbury House Foundation

4025 Tonawanda Drive
Des Moines, IA 50312
Tel: 515-274-1777
www.salisburyhouse.org

State Historical Society of Iowa

600 East Locust Street
Des Moines, IA 50319
Tel: 515-281-5111
www.iowahistory.org

Audubon County Historical Society, Courthouse Museum

East Washington and Kilwoth Street
Exira, IA 50076
Tel: 712-563-3984

Fort Dodge Historical Museum

South Kenyon & Museum Road
Fort Dodge, IA 50501
Tel: 515-573-4231
www.fortmuseum.com

Garnavillo Historical Museum

205 North Washington
Garnavillo, IA 52049
Tel: 563-964-2607

University of Iowa Hospitals and Clinics Medical Museum

200 Hawkins Drive 8014 RCP
Iowa City, IA 52242
Tel: 319-356-1616
www.uihealthcare.com/depts/medmuseum

University of Iowa Museum of Art

150 North Riverside Drive
Iowa City, IA 52242-1789
Tel: 319-335-1727 Fax: 319-335-3677
www.uiowa.edu/uima
Hours: Wed–Sun 12–5 pm, Thu–Fri 12–9 pm
Institution type: University museum
🖐

Kellogg Historical Society

218 High Street
Kellogg, IA 50135
Tel: 641-526-3430

Van Buren County Historical Society Museum

801 First Street
Keosauqua, IA 52565
Tel: 319-293-3211

Liberty Hall Historic Center

RR 1, Box 2
Lamoni, IA 50140
Tel: 641-784-6133

Pocahontas County Iowa Historical Society Museum

272 North 3rd Street
Laurens, IA 50554-1017
Tel: 712-845-2577

Jackson County Historical Museum

1212 East Quarry, Fairgrounds
Maquoketa, IA 52060
Tel: 563-652-5020

Historical Society of Marshall County

202 East Church Street
Marshalltown, IA 50158
Tel: 515-752-6664

Community Historical Museum

101 Main Street
Maxwell, IA 50161
Tel: 641-385-2376

Steamboat Bertrand Museum

1434 316th Lane
Missouri Valley, IA 51555
Tel: 712-642-4121 Fax: 712-642-5427
www.fws.gov/refuges/generalInterest/
    steamBoatBertrand.html
Hours: Mon–Sun 9–4:30 pm
Contact: Jennifer Stafford
Institution type: Federal museum
Collection type: Clothing, accessories, general textiles
Description: 1850–1899. Cargo that was excavated out of the hold of a steamboat that sank in the Missouri River on April 1, 1865, including securely dated men's work and dress clothing, sewing notions, footwear, headwear, textiles, and accessories.

$

Harlan-Lincoln House

101 West Broad Street
Mount Pleasant, IA 52641
Tel: 319-385-8021

Muscatine Art Center

THE COSTUMES OF LAURA MUSSER
1314 Mulberry Avenue
Muscatine, IA 52761
Tel: 563-263-8282 Fax: 563-263-4702
www.muscatineartcenter.org
Hours: Tue–Fri 10–5 pm, Thu 7–9 pm, Sat–Sun 1–5 pm
Contact: Virginia L. Cooper
Institution type: Art museum, history museum, historic house, city museum
Collection type: Clothing, accessories, costumes, general textiles, quilts
Description: 1850–1960. More than 1,000 items including women's dresses and accessories, children's clothing and accessories, and men's costumes, all from circa 1860 to 1930, the majority from the turn of the century. The costumes are primarily Iowa pieces. Many of Laura Musser's dresses were made in Chicago. Original textiles from the Musser home, as well as coverlet and quilt collections.

Muscatine History and Industry Center

117 West 2nd Street
Muscatine, IA 52761
Tel: 563-263-1052
www.muscatinehistory.org

American Maid pearl button card, circa 1920. Courtesy of Muscatine History and Industry Center.

Hours: Tue–Sat 12–4 pm
Contact: Melanie Alexander
Institution type: History museum, city museum
Collection type: Accessories
Description: 1915–1960. Artifacts relate to pearl button industry and include factory equipment, finished buttons, button cards, button company memorabilia, button blanks, mussel shells, and a clamming boat.

Chickasaw County Historical Society Museum, Bradford Village
2729 Cheyenne Avenue
Nashua, IA 50658
Tel: 641-435-2567

Nishna Heritage Museum
123 Main Street
Oakland, IA 51560
Tel: 712-482-6802

Mitchell County Historical Society Museum
821 Poplar Avenue
Osage, IA 50461-8557
Tel: 515-732-3059

Airpower Museum
22001 Bluegrass Road
Ottumwa, IA 52501-8569
Tel: 641-938-2773
www.aaa-apm.org/apm/index.html

Wapello County Historical Museum
210 West Main Street
Ottumwa, IA 52501
Tel: 641-682-8676
Hours: Call for hours
Contact: Curator of collections
Institution type: History museum
Collection type: Clothing, accessories, quilts
Description: 1800–present. More than 2,000 items including clothing brought by pioneers, limited to Wapello County; large selection of infant wear; large selection of hats and shoes for women and children; and quilts and coverlets.

$

Scholte House Museum
728 Washington
Pella, IA 50219
Tel: 641-628-3684

Calhoun County Museum
150 East High Street, U.S. Highway 20
Rockwell City, IA 50579
Tel: 712-297-8139

McCallum Museum
Sibley City Park
Sibley, IA 51249
Tel: 712-754-3882
www.osceolacountyia.com/info/museums.htm

Sioux City Public Museum
2901 Jackson Street
Sioux City, IA 51104-3697
Tel: 712-279-6174
www.sioux-city.org/museum

Tama County Historical Museum
200 North Broadway
Toledo, IA 52342
Tel: 515-484-6767

Living History Farms
2600 111th Street
Urbandale, IA 50322
Tel: 515-278-5286 Fax: 515-278-9808
www.livinghistoryfarms.org
Hours: Mon–Sun 9–5 pm (May–Oct)
Contact: Deb Irving
Institution type: History museum
Collection type: Clothing, accessories, uniforms, costumes, general textiles, quilts, flags
Description: 1800–present. More than 340 quilts and many quilting related items, including books and tools, as well as thousands of clothing items, household items, blankets, coverlets, and paisley shawls. Many items have an Iowa connection.

$

H. W. Grout Museum District
503 South Street
Waterloo, IA 50701
Tel: 319-234-6357 Fax: 319-236-0500
www.groutmuseumdistrict.org
Hours: Tue–Fri 9–5 pm
Contact: Lorraine L. Ihnen

Institution type: History museum, historic house

Collection type: Clothing, accessories, uniforms, general textiles, quilts, flags

Description: Pre-1700–present. More than 100 quilts and coverlets; clothing, 1800–present; Victorian clothing of women and children; military uniforms from the Civil War to the Korean War; U.S. flags from the Civil War to the present; and accessories, including shoes, hats, purses, and jewelry, 1800–present.

$ ✍

Herbert Hoover Presidential Library-Museum

210 Parkside Drive
West Branch, IA 52358
Tel: 319-643-5301
www.hoover.archives.gov

Hours: Mon–Sun 9–5 pm

$ ✍

Madison County Historical Society

815 South 2nd Avenue
Winterset, IA 50273
Tel: 515-462-2134

KANSAS

Dickinson County Historical Society
412 South Campbell Street
Abilene, KS 67410
Tel: 785-263-2681 Fax: 785-263-0380
www.heritagecenterdk.com
Hours: Mon–Fri 9–4 pm, Sat 10–5 pm, Sun 1–5 pm
Contact: Jeff Sheets
Institution type: History museum, historical society, county museum
Collection type: Clothing, uniforms, general textiles, quilts
Description: 1850–present. Clothing, 1870s–1950s; quilts, 1851–1970; and uniforms, 1898–Vietnam War.
$

Dwight D. Eisenhower Library and Museum
200 SE 4th Street
Abilene, KS 67410
Tel: 785-263-4751 Fax: 785-263-4218
www.dwightdeisenhower.com
Hours: Sun–Sat 9-4:45 pm
Contact: Dennis H. J. Medina
Institution type: History museum, historic house, federal museum
Collection type: Clothing, accessories, uniforms
Description: 1900–present. Collection includes 300 dresses and accessories worn by Mamie Eisenhower from 1916 to 1979 and various uniforms from divisions of military service during World War II era.
$

The Fashion Museum
212 North Broadway Street
Abilene, KS 67410
Tel: 785-263-7997
Hours: Thu–Sat 10–4 pm, Sun 1–4 pm
Contact: Jill Crist
Institution type: History museum
Collection type: Clothing, accessories, uniforms
Description: 1850–present. Women's, men's, and children's clothing from 1870 through 1980. Museum maintains collection for exhibits only plus an educational collection that can be used for hands-on learning purposes.
$

Wabaunsee County Historical Museum
227 Missouri Street
Alma, KS 66401
Tel: 785-765-2200

Cherokee Strip Land Rush Museum
31639 U.S. Highway 77
Arkansas City, KS 67005
Tel: 316-442-6750
http://arkcity.org/index.asp?ID=216

Atchison County Historical Society
200 South 10th Street
Atchison, KS 66002
Tel: 913-367-6238
www.atchisonhistory.org

CSA Region VII Southwest

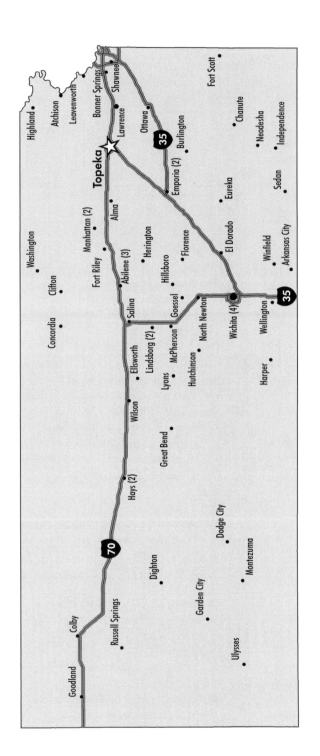

Population

- 0 - 50,000
- 50,001 - 100,000
- 100,001 - 250,000
- 250,001 - 500,000
- > 500,000
☆ State Capital

Wyandotte County Museum
631 North 126th Street
Bonner Springs, KS 66012
Tel: 913-721-1078

Coffey County Historical Society and Museum
1101 Neosho Street
Burlington, KS 66839
Tel: 620-364-2653 Fax: 620-364-8933
www.coffeycountymuseum.org

Martin and Osa Johnson Safari Museum
111 North Lincoln Avenue
Chanute, KS 66720
Tel: 620-431-2730
www.safarimuseum.com

Clifton Community Historical Society
108 Clifton Street
Clifton, KS 66937-0223
Tel: 785-455-2296

Prairie Museum of Art and History
1905 South Franklin
Colby, KS 67701
Tel: 785-462-4590 Fax: 785-462-4590
www.prairiemuseum.org

Cloud County Historical Society Museum
635 Broadway
Concordia, KS 66901
Tel: 785-243-2866

Lane County Historical Museum
333 North Main Street
Dighton, KS 67839
Tel: 620-397-5652

Boot Hill Museum
500 West Wyatt Earp Boulevard
Dodge City, KS 67801
Tel: 620-227-8188
www.boothill.org

Kansas Oil Museum
383 East Central Avenue
El Dorado, KS 67042
Tel: 316-321-9333
http://skyways.lib.ks.us/museums/kom/index.html

Hodgen House Museum Complex
104 West Main
Ellsworth, KS 67439
Tel: 785-472-3059

Emporia State University
1200 Commercial Drive
Emporia, KS 66801
Tel: 620-341-5325
www.emporia.edu/theatre

Lyon County Historical Society and Museum
118 East 6th Avenue
Emporia, KS 66801
Tel: 620-342-0933

Greenwood County Historical Society
120 West 4th Street
Eureka, KS 67045-1445
Tel: 620-583-6682

Harvey House Museum
221 Marion
Florence, KS 66851
Tel: 620-878-4296

U.S. Cavalry Museum
Fort Riley, Building 205
Fort Riley, KS 66442
Tel: 785-239-2737
www.uscavalry.org

Fort Scott National Historic Site
Old Fort Boulevard
Fort Scott, KS 66701
Tel: 620-223-0310 Fax: 620-223-0188
www.nps.gov/fosc
Hours: Mon–Sun 8–5 pm (Apr–Oct), 9–5 pm (Nov–Mar)
Contact: Kelley Collins or Alan Chilton
Institution type: History museum, historic house, federal museum
Collection type: Clothing, accessories, uniforms, costumes, general textiles
Description: 1800–1899. Objects representing the U.S. Army, primarily from 1842 to 1853, and personal possessions representing home life as well as military objects.
$ ✎

Finney County Museum

403 South 4th Street
Garden City, KS 67846
Tel: 620-272-3664
www.finneycounty.org/history.asp

Wedding photograph of Sara Schroeder and Heinrich J. S. Schmidt, 1900. Courtesy of Mennonite Heritage Museum.

Mennonite Heritage Museum

200 North Poplar Street
Goessel, KS 67053
Tel: 620-367-8200
http://heritagemuseum.mennonite.net
Hours: Tue–Fri 10–4:30, Sat–Sun 1–4:30 pm
(May–Sep); Tue–Fri 12–4 pm, Sat–Sun 1–4
pm (Mar–Apr, Oct–Dec), and by appointment
Contact: Darlene Schroeder
Institution type: History museum, historic house
Collection type: Clothing, accessories
Description: 1850–1950. Clothes worn by Mennonite immigrants from 1874 to 1930,
including black haubes (lace caps), black wedding dress, black fur coat, boys' knickers and
jacket, 2 long skirted baby dresses, 2 death
shrouds, white wedding dress, nurse's uniform
with cap and capes, long fur coat, and indigo
print aprons from Russia.
$ ✍

High Plains Museum

1717 Cherry
Goodland, KS 67735
Tel: 785-899-4595

Barton County Historical Society Village and Museum

85 South Highway 281
Great Bend, KS 67530
Tel: 620-793-5125
www.bartoncountymuseum.org

Harper City Historical Society

804 East 12th Street
Harper, KS 67058
Tel: 620-896-2304

Wedding dress, circa 1920. Courtesy of Ellis County Historical Society.

Ellis County Historical Society

100 West 7th Street
Hays, KS 67601
Tel: 785-628-2426 Fax: 785-628-0386
www.elliscountyhistoricalmuseum.org
Hours: Tue–Fri 10–5 pm
Contact: Erin Hammer
Institution type: County museum
Collection type: Clothing, accessories, uniforms,
costumes, general textiles, quilts, flags
Description: 1850–present. Collection includes
89 quilts and 83 wedding gowns dating from
the 1880s to the present and other items of
dress and appearance.
$ ✍

Fort Hays State Historic Site

1472 Highway 183 Alt
Hays, KS 67601-9212
Tel: 785-625-6812 Fax: 785-625-4785
www.kshs.org/places/forthays
Hours: Tue–Sat 9–5 pm, Sun–Mon 1–5 pm
Contact: Robert Wilhelm
Institution type: History museum, historic house, state museum
Collection type: Clothing, accessories, uniforms, costumes, quilts
Description: 1850–1899. Collection includes 2 bustle dresses, 1 partial 1880 infantry uniform and accoutrements, 1 quilt, and several women's clothing accessories, primarily jewelry. Other items include collection of reproduction military uniforms and women's dresses.

$

Tri-County Historical Society and Museum

200 Washington Avenue
Herington, KS 67449-3060
Tel: 785-258-2842

Native American Heritage Museum at Highland Mission State Historic Site

1737 Elgin Road
Highland, KS 66035
Tel: 785-442-3304
www.kshs.org/places/nativeamerican/friends.htm

Hillsboro Museums

501 South Ash
Hillsboro, KS 67063
Tel: 620-947-3775

Reno County Museum

100 South Walnut
Hutchinson, KS 67501
Tel: 620-662-1184

Independence Historical Museum

123 North 8th Street
Independence, KS 67301
Tel: 620-331-3515

Watkins Community Museum of History

1047 Massachusetts Street
Lawrence, KS 66044
Tel: 785-841-4109 Fax: 785-841-9547
www.watkinsmuseum.org

Hours: Tue–Wed 10–6 pm, Thu 10–9 pm, Fri 10–5 pm, Sat 10–4 pm
Contact: Alison Miller
Institution type: History museum, county museum
Collection type: Clothing, accessories, uniforms, costumes
Description: 1850–present. Variety of items from mid-nineteenth century to the present includes ones of importance to Douglas County history, including those worn by local icon Leo Beurman and dresses worn to events hosted by Abraham Lincoln. Collection is strong in twentieth-century items. Other items include uniforms, outerwear, and accessories.

Carroll Mansion, Leavenworth County Historical Society

1128 5th Avenue
Leavenworth, KS 66048
Tel: 913-682-7759 Fax: 913-682-2089
Hours: Tue–Sat 10:30–4:30 pm (Apr–Nov); Tue–Sat 1–4:30 pm (Dec–Mar)
Collection type: Clothing, accessories, uniforms
Institution type: History museum, historic house
Description: 1850–1960. Clothing dates from 1850 through 1930, mainly Victorian era and from Leavenworth County, Kansas. More than 1,000 articles of clothing and underwear, including dresses, men's suits, military uniforms, and children's clothes. Collection of accessories includes shoes, silk stockings, hats, and petticoats.

$

Birger Sandzen Memorial Gallery

401 North 1st Street
Lindsborg, KS 67456
Tel: 785-227-2220
www.sandzen.org

McPherson County Old Mill Museum

120 East Mill Street
Lindsborg, KS 67456
Tel: 785-227-3595 Fax: 785-227-2810
www.oldmillmuseum.org

Coronado-Quivira Museum

105 West Lyon
Lyons, KS 67554
Tel: 620-257-3941

Wedding dress worn by three generations, 1909, 1945, 1969. Courtesy of Kansas State University Historic Costume and Textile Museum.

Kansas State University Historic Costume and Textile Museum

225 Justin Hall, KSU Campus
Manhattan, KS 66506
Tel: 785-532-6993
www.ksu.edu/humec/atid/historic

Hours: By appointment
Contact: Marla Day
Institution type: University museum
Collection type: Clothing, accessories, general textiles
Description: 1850–present. More than 17,000 clothing and textile artifacts. Museum is dedicated to the collection and preservation of clothing and textile items of historic and artistic value to facilitate educational, research, and extension activities.

Riley County Historical Society

2309 Claflin Road
Manhattan, KS 66502
Tel: 785-565-6490
www.rileycgs.com

McPherson Museum

1130 East Euclid Street
McPherson, KS 67460
Tel: 620-241-8464
www.mcphersonmuseum.org

Stauth Memorial Museum

111 North Aztec Street
Montezuma, KS 67867
Tel: 620-846-2527

Norman #1 Oil Well Museum

106 South 1st Street
Neodesha, KS 66757
Tel: 620-325-5316

Indigo print apron from Russian Mennonite immigrant woman, 1874. Courtesy of Kauffman Museum.

Kauffman Museum

Bethel College, 2801 North Main
North Newton, KS 67117-0531
Tel: 316-283-1612 Fax: 316-283-2107
www.bethelks.edu/kauffman

Hours: Tue–Fri 9:30–4:30 pm, Sat–Sun 1:30–4:30 pm
Institution type: History museum, university museum
CROSS-CULTURAL TEXTILES AND CLOTHING COLLECTION
Contact: Rachel Pannabecker
Collection type: Clothing, accessories, general textiles
Description: 1850–1960. Historic artifacts collected by Mennonites, with particular strengths in pre-revolutionary central China, the first half of the twentieth century in central India, mid-twentieth-century central Congo (systematic collection of Pende masks), and nineteenth-century to early-twentieth-century Northern Cheyenne nation.

$ 🔊

MENNONITE HISTORY AND LIFE COLLECTION

Contact: Rachel Pannabecker

Collection type: Clothing, accessories, general textiles

Description: 1850–present. Artifacts from Mennonites who settled in Kansas and nearby central Plains states in the 1870s and 1880s, including German-speaking families who emigrated from Prussia and Russia and German-speaking Mennonites who had emigrated earlier from Switzerland, Germany, and the Netherlands by way of Pennsylvania, Ohio, Indiana, Illinois, Iowa, and Missouri.

Old Depot Museum

135 West Tecumseh

Ottawa, KS 66067

Tel: 785-242-1232 Fax: 785-242-1267

www.old.depot.museum

Hours: Records Center: Mon–Fri 9–5 pm; Museum: Tue–Sun 10–4 pm

Contact: Deborah Barker

Institution type: History museum, county museum

Collection type: Clothing, accessories, uniforms, general textiles, quilts

Description: 1800–present. Collection includes 75 quilts, 1850s–1970s; women's outerwear, 1850s–1970s; and woven coverlets, 1810–1850.

$ 🖎

Butterfield Trail Historical Museum

Broadway and Hilts Street

Russell Springs, KS 67755

Tel: 785-751-4242

Smoky Hill Museum

211 West Iron Avenue

Salina, KS 67401

Tel: 785-309-5776

www.smokyhillmuseum.org

Emmett Kelly Historical Museum

202 East Main

Sedan, KS 67361

Tel: 316-725-3470

www.emmettkellymuseum.org

Johnson County Museums

6305 Lackman Road

Shawnee, KS 66217

Tel: 913-631-6709

www.jocomuseum.org

Evening gown worn by Mrs. Ivison Scott Hanna, 1890–1899. Courtesy of Kansas Museum of History.

Kansas Museum of History

6425 SW 6th

Topeka, KS 66615

Tel: 785-272-8681 Fax: 785-272-8682

www.kshs.org

Hours: Tue–Sat 9–5 pm, Sun 1–5 pm

Contact: Laura Vannorsdel

Institution type: History museum, state museum

Collection type: Clothing, accessories, uniforms, costumes, general textiles, quilts, flags

Description: 1800–present. Collection depicts Kansas culture, focusing on daily life and settlement, from wedding dresses and formal gowns to band uniforms and casual apparel, heavily weighted to late-nineteenth- and early-twentieth-century pieces. Collection includes one of the nation's largest groupings of Civil War flags associated with African American regiments. Interesting artifacts include garments worn by temperance advocate Carrie Nation, some Ku Klux Klan robes, and a 1902 costume dress printed with newspaper text.

$ 🖎

Grant County Museum

300 East Oklahoma
Ulysses, KS 67880
Tel: 620-356-3009

Washington County Historical Society

206-208 Ballard
Washington, KS 66968
Tel: 785-325-2198

Chisholm Trail Museum

502 North Washington
Wellington, KS 67152
Tel: 620-326-3820
Hours: Mon–Sun 1–4 pm (Jun–Aug); Sat–Sun
1–4 pm (mid-Apr–May, Sep–Nov)
Contact: Collections manager
Institution type: History museum
Collection type: Clothing, uniforms
Description: 1900–present. Small collection of
clothing and textile objects includes military
uniforms, mostly World War II; local school
related clothing and uniforms; railroad and
conductor uniforms; and civilian clothing,
suits, and dresses.

Indian Center Museum

650 North Seneca
Wichita, KS 67203
Tel: 316-262-5221

Old Cowtown Museum

1871 Sim Park Drive
Wichita, KS 67203
Tel: 316-264-0671
www.old-cowtown.org

Wichita Center for the Arts

9112 East Central
Wichita, KS 67206
Tel: 316-634-2787
www.wcfta.com

Wichita-Sedgwick County Historical Museum Association

204 South Main
Wichita, KS 67202
Tel: 316-265-9314
www.wichitahistory.org

Wilson Czech Opera House

415 27th Street, Old Highway 40
Wilson, KS 67490
Tel: 785-658-3505
Hours: Mon–Fri 10–12 pm and 1–4 pm
Institution type: History museum

Cowley County Historical Society Museum

1011 Mansfield Street
Winfield, KS 67156
Tel: 620-221-4811
www.cchsm.com
Hours: Tue 8:30–11:30 am, Sat–Sun 2–5 pm
Institution type: History museum

Highlands Museum and Discovery Center
1620 Winchester Avenue
Ashland, KY 41101
Tel: 606-329-8888
www.highlandsmuseum.com

Berea College Doris Ulmann Galleries
Corner of Chestnut and Elipse Streets
Berea, KY 40403
Tel: 859-985-3000

The Kentucky Library and Museum
1 Big Red Way
Western Kentucky University
Bowling Green, KY 42101
Tel: 502-745-6258

Riverview at Hobson Grove
1100 West Main Avenue
Bowling Green, KY 42101
Tel: 270-843-5565
www.bgky.org/riverview.htm

Dinsmore Homestead Foundation
5656 Burlington Pike
Burlington, KY 41005
Tel: 859-586-6117
www.dinsmorefarm.org

Columbus-Belmont Civil War Museum
Columbus-Belmont State Park, 350 Park Road
Columbus, KY 42032
Tel: 270-677-2327
http://parks.ky.gov/stateparks/cb/index.htm

Behringer-Crawford Museum
1600 Montague Road, Devou Park
Covington, KY 41012
Tel: 859-491-4003 Fax: 859-491-4006
www.bcmuseum.org
Hours: Tue–Fri 10–5 pm, Sat–Sun 1–5 pm
Institution type: History museum, historic house
$ ✍

Dawson Springs Museum and Art Center
127 South Main Street
Dawson Springs, KY 42408
Tel: 270-797-3503

Kentucky Historical Society
100 West Broadway
Frankfort, KY 40601
Tel: 502-564-1792
www.history.ky.gov
Hours: Tue–Sat 10–5 pm, Sun 1–5 pm
Contact: Collections manager
Institution type: History museum, historical
society, state museum
Collection type: Clothing, accessories, uniforms,
costumes, general textiles, quilts, flags
Description: 1750–present. Clothing and textile
holdings of 9,300 objects are recognized
regionally and nationally for their depth and
quality. Collection includes men's, women's,
and children's clothing and accessories and uniforms and quilts.
$ ✍

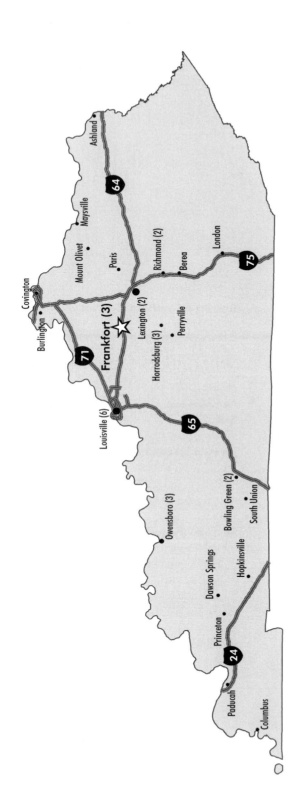

CSA Region VI Southeast

Population

● 0 - 50,000
● 50,001 - 100,000
● 100,001 - 250,000
● 250,001 - 500,000
● > 500,000
☆ State Capital

Kentucky Military History Museum

125 East Main Street
Frankfort, KY 40601
Tel: 502-564-1792
www.history.ky.gov

Liberty Hall Historic Site

218 Wilkinson Street
Frankfort, KY 40601
Tel: 502-227-2560 Fax: 502-227-3348
www.libertyhall.org
Hours: Tue–Sat 10:30–4 pm, Sun 12–4 pm
Institution type: Historic house
$ ✍

Morgan Row Museum and Research Center

220 South Chiles Street
Harrodsburg, KY 40330
Tel: 859-734-5985

Old Fort Harrod State Park Mansion Museum

U.S. 68
Harrodsburg, KY 40330
Tel: 859-734-3314
http://parks.ky.gov/stateparks/fh/

Shaker bonnet, circa 1870. Courtesy of Shaker Village of Pleasant Hill.

Shaker Village of Pleasant Hill

3501 Lexington Road
Harrodsburg, KY 40330
Tel: 859-734-5411 Fax: 859-734-7278
www.shakervillageky.org

Hours: Mon–Sun 10–5 pm (seasonal hours)
Contact: Larrie Curry
Institution type: History museum
Collection type: Clothing, accessories, costumes, general textiles
Description: 1800–1914. Shaker textiles, including silk scarves, dresses, straw bonnets, parts of costumes, clothing accessories, and shoes. Approximately one-fourth of collection is bedding and floor coverings.
$ ✍

Pennyroyal Area Museum

217 East 9th Street
Hopkinsville, KY 42240
Tel: 270-887-4270

Hat by Balenciaga owned by Mona von Bismarck, circa 1960. Courtesy of University of Kentucky.

University of Kentucky

BETTY D. EASTIN HISTORIC COSTUME COLLECTION

318 Erikson Hall
Lexington, KY 40506
Tel: 859-257-4917 Fax: 859-257-1275
www.uky.edu/Design/IDMTweb/IDMT_Index.htm
Hours: By appointment
Contact: Department of Merchandising, Apparel and Textiles
Institution type: University collection
Collection type: Clothing, accessories, general textiles
Description: 1850–present. Of note in the university costume collection are 19 garments of Madame Belle Brezing (1860–1940); garments and hats of Countess Mona Travis Strader Schlesinger Bush Williams von Bismarck (1897–1983); 500 hats from 1878 to the 1970s; and a 440-piece doll collection.
✍

William S. Webb Museum of Anthropology

University of Kentucky
211 Lafferty
Lexington, KY 40506-0024
Tel: 859-257-2710
www.uky.edu/ArtsSciences/Anthropology/
Museum/History.htm
Hours: Mon–Fri 8–4:30 pm
Contact: Collections manager
Institution type: University museum
Collection type: General textiles
Description: Pre-1700–1900. Archeological and ethnographic materials, particularly artifacts collected in surveys throughout Kentucky. Primary goals of the museum are education and research. Museum maintains regular exhibits.

Mountain Life Museum, Levi Jackson Park

998 Levi Jackson Mill Road
London, KY 40744
Tel: 606-878-8000
http://parks.ky.gov/stateparks/lj/index.htm

Farmington Historic Home

3033 Bardstown Road
Louisville, KY 40205
Tel: 502-452-9920

Filson Historical Society

1310 South 3rd Street
Louisville, KY 40208
Tel: 502-635-5083 Fax: 502-635-5086
www.filsonhistorical.org
Hours: Mon–Fri 9–5 pm, Sat 9–12 pm
Contact: James J. Holmberg

The Joseph A. Callaway Archaeological Museum

Southern Baptist Theological Seminary, 2825
Lexington Road
Louisville, KY 40280
Tel: 502-897-4011

Kentucky Derby Museum

704 Central Avenue, Gate 1, Churchill Downs
Louisville, KY 40201
Tel: 502-637-1111
www.derbymuseum.org

Locust Grove

561 Blankenbaker Lane
Louisville, KY 40207
Tel: 502-897-9845
www.locustgrove.org

Portland Museum

2308 Portland Avenue
Louisville, KY 40212
Tel: 502-776-7678
www.goportland.org

The Museum Center

215 Sutton Street
Maysville, KY 41056
Tel: 606-564-5865 Fax: 606-564-4372
www.masoncountymuseum.org
Hours: Mon–Fri 9–4 pm, Sat 10–4 pm (Feb–Dec)
Contact: Sue Ellen Grannis
Institution type: Art museum, history museum
Collection type: Clothing, accessories, uniforms, general textiles, quilts, flags
Description: 1800–present. Regional focus of five counties in Kentucky and two in Ohio. Holdings include 33 uniforms from the World Wars and Korean War, including a WAC uniform; 61 items of underwear and 285 of outerwear; 30 quilts; 141 accessories; 1 brocade fragment from the wedding dress of Mary Keith Randolph, grandmother of Chief Justice Randolph Marshall; and substantial collection of beaded purses and fans.

$

Blue Licks Battlefield Museum

Blue Licks Battlefield Park, Highway 68
Mount Olivet, KY 41064
Tel: 859-289-5507
www.state.ky.us/bluelick.htm

International Blue Grass Music Museum

207 East 2nd Street
Owensboro, KY 42303
Tel: 270-926-7891
www.bluegrass-museum.org

Owensboro Area Museum of Science and History

220 Daviess Street
Owensboro, KY 42303
Tel: 270-687-2732

Owensboro Museum of Fine Art

901 Frederica Street
Owensboro, KY 42301
Tel: 270-685-3181

Museum of the American Quilter's Society

215 Jefferson Street
Paducah, KY 42001
Tel: 270-442-8856
www.quiltmuseum.org

Hopewell Museum

800 Pleasant Street
Paris, KY 40361
Tel: 859-987-7274

Perryville Battlefield Museum

1825 Battlefield Road
Perryville, KY 40468
Tel: 859-332-8631
http://parks.ky.gov/statehistoricsites/pb/
index.htm

Adsmore Museum

SMITH-GARRETT FAMILY COLLECTION
304 North Jefferson Street
Princeton, KY 42445
Tel: 270-365-3114 Fax: 270-365-3310
www.adsmore.org
Hours: Tue–Sat 11–4 pm, Sun 1:30–4 pm
Contact: Ardell Jarratt

Institution type: History museum
Collection type: Clothing, accessories, general textiles, quilts
Description: 1800–1960. Samplers, extensive table linens, quilts, and clothing, including items worn by Governor John Osborne and his wife, Selena Smith, when he was undersecretary of state in the Wilson administration.
$ ✍

Fort Boonesboro Museum

4375 Boonesboro Road
Richmond, KY 40475
Tel: 859-527-3131
www.kystateparks.com/stateparks/fb

White Hall State Historic Site

500 White Hall Shrine Road
Richmond, KY 40475
Tel: 859-623-9178
http://parks.ky.gov/statehistoricsites/wh/
index.htm

Shaker Museum at South Union

850 Shaker Museum Road
South Union, KY 42283
Tel: 502-542-4167
www.logantele.com/~shakmus

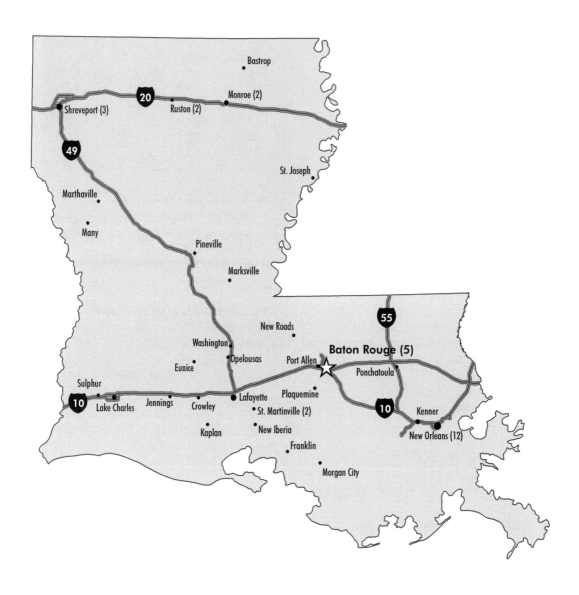

Bastrop

Monroe (2)

20

Shreveport (3)   Ruston (2)

49

St. Joseph

Marthaville

Many

Pineville

Marksville

New Roads

55

Washington

Baton Rouge (5)

Eunice   Opelousas   Port Allen

Ponchatoula

Sulphur

Plaquemine

10   Lake Charles   Jennings   Crowley   Lafayette

St. Martinville (2)

Kenner

10

Kaplan   New Iberia

New Orleans (12)

Franklin

Morgan City

Population

- 0 - 50,000
- 50,001 - 100,000
- 100,001 - 250,000
- 250,001 - 500,000
- \> 500, 000

☆ State Capital

CSA Region VI Southeast

LOUISIANA

Snyder Museum and Creative Arts Center

1620 East Madison Avenue

Bastrop, LA 71220

Tel: 318-281-8760

**Louisiana Naval War Memorial
and USS Kidd**

305 South River Road

Baton Rouge, LA 70802

Tel: 225-342-1942

www.usskidd.com

**Louisiana Old State Capitol, Center for
Political and Governmental History**

100 North Boulevard

Baton Rouge, LA 70801

Tel: 225-342-0500

www.sos.louisiana.gov/museums/osc/osc/
osc-index.htm

**Louisiana State University Textile and
Costume Museum**

140 Human Ecology Building

Baton Rouge, LA 70803

Tel: 225-578-5992 Fax: 225-578-2697

www.textilemuseum.huec.lsu.edu

Hours: Mon–Fri 8–4:30 pm

Contact: Pamela P. Rabalais

Institution type: University museum

Collection type: Clothing, uniforms, costumes,
general textiles

Description: Pre-1700–present. Prehistoric and
ethnic textiles and costume as well as contemporary high fashions and high-tech textiles.

Girl's dress, circa 1900. Courtesy of Louisiana State University Textile and Costume Museum.

Collection contains apparel, accessories, household textiles, piece goods, books, patterns, and
items related to textile and apparel production,
use, and care. The Louisiana Acadian handspun and hand-woven textile artifacts are of
regional significance.

Magnolia Mound Plantation

2161 Nicholson Drive

Baton Rouge, LA 70802

Tel: 225-343-4955 Fax: 225-343-6739

www.magnoliamound.org

Hours: Tue–Sun 10–4 pm

Contact: Carey Coxe, Director

Institution type: Historic house

Collection type: Clothing, general textiles, quilts

Description: 1800–1849. Primarily bedding and quilts, with a few pieces of clothing.

$ ✍

Rural Life Museum and Windrush Gardens

4560 Essen Lane
Baton Rouge, LA 70809
Tel: 225-765-2437
http://rurallife.lsu.edu

Crystal Rice Plantation

6428 Airport Road
Crowley, LA 70526
Tel: 318-783-6417
www.crystalrice.com

The Eunice Museum

220 South C. C. Duson Drive
Eunice, LA 70535
Tel: 337-457-6540
www.eunice-la.com/historic.html
Hours: Tue–Sat 8–12 pm, 1–5 pm
$ ✍

House of Needlework

610 St. Mary Parish Road 131
Franklin, LA 70538
Tel: 337-836-5442
Hours: By appointment
✍

W. H. Tupper General Merchandise Museum

311 North Main Street
Jennings, LA 70546
Tel: 337-821-5532
www.tuppermuseum.com
Hours: Mon–Fri 9–5 pm
✍

Le Musee de la Ville de Kaplan

405 North Cushing Avenue
Kaplan, LA 70548
Tel: 337-643-1528
www.tourlouisiana.com/kaplan_museum.htm
Hours: Mon–Fri 8–4 pm
$ ✍

Mardi Gras Museum and Rivertown Museums

405 Williams Boulevard
Kenner, LA 70062
Tel: 504-468-7231
www.rivertownkenner.com/mgmus.html

Alexandre Mouton House and Lafayette Museum

1122 Lafayette Street
Lafayette, LA 70501
Tel: 337-234-2208

Imperial Calcasieu Museum

204 West Sallier Street
Lake Charles, LA 70601
Tel: 337-430-0043

The Robert Gentry Museum

867 San Antonio Avenue
Many, LA 71449
Tel: 318-256-0523
Hours: Mon–Fri 8–5 pm, Sat 9–4 pm
$ ✍

Tunica-Biloxi Native American Museum

150 Melancon Road
Marksville, LA 71351
Tel: 318-253-8174
www.tunica.org/museum.htm

Rebel State Historic Site and Louisiana Country Music Museum

1260 Highway 1221
Marthaville, LA 71450
Tel: 318-472-6255
www.lastateparks.com/rebel/rebel.htm

Aviation and Military Museum of Louisiana

701 Kansas Lane
Monroe, LA 71213
Tel: 318-361-9020

Northeast Louisiana Delta African American Heritage Museum

503 Plum Street
Monroe, LA 71202
Tel: 318-323-1167

Cypress Manor and Mardi Gras Museum

715 Second Street
Morgan City, LA 70380
Tel: 985-380-4651
www.louisianamardigras.com
Hours: Tue–Sat 10–5, Sun 1–5 pm
$ ✍

Shadows on the Teche

317 East Main Street
New Iberia, LA 70560
Tel: 337-369-6446 Fax: 337-365-5213
www.shadowsontheteche.org
Hours: Mon–Sun 9–5 pm
Contact: Pat Kahle
Institution type: Historic house
Collection type: Clothing, accessories, general textiles, quilts
Description: 1800–1960. Clothing and household linens belonging to four generations of the Weeks family, who lived at Shadows from 1834 to 1958.
$ ✍

Backstreet Cultural Museum

1116 St. Claude Street
New Orleans, LA 70116
Tel: 504-522-4806
www.backstreetculturalmuseum.com
Hours: Tue–Sat 10–5 pm

Catholic Cultural Heritage Center

1100 Chartres Street
New Orleans, LA 70116
Tel: 504-529-3040

Confederate Museum

929 Camp Street
New Orleans, LA 70130
Tel: 504-523-4522
www.confederatemuseum.com

Germaine Wells Mardi Gras Museum

Arnaud's Restaurant, 813 Bienville Street
New Orleans, LA 70112
Tel: 504-523-5433
www.arnauds.com/museum.html

Hermann-Grima and Gallier Historic Houses

820 St. Louis Street
New Orleans, LA 70112
Tel: 504-525-5661 Fax: 504-568-9735
www.hgghh.org
Hours: Mon–Sun 10–4 pm
Contact: Jan Bradford
Institution type: Historic house
Collection type: General textiles
Description: 1800–1900. Holdings include furniture, decorative arts, and kitchen collections.
$ ✍

Jackson Barracks Military Museum

6400 St. Claude Avenue
New Orleans, LA 70117
Tel: 504-865-5110
www.la.ngb.army.mil/dmh/index.htm
Hours: Mon–Fri 8–4 pm, Sat by appointment

Longue Vue House and Gardens

7 Bamboo Road
New Orleans, LA 70124
Tel: 504-488-5488
www.longuevue.com

Bracelet, hair and gold, mid-nineteenth century. Courtesy of Louisiana State Museum.

Louisiana State Museum

751 Chartres Street
New Orleans, LA 70176
Tel: 504-568-6968
http://lsm.crt.state.la.us
Hours: Tue–Sun 9–5 pm
Contact: Wayne Phillips
Institution type: History museum, state museum
Collection type: Clothing, accessories, uniforms, costumes, general textiles, quilts, flags
Description: 1700–present. Objects from late eighteenth century to the present, with

majority having a Louisiana provenance. Of the approximately 15,000 objects in the collection, one third is the costumes and accessories collection, one third is the textile collection, and one third is the Carnival collection.

$

Middle American Research Institute and Museum

6823 St. Charles Avenue
New Orleans, LA 70118
Tel: 504-865-5110

The National D-Day Museum

945 Magazine Street
New Orleans, LA 70130
Tel: 504-527-6012
www.ddaymuseum.org

New Orleans Fire Department Museum and Educational Center

1135 Washington Avenue
New Orleans, LA 70130
Tel: 504-896-4756
www.neworleansmuseums.com/
familymuseums/firemuseum.htm

Pitot House Museum

1440 Moss Street
New Orleans, LA 70119
Tel: 504-482-0312

Pointe Coupee Museum

8348 False River Road
New Roads, LA 70760
Tel: 225-638-7788

Opelousas Museum and Interpretive Center

315 North Main Street
Opelousas, LA 70570
Tel: 337-948-2589
www.cityofopelousas.com/tourism_
INTmuseum.htm

Louisiana Maneuvers and Military Museum

409 F Street
Pineville, LA 71423
Tel: 318-641-5733

www.la.ngb.army.mil/dmh/immm.htm
Hours: Mon–Fri 7:30–4 pm

Iberville Museum

57735 Main Street
Plaquemine, LA 70764
Tel: 225-687-7197
www.parish.iberville.la.us/municipalities/
plaquemine/oldch.htm
Hours: Tue–Sat 10–4 pm

Collinswood School Museum

165 East Pine Street
Ponchatoula, LA 70454
Tel: 985-386-6794
www.ponchatoula.com/museum.html
Hours: Fri–Sat 10–4 pm, Tue–Thu flexible hours

West Baton Rouge Museum

845 North Jefferson Avenue
Port Allen, LA 70767
Tel: 225-336-2422
www.westbatonrougemuseum.com

Lincoln Parish Museum and Historical Society

609 North Vienna Street
Ruston, LA 71270
Tel: 318-251-0018

North Louisiana Military Museum

201 Memorial Drive
Ruston, LA 71270
Tel: 318-255-3196
www.sec.state.la.us/museums/military/
military-index.htm
Hours: Mon–Fri 10–6:30 pm, Sat 10–5 pm, Sun 1–5 pm

$

Ark-La-Tex Antique and Classic Vehicle Museum

601 Spring Street
Shreveport, LA 71101
Tel: 318-222-0227 Fax: 318-222-5042
www.carmuseum.org
Hours: Mon–Sat 9–5 pm, Sun 1–5 pm
Contact: Jan Pettiet
Institution type: History museum, historic house

Driver coat, hat, and goggles in 1914 Ford Model T Speedster, circa 1918. Courtesy of Ark-La-Tex Antique and Classic Vehicle Museum.

Collection type: Clothing, accessories, costumes
Description: 1915–present. Approximately 300 costumes and vintage clothing, most are American, a few Spanish and Indian, 1920s to the present. Clothing collection complements classic and antique vehicles and includes a Mae West costume.

$ 🖋

Pioneer Heritage Center, LSU-Shreveport
1 University Place
Shreveport, LA 71115
Tel: 318-797-5332
www.lsus.edu/map

Spring Street Historical Museum
525 Spring Street
Shreveport, LA 71101
Tel: 318-424-0964 Fax: 318-424-0964
www.springstreetmuseum.com
Hours: Tue–Sat 10–3:30 pm
Institution type: History museum
$ 🖋

Tensas Parish Library and Plantation Museum
135 Plank
St. Joseph, LA 71366
Tel: 318-766-3781

Longfellow-Evangeline State Historic Site
1200 North Main Street
St. Martinville, LA 70582
Tel: 337-394-3754
www.lastateparks.com/longfell/longfell.htm

Petit Paris Museum
103 South Main Street
St. Martinville, LA 70582
Tel: 337-394-7334

Brimstone Museum
800 Picard Road
Sulphur, LA 70663
Tel: 318-527-7142

Washington Museum and Tourist Center
402 North Main Street
Washington, LA 70589
Tel: 337-826-3627

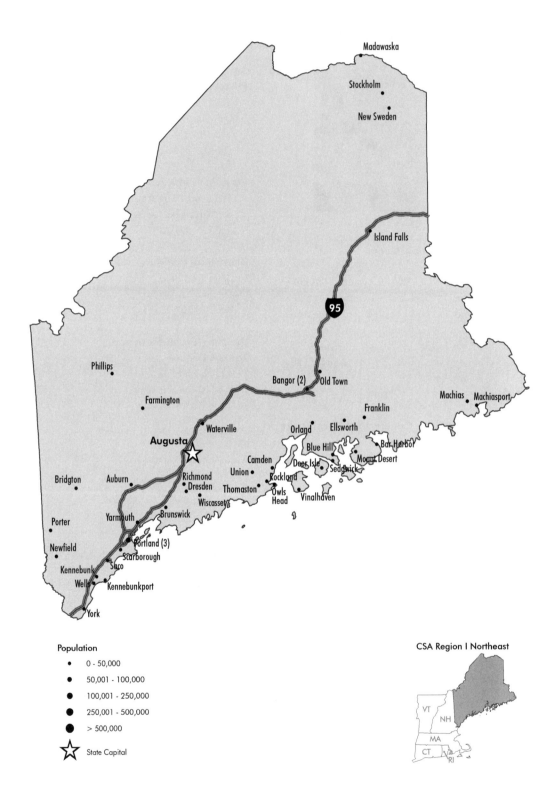

Madawaska

Stockholm

New Sweden

Island Falls

95

Phillips

Farmington

Bangor (2) Old Town

Machias Machiasport

Waterville

Franklin

Orland Ellsworth

Augusta

Blue Hill Bar Harbor

Camden

Mount Desert

Bridgton

Auburn

Richmond
Dresden

Union

Deer Isle
Sedgwick

Rockland

Thomaston

Owls
Head

Wiscasset

Vinalhaven

Porter

Yarmouth

Brunswick

Newfield

Portland (3)

Scarborough

Kennebunk

Saco

Wells

Kennebunkport

York

Population

●   0 - 50,000

●   50,001 - 100,000

●   100,001 - 250,000

●   250,001 - 500,000

●   > 500,000

☆   State Capital

CSA Region I Northeast

VT
NH
MA
CT
RI

MAINE

Androscoggin Historical Society

County Building, 2 Turner Street
Auburn, ME 04210-5978
Tel: 207-784-0586
www.rootsweb.com/~meandrhs
Hours: Wed–Fri 9–12 pm, 1–5 pm
Contact: Executive secretary
Institution type: History museum
Collection type: Clothing, accessories, uniforms, costumes, general textiles, flags
Description: 1760–present. Collection reflects local history of Androscoggin County, Maine.

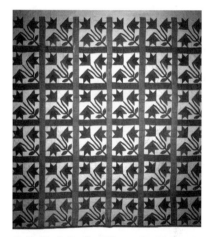

Quilt, North Carolina Lily pattern, 1880–1900. Courtesy of Maine State Museum.

Detail, Maine Militia color, 1822. Courtesy of Maine State Museum.

Maine State Museum

83 State House Station
Augusta, ME 04333
Tel: 207-287-2301 Fax: 207-287-6633
www.maine.gov/museum
Hours: Tue–Fri 9–5 pm, Sat 10–4 pm
Institution type: History museum, state museum
$

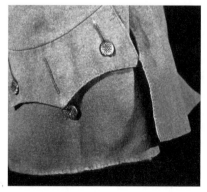

Detail, U.S. Marine vest, 1778. Courtesy of Maine State Museum.

CLOTHING COLLECTION

Contact: Julia A. Hunter

Collection type: Clothing, accessories, uniforms

Description: 1760–1960. Collection represents what Maine people of all ages wore in many situations. The military collections include the earliest U.S. Marine jacket in a museum collection. Especially broad selection from the mid-nineteenth century ranges from a denim man's work smock to the gown worn by Mrs. Hannibal Hamlin when she was presented at the royal court of Spain.

EMBROIDERY COLLECTION

Contact: Julia A. Hunter

Collection type: Clothing, accessories, general textiles

Description: 1760–present. Collection crosses multiple boundaries within the overall textile collections, everything from 23 early- to mid-nineteenth-century schoolgirl samplers to a professionally embroidered man's vest worn in a 1773 wedding. Most examples were worked in Maine; many adorn clothing or other functional pieces such as towels or blankets.

FLAG COLLECTION

Contact: Laureen LaBar

Collection type: Flags

Description: 1800–present. Flags were either used in Maine or by Maine people acting in other places. Collection contains more than 330 pieces, including 122 flags from the Civil War as well as national and state flags, temperance banners, militia banners, shipyard house flags, and political banners from the early nineteenth century through the late twentieth century.

MADE IN MAINE

Contact: Edwin A. Churchill

Collection type: General textiles

Description: 1760–1960. The Made in Maine collection is about how Maine people have made their livelihoods from the late eighteenth century to the mid-twentieth century. Textile production is shown, complete with an assortment of looms, tools, and machinery, from small in-home operations to a multi-storied woolen mill.

QUILTS AND BLANKETS COLLECTION

Contact: Julia A. Hunter

Collection type: General textiles, quilts

Description: 1760–present. Collection contains 80 quilts, 30 quilt fragments, and 30 blankets, all produced in Maine, which are a good representative cross-section of techniques across time. Holdings date 1790s–1990s, with oldest example being an all-wool quilt from Matinicus Island. Holdings include crazy quilts. This is an actively growing collection; the latest acquisition is a large 1820s crewel decorated quilt with wool embroidery on wool squares.

RUG COLLECTION

Contact: Julia A. Hunter

Collection type: General textiles

Description: 1850–1960. All the rugs have Maine-use history; some in-grain carpet examples from the second half of the nineteenth century may have been produced elsewhere. Collection includes a variety of nineteenth- and twentieth-century penny rugs, woven rag rugs, and hooked rugs. Museum recently acquired the majority of the surviving stencils from the seminal 1870s E. S. Frost and Company operation.

Bangor Museum and Center for History

QUIPUS COLLECTION

6 State Street

Bangor, ME 04401

Tel: 207-942-1900 Fax: 207-941-0266

www.bangormuseum.org

Hours: Tue–Fri 10–4 pm, Sat 12–4 pm

Contact: Dana Lippitt

Institution type: History museum

Collection type: Clothing, accessories, uniforms, costumes, general textiles, quilts, flags

Description: 1800–present. Clothing and accessories from the Quipus Ladies Club, founded circa 1912. Varied selection of quilts, flags, and uniforms in the remainder of the museum's collections.

✍

Isaac Farrar Mansion

17 2nd Street

Bangor, ME 04401

Tel: 207-941-2808 Fax: 207-941-2812

William Otis Sawtelle Collections and Research Center

Acadia National Park, Route 233,

Eagle Lake Road

Bar Harbor, ME 04609

Tel: 207-288-5463

www.nps.gov/acad/rm/curatprog.htm

Parson Fisher House

44 Mines Road
Blue Hill, ME 04614
Tel: 207-374-2459
www.jonathanfisherhouse.org

Bridgton Historical Society

U.S. Route 302 and Gibbs Avenue
Bridgton, ME 04009
Tel: 207-647-3699
www.megalink.net/~bhs

Pejepscot Historical Society

159 Park Row
Brunswick, ME 04011
Tel: 207-729-6606
www.curtislibrary.com/pejepscot.htm

Old Conway Homestead Complex and Museum

U.S. Route 1, Camden-Rockport Lane
Camden, ME 04853
Tel: 207-236-2257

Deer Isle Historical Society

416 Sunset Road
Deer Isle, ME 04627
Tel: 207-367-8978
Institution type: Art museum, history museum, historic house
Hours: Tue, Fri 1–4 pm (Jul–mid Sep); Mon, Thu 1–4 pm (Winter)
Collection type: Clothing, accessories, uniforms, costumes, general textiles, quilts, flags
Description: 1700–1960. Quilts, gowns, and uniforms representing Island history circa 1800 through World War II.

✍

Powanlborough Court House

Courthouse Road Route 128
Dresden, ME 04342
Tel: 207-882-6817
www.lincolncountyhistory.org

Woodlawn Museum and The Black House

19 Black House Road
Ellsworth, ME 04605
Tel: 207-667-8671 Fax: 207-667-7590
www.woodlawnmuseum.com
Hours: May–Oct Tue–Sat 10–5 pm, Sun 1–4 pm
Contact: Rosamond Rea

Institution type: Historic house
Collection type: Clothing, general textiles
Description: 1800–1914. Original contents of a historic house (1827–1928) include bed hangings, window treatments, embroideries (eighteenth century), samplers, some clothing, tapestry, and assorted incidentals such as sheets, towels, bedspreads, and doilies.

$ ✍

Nordica Homestead

116 Nordica Lane
Farmington, ME 04938
Tel: 207-778-2042

Franklin Historical Society

Route 200
Franklin, ME 04634
Tel: 207-565-2223

John E. and Walter D. Webb Museum of Vintage Fashion

10 Sherman Street, Route 2
Island Falls, ME 04747
Tel: 207-463-2404

Brick Store Museum

117 Main Street
Kennebunk, ME 04043
Tel: 207-985-4802
www.brickstoremuseum.org

Kennebunkport Historical Society

125 North Street
Kennebunkport, ME 04046
Tel: 207-967-2751
www.kporthistory.org

Burnham Tavern

Main Street
Machias, ME 04654
Tel: 207-255-4432
www.burnhamtavern.com

Machiasport Historical Society

Route North 92
Machiasport, ME 04655-0301
Tel: 207-255-8461

Tante Blanche Museum

U.S. Highway 1
Madawaska, ME 04756
Tel: 207-728-4518

Mount Desert Island Historical Society
373 Sound Drive
Mount Desert, ME 04660
Tel: 207-276-9323
www.mdihistory.org/museum.html

New Sweden Historical Society
110 Station Road
New Sweden, ME 04762
Tel: 207-896-3018

Willowbrook at Newfield
Route 11 and Elm Street
Newfield, ME 04056
Tel: 207-793-2784
www.willowbrookmuseum.org

Old Town Museum
153 Main Street
Old Town, ME 04468
Tel: 207-827-7256

Orland Historical Society
Castine Road
Orland, ME 04472
Tel: 207-469-2476

Owls Head Transportation Museum
Route 73
Owls Head, ME 04854
Tel: 207-594-4418
www.ohtm.org

Phillips Historical Society
Pleasant Street
Phillips, ME 04966
Tel: 207-639-5013

Parsonsfield-Porter Historical Society
92 Main Street
Porter, ME 04068
Tel: 207-625-4667

Maine Historical Society
489 Congress Street
Portland, ME 04108
Tel: 207-774-1822 Fax: 207-775-4301
www.mainehistory.org
Hours: Mon–Sun, 10–5 pm
Contact: John Mayer, Curator; Holly Hurd-
Forsyth, Registrar

Wedding dress, 1912. Courtesy of Maine Historical Society.

Institution type: History museum, historic house, state museum
Collection type: Clothing, accessories, uniforms, general textiles, quilts, flags
Description: Pre-1700–present. The Maine Historical Society, founded in 1822, is the third oldest organization of its kind in the United States. Collections document the state's social, economic, political, and cultural history from the seventeenth century through the twentieth century. Textiles are an important component of the collections, with significant holdings of clothing, quilts, and samplers from Maine.
$ ✍

Tate House
1270 Westbrook Street
Portland, ME 04102
Tel: 207-774-9781
www.tatehouse.org

Victoria Mansion
109 Danforth Street
Portland, ME 04101
Tel: 207-772-4841
www.victoriamansion.org

CHTJ Southard House Museum
75 Main Street
Richmond, ME 04357
Tel: 207-737-8202

Farnsworth Museum
16 Museum Street
Rockland, ME 04841
Tel: 207-596-6457 Fax: 207-596-0509
www.farnsworthmuseum.org

Hours: Tue–Sat 10–5 pm, Sun 1–5 pm (vary by season)

Contact: Janice Kasper, Curator of Historic Sites

Institution type: Art museum, historic house

Collection type: Clothing, accessories, general textiles

Description: 1850–1914. Intact Victorian home includes all furnishings from the Farnsworth family (1850–1935). Period rugs, draperies, upholstery, bedding, and needlework, with a separate collection of nineteenth-century clothing from the Rockland area.

$ ✍

Saco Museum

371 Main Street

Saco, ME 04072

Tel: 207-283-3861

www.sacomuseum.org/about-museum.shtml

Scarborough Historical Museum

649A U.S. Route 1 Dunstan

Scarborough, ME 04070

Tel: 207-883-3539

Sedgwick-Brooklin Historical Society

Route 172

Sedgwick, ME 04676

Tel: 207-359-2547

Stockholm Historical Society Museum

280 Main Street

Stockholm, ME 04783

Tel: 207-896-5759

Montpelier—The General Henry Knox Museum

30 High Street

Thomaston, ME 04861

Tel: 207-354-8062

www.generalknoxmuseum.org

Matthews Museum of Maine Heritage

Union Fairgrounds

Union, ME 04862

Tel: 207-785-3321

Vinalhaven Historical Society Museum

High Street

Vinalhaven, ME 04863

Tel: 207-863-4410

www.midcoast.com/~vhhissoc

Redington Museum

62 Silver Street

Waterville, ME 04901

Tel: 207-872-9439

http://users.adelphia.net/~lheureux/gnrlinfo.html

Historical Society of Wells and Ogunquit

Route 1, 938 Post Road

Wells, ME 04090

Tel: 207-646-4775

Lincoln County Historical Association

133 Federal Street

Wiscasset, ME 04578

Tel: 207-882-6817 Fax: 207-882-6817

www.lincolncountyhistory.org

Museum of Yarmouth History

215 Main Street

Yarmouth, ME 04096

Tel: 207-846-6259

Old York Historical Society

207 York Street

York, ME 03909

Tel: 207-363-4974 Fax: 207-363-4021

www.oldyork.org

Hours: Mon–Sat, 10–5 pm (Jun–mid Oct)

Contact: Thomas Johnson, Curator; Cynthia Young, Registrar

Institution type: History museum, historic house

Collection type: Clothing, accessories, general textiles, quilts

Description: 1700–1960. More than 4,000 historic textiles, focusing on York's past. Items include Bulman bedhangings (circa 1740), the most complete set of eighteenth-century hand-worked bedhangings in North America; 71 quilts (eighteenth century–1940s); fashion-ethnological costume collection of Miss Elizabeth Perkins (1869–1952); and 345 textile related tools. Strengths are in early federal through first-quarter twentieth century costumes.

$ ✍

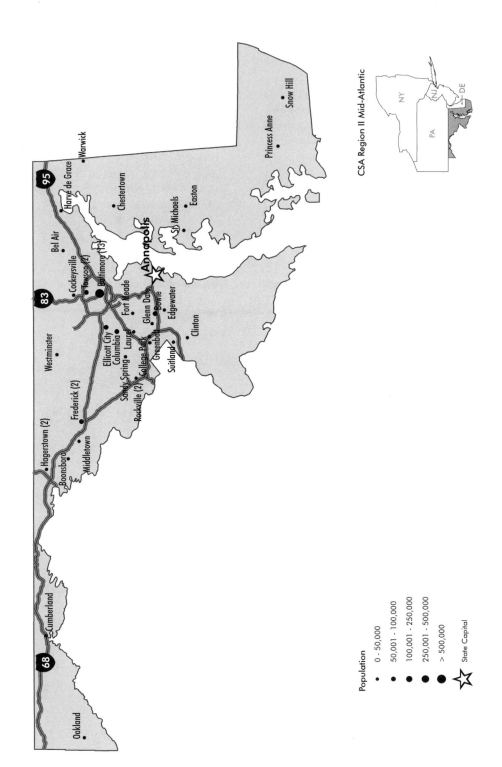

CSA Region II Mid-Atlantic

NY
PA
NJ
DE

Snow Hill

Princess Anne

Warwick

Harve de Grace

Chestertown

Easton

St. Michaels

Annapolis

Bel Air

Cockeysville

Towson (2)

Baltimore (13)

Fort Meade

Glenn Dale

Bowie

Edgewater

Clinton

Westminster

Ellicott City

Columbia

Laurel

College Park

Greenbelt

Suitland

Sandy Spring

Rockville (2)

Frederick (2)

Hagerstown (2)

Middletown

Boonsboro

Cumberland

Oakland

Population

• 0 - 50,000
• 50,001 - 100,000
● 100,001 - 250,000
● 250,001 - 500,000
● > 500,000
☆ State Capital

MARYLAND

U.S. Naval Academy Museum
118 Maryland Avenue
Annapolis, MD 21402
Tel: 410-293-2108
www.usna.edu/Museum

The B & O Railroad Museum
901 West Pratt Street
Baltimore, MD 21223
Tel: 410-752-2490
www.borail.org

The Babe Ruth Birthplace and Museum
216 Emory Street
Baltimore, MD 21230
Tel: 410-727-1539
www.baberuthmuseum.com

Baltimore Maritime Museum
Pier 3 and 5, Pratt Street
Baltimore, MD 21202
Tel: 410-396-3453
www.baltomaritimemuseum.org

Baltimore Museum of Art
10 Art Museum Drive
Baltimore, MD 21218
Tel: 410-396-6300
www.artbma.org

Eubie Blake National Jazz Institute and Cultural Center
847 North Howard Street
Baltimore, MD 21201
Tel: 410-625-3113
www.eubie.org

Evergreen House, Johns Hopkins University
4545 North Charles Street
Baltimore, MD 21210
Tel: 410-516-0341
www.jhu.edu/historichouses

Fort McHenry National Monument and Historic Shrine
2400 East Fort Avenue
Baltimore, MD 21230
Tel: 410-962-4290
www.nps.gov/fomc

Jewish Museum of Maryland
15 Lloyd Street
Baltimore, MD 21202
Tel: 410-732-6400
www.jewishmuseummd.org

The Lacrosse Museum and National Hall of Fame
113 West University Parkway
Baltimore, MD 21210
Tel: 410-235-6882x100
www.lacrosse.org/museum/index.phtml

Baltimore album quilt, Mary Simon design, 1852. Courtesy of Maryland Historical Society.

Gown of Margaret Tilghman Carroll, circa 1770. Courtesy of Mount Clare Museum House.

Maryland Historical Society

201 West Monument Street
Baltimore, MD 21201
Tel: 410-685-3750
www.mdhs.org
Hours: Tue–Sun 10–5 pm
Contact: Nancy Davis, Deputy Director
Institution type: History museum, historic house, state museum
Collection type: Clothing, accessories, uniforms, quilts, flags
Description: 1700–present. More than 10,000 items dating from 1730 to the present. Items include quilts, including one of the largest collections of Baltimore Album quilts; women's and men's clothing and accessories; military uniforms; children's and infants' clothing and accessories; rugs; flags and banners; samplers; curtains and bedhangings; coverlets; blankets; and tablecloths.

$ 🖊

Mount Clare Museum House

1500 Washington Boulevard
Baltimore, MD 21230
Tel: 410-837-3262 Fax: 410-837-0251
www.mountclare.org
Hours: Tue–Sat 11–4 pm
Contact: Carolyn Adams
Institution type: History museum, historic house
Collection type: Clothing, accessories, costumes, general textiles
Description: 1760–1899. Collection interprets life on a Maryland plantation from 1760 to 1850 and includes clothing for men, women, and children from the late eighteenth century

through the late nineteenth century. Centerpiece of the collection is a sack back ball gown made for Margaret Tilghman Carroll and worn at the birthday celebration of Queen Charlotte in 1771.

$ 🖊

Star Spangled Banner Flag House and 1812 Museum

844 East Pratt Street
Baltimore, MD 21202
Tel: 410-837-1793
www.flaghouse.org

Coptic fragment, sixth century. Courtesy of Walters Art Museum.

Walters Art Museum

600 North Charles Street
Baltimore, MD 21201
Tel: 410-547-9000 Fax: 410-783-7969
www.thewalters.org
Hours: Wed–Sun 10–5 pm
Contact: Joan Elizabeth Reid, Registrar
Institution type: Art museum
Collection type: General textiles

Description: Pre-1700–1799. Collection includes
Coptic textiles, Islamic carpets, Renaissance
and Baroque liturgical dress and individual textiles, and eighteenth-century lace.

$ ✍

Historical Society of Harford County

143 North Main Street
Bel Air, MD 21014
Tel: 410-838-7691
www.harfordhistory.net
Hours: Tue , Thu 10–12 pm, 1–2:30 pm, Wed
8–2 pm, 4th Sat 10–2 pm
Institution type: History museum, county
museum

Boonsborough Museum of History

113 North Main Street
Boonsboro, MD 21713
Tel: 301-432-6969

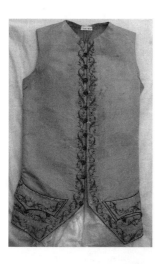

*Waistcoat, circa
1770. Courtesy of
Belair Mansion
and Stable.*

Belair Mansion and Stable

12207 Tulip Grove Drive
Bowie, MD 20715
Tel: 301-809-3089 Fax: 301-809-2308
www.cityofbowie.org/comserv/museums.htm
Hours: Wed–Sun 12–4 pm
Contact: Pam Williams
Institution type: Historic house, city museum
Collection type: Clothing
Description: 1750–1960. Collections contain gen-
eral interpretive objects, including art and tex-
tiles.

✍

Museum at the Geddes-Piper House

101 Church Alley
Chestertown, MD 21620
Tel: 410-778-3499 Fax: 410-778-3747
www.hskcmd.com
Hours: Tue–Fri 9:30–4:30 pm
Contact: Helen Fritz, Museum Chair
Institution type: Historic house, county museum
Collection type: Clothing, accessories, uniforms,
general textiles, flags
Description: 1760–1960. Collection includes one
wedding dress dating between 1760 and 1799,
children's clothing, accessories, and U.S. Navy
and Red Cross uniforms.

$ ✍

Surratt House Museum

9118 Brandywine Road
Clinton, MD 20735
Tel: 301-868-1121
www.surratt.org

Baltimore County Historical Society

9811 Van Buren Lane
Cockeysville, MD 21030
Tel: 410-666-1876
www.baltocohistsoc.org

College Park Aviation Museum

1985 Corporal Frank Scott Drive
College Park, MD 20740
Tel: 301-864-6029
www.collegeparkaviationmuseum.com

Howard County Center of African American Culture

5434 Vantage Point Road
Columbia, MD 21044
Tel: 410-715-1921

Allegany County Historical Society

218 Washington Street
Cumberland, MD 21502
Tel: 301-777-8678 Fax: 301-777-8678
www.historyhouse.allconet.org
Hours: Tue–Sat 10–5 pm
Contact: Sharon Neals
Institution type: Historic house
Collection type: Clothing, accessories, uniforms,
costumes, general textiles, quilts, flags
Description: 1760–present. Women's clothing
from the mid-1800s to the present, a few men's

and children's objects, infants' clothing, military uniforms from several time periods, quilts, and coverlets.

$ ✑

Historical Society of Talbot County

25 South Washington Street
Easton, MD 21601
Tel: 410-822-0773
www.hstc.org

Historic London Town and Gardens

839 Londontown Road
Edgewater, MD 21037
Tel: 410-222-1919
www.historiclondontown.com

Howard County Historical Society

8328 Court Avenue
Ellicott City, MD 21041
Tel: 410-750-0370

Fort George G. Meade Museum

4674 Griffin Avenue
Fort Meade, MD 20755
Tel: 301-677-6966
www.smallmuseum.org/meade.htm

The Barbara Fritchie House

154 West Patrick Street
Frederick, MD 21701
Tel: 301-698-0630

Juliannea Hoffman sampler, 1822. Courtesy of Historical Society of Frederick County.

Historical Society of Frederick County

24 East Church Street
Frederick, MD 21701
Tel: 301-663-1188 Fax: 301-663-0526
www.hsfcinfo.org

Hours: Mon–Sat 10–4 pm, Sun 1–4 pm
Contact: Heidi Campbell-Shoaf
Institution type: History museum
Collection type: Clothing, accessories, uniforms, general textiles, quilts
Description: 1800–present. Clothing, accessories, shoes, uniforms, and household textiles (quilts, coverlets, samplers) made or used by people in Frederick County.

$ ✑

Marietta House Museum

5626 Bell Station Road
Glenn Dale, MD 20769
Tel: 301-464-5291
www.pgparks.com/places/eleganthistoric/marietta_intro.html

Greenbelt Museum

15 Crescent Road
Greenbelt, MD 20770
Tel: 301-474-1936
www.ci.greenbelt.md.us/about_greenbelt/museum.htm

Jonathan Hager House and Museum

110 Key Street
Hagerstown, MD 21740
Tel: 301-739-8393

Wedding dress, 1857. Courtesy of Washington County Historical Society, The Miller House and Gardens.

The Miller House and Gardens

135 West Washington Street
Hagerstown, MD 21740
Tel: 301-797-8782 Fax: 301-797-9509
www.rootsweb.com/~mdwchs/miller.htm
Hours: Wed–Sat 1–4 pm (Apr–Dec) and by appointment

Contact: Jennifer L. Dintaman
Institution type: History museum, historic house
Collection type: Clothing, accessories, uniforms, costumes, general textiles, quilts, flags
Description: 1760–1960. Period clothing and accessories, mostly women's circa 1800–1940s; some men's attire; military uniforms dating from the late nineteenth century to World War II with Washington County connections; and locally made quilts and coverlets.

$ ✍

Steppingstone Museum
461 Quaker Bottom Road
Havre de Grace, MD 21078
Tel: 410-939-2299
www.steppingstonemuseum.org

The Laurel Museum
817 Main Street
Laurel, MD 20707
Tel: 301-725-7975
www.laurelhistory.org

Middletown Valley Historical Society
305 West Main Street
Middletown, MD 21769
Tel: 301-371-7582

Garrett County Historical Museum
107 South 2nd Street
Oakland, MD 21550
Tel: 301-334-3226

Teackle Mansion
11736 Mansion Street
Princess Anne, MD 21853
Tel: 410-651-2238

Latvian Museum
400 Hurley Avenue
Rockville, MD 20850
Tel: 301-340-1914
www.alausa.org/read.php?p=museums

Montgomery County Historical Society
111 West Montgomery Avenue
Rockville, MD 20850
Tel: 301-340-2825
www.montgomeryhistory.org
Hours: Tue–Sun 12–4 pm
Contact: Joanna Church

Institution type: Historic house, county museum
Collection type: Clothing, accessories, uniforms, general textiles, quilts, flags
Description: 1800–present. Objects worn and used by Montgomery County residents. Strengths are women's clothing and accessories, circa 1850–1950, and quilts. Collection includes smaller number of men's and children's clothing, military uniforms, and general household textiles.

$ ✍

Sandy Spring Museum
17901 Bentley Road
Sandy Spring, MD 20860
Tel: 301-774-0022
www.sandyspringmuseum.org

Julia A. Purnell Museum
208 West Market Street
Snow Hill, MD 21863
Tel: 410-632-0515 Fax: 410-632-0515
www.purnellmuseum.com
Hours: Tue–Sat 10–4 pm, Sun 1–4 pm (Apr–Oct)
Institution type: Art museum, history museum, city museum

$ ✍

JULIA A. PURNELL COLLECTION
Contact: Mary St. Hippolyte
Collection type: General textiles, quilts
Description: 1800–1960. Needle art of Julia Purnell, including embroidered architectural scenes, quilts, and dolls.

WORCESTER COUNTY COLLECTION
Contact: Mary St. Hippolyte
Collection type: Clothing, accessories, uniforms, general textiles
Description: 1700–present. Victorian mourning attire and accessories; Victorian underwear and gowns; and Worcester County artifacts, including textiles and clothing.

Museum of Historical Costumes
400 St. Mary's Square
St. Michaels, MD 21663
Hours: By appointment
Contact: Millie Curtis, Owner and Curator
Institution type: History museum, historic house
Collection type: Clothing, accessories, uniforms, quilts
Description: 1800–1959. Clothing, accessories, uniforms, and quilts in a historic house on St.

Mary's Square. Each room displays appropriate historical fashions and accessories. Oldest garment is a dress from Thomas Jefferson's daughter, circa 1820. Other items include collection of 1920s clothing and accessories and large collection of hats.

Cultural Resources Center, National Museum of the American Indian, Smithsonian Institution

4220 Silver Hill Road
Suitland, MD 20746
Tel: 301-238-1435
www.americanindian.si.edu
Hours: By appointment only
Contact: Pat Nietfield
Institution type: Federal research center
Collection type: Clothing, accessories
Description: Pre-1700–present. State-of-the-art collections and research facility supports National Museum of the American Indian. More than 800,000 works of aesthetic, cultural, historical, and spiritual significance spanning more than 10,000 years of Native heritage. Public tours on the last Friday of each month at 2 pm for adults over the age of 18 years by appointment only. School groups are encouraged to visit the NMAI's facilities in Washington, DC, or New York City. Plan at least two months in advance to set up a research visit or schedule a tour.

Asian Arts and Culture Center, Towson University

8000 York Road
Towson, MD 21252
Tel: 410-704-2807
www.towson.edu/tu/asianarts

Hampton National Historic Site

535 Hampton Lane
Towson, MD 21286
Tel: 410-823-1309
www.nps.gov/hamp/home.htm

Old Bohemia Historical Society

Bohemia Church Road
Warwick, MD 21912
Tel: 302-378-5800
www.stdennischurch.org/OLDBOHEMIA
.htm

Historical Society of Carroll County

210 East Main Street
Westminster, MD 21157
Tel: 410-848-6494
www.carr.org/hscc

MASSACHUSETTS

The Bartlett Museum
270 Main Street
Amesbury, MA 01913
Tel: 978-388-4528

Whittier House Association
86 Friend Street
Amesbury, MA 01913
Tel: 978-388-1337

Amherst History Museum
67 Amity Street
Amherst, MA 01002
Tel: 413-256-0678 Fax: 413-256-0672
www.amhersthistory.org
Hours: Wed–Sat 12:30–3:30 pm (May–Nov)
Institution type: History museum, historic house
Contact: Fiona Russel
$ ✍

Andover Historical Society
97 Main Street
Andover, MA 01810
Tel: 978-475-2236 Fax: 978-470-2741
http://mysite.verizon.net/vze2t6hv
Hours: Tue–Fri 1–4 pm, and by appointment
Contact: Barbara Brown, Collections Manager
Institution type: History museum, historic house
Collection type: Clothing, accessories, uniforms, general textiles, quilts
Description: 1800–1914. Collection contains more than 1,500 pieces, most of Andover, Massachusetts, origin. Men's, women's, and children's outerwear and underwear with heavy emphasis on the nineteenth century, everyday wear, and formal wear. Accessories include hats, gloves, shoes, laces, collars, cuffs, and shawls. Military uniforms date from pre-1800, with most of the uniforms from the World Wars. Quilts and textiles collections emphasize textiles manufactured by the local woolen and linen mills.
$ ✍

Arlington Historical Society
7 Jason Street
Arlington, MA 02476
Tel: 781-648-4300
www.arlingtonhistorical.org

Attleboro Museum and Center for the Arts
86 Park Street
Attleboro, MA 02703
Tel: 508-222-2644

Barre Historical Society
18 Common Street
Barre, MA 01005
Tel: 978-355-4067

The Stone House Museum
20 Maple Street
Belchertown, MA 01007
Tel: 413-323-6573
www.stonehousemuseum.org
Hours: Wed and Sat 2–5 pm (mid-May–Oct), and by appointment

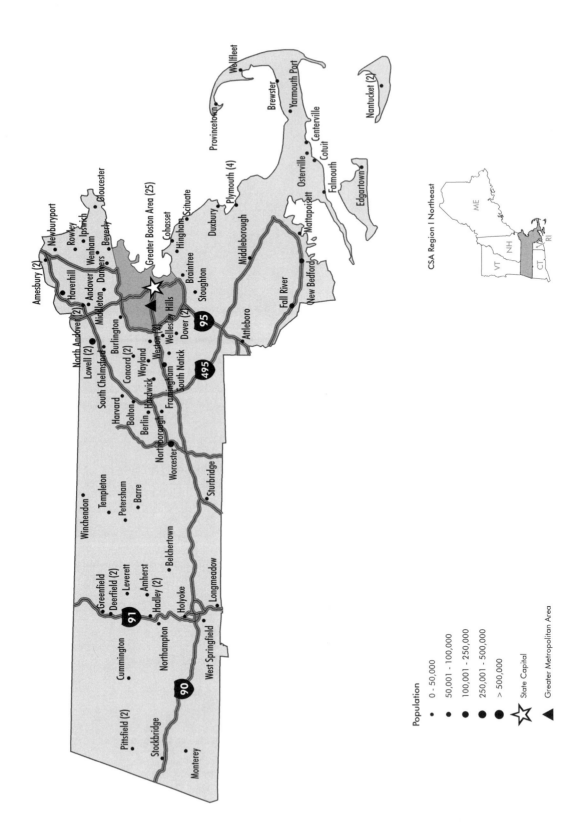

Population

- 0 - 50,000
- 50,001 - 100,000
- 100,001 - 250,000
- 250,001 - 500,000
- > 500,000

☆ State Capital

◄ Greater Metropolitan Area

CSA Region I Northeast

Amesbury (2)
Newburyport
Rowley
Ipswich
Wenham
Beverly
Gloucester
Greater Boston Area (25)
Cohasset
Hingham
Scituate
Duxbury
Middleborough
Provincetown
Wellfleet
Brewster
Yarmouth Port
Nantucket (2)
Centerville
Osterville
Cotuit
Falmouth
Edgartown
Mattapoisett
New Bedford (2)
Fall River
Attleboro
Stoughton
Braintree
Wellesley Hills
Dover (2)
Haverhill
Andover
Middleton
Danvers
North Andover
Lowell (2)
Burlington
South Chelmsford
Concord (2)
Wayland
Weston (3)
South Natick
Framingham
Hardwick
Harvard
Bolton
Berlin
Northborough
Sturbridge
Worcester
Winchendon
Templeton
Petersham
Barre
Belchertown
Longmeadow
Greenfield
Deerfield (2)
Leverett
Amherst
Hadley (2)
Holyoke
Northampton
West Springfield
Cummington
Stockbridge
Monterey
Pittsfield (2)

91
90
95
495

ME
NH
VT
CT
RI

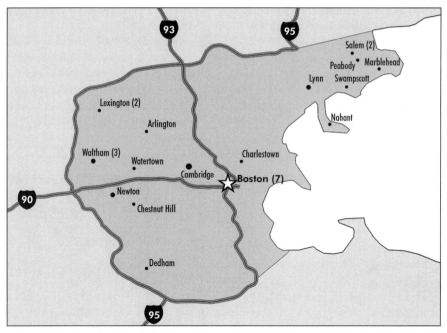

Greater Boston Metropolitan Area (24)

Contact: Caren Anne Harrington
Institution type: History museum, historic house
Collection type: Clothing, accessories, uniforms, costumes, general textiles, quilts, flags
Description: 1760–1960. New England Historic house (1827) collection includes quality textile pieces, both dress and flat textiles. Majority of items are from the early nineteenth century to 1950. Dress relates heavily to Connecticut River Valley residents. More than 100 hats as well as jewelry, parasols, fans, shoes, canes, capes, gloves, stockings, underwear, quilts, samplers, household linens, including bed hangings, and coverlets. Other items include World War I and World War II military uniforms and a considerable collection of dolls and doll clothing.

$ ✐

Berlin Art and Historical Collections
4 Woodward Avenue
Berlin, MA 01503
Tel: 978-838-2502

Beverly Historical Society and Museum
117 Cabot Street
Beverly, MA 01915

Tel: 978-922-1186
www.beverlyhistory.org

Bolton Historical Society
Sawyer House, 676 Main Street
Bolton, MA 01740
Tel: 978-779-6392

Boston National Historical Park
Charlestown Navy Yard
Boston, MA 02129
Tel: 617-242-5642
www.nps.gov/bost

The Bostonian Society—Old State House Museum
206 Washington Street
Boston, MA 02109
Tel: 617-720-1713 Fax: 617-720-3289
www.bostonhistory.org
Hours: Mon–Sun 9–5 pm
Contact: Rainey Tisdale
Institution type: History museum
Collection type: Clothing, accessories, uniforms, general textiles, flags
Description: Pre-1700–present. Textiles related to Boston history, including flags, military uni-

forms, and some clothing and accessories. Emphasis is on Revolutionary era and the nineteenth century. Significant pieces include Liberty Free flag, John Hancock's coat, 1735 embroidered wedding dress, and 1775 embroidered map of Boston Harbor.

$ ✍

Historic New England
141 Cambridge Street
Boston, MA 02114
Tel: 617-227-3956
www.historicnewengland.org

John F. Kennedy Library and Museum
Columbia Point
Boston, MA 02125
Tel: 617-929-4500
www.jfklibrary.org

Evening dresses by Charles James, 1950–1951. Courtesy of Museum of Fine Arts, Boston.

Museum of Fine Arts, Boston
DEPARTMENT OF TEXTILES AND
FASHION ARTS
465 Huntington Avenue
Boston, MA 02115
Tel: 617-369-3963 Fax: 617-262-6549
www.mfa.org
Hours: Mon–Tue, Sat–Sun 10–4:45 pm, Wed–Fri
10–9:45 pm
Contact: Pam Parmal, Curator

Institution type: Art museum
Collection type: Clothing, accessories, uniforms, general textiles, flags
Description: Pre-1700–present. Encyclopedic collection of textiles and fashion arts, including accessories. Collection contains more than 400 pairs of shoes, with strengths in Western fashionable shoes from the seventeenth century through the early twentieth century.

$ ✍

Wedding dresses, circa 1810-1830. Courtesy of The National Society of Colonial Dames of America in the Commonwealth of Massachusetts.

The National Society of Colonial Dames of America in the Commonwealth of Massachusetts
55 Beacon Street
Boston, MA 02108-3595
Tel: 617-742-3190 Fax: 617-722-9702
www.nscda.org/ma
Hours: Vary (May–Oct)
Contact: Joan T. Walther
Institution type: Historic house
Collection type: Clothing, accessories
Description: 1750–present. 6,500 items of clothing and textiles donated by Colonial Dames since 1940. Strengths are in women's clothes, dresses, hats, underwear, and accessories. Greatest strength is in nineteenth-century dresses.

$ ✍

The Sports Museum of New England

1 Fleet Center
Boston, MA 02134
Tel: 617-624-1105
www.sportsmuseum.org

Braintree Historical Society

31 Tenney Road
Braintree, MA 02184
Tel: 781-848-1640

New England Fire and History Museum

1439 Main Street
Brewster, MA 02631
Tel: 508-896-5711

Burlington Historical Museum

Town Hall, 29 Center Street
Burlington, MA 01803
Tel: 781-272-1049

Delaware skin hunting pouch, circa 1839. Courtesy of Peabody Museum of Archaeology and Ethnology.

Peabody Museum of Archaeology and Ethnology

11 Divinity Avenue
Cambridge, MA 02138
Tel: 617-496-1027
www.peabody.harvard.edu
Hours: Mon–Sun 9–5 pm
Contact: Pamela Gerardi
Institution type: University museum
Collection type: Clothing, accessories, costumes, general textiles
Description: Pre-1700–present. Textiles from around the world, especially Southwest U.S.

blankets and rugs, kuba cloth from Africa, molas and huipils from Central America, archaeological textiles from Peru, and tribal textiles from Southeast Asia and Siberia.
$ 🖎

Centerville Historical Museum

513 Main Street
Centerville, MA 02632
Tel: 508-775-0331

Bunker Hill Museum

43 Monument Square
Charlestown, MA 02129
Tel: 617-242-5641
www.nps.gov/bost

McMullen Museum of Art, Boston College

Devlin Hall, 140 Commonwealth Avenue
Chestnut Hill, MA 02167
Tel: 617-552-8587
www.bc.edu/bc_org/avp/cas/artmuseum

Cohasset Museum

106 South Main Street
Cohasset, MA 02446
Tel: 781-383-1434
www.cohassethistoricalsociety.org
Hours: Mon–Fri 10–4 pm
Contact: Paula Morse
Institution type: History museum
Collection type: Clothing, accessories, uniforms, costumes, general textiles, quilts
Description: 1799–present. Women's day and evening dresses, outerwear and ball gowns, undergarments, men's and children's clothing and uniforms dating from 1820–1960s. Large number of accessories including hats, gloves, shoes, bags, fans, jewelry, parasols, and walking sticks. Quilts and samplers.
$ 🖎

Concord Mansion Museum

200 Lexington Road
Concord, MA 01742
Tel: 978-369-9763
www.concordmuseum.org
Hours: Mon–Sat 11–4 pm, Sun 1–4 pm (Jan–Mar); Mon–Sat 9–5, Sun 12–5 pm (Apr–Dec)
$ 🖎

Ralph Waldo Emerson House

28 Cambridge Turnpike at Lexington Road
Concord, MA 01742
Tel: 978-369-2236

Historical Society of Santuit and Cotuit

1148 Main Street
Cotuit, MA 02635
Tel: 508-428-0461

Kingman Tavern Historical Museum

41 Main Street
Cummington, MA 01026
Tel: 413-634-5527

Danvers Historical Society

9 Page Street
Danvers, MA 01923
Tel: 978-777-1666
www.danvershistory.org

Dedham Historical Society

612 High Street
Dedham, MA 02026
Tel: 781-326-1385 Fax: 781-326-5762
www.dedhamhistorical.org
Hours: Tue–Fri 9–4 pm, even-dated Sats 1–4 pm
Contact: Virginia Parker
Institution type: History museum
Collection type: Clothing, accessories, uniforms,
costumes, general textiles, flags
Description: Pre-1700–1914. Broad range of costumes and textiles.
$ ✍

Historic Deerfield

HELEN GEIER FLYNT TEXTILE
COLLECTION
Flynt Center
Deerfield, MA 01342
Tel: 413-774-5581 Fax: 413-775-7224
www.historic-deerfield.org
Hours: Mon–Sun 9:30–4:30 pm
Contact: Edward F. Maeder
Institution type: History museum, historic house
Collection type: Clothing, accessories, costumes,
general textiles
Description: Pre-1700–1899. Costume and textiles, circa 1600–1860; European and colonial
women's gowns and men's suits; and eighteenth-century embroidery, bed covers, woven

Man's waistcoat, circa 1745–1760. Courtesy of Historic Deerfield.

textiles, samplers, shoes, hats, and costume
accessories. Emphasis is on New England and
the Connecticut River Valley.
$ ✍

Memorial Hall Museum

8 Memorial Street
Deerfield, MA 01342
Tel: 413-774-3768 Fax: 413-774-7070
www.deerfield-ma.org
Hours: Mon–Sun 9:30–4:30 pm (May–Oct)
Contact: Suzanne L. Flynt
Institution type: Art museum, history museum,
historic house
Collection type: Clothing, accessories, quilts
Description: 1700–1960. Everyday clothing and
accessories from western Massachusetts, quilts,
and items from the Deerfield Society of Blue
and White Embroidery.
$ ✍

Dover Historical Society

107 Dedham Street
Dover, MA 02030
Tel: 508-785-1832
www.doverhistoricalsociety.org
Hours: Sat 1–4 pm (Spring and Fall)
Contact: Shirley McGill; Glenda Mattes
Institution type: History museum, historic house,
city museum
Collection type: Clothing, accessories, uniforms,
costumes, general textiles, quilts, flags
Description: 1700–present. Diverse collection
includes unique quilts made to commemorate
town history. Sampler collection related to

early Dover residents, circa 1800s; U.S. flags, the most special being a handmade one from the Civil War era; wedding dresses from the late nineteenth century and early twentieth century; and collection of beaded bags, lace, head coverings, and shoes. Clothing collection covers a wide range of years and uses, from the fancy party dress to everyday wear.

✍

Sawin Memorial Museum
80 Dedham Street
Dover, MA 02030
Tel: 508-785-1832

Duxbury Historical Society
479 Washington Street
Duxbury, MA 02332
Tel: 781-934-5949
http://duxburyhistory.org

Waistcoat, wedding vest of Jabez Athearn, 1705. Courtesy of Martha's Vineyard Historical Society.

Martha's Vineyard Historical Society
59 School Street
Edgartown, MA 02539
Tel: 508-627-4441 Fax: 508-627-4436
www.marthasvineyardhistory.org
Hours: Tue–Sat 10–5 pm (Summer); Wed–Fri 1–4 pm, Sat 10–4 pm (Winter)
Contact: Jill Bouck, Curator; Dana Costanza, Assistant Curator
Institution type: History museum, historic house
Collection type: Clothing, accessories, uniforms, costumes, general textiles, quilts, flags

Description: 1700–present. Women's nineteenth-century dresses and accessories, men's clothing and accessories, children's clothing, textiles, flags, and needlework.

$ ✍

The Fall River Historical Society Museum
451 Rock Street
Fall River, MA 02720
Tel: 508-679-1071
www.lizzieborden.org

Falmouth Historical Society
55–65 Palmer Avenue
Falmouth, MA 02541
Tel: 508-548-4857
www.falmouthhistoricalsociety.org

Bonnet, straw layered poke bonnet with silk lining and ribbons, circa 1853–1855. Courtesy of Framingham Historical Society and Museum.

Framingham Historical Society and Museum
16 Vernon Street
Framingham, MA 01703
Tel: 508-872-3780 Fax: 508-872-3780
www.framinghamhistory.org
Hours: Wed–Thu 10–4 pm, Sat 10–1 pm
Contact: Dana Dauterman Ricciardi, Curator
Institution type: History museum
Collection type: Clothing, accessories, uniforms, general textiles, flags
Description: 1760–present. Strengths include nineteenth-century clothing and accessories— straw bonnets and hats in particular. Collection contains uniforms, riding habits, gowns, coats, capes, dresses, skirts, jackets, vests, pants,

tunics, bodices, dressing gowns, nightgowns, undergarments, shoes, pockets, handbags, and fans.

✍

Cape Ann Historical Museum
FOLLY COVE DESIGNERS COLLECTION
27 Pleasant Street
Gloucester, MA 01930
Tel: 978-283-0455 Fax: 978-283-4141
www.capeannhistoricalmuseum.org
Hours: Tue–Sat 10–5 pm
Contact: James Craig
Institution type: Art museum, history museum, historic house
Collection type: Clothing, accessories, uniforms, general textiles, flags
Description: 1700–present. More than 400 clothing articles and accessories (mostly women's and children's), samplers, flags, and uniforms pertaining to Cape Ann area. Of special interest is a British coat-hardee from the War of 1812, issued to the 104th New Brunswick Regiment, one of only seven such uniforms known to exist in the world (only one in North America).

1915–present. The Folly Cove Designers Collection offers a broad assortment of block print textiles including placemats, curtains, skirts, table runners, dishcloths, and household linens made specifically within the Folly Cove area of Gloucester, Massachusetts, between the years 1941 and 1969.

$ ✍

Historical Society of Greenfield
43 Church Street
Greenfield, MA 01302
Tel: 413-774-3663

Hadley Farm Museum
147 Russell Street
Hadley, MA 01035
Tel: 413-586-1812

Porter-Phelps-Huntington Foundation
130 River Drive
Hadley, MA 01035
Tel: 413-584-4699
Hours: Sat–Wed 1–4:30 pm
Contact: Susan Lisk
Institution type: Historic House

Collection type: Clothing, accessories, costumes, general textiles
Description: 1700–1960
$ ✍

Hardwick Historical Society
On Hardwick Commons
Hardwick, MA 01037
Tel: 413-477-6635

Harvard Historical Society
215 Still River Road
Harvard, MA 01451
Tel: 978-456-8285
www.harvardhistory.org
Hours: Vary by season
Contact: Melanie Clifton-Harvey
Institution type: Art museum, history museum, historic house, city museum
Collection type: Clothing, accessories, uniforms
Description: 1850–1960. Mostly New England costume from 1900 to 1930 and some Shaker costume and military attire. Most pieces are women's fashion from the late nineteenth century.

✍

Haverhill Historical Society
240 Water Street
Haverhill, MA 01830
Tel: 978-374-4626
www.haverhillhistory.org

The Old Ordinary
21 Lincoln Street
Hingham, MA 02043
Tel: 781-794-0013
www.hinghamhistorical.org
Hours: Tue–Sat 1:30–4:30 pm (Jun–Sep)
Contact: Paula Morse
Institution type: History museum, historic house
Collection type: Clothing, accessories, uniforms, costumes, general textiles, quilts
Description: 1760–1915. Eighteenth- and nineteenth-century gowns, lingerie, shoes, accessories, and quilts.
$ ✍

Wistariahurst Museum
238 Cabot Street
Holyoke, MA 01040
Tel: 413-534-2216
www.wistariahurst.org

Ipswich Historical Society

54 South Main
Ipswich, MA 01938
Tel: 978-356-2811
www.ipswichma.com/directory/ihs.asp

Leverett Historical Society

North Leverett Road
Leverett, MA 01054
Tel: 413-548-9082

Lexington Historical Society

1332 Massachusetts Avenue
Lexington, MA 02420
Tel: 781-862-1703
www.lexingtonhistory.org

National Heritage Museum

33 Marrett Road
Lexington, MA 02421
Tel: 781-861-6559 Fax: 781-861-9846
www.monh.org
Hours: Mon–Sat 10–5 pm, Sun 12–5 pm
Contact: Hilary Anderson, Director of Collections
and Exhibitions
Institution type: History museum
Collection type: Clothing, accessories, uniforms,
costumes, general textiles, quilts, flags
Description: 1700–present. Large collection of
eighteenth- to twentieth-century American
costumes and textiles. Strengths in fraternal
costumes and regalia and American quilts and
coverlets.

Richard Salter Storrs House

697 Longmeadow Street
Longmeadow, MA 01106
Tel: 413-567-3600
www.longmeadow.org/hist_soc/histsoc_main
.html

American Textile History Museum

491 Dutton Street
Lowell, MA 08154
Tel: 978-441-0400 Fax: 978-441-1412
www.athm.org
Hours: Tue–Fri 9–4 pm, Sat–Sun 10–5 pm
Contact: Karen Herbaugh, Curator; Clare
Sheridan, Librarian
Institution type: History museum

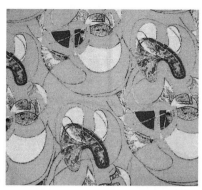

Textile sample, 1950s. Courtesy of American Textile History Museum.

Collection type: Clothing, accessories, general textiles, quilts
Description: 1750–1960. Printed cottons and
everyday clothing; hundreds of printed cotton
sample books, 1870s–1940s; coverlets; and
cloth printing and producing machinery and
tools. Extensive library resources include
books, images, and manuscripts relating to textiles.

$ ✍

Quilt, Burgoyne Surrounded variation, 1870–1900. Courtesy of New England Quilt Museum.

New England Quilt Museum

18 Shattuck Street
Lowell, MA 01852
Tel: 978-452-4207 Fax: 978-452-5405
www.nequiltmuseum.org
Hours: Tue–Sat 10–4 pm (Jan–Apr); Tue–Sat
10–4 pm, Sun 12–4 pm (May–Dec)
Contact: Anita B. Loscalzo, Curator
Institution type: History museum

Collection type: Quilts

Description: 1760–present. Museum actively collects and preserves antique and contemporary quilts and quilt related items. Permanent collection ranges from whole-cloth quilts made in the late eighteenth century to contemporary quilts made by highly regarded art quilters.

$ ✍🏻

Lynn Museum

125 Green Street
Lynn, MA 01901
Tel: 781-592-2465
www.lynnmuseum.org

Marblehead Museum and Historical Society

170 Washington Street
Marblehead, MA 01945
Tel: 781-631-7945
www.marbleheadmuseum.org

Mattapoisett Museum and Carriage House

5 Church Street
Mattapoisett, MA 02739
Tel: 508-758-2844

Middleborough Historical Association

Jackson Street
Middleborough, MA 02346
Tel: 508-947-1969

Lura Watkins Museum and Middleton Historical Society

Pleasant Street
Middleton, MA 01949
Tel: 978-774-9301
www.flintlibrary.org/history.htm

The Bidwell House

The Casino, Congress Park
Monterey, MA 01245-0537
Tel: 413-528-6888
www.bidwellhousemuseum.org

Nahant Historical Society

41 Valley Road
Nahant, MA 01908
Tel: 781-581-2727
www.NahantHistory.org
Hours: Wed 10–4 pm, 1st Sun 1–4 pm

Institution type: History museum, city museum
✍🏻

Egan Institute

The Coffin School
4 Winter Street
Nantucket, MA 02554
Tel: 508-228-2505
www.eganinstitute.com

Nantucket Historical Association

15 Broad Street
Nantucket, MA 02554
Tel: 508-228-1894 Fax: 508-228-5618
www.nha.org
Hours: Mon–Sun 10–5 pm (Summer); Mon–Sun 11–4 pm (Winter)
Contact: Niles Parker, Tony Dumitru, Mark Wilson
Institution type: Historic house
Collection type: Clothing, accessories, costumes, general textiles, flags
Description: 1700–present. Collection contains maritime art and decorative arts, including clothing and accessories.

$ ✍🏻

The Rotch-Jones-Duff House and Garden Museum

396 County Street
New Bedford, MA 02740
Tel: 508-997-1401
www.rjdmuseum.org

Cushing House Museum and Historical Society of Old Newbury

98 High Street
Newburyport, MA 01950
Tel: 978-462-2681
www.newburyhist.com

Newton History Museum at the Jackson Homestead

527 Washington Street
Newton, MA 02458
Tel: 617-796-1450 Fax: 617-552-7228
www.newtonhistorymuseum.org
Hours: Tue–Sat 11–5 pm, Sun 2–5 pm
Contact: Sheila M. Sibley, Curator of Objects and Education
Institution type: History museum, city museum
Collection type: Clothing, accessories, uniforms, costumes, general textiles, quilts, flags

West African cloth sample sent to William B. Dodge, circa 1800–1840. Courtesy of Newton History Museum.

Description: 1760–present. Collection reflects the people and history of Newton, emphasizing and illustrating Newton as an evolving suburban community of diverse populations. Costumes, clothing, and accessories representative of Newton residents; textiles, quilts, samplers, and lace created and owned by local residents. Majority of these clothing and textile collections (approximately 6,500 items) date between 1800 and 1900.

$ ✍

North Andover Historical Society
153 Academy Road
North Andover, MA 01845
Tel: 978-686-4035
www.essexheritage.org/visiting/placestovisit/
    listofsitesbycommunity/north_andover_hist
    _soc.shtml

The Stevens-Coolidge Place
137 Andover Street
North Andover, MA 01845
Tel: 978-682-3580

Historic Northampton
46 Bridge Street
Northampton, MA 01060
Tel: 413-584-6011
www.historic-northampton.org

Northborough Historical Society
50 Main Street
Northborough, MA 01532
Tel: 508-393-6298
www.northboroughhistsoc.org

Osterville Historical Society
155 West Bay Road
Osterville, MA 02655

Tel: 508-428-5861
www.osterville.org

Peabody Historical Society and Museum
35 Washington Street
Peabody, MA 01960
Tel: 978-531-0805
www.peabodyhistorical.org

Petersham Historical Society
10 North Main Street
Petersham, MA 01366
Tel: 978-724-3380

Berkshire Historical Society
780 Holmes Road
Pittsfield, MA 01201
Tel: 413-442-1793 Fax: 413-443-1449
www.berkshirehistory.org
Hours: Mon–Fri 9–5 pm
Contact: Catherine Reynolds, Curator
Institution type: Historic house
Collection type: Clothing, accessories, uniforms, general textiles, quilts, flags
Description: 1800–1960. Items owned by Berkshire County residents in the nineteenth century and early twentieth century. Utilitarian items but mostly very high end shoes, hats, gloves, coats, and many other accessories. Most are women's clothing items. More than 40 wedding dresses with exquisite details—beads, embroidery, and lace—and 40 quilts from the early nineteenth century and later.

$ ✍

Hancock Shaker Village
Route 20
Pittsfield, MA 01202
Tel: 413-443-0188
www.hancockshakervillage.org

Howland House
35 Sandwich Street
Plymouth, MA 02360
Tel: 508-746-9590

Pilgrim Hall Museum
75 Court Street
Plymouth, MA 02360
Tel: 508-746-1620
www.pilgrimhall.org

Plimoth Plantation
137 Warren Avenue
Plymouth, MA 02362
Tel: 508-746-1622x8249
www.plimoth.org

Plymouth Antiquarian Society
6 Court Street
Plymouth, MA 02360
Tel: 508-746-0012

Pilgrim Monument and Provincetown Museum
High Pole Hill
Provincetown, MA 02657
Tel: 508-487-1310
www.pilgrim-monument.org

Rowley Historical Society
233 Main Street
Rowley, MA 01969
Tel: 508-948-7483

Peabody Essex Museum
East India Square
Salem, MA 01970-3783
Tel: 978-745-1876
www.pem.org

The Stephen Phillips Memorial Trust House
34 Chestnut Street
Salem, MA 01970
Tel: 978-744-0440
www.phillipsmuseum.org

Scituate Historical Society
43 Cudworth Road
Scituate, MA 02066
Tel: 781-545-1083
www.scituatehistoricalsociety.org

Chelmsford Historical Society
40 Byam Road
South Chelmsford, MA 01824
Tel: 978-256-2311
www.chelmhist.org

Natick Historical Society and Museum
58 Eliot Street
South Natick, MA 01760

Tel: 508-647-4841
www.natickhistory.com/index.shtml

Naumkeag
CHOATE FAMILY COLLECTION
5 Prospect Hill Road
Stockbridge, MA 01262
Tel: 413-298-8123 Fax: 413-298-5239
www.thetrustees.org/pages/335_naumkeag.cfm
Hours: Mon–Sun 10–5 pm (Memorial Day–Columbus Day)
Contact: Will Garrison
Institution type: Historic house
Collection type: Clothing, accessories, quilts
Description: 1700–1960. Bed covers, eighteenth-century tapestry, and quilts.
$ ✍

Stoughton Historical Society
6 Park Street
Stoughton, MA 02072
Tel: 781-344-5456

Man's outfit, circa 1835, and woman's gown, circa 1820. Courtesy of Old Sturbridge Village.

Old Sturbridge Village
1 Old Sturbridge Village Road
Sturbridge, MA 01566
Tel: 508-347-3362
www.osv.org
Hours: Mon–Sun 9:30–5 pm, vary seasonally
Contact: Aimee E. Newell
Institution type: History museum

Collection type: Clothing, accessories, costumes, general textiles, quilts

Description: 1760–1849. More than 7,500 pieces, including costumes and domestic textiles with focus on rural New England during the period from 1790 to 1840, with particular interest in everyday items.

$ ✍

Swampscott Historical Society

99 Paradise Road
Swampscott, MA 01907
Tel: 781-599-1297

Narragansett Historical Society

1 Boynton Road
Templeton, MA 01468
Tel: 978-939-2251

Gore Place

52 Gore Street
Waltham, MA 02453
Tel: 718-894-2798
www.goreplace.org

Waltham Historical Society

190 Moody Street
Waltham, MA 02453
Tel: 781-894-2798
www.walthamhistoricalsociety.org

The Waltham Museum

196 Charles Street
Waltham, MA 02543
Tel: 781-893-8017
www.walthammuseum.com

Armenian Library and Museum of America

65 Main Street
Watertown, MA 02472
Tel: 617-926-2562x25 Fax: 617-926-0175
www.armenianlibraryandmuseum.org
Hours: Sun, Fri 1–5 pm, Tue 1–9 pm
Institution type: History museum

$ ✍

Wayland Historical Society

12 Cochituate Road
Wayland, MA 01778
Tel: 508-358-7959
http://j.w.d.home.comcast.net/whs
Hours: Tue, Fri 9:30–12 pm, and by appointment
Contact: Gloria Backman
Institution type: History museum, historic house
Collection type: Clothing, accessories, uniforms, costumes, general textiles, flags
Description: 1700–1960. Clothing and accessories with a Wayland connection.

✍

Wellesley Historical Society

OLDHAM LACE COLLECTION
229 Washington Street
Wellesley Hills, MA 02481
Tel: 781-235-6690 Fax: 781-239-0660
www.wellesleyhsoc.com
Hours: Wed and Fri 1–4 pm, Thu 1–7 pm, Sat 1–3 pm (Sep–May)
Contact: Laurel Nilsen Sparks
Institution type: Art museum, history museum, historic house
Collection type: Clothing, accessories, uniforms, general textiles
Description: Pre-1700–present. Women's clothing, children's clothing, and accessories with more than 1,000 artifacts. Oldham Lace Collection has lace collars, cuffs, lace samples, and lace-making tools with 2,000 artifacts.

✍

Wellfleet Historical Society Museum

266 Main Street
Wellfleet, MA 02667
Tel: 508-349-2954
www.wellfleethistoricalsociety.com

Wenham Museum

132 Main Street
Wenham, MA 01984
Tel: 978-468-2377
www.wenhammuseum.org

Ramapogue Historical Society

70 Park Street
West Springfield, MA 01090
Tel: 413-734-8322

Golden Ball Tavern Museum
662 Boston Post Road
Weston, MA 02493
Tel: 781-894-1751
www.goldenballtavern.org

Museum of the Weston Historical Society
358 Boston Post Road
Weston, MA 02193
Tel: 617-237-1447

Winchendon Historical Society
151 Front Street
Winchendon, MA 01475
Tel: 978-297-2142

Worcester Historical Museum
30 Elm Street
Worcester, MA 01609
Tel: 617-753-8278
www.worcesterhistory.org

Historical Society of Old Yarmouth
11 Strawberry Lane
Yarmouth Port, MA 02675
Tel: 508-362-3021
www.hsoy.org

MICHIGAN

Brueckner Museum of the Starr Commonwealth
13725 Starr Commonwealth Road
Albion, MI 49224
Tel: 517-629-5591

Gardner House Museum
509 South Superior Street
Albion, MI 49224
Tel: 517-629-5100
www.forks.org/history

Jesse Besser Museum
491 Johnson Street
Alpena, MI 49707
Tel: 989-356-2202 Fax: 989-356-3133
www.bessermuseum.org

Kelsey Museum of Archaeology
434 South State Street
Ann Arbor, MI 48109
Tel: 734-764-9304

The University of Michigan Museum of Art
525 South State Street
Ann Arbor, MI 48109
Tel: 734-764-0395
www.umich.edu/~umma

Historical Museum of Bay County
321 Washington Avenue
Bay City, MI 48708
Tel: 989-893-5733
www.bchsmuseum.org

Bay View Historical Museum
Bay View Association Encampment 1715
Bay View, MI 49770
Tel: 231-347-6225

Morton House Museum
501 Territorial
Benton Harbor, MI 49022
Tel: 616-925-7011
www.parrett.net/~morton
Hours: Thu 1–4 pm, Sun 2–4 pm (Apr–Oct)
Institution type: Historic house
$

Benzie Area Historical Museum
6941 Traverse Avenue
Benzonia, MI 49616
Tel: 231-882-5539
Hours: Mon–Sat 11–5 pm (May–Nov)
Contact: Kathleen Osterhaus
Institution type: History museum
Collection type: Quilts
Description: 1760–present. Quilts from the local community that show the history of the area, from signature quilts to quilts that were made as gifts.

1839 Courthouse Museum
313 North Cass
Berrien Springs, MI 49103
Tel: 616-471-1202
www.berrienhistory.org

Marquette

Ishpeming

75

Drummond Island

Mackinac Island

Harbor Springs

Rogers City

Leland
Bay View
East Jordan
Gaylord

Alpena

Traverse City

Benzonia

Cadillac

East Tawas

Manistee

Port Austin

Ludington

Big Rapids

Sebewaing

Midland
Bay City
Saginaw
Frankenmuth
Port Sanilac

St. Johns
Owosso
Flint (2)

Grand Haven
Grand Rapids (2)

69

Holland

Oxford

Douglas
Hastings
Lansing
East Lansing
Fenton

South Haven
Delton
Kalamazoo (2)
Charlotte
Albion (2)
Dexter
Ann Arbor (2)

Benton Harbor

94

Marshall (2)

Jackson
Ypsilanti
Willow Run
Airport
Greater
Detroit
Area (20)

Berrien Springs
Niles
Constantine
Hanover
Monroe

Population

- • 0 - 50,000
- • 50,001 - 100,000
- ● 100,001 - 250,000
- ● 250,001 - 500,000
- ● > 500,000
- ☆ State Capital
- ▲ Greater Metropolitan Area

CSA Region III Midwest

162 ■ **Michigan**

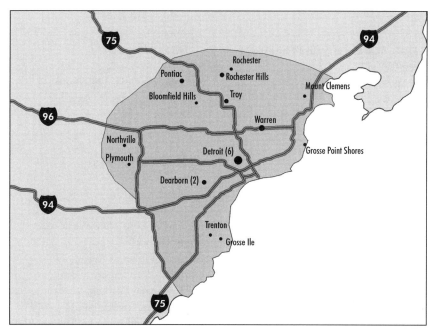

Greater Detroit Metropolitan Area (20)

Mecosta County Historical Museum

129 South Stewart Street
Big Rapids, MI 49307
Tel: 616-592-5091

Cranbrook Art Museum

39221 Woodward Avenue
Bloomfield Hills, MI 48303
Tel: 248-645-3361
www.cranbrookart.edu/museum

Wexford County Historical Society

127 Beech Street
Cadillac, MI 49601
Tel: 231-775-1717 Fax: 231-775-0888

Courthouse Square Association

100 West Lawrence Avenue
Charlotte, MI 48813
Tel: 517-543-6999 Fax: 517-543-6999
www.visitcourthousesquare.org

John S. Barry Historical Society

300 North Washington
Constantine, MI 49042
Tel: 269-435-5825

Dearborn Historical Museum

915 Brady Street
Dearborn, MI 48124
Tel: 313-565-3000 Fax: 313-565-4848
www.cityofdearborn.org/departments/
	historicalmuseum/faq.shtml
Hours: Mon–Fri 9–5 pm, Sat 1–5 pm
Contact: Bernice Carden
Institution type: City museum
Collection type: Clothing, accessories, uniforms,
	costumes, general textiles
Description: 1800–present
✍

Henry Ford Museum and Greenfield Village

20900 Oakwood Boulevard
Dearborn, MI 48124
Tel: 313-982-6100 Fax: 313-982-6250
www.hfmgv.org
Hours: Mon–Sun 9:30–5 pm
Contact: Nancy Bryk; contact Access Services
	Department to make research arrangements
Institution type: History museum, historic house,
	city museum
Collection type: Clothing, accessories, uniforms,
	costumes, general textiles, quilts, flags

Description: 1800–present. More than 15,000 items with broad range of objects.

$ ✍

Bernard Historical Society and Museum

7135 West Delton Road
Delton, MI 49046
Tel: 616-623-5451

Black Legends of Professional Basketball

8900 East Jefferson, Suite 328
Detroit, MI 48214
Tel: 313-822-8208 Fax: 313-822-8227

Detroit Historical Museum

5401 Woodward Avenue
Detroit, MI 48202
Tel: 313-297-8378 Fax: 313-297-8361
www.detroithistorical.org
Hours: Tue–Fri 9:30–5 pm, Sat 10–5 pm, Sun 11–5 pm
Contact: Patience Nauta
Institution type: History museum, historic house, city museum
Collection type: Clothing, accessories, uniforms, costumes, general textiles, quilts, flags
Description: 1800–present. Comprehensive collection reflects two hundred years of life in Detroit, including a broad range of social levels, Detroit retailers and dressmakers, and American and European designers. Collection includes accessories; military items from the Civil War through the 1960s; quilts, domestic textiles, and samplers; outerwear and furs; children's clothing from 1849 to 1940; and menswear from 1800 through the 1990s.

$ ✍

Detroit Institute of Arts

5200 Woodward Avenue
Detroit, MI 48202
Tel: 313-833-7900
www.dia.org

International Gospel Music Hall of Fame and Museum

18301 West McNichols
Detroit, MI 48219
Tel: 313-592-0017 Fax: 313-592-8762
www.igmhf.org

International Institute of Metropolitan Detroit

111 East Kirby
Detroit, MI 48202
Tel: 313-871-8600

Motown Historical Museum

2648 West Grand Boulevard
Detroit, MI 48208
Tel: 313-875-2264

Dexter Area Museum

3443 Inverness
Dexter, MI 48130
Tel: 313-577-2872
www.hvcn.org/info/dextermuseum
Hours: Fri–Sat 1–3 pm
Contact: Nina Rackham
Institution type: History museum
Collection type: Clothing, accessories, uniforms, general textiles, flags
Description: 1800–present. Uniforms from the Civil War to the present and clothing from local residents from 1830 to 1930.

✍

Keewatin Maritime Museum

Harbour Village
Union Street and Blue Star Highway
Douglas, MI 49406
Tel: 616-857-2464
www.keewatinmaritimemuseum.com

Drummond Island Historical Museum

Water Street
Drummond Island, MI 49726
Tel: 906-493-5746
www.drummondislandnews.com/history.html

East Jordan Portside Art and Historical Museum

1787 South M-66 Highway
East Jordan, MI 49727
Tel: 231-536-2363

The Michigan State University Museum

West Circle Drive
East Lansing, MI 48824
Tel: 517-355-2370
www.museum.msu.edu

Iosco County Historical Museum

405 West Bay Street
East Tawas, MI 48730
Tel: 989-362-8911
www.ioscomuseum.org

The Pioneer Memorial Association of Fenton and Mundy Townships

2436 North Long Road
Fenton, MI 48430
Tel: 810-629-7748

Flint Institute of Arts

1120 East Kearsley Street
Flint, MI 48503
Tel: 810-234-1695
www.flintarts.org

Sloan Museum

1221 East Kearsley Street
Flint, MI 48503
Tel: 810-237-3450
www.sloanmuseum.com

Frankenmuth Historical Association

613 South Main
Frankenmuth, MI 48734
Tel: 989-652-9701 Fax: 989-652-9390
http://frankenmuth.michigan.museum
Hours: Vary by season, call for hours
Contact: Mary Nuechterlein
Institution type: History museum, city museum
Collection type: Clothing, accessories, uniforms, general textiles, flags
Description: 1850–present. Collection is typical of a Midwest United States historical museum. Exceptions are items that relate to the German American heritage of the community, including aprons and shawls, "Baenderhaube," and wedding and capping ceremony hats.
$ 🖎

Tri-Cities Museum

200 Washington Avenue
Grand Haven, MI 49417
Tel: 616-842-0700 Fax: 616-842-3698
www.tri-citiesmuseum.org

The Grand Rapids Art Museum

155 Division North
Grand Rapids, MI 49503
Tel: 616-831-1000
www.gramonline.org

Bridal party outfits, circa 1950. Courtesy of Public Museum of Grand Rapids.

Public Museum of Grand Rapids

272 Pearl Street NW
Grand Rapids, MI 49504
Tel: 616-456-3977 Fax: 616-456-3873
www.grmuseum.org
Hours: Mon–Sat 9–5 pm, Sun 12–5 pm
Contact: Veronica Kandl
Institution type: History museum, county museum, city museum
Collection type: Clothing, accessories, uniforms, general textiles, quilts
Description: 1850–present. Collection includes clothing worn by middle class west Michigan area women, wedding dresses from 1850 to 1970, and 1920s evening dresses. The Scassi Archive Collection includes 30 pieces. Other items include male military uniforms from 1820 through Desert Storm, with the largest concentration during World War I and World War II. Collection also includes more than 100 quilts, made primarily in the Midwest, with examples of whole-cloth, pieced, appliquéd, and tied. Majority are crazy quilts from the late 1800s. Accessories include examples of American used hats, shoes, fans, and purses.
$ 🖎

Grosse Ile Historical Society

East River and Grosse Ile Parkway
Grosse Ile, MI 48138
Tel: 734-675-1250

Edsel and Eleanor Ford House

1100 Lake Shore Road
Grosse Pointe Shores, MI 48236

Tel: 313-884-4222 Fax: 313-884-5977
www.fordhouse.org
Hours: Tue–Sat 9:30–6 pm, Sun 11:30–6 pm
(Apr–Dec); Tue–Sun 11:30–6 pm (Jan
15–Mar)
Institution type: History museum, historic house
$

Wedding clothing, 1947. Courtesy of Hanover-Horton Area Historical Society.

Hanover-Horton Area Historical Society

105 Fairview
Hanover, MI 49241
Tel: 517-563-8927 Fax: 517-563-8927
www.conklinreedorganmuseum.org
Hours: Sun 1–5 pm (Apr–Oct)
Contact: Joyce G. Kent
Institution type: History museum, historic house
Collection type: Clothing, accessories, uniforms,
general textiles, quilts, flags
Description: 1800–present. Dresses of early set-
tlers; several veterans' uniforms; small quilt col-
lection, mostly crazy or friendship quilts from
local ancestors; local firefighter's uniform;
household textiles (1900–1950); and flags.
$ 🖉

Andrew J. Blackbird Museum

368 East Main Street
Harbor Springs, MI 49740
Tel: 231-526-0612 Fax: 231-526-2705

Historic Charlton Park Village and Museum

2545 South Charlton Park Road
Hastings, MI 49058
Tel: 269-945-3775 Fax: 269-945-0390
www.charltonpark.org

The Holland Museum

31 West 10th Street
Holland, MI 49423
Tel: 616-394-1362
www.hollandmuseum.org

U.S. National Ski Hall of Fame and Museum

610 Palms
Ishpeming, MI 49849
Tel: 906-485-6323
www.skihall.com

Ella Sharp Museum

3225 4th Street
Jackson, MI 49203
Tel: 517-787-2933
www.ellasharp.org

John E. Gray Memorial Museum

8119 6th Street
Kalamazoo, MI 49009
Tel: 269-344-2107

Kalamazoo Valley Museum

230 North Rose Street
Kalamazoo, MI 49007
Tel: 269-373-7987 Fax: 269-373-7997
http://kvm.kvcc.edu

Michigan Historical Museum

702 West Kalamazoo Street
Lansing, MI 48915
Tel: 517-373-1509
www.michiganhistory.org
Hours: Mon–Fri 8–5 pm
Contact: Eve Weipert
Institution type: History museum, state museum
Collection type: Clothing, accessories, uniforms,
costumes, general textiles, quilts, flags
Description: 1800–present. Wedding dresses from
various time periods, clothing belonging to
Michigan's governors and First Ladies, Civil
War battle flags, and military uniforms. Quilt
and coverlet collection contains more than 300
pieces, including coverlets dating from 1790 to
1850 and quilts dating from 1837 to 1935.
Quilt featured was made by Olivia Rich Hall,
circa 1815–1830, and brought to Mount
Clemens via the Erie Canal before Michigan
became a state in 1837.

🖉

Leelanau Historical Museum

203 East Cedar Street
Leland, MI 49654
Tel: 231-256-7475
www.leelanauhistory.org
Hours: Tue–Sat 10–4 pm
Contact: Laura Quackenbush
Institution type: History museum
Collection type: Clothing, accessories, uniforms, general textiles, flags
Description: 1850–1960. Clothing and household linens.
$ ✍

Historic White Pine Village

1687 South Lakeshore Drive
Ludington, MI 49431
Tel: 231-843-4808
www.historicwhitepinevillage.org

Stuart House Museum of Astors

Market Street
Mackinac Island, MI 49757
Tel: 906-847-3808

Manistee County Historical Museum

425 River Street
Manistee, MI 49660
Tel: 231-723-5531

Marquette County History Museum

213 North Front Street
Marquette, MI 49855
Tel: 906-226-3571
www.marquettecohistory.org

American Museum of Magic

107 East Michigan
Marshall, MI 49068
Tel: 616-781-7666

Honolulu House Museum

107 North Kalamazoo
Marshall, MI 49068
Tel: 616-781-8544
www.marshallhistoricalsociety.org

Midland County Historical Society

1801 West St. Andrews Road
Midland, MI 48640
Tel: 989-631-5931 Fax: 989-631-7890
www.mcfta.org

Monroe County Historical Museum

126 South Monroe Street
Monroe, MI 48161
Tel: 734-240-7780 Fax: 734-240-7788

Crocker House

15 Union Street
Mount Clemens, MI 48043
Tel: 810-465-2488

Fort St. Joseph Museum

508 East Main Street
Niles, MI 49120
Tel: 269-683-4702 Fax: 269-684-3930
www.ci.niles.mi.us/living/museum.htm

Mill Race Historical Village

Griswold Street
Northville, MI 48167
Tel: 248-348-1845 Fax: 248-348-0056

The Movie Museum

318 East Oliver Street
Owosso, MI 48867
Tel: 989-725-7621
Hours: By appointment
Contact: Don Schneider, President
Institution type: Theater museum, city museum
Collection type: Clothing, accessories, uniforms, costumes
Description: 1850–present. Collection contains movie and theater costumes, accessories, and jewelry, including 12 complete World War I U.S. Army uniforms from *The Big Parade* (1925). Costumes from twenty movie stars, including Valentino, Gable, Bartholomeo, Byington, and Pickford. Access to collection is limited.
$ ✍

Northeast Oakland Historical Museum

1 North Washington Street
Oxford, MI 48371
Tel: 800-628-8413

Plymouth Historical Museum

155 South Main Street
Plymouth, MI 48170
Tel: 734-455-7797
www.plymouthhistory.org

Pine Grove Historical Museum
405 Oakland Avenue
Pontiac, MI 48342
Tel: 248-338-6732
www.wwnet.net/~ocphs/museum.html

Huron City Museums
7995 Huron City Road
Port Austin, MI 48467
Tel: 989-428-4123
http://huroncitymuseums.com

Sanilac County Historical Museum and Village
228 South Ridge Street
Port Sanilac, MI 48469
Tel: 810-622-9946

Meadow Brook Hall
Oakland University
480 South Adams Road
Rochester, MI 48309
Tel: 248-370-3140
www.meadowbrookhall.org

Rochester Hills Museum at Van Hoosen Farm
1005 Van Hoosen Road
Rochester Hills, MI 48306
Tel: 248-656-4663 Fax: 248-608-8198
www.rochesterhills.org/city_services/museum/
overview.asp
Hours: Wed–Sat 1–4 pm
Contact: Michelle Akers-Berg, Curator
Institution type: Historic house, city museum
Collection type: General textiles
Description: 1850–present. Items in collection are mostly from the Greater Rochester area, with pieces dating back to 1850. Collection includes Van Doren coverlets, items of Dr. Bertha Van Hoosen, Van Hoosen Farm textiles, and items from the Rochester centennial celebration of 1969.
$ 🖾

Presque Isle County Historical Museum
176 West Michigan Avenue
Rogers City, MI 49779
Tel: 517-734-4121

Castle Museum of Saginaw County History
500 Federal Avenue
Saginaw, MI 48607
Tel: 989-752-2861

Luckhard Museum—The Indian Mission
612 East Bay Street
Sebewaing, MI 48759
Tel: 989-883-2539

Michigan Maritime Museum
260 Dychman Avenue
South Haven, MI 49090
Tel: 269-637-8078
www.michiganmaritimemuseum.org

Paine Gilliam Scott Museum
106 Maple Avenue
St. Johns, MI 48879
Tel: 989-224-2894

Con Foster Museum
181 East Grandview Parkway
Traverse City, MI 49684
Tel: 231-995-0313

Trenton Historical Museum
306 St. Joseph
Trenton, MI 48183
Tel: 734-675-2130

Troy Museum and Historic Village
60 West Wattles Road
Troy, MI 48098
Tel: 248-524-3570
www.ci.troy.mi.us/parks/museum
Hours: Tue–Sat 9–5:30 pm, Sun 1–5 pm
Contact: William Boardman, Collection Manager
Institution type: County museum
Collection type: Clothing, accessories, uniforms, general textiles, quilts
Description: 1800–1960. Women's clothing, mid-1800s–1910, and men's and children's clothing.
🖾

Ukrainian-American Museum and Archives
Ukrainian Cultural Center, 26601 Ryan Road
Warren, MI 48091
Tel: 810-757-8130

Yankee Air Force Museum
  H-2041 A Street
  Willow Run Airport, MI 48112
  Tel: 734-483-4030
  www.yankeeairmuseum.org

Ypsilanti Historical Museum
  220 North Huron Street
  Ypsilanti, MI 48197
  Tel: 734-482-4990
  www.ypsilantihistoricalsociety.org

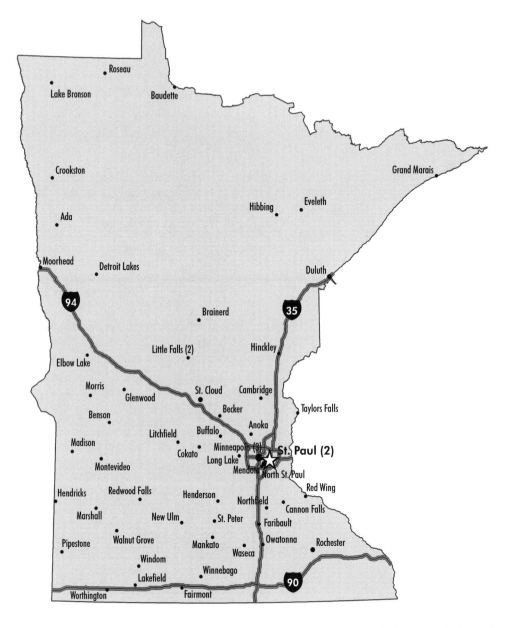

Roseau

Lake Bronson · Baudette

Crookston

Ada

Moorhead · Detroit Lakes

Grand Marais

Hibbing · Eveleth

Duluth

94

35

Brainerd

Little Falls (2) · Hinckley

Elbow Lake

Morris · St. Cloud · Cambridge
Glenwood · Becker · Taylors Falls

Benson · Anoka
Litchfield · Buffalo
Madison · Minneapolis (9) · St. Paul (2)
Cokato · Long Lake · Mendota · North St. Paul
Montevideo · Red Wing

Hendricks · Redwood Falls · Henderson · Northfield
Marshall · Cannon Falls
New Ulm · St. Peter · Faribault
Pipestone · Walnut Grove · Owatonna · Rochester
Mankato · Waseca
Windom · Winnebago
Lakefield · **90**
Worthington · Fairmont

Population

- 0 - 50,000
- 50,001 - 100,000
- 100,001 - 250,000
- 250,001 - 500,000
- > 500,000
- ☆ State Capital

MINNESOTA

Memorial Museum
  409 East 1st Avenue
  Ada, MN 56510
  Tel: 218-784-7311

Anoka County Historical and Genealogical Society
  2135 3rd Avenue North
  Anoka, MN 55303
  Tel: 763-421-0600

Lake of the Woods County Museum
  119 8th Avenue SE
  Baudette, MN 56623
  Tel: 218-634-1200
  www.lakeofthewoodsmn.com/museum.asp
  Hours: Tue–Sat 10–4 pm, (May 15–Oct 1)
  Contact: Marlys L. Hirst, Director
  Institution type: County museum
  Collection type: Clothing
  Description: 1900–1960. Women's, men's, and children's clothing.
  ✍

Sherburne County Historical Society
  13122 1st Street
  Becker, MN 55308
  Tel: 763-261-4433
  www.rootsweb.com/~mnschs

Swift County Historical Society
  2135 Minnesota Avenue, Building 2
  Benson, MN 56215
  Tel: 320-843-4467

Crow Wing County Historical Society
  320 Laurel
  Brainerd, MN 56401
  Tel: 218-829-3268 Fax: 218-828-4434
  Hours: Tue–Fri 1–5 pm, Sat 10–2 pm (Labor Day–Memorial Day); Mon–Fri 10–4 pm (Memorial Day–Labor Day)
  Contact: Mary Lou Moudry
  Institution type: History museum, historic house, county museum
  Collection type: Clothing, accessories, uniforms, general textiles
  Description: 1850–present.
  $ ✍

Wright County Historical Society
  2001 Highway 25 North
  Buffalo, MN 55313
  Tel: 763-682-7323 Fax: 763-682-8945
  Hours: Mon–Fri 8–4:30 pm (Oct–May), Mon–Fri 8–4:30 pm, Sat 8–4 pm (Jun–Sep)
  Contact: Curator
  Institution type: County museum
  Collection type: Clothing, accessories, uniforms, general textiles, flags
  Description: 1850–present.
  ✍

Isanti County Historical Society
  33525 Flanders Street NE
  Cambridge, MN 55008
  Tel: 763-689-4229 Fax: 763-552-0740
  www.ichs.ws
  Hours: Mon, Tue, Fri 9–4:30 pm, 2nd Sat 9–1 pm

Contact: Curator
Institution type: History museum
Collection type: Clothing, accessories, uniforms, costumes, general textiles, quilts, flags
Description: 1850–present. Clothing, uniforms both military and civilian, general textiles, flags, folk costume, quilts, and accessories from families in Isanti County. Collection started in 1965 with clothing dating back to late 1800s.

Cannon Falls Area Historical Museums
208 West Mill Street
Cannon Falls, MN 55009
Tel: 507-263-4080

Cokato Museum
175 West 4th Street
Cokato, MN 55321
Tel: 320-286-2427
www.cokato.mn.us/cmhs

Polk County Historical Society
U.S. 2 East
Crookston, MN 56716
Tel: 218-281-1038
www.crookston.com

Becker County Historical Society
915 Lake Avenue
Detroit Lakes, MN 56502
Tel: 218-847-2938

Tweed Museum of Art
1201 Ordean Court
Duluth, MN 55812
Tel: 218-726-7056 Fax: 218-726-8503
www.d.umn.edu/tma
Hours: Tue 9–8 pm, Wed–Fri 9–4:30 pm, Sat–Sun 1–5 pm
Contact: Peter Spooner, Curator
Institution type: Art museum, university museum
Collection type: General textiles
Description: 1960–present. Fiber arts represent a small portion of the fine art in the collection.

Grant County Historical Society
115 Second Street NE
Elbow Lake, MN 56531
Tel: 218-685-4864
www.rootsweb.com/~mngrant/hist.htm

Hours: Mon–Fri 10–12 pm, 1–4 pm
Contact: Patricia Benson, Director and Curator
Institution type: History museum, county museum
Collection type: Clothing, uniforms, general textiles, quilts
Description: 1850–present. Military uniforms, wedding dresses, general clothing, and quilts.
$ 🖐️

United States Hockey Hall of Fame
801 Hat Trick Avenue
Eveleth, MN 55734
Tel: 218-744-5167
www.ushockeyhall.com

Pioneer Museum
304 East Blue Earth Avenue
Fairmont, MN 56031
Tel: 507-235-5178
www.co.martin.mn.us/mchs

Rice County Museum of History
1814 NW 2nd Avenue
Faribault, MN 55021
Tel: 507-332-2121

Pope County Historical Society
809 South Lakeshore Drive
Glenwood, MN 56334
Tel: 320-634-3293
Hours: Tue–Sat 10–5 pm
Contact: Merlin Peterson
Institution type: County museum
Collection type: Clothing, uniforms, costumes, general textiles, flags
Description: 1800–present.
$ 🖐️

Cook County Historical Museum
8 Broadway
Grand Marias, MN 55604
Tel: 218-387-2883

Sibley County Historical Museum
700 Main Street
Henderson, MN 56044
Tel: 507-248-3434
www.history.sibley.mn.us
$ 🖐️

Lincoln County Pioneer Museum
610 West Elm
Hendricks, MN 56136
Tel: 507-275-3537

Hibbing Historical Society and Museum
400 East 23rd Street
Hibbing, MN 55746
Tel: 218-263-8522

Hinckley Fire Museum
106 Old Highway 61
Hinckley, MN 55037
Tel: 320-384-7338

Kittson County History Center Museum
332 East Main Street
Lake Bronson, MN 56734
Tel: 218-754-4100

**Jackson County Historical Society
and Museum**
307 North Highway 86
Lakefield, MN 56150
Tel: 507-662-5505

Meeker County Museum and GAR Hall
308 North Marshall
Litchfield, MN 55355
Tel: 320-693-8911
www.garminnesota.org
Hours: Tue–Sun 12–4 pm
Contact: Cheryl Bulau, Director
Institution type: History museum, historic house, county museum
Collection type: Clothing, uniforms, flags
Description: 1800–1960. Uniforms from Spanish-American War, World War I, World War II, Korean War, Vietnam War, and Gulf War. Holdings include small collection of wedding dresses, 1838–1965, and clothing from pre-1950.
✍🏻

**Charles A. Weyerhaeuser
Memorial Museum**
2151 South Lindbergh Drive
Little Falls, MN 56345
Tel: 320-632-4007

Morrison County Historical Society
2151 Lindbergh Drive South
Little Falls, MN 56345-0239
Tel: 320-632-4007
www.morrisoncountyhistory.org
Hours: Tue–Sat 10–5 pm
Contact: Ann Marie Johnson
Institution type: History museum, county museum
Collection type: Clothing, accessories, uniforms, costumes, general textiles, flags
Description: 1850–present
✍🏻

**Western Hennepin County Pioneers
Association**
1953 West Wayzata Boulevard
Long Lake, MN 55356
Tel: 952-473-6557

Lac Qui Parle County Historical Society
250 8th Avenue South
Madison, MN 56256
Tel: 612-598-7678

Blue Earth County Historical Society
415 East Cherry Street
Mankato, MN 56001
Tel: 507-345-5566
www.rootsweb.com/~mnbechs/welcome.html
Hours: Tue–Sat 10–4 pm
Contact: Jessica Potter
Institution type: History museum, historic house, county museum
Collection type: Clothing, accessories, uniforms, costumes, general textiles, flags
Description: 1800–present. Collection represents Blue Earth County in southern Minnesota and items brought to area by early settlers. Large representation of 1890–1919 adult and children's clothing.
$ ✍🏻

Southwest Minnesota State University
Department of Theater, 1501 State Street
Marshall, MN 56258
Tel: 507-537-6273 Fax: 507-537-7014
www.southwestmsu.edu/thtr
Hours: Vary
Contact: Sheila Tabaka
Institution type: University collection

Collection type: Clothing, costumes
Description: 1900–present. Theatrical costuming includes several interesting items and garments dating to the late 1800s.

Sibley Historic Site
1357 Sibley Memorial Highway
Mendota, MN 55150
Tel: 651-452-1596
www.mnhs.org/places/sites/shs

American Swedish Institute
2600 Park Avenue
Minneapolis, MN 55407
Tel: 612-871-4907
www.americanswedishinst.org

Hennepin History Museum
2303 3rd Avenue South
Minneapolis, MN 55404
Tel: 612-870-1329
www.hhmuseum.org

The Minneapolis Institute of Arts
2400 3rd Avenue South
Minneapolis, MN 55404
Tel: 612-870-3000

Chippewa County Historical Society
151 Pioneer Drive
Montevideo, MN 56265
Tel: 320-269-7636
Hours: Mon–Fri 9–5 pm
Institution type: County museum
$

Clay County Museum
202 1st Avenue North
Moorhead, MN 56560
Tel: 218-299-5520
www.info.co.clay.mn.us/history

Stevens County Historical Society Museum
116 West 6th Street
Morris, MN 56267
Tel: 320-589-1719
Hours: Mon–Fri 9–5 pm
Contact: Joan Boleman, Collections Registrar
Institution type: History museum, historic house, county museum

Collection type: Clothing, accessories, uniforms, general textiles, flags
Description: 1800–present. Museum started as a World War I collection, and now collects Stevens County related items.

Brown County Historical Society Museum
2 North Broadway
New Ulm, MN 56073
Tel: 507-233-2616 Fax: 507-354-1068
www.browncountyhistorymnusa.org
Hours: Mon–Fri 9–4 pm, Sat 1–5 pm (Winter); Mon–Fri 9–4 pm, Sat–Sun 1–5 pm (Summer)
Contact: Pam Krzmarzick
Institution type: History museum, county museum
Collection type: Clothing, accessories
Description: 1800–present. General history collection emphasizes Brown County related materials. Women's clothing from the late 1800s to the early 1900s is the strength.
$

North Star Museum of Boy Scouting and Girl Scouting
2640 East Seventh Avenue
North St. Paul, MN 55109
Tel: 651-748-2880
www.nssm.org

Northfield Historical Society Museum
408 Division Street
Northfield, MN 55057
Tel: 507-645-9268
www.northfieldhistory.org

Owatonna Arts Center
435 Garden View Lane
Owatonna, MN 55060
Tel: 507-451-0533

Pipestone County Museum
113 South Hiawatha Avenue
Pipestone, MN 56164
Tel: 507-825-2563 Fax: 507-825-2563
http://pipestoneminnesota.com/museum
Hours: Mon–Fri 10–5 pm (Memorial Day–Labor Day)
Contact: Susan Hoskins
Institution type: History museum

Collection type: Clothing, accessories, uniforms, costumes, general textiles, flags
Description: 1850–present.

$

Goodhue County Historical Society

1166 Oak Street
Red Wing, MN 55418
Tel: 651-388-6024 Fax: 651-388-3577
www.goodhuehistory.mus.mn.us
Hours: Tue–Fri 10–5 pm, Sat–Sun 1–5 pm
Contact: Char Henn
Institution type: History museum, county museum
Collection type: Clothing, accessories, uniforms, general textiles, quilts
Description: 1850–present. More than 150,000 artifacts and photos detailing county history from its prehistory to the present. Special exhibits reflect the wide variety of items in collection.

$

Redwood County Historical Society

33965 Laser Avenue
Redwood Falls, MN 56283
Tel: 507-637-3329

Olmsted County Historical Society

1195 West Circle Drive SW
Rochester, MN 55902
Tel: 507-282-9447
www.olmstedhistory.com

Roseau County Historical Museum and Research Center

307 Third Avenue NW
Roseau, MN 56751
Tel: 218-463-1918
www.roseaucohistoricalsociety.org

St. Cloud State University

ANTIQUES CLOSET
720 4th Avenue South
St. Cloud, MN 56301
Tel: 320-308-2223
www.stcloudstate.edu/default.asp
Hours: Mon–Fri 8–5 pm, studio during school year only
Contact: Costume studio supervisor
Institution type: University collection

Collection type: Clothing, accessories
Description: 1850–1960. Study collection is mostly items acquired by a former faculty member, Harvey Jurek.

Dress, Elsa Schiaparelli Fall 1938 Collection. Courtesy of The Goldstein Museum of Design.

The Goldstein Museum of Design, University of Minnesota

244 McNeal Hall, 1985 Buford
St. Paul, MN 55108
Tel: 612-624-7434 Fax: 612-624-2750
http://goldstein.che.umn.edu
Hours: Mon–Wed 10–4 pm, Thu 10–8 pm, Sat–Sun 1:30–4:30 pm
Contact: Marilyn Delong; Kathleen Campbell
Institution type: University museum
Collection type: Clothing, accessories, general textiles
Description: 1760–present. Historic and ethnic apparel, twentieth-century designer fashion, accessories, and Euro-American and ethnic textiles.

Minnesota Historical Society

345 Kellogg Boulevard West
St. Paul, MN 55102
Tel: 651-297-8094 Fax: 651-297-2967
www.mnhs.org
Hours: Tue 12–8 pm, Wed–Sat 9–8 pm
Contact: Linda McShannock
Institution type: History museum, state museum
Collection type: Clothing, accessories, costumes, general textiles, quilts

Description: 1800–present. More than 25,000 objects reflect occupational dress, sports clothing, formal wear, special occasion, and everyday clothing and accessories. Collection includes Munsingwear knitwear, St. Paul Winter Carnival sportswear, governors' wives' gowns, farm clothing, jewelry, shoes, military apparel, and general store merchandise representing Minnesota's apparel manufacturers, tailors, seamstresses, dressmakers, and fiber artists.

Nicollet County Historical Society
Treaty Site History Center
1851 North Minnesota Avenue
St. Peter, MN 56082
Tel: 507-934-2160
www.tourism.st-
   peter.mn.us/sections/history.php
Hours: Tue–Sat 10–4 pm, Sun 1–4 pm

The Historic W. H. C. Folsom House Museum
272 West Government Road
Taylors Falls, MN 55084
Tel: 651-465-3125

Laura Ingalls Wilder Museum and Tourist Center
330 8th Street
Walnut Grove, MN 56180
Tel: 507-859-2358
www.walnutgrove.org

Waseca County Historical Society
315 2nd Avenue NE
Waseca, MN 56093
Tel: 507-835-7700
www.historical.waseca.mn.us

Cottonwood County Historical Society
812 4th Avenue
Windom, MN 56101
Tel: 507-831-1134 Fax: 507-831-2665
Hours: Mon–Fri 8–4 pm
Contact: Linda Fransen
Institution type: Art museum, history museum, county museum
Collection type: Clothing, uniforms, general textiles, flags
Description: 1850–present. Strengths include wedding dresses, baptism and confirmation clothing, and military uniforms.

Winnebago Area Museum
18 1st Avenue NE
Winnebago, MN 56098
Tel: 507-893-4660
Hours: Tue–Fri, hours vary per day
Collection type: Clothing, accessories, uniforms, general textiles, quilts, flags
Institution type: History museum, historic house, city museum
Description: 1850–present. Quilts from the prairie; World War I and World War II uniforms; hats; and vintage clothing, including wedding dresses and suits.

Nobles County Historical Society
407 12th Street, Suite 2
Worthington, MN 56187
Tel: 507-376-4431

MISSISSIPPI

Wedding dress, circa 1870. Courtesy of Amory Regional Museum.

Amory Regional Museum

715 South 3rd Street
Amory, MS 38821
Tel: 662-256-2761 Fax: 662-256-2761
www.amoryms.us
Hours: Tue–Fri 9–5 pm, Sat–Sun 1–5 pm
Contact: Lynn Millender
Institution type: History museum, city museum
Collection type: Clothing, uniforms, general textiles
Description: 1850–present. Military uniforms; baby clothes of the Depression era and earlier; and skirts, dresses, and blouses of the early 1900s. Two collections of note are the Lottie Trapp Collection of 46 textile items and the Myrtle Mayfield Collection of 143 items, including clothing and household textiles.

The Ethel Wright Mohomed Stitchery Museum

307 Central
Belzoni, MS 39038
Tel: 601-960-1457
www.mamasdreamworld.com
Hours: By appointment only
$

Beauvoir, the Jefferson Davis Home and Presidential Library

2244 Beach Boulevard
Biloxi, MS 39531
Tel: 228-388-9074
www.beauvoir.org

Mardi Gras Museum

119 Rue Magnolia
Biloxi, MS 39530
Tel: 228-435-6245

Delta Blues Museum

#1 Blues Alley
Clarksdale, MS 38614
Tel: 662-627-6820
www.deltabluesmuseum.org

Northeast Mississippi Museum

204 East 4th Street
Corinth, MS 38834
Tel: 662-287-3120

Holly Springs

Corinth

55

Clarksdale

Amory

Greenwood

Starkville

Belzoni

Jackson (3) ⭐

Meridian

20

Port Gibson

Taylorsville

Washington

Natchez

55

59

Biloxi (2)

10

Population

- •   0 - 50,000
- •   50,001 - 100,000
- ●   100,001 - 250,000
- ●   250,001 - 500,000
- ●   > 500,000
- ☆   State Capital

CSA Region VI Southeast

KY   WV   VA

AR   TN   NC

SC

LA   AL   GA

FL

Cottonlandia Museum

1608 Highway 82 West
Greenwood, MS 38930
Tel: 662-453-0925

Marshall County Historical Museum

111 Van Doren Avenue
Holly Springs, MS 38635
Tel: 601-252-3669

Manship House Museum

420 East Fortification Street
Jackson, MS 39202
Tel: 601-961-4724 Fax: 601-354-6043
www.mdah.state.ms.us/museum/manship.html
Hours: Tue–Fri 9–4 pm, Sat 10–4 pm
Contact: Jean Schott
Institution type: History museum, state museum
Collection type: General textiles
Description: 1800–1899. Collection includes nineteenth-century furnishings and decorative arts.

Museum of the Southern Jewish Experience

4915 I-55 North, Suite 204B
Jackson, MS 39206
Tel: 601-362-6357 Fax: 601-366-6293
www.msje.org/museum.html
Hours: By appointment
Contact: Macy B. Hart, CEO
Institution type: Art museum, history museum
Collection type: Clothing, costumes, general textiles, quilts
Description: 1850–present. Textile objects from clothing to quilts to Judaica from Jewish communities in the twelve states between Texas and Virginia.

$

Old Capital Museum of Mississippi History

100 South State Street
Jackson, MS 39205
Tel: 601-359-6920
www.mdah.state.ms.us/museum
Hours: Mon–Fri 8–5 pm
Contact: M. Wright
Institution type: History museum
Collection type: Clothing, uniforms, costumes, general textiles, quilts, flags

Description: 1781–1960. More than 970 objects from the state of Mississippi or surrounding states. Collection includes 200 quilts and Confederate flags, uniforms, and other textiles.

Jimmie Rodgers Museum

1725 Jimmie Rodgers Drive
Meridian, MS 39304
Tel: 601-485-1808

Rosalie Mansion

100 Orleans Street
Natchez, MS 39120
Tel: 601-445-4555
www.rosaliemansion.com

Grand Gulf Military State Park Museum

12006 Grand Gulf Road
Port Gibson, MS 39150
Tel: 601-437-2929
www.grandgulfpark.state.ms.us

Oktibbeha County Heritage Museum

206 Fellowship Street
Starkville, MS 39759
Tel: 601-323-0211

Watkins Museum

Eureka Street
Taylorsville, MS 39168
Tel: 601-785-9816

Historic Jefferson College

Highway 61
Washington, MS 39190
Tel: 601-442-2901 Fax: 601-442-2902
www.mdah.state.ms.us/hprop/hjc.html
Hours: Mon–Sat 9–5 pm, Sun 1–5 pm
Contact: Anne Gray, Historian II
Institution type: State museum
Collection type: Accessories, uniforms
Description: 1850–present. Uniforms and accessories relating to Jefferson Military College, including hats, caps, medals with ribbons, and patches dating from 1893 to 1964.

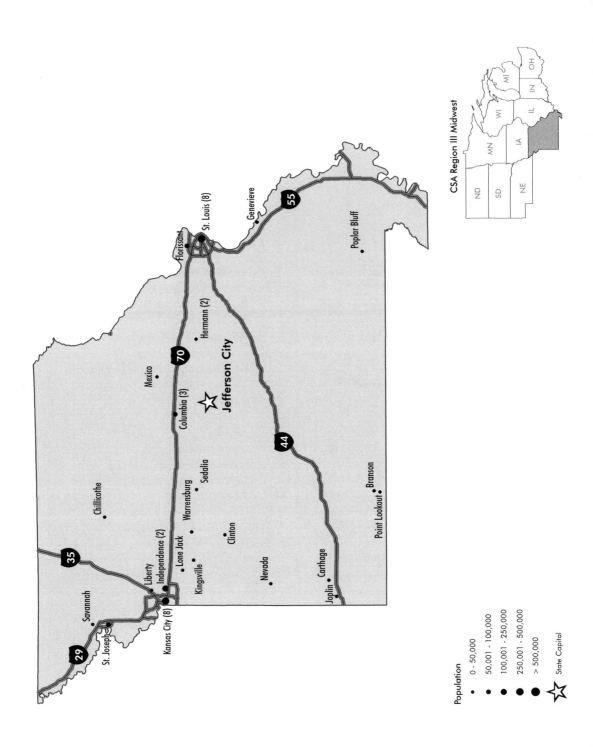

CSA Region III Midwest

Population
• 0 - 50,000
• 50,001 - 100,000
● 100,001 - 250,000
● 250,001 - 500,000
● > 500,000
☆ State Capital

MISSOURI

The Roy Rogers-Dale Evans Museum and Theater

3950 Green Mountain Drive
Branson, MO 65616
Tel: 417-339-1900
www.royrogers.com/museum-index.html

Powers Museum

1617 West Oak
Carthage, MO 64836
Tel: 417-358-2667 Fax: 417-359-9627
www.powersmuseum.com
Hours: Tue–Sat 11–4 pm (Mar–May, mid-Oct–mid-Dec); Tue–Sat 11–5 pm, Sun 1:30–4:30 pm (Jun–mid-Oct)
Contact: Michele Hansford
Institution type: City museum
Collection type: Clothing, accessories, uniforms, costumes, general textiles, quilts, flags
Description: 1850–present. Strengths are in twentieth-century women's clothing, fashion accessories, bed coverings, and household textiles used or created in Carthage, Missouri. Majority of items are from one local family and include music performance costumes and related items. Holdings include photographic collection with fashion images, 1840s–1950s.
$ ✍🏻

The Grand River Historical Society and Museum

1401 Forest Drive
Chillicothe, MO 64601
Tel: 660-646-3430

Henry County Museum and Cultural Arts Center

203 West Franklin Street
Clinton, MO 64735
Tel: 660-885-8414

Museum of Art and Archaeology, University of Missouri–Columbia

University Avenue and 9th Street,
1 Pickard Hall
Columbia, MO 65211
Tel: 573-882-3591 Fax: 573-884-4039
www.mumaa.missouri.edu
http://maa.missouri.edu/education/academic.html
Hours: Tue–Fri 9–4 pm, Sat–Sun 12–4 pm
Institution type: Art museum, university museum
✍🏻
COPTIC TEXTILES AND
PRE-COLUMBIAN TEXTILES
Contact: Benton Kidd
Collection type: General textiles
Description: Pre-1700. 36 ancient Coptic textile fragments and 158 pre-Columbian textiles and fragments.
EUROPEAN TAPESTRIES
Contact: Joan Stack
Collection type: General textiles
Description: Pre-1700–present. 3 European tapestries.
CHINESE AND JAPANESE ROBES,
INDONESIAN TEXTILES
Contact: Jeff Wilcox, Registrar
Collection type: General textiles

Description: Pre-1700–present. Two separate collections include 65 Chinese and Japanese robes and 13 Indonesian textiles.

Wedding dress designed by Mary McFadden, 1985. Courtesy of Stephens College.

Western wear, circa 1980s. Courtesy of University of Missouri–Columbia.

University of Missouri–Columbia
HISTORIC COSTUME AND TEXTILE COLLECTION
137 Stanley Hall
Columbia, MO 65211
Tel: 573-882-7317 Fax: 573-882-3289
http://web.missouri.edu/~tam/coll_home.htm
Hours: By appointment
Contact: Laurel E. Wilson
Institution type: University collection
Collection type: Clothing, accessories, uniforms, general textiles, quilts
Description: 1800–present. Men's garments and accessories used by prominent and ordinary Missourians. Unusually rare are 3 pairs of men's long underwear from the nineteenth century. Collection also contains 58 quilts made over the course of one hundred years by three generations of one farm family; everyday clothing from the 1930s and 1940s; designer garments and accessories from the 1930s through the 1980s; "Mother Hubbards"; household textiles such as nineteenth-century bed coverings; and ethnographic pieces.

Florissant Valley Historical Society
1896 South Florissant Road
Florissant, MO 63031
Tel: 314-524-1100
Hours: Sun 12–5 pm, and by appointment
Contact: Mary Kay Gladbach
Institution type: History museum

Stephens College, Costume Research Library
1200 East Broadway
Columbia, MO 65215
Tel: 573-876-7218
Hours: By appointment
Contact: Monica Phillippe McMurry
Institution type: University collection
Collection type: Clothing, accessories
Description: 1850–1960. Dress of American designers and women is central to the mission of the Stephens College Costume Research Library in Columbia, Missouri. Begun in 1958, the Costume Research Library now showcases nearly 12,000 artifacts of vernacular dress.

Collection type: Clothing, accessories
Description: 1850–1960. A century of wedding dresses, graduation dresses, some children's clothing, Halloween costumes, and hats.

✍🏻

National Society of the Colonial Dames of America in Missouri

1165 Main Street
Genevieve, MO 63670-1630
Tel: 575-883-3105
Hours: Mon–Sun 11–4 pm
Contact: Lorraine Stange
Institution type: History museum, historic house
Description: 1760–1799. The house and clothing and textiles collection are in a French colonial style.

$ ✍🏻

Deutschheim State Historic Site

109 West 2nd Street
Hermann, MO 65041
Tel: 573-486-2200
www.mostateparks.com/deutschheim.htm

Historic Hermann Museum

312 Schiller Street
Hermann, MO 65041
Tel: 573-486-2017
www.hermannmissouri.com

Shoes, white suede and brown alligator, 1949. Courtesy of Harry S. Truman National Historic Site.

Harry S. Truman National Historic Site

223 North Main Street
Independence, MO 64050
Tel: 816-254-2720 Fax: 816-254-4491
www.nps.gov/hstr
Hours: Tue–Sun 8:30–5 pm (Labor Day–Memorial Day)
Contact: Carol J. Dage

Institution type: Historic house, federal museum
Collection type: Clothing, accessories, general textiles
Description: 1900–1980. Clothing and accessories from the Truman family, with emphasis on Harry Truman's clothing from 1930 to 1970. Garments include suits, pants, dress shirts, sport shirts, pajamas, and dressing gowns. Limited number of garments belonging to Bess and Margaret Truman, including dresses and formal gowns. Accessories include hats, shoes, belts, canes, socks, and handkerchiefs. Household textiles include bedding and window and floor coverings.

$ ✍🏻

National Frontier Trails Museum

318 West Pacific
Independence, MO 64050
Tel: 816-325-7575
www.ci.independence.mo.us/nftm

Cole County Historical Society

GOWNS OF THE FIRST LADIES OF MISSOURI
109 Madison Street
Jefferson City, MO 65101
Tel: 573-635-1850
Hours: Mon–Thu 8:30–2:30 pm
Contact: Anne Gue; Gerri Rozier
Institution type: History museum, historic house, county museum
Collection type: Clothing, accessories
Description: 1800–present.

$ ✍🏻

Dorothea B. Hoover Historical Museum

504 Schifferdecker
Joplin, MO 64802
Tel: 417-623-1180
www.joplinmuseum.org/about.htm

The American Jazz Museum

1616 East 18th Street
Kansas City, MO 64108
Tel: 816-474-8463
www.americanjazzmuseum.com

American Royal Museum and Visitors Center

1701 American Royal Court
Kansas City, MO 64102

Tel: 816-221-9800
www.americanroyal.com

Arabia Steamboat Museum
400 Grand Boulevard
Kansas City, MO 64106
Tel: 816-471-1856 Fax: 816-471-1616
www.1856.com
Hours: Mon–Sat 10–5:30 pm, Sun 12–5 pm
Contact: Greg Hawley
Institution type: History museum
Collection type: Clothing, accessories, general textiles
Description: 1850–1899. On September 5, 1856, the Steamboat Arabia was en route with goods for general stores in Iowa and Nebraska, and the boat sank. On board were 5,000 shoes (950 on display), coats, pants, socks, and bolts of fabric.
$ ✍

John Wornall House Museum
6115 Wornall Road
Kansas City, MO 64113
Tel: 816-444-1858
www.wornallhouse.org

Liberty Memorial Museum of World War I
100 West 26th Street
Kansas City, MO 64108
Tel: 816-784-1918 Fax: 816-784-1929
www.libertymemorialmuseum.org
Hours: Tue–Sun 10–5 pm
Contact: Doran L. Cart, Curator
Institution type: History museum, city museum
Collection type: Accessories, uniforms
Description: 1914–1919. 175,000 items exclusive to WWI. Strengths include uniforms, weapons, accoutrements, posters, documents, and photographs.
$ ✍

The Nelson-Atkins Museum of Art
4525 Oak Street
Kansas City, MO 64111
Tel: 816-561-4000
www.nelson-atkins.org

Piper Memorial Medical Museum
St. Joseph Health Center
1000 Carondelet Drive
Kansas City, MO 64114
Tel: 816-943-2183 Fax: 816-943-2796
Hours: Mon–Sun 8–8 pm
Contact: Joan Hilger-Mullen
Institution type: History museum
Collection type: Clothing, accessories, uniforms, flags
Description: 1900–present. Medical uniforms from two Catholic hospitals in Kansas City. Collection includes nursing sister's habit (1950s); student nurse uniforms (1910–1960); nurses' capes (1930–1960); nurses' caps (1910–1960); nurses' shoes (1910); surgical scrub suit (1990s); canvas straitjacket (1950s); and silk "Sodality of Mary" banner (1940s).
✍

Ensemble of Country and Western singers Kit and Kay, circa 1937–1942. Courtesy of Union Station Kansas City.

Union Station Kansas City
30 West Pershing Road
Kansas City, MO 64108
Tel: 816-460-2052 Fax: 816-460-2260
www.unionstation.org
Hours: Mon–Sun 10–5 pm (Winter); 10–6 pm (Summer)
$ ✍

KANSAS CITY MUSEUM CLOTHING AND ACCESSORIES COLLECTION

Contact: Denise Morrison

Collection type: Clothing, accessories, uniforms, costumes

Description: 1800–present. Historical artifacts that tell the story of Kansas City and its inhabitants. Large clothing and textile collection with more than 10,000 items includes men's, women's, and children's clothing and accessories.

KANSAS CITY MUSEUM QUILT COLLECTION

Contact: Anne Jones, Collections Manager

Collection type: Quilts

Description: 1760–1960. Collection contains quilt styles, from the fancy show pieces to utilitarian quilts, from the eighteenth century to the early twentieth century. Examples of nineteenth-century appliqué and pieced and appliquéd quilts with provenance. Quilts include a Star of Bethlehem with flags quilt (1852), a blue and white pieced Sawtooth (1840–1865), crazy quilt with fans (1880–1910), and an embroidered World War I commemorative quilt (1917–1918).

KANSAS CITY MUSEUM SAMPLERS

Collection type: General textiles

Description: 1760–present. Sampler collection shows the variety of styles utilized by women over a two-hundred-year span. Examples include young girls' first endeavors to pictorials made by experienced hands. Other items include Berlin work and samplers worked on Bristol board.

Nance Museum and Library of Antiquity

497 NW 2001st Road
Kingsville, MO 64061
Tel: 816-697-2526

Clay County Historical Museum

14 North Main
Liberty, MO 64068
Tel: 816-792-1849

Civil War Museum of Lonejack, Jackson County

301 South Bynum Road
Lone Jack, MO 64070
Tel: 816-697-8833

Audrain Historical Museum, Graceland

501 South Muldrow
Mexico, MO 65265
Tel: 573-581-3910
www.audrain.org

Bushwhacker Museum

231 North Main Street
Nevada, MO 64772
Tel: 417-667-9602
www.bushwhacker.org

The Ralph Foster Museum

College of the Ozarks, 1 Cultural Court
Point Lookout, MO 65726
Tel: 417-334-6411
www.rfostermuseum.com

Margaret Harwell Art Museum

421 North Main Street
Poplar Bluff, MO 63901
Tel: 573-686-8002
www.mham.org

Andrew County Museum and Historical Society

202 East Duncan Drive
Savannah, MO 64485
Tel: 816-324-4720
www.savannahmo.net/museums.html

Pettis County Historical Society

311 West 3rd
Sedalia, MO 65301
Tel: 660-826-1314

The Albrecht-Kemper Museum of Art

2818 Frederick Avenue
St. Joseph, MO 64506
Tel: 816-233-7003
www.albrecht-kemper.org

Campbell House Museum

1508 Locust Street
St. Louis, MO 63103
Tel: 314-421-0325 Fax: 314-421-0113
http://stlouis.missouri.org/501c/chm
Hours: Wed–Sat 10–4 pm, Sun 12–4 pm
Contact: Andy Hahn
Institution type: Art museum, history museum, historic house

Collection type: Clothing, accessories, general textiles

Description: 1850–1960.

$

Chatillon-DeMenil Mansion

3352 DeMenil Place
St. Louis, MO 63118
Tel: 314-771-5828
www.chatillondemenilhouse.com

Eugene Field House and St. Louis Toy Museum

634 South Broadway
St. Louis, MO 63102
Tel: 314-421-4689
www.eugenefieldhouse.org

International Bowling Museum and Hall of Fame

111 Stadium Plaza
St. Louis, MO 63102
Tel: 314-231-6340
www.bowlingmuseum.com

Jefferson Barracks Historic Site

533 Grant Road
St. Louis, MO 63125
Tel: 314-544-5714
www.co.st-louis.mo.us/parks/j-b.html

Missouri Historical Society

5700 Lindell Boulevard
St. Louis, MO 63112
Tel: 314-746-4599
www.mohistory.org

Hours: Wed–Mon 10–6 pm, Tue 10–8 pm

Contact: Shannon Berry

Institution type: History museum

Collection type: Clothing, accessories, uniforms, costumes, general textiles, quilts, flags

Description: 1760–present. More than 16,000 pieces of clothing and textiles, dating from the late eighteenth century to the present, including men's, women's, and children's clothing and accessories. Strengths include women's clothing and accessories (especially late nineteenth to early twentieth century), St. Louis designers and manufacturers, Veiled Prophet gowns, quilts, and Missouri related military uniforms and flags.

Samuel Cupples House of St. Louis University

221 North Grand Boulevard
St. Louis, MO 63103
Tel: 314-977-3575
www.slu.edu/the_arts/cupples

St. Louis Art Museum

#1 Fine Arts Drive
St. Louis, MO 63110
Tel: 314-721-0072 Fax: 314-721-6172
www.stlouis.art.museum

Hours: Tue–Sat 10–5 pm

Contact: Zoe Perkins

Institution type: City museum

Collection type: General textiles

Description: Pre-1700–present. Flat textile collection includes pre-Columbian to contemporary fiber art.

Saudi Arabian woman's headdress with beadwork and coins, twentieth century. Courtesy of Central Missouri State University Archives and Museum.

Central Missouri State University Archives and Museum

Kirkpatrick Library Room 1470
Warrensburg, MO 64093
Tel: 660-543-4649
www.cmsu.edu/archmusm

Hours: Mon–Fri 8–4 pm (during semester)

Institution type: University museum

HAYMAKER COLLECTION

Contact: Amber R. Clifford

Collection type: Clothing, accessories, costumes, general textiles

Description: 1850–present. Costumes and textiles

from Guatemala and neighboring Central American countries, including complete indigenous Guatemalan costumes, traditional textiles and accessories, and fabric dolls.

NANCE ASIAN COLLECTION

Contact: Amber R. Clifford

Collection type: Clothing, accessories, costumes

Description: 1900–present. Southeast Asian costumes, textiles, and accessories, including Sri Lankan and Indonesian puppets and masks, Chinese and Indian fabrics, and a large collection of batiks from Sri Lanka.

NANCE MIDDLE EASTERN COLLECTION

Contact: Amber R. Clifford

Collection type: Clothing, accessories, costumes, general textiles, flags

Description: 1900–present. Middle Eastern costumes and textiles, focusing on Saudi Arabian and Bedouin cultures collected from 1945 to 1983 on site. Collection also includes traditional costumes and clothing, Bedouin weaving, and a complete Bedouin tent.

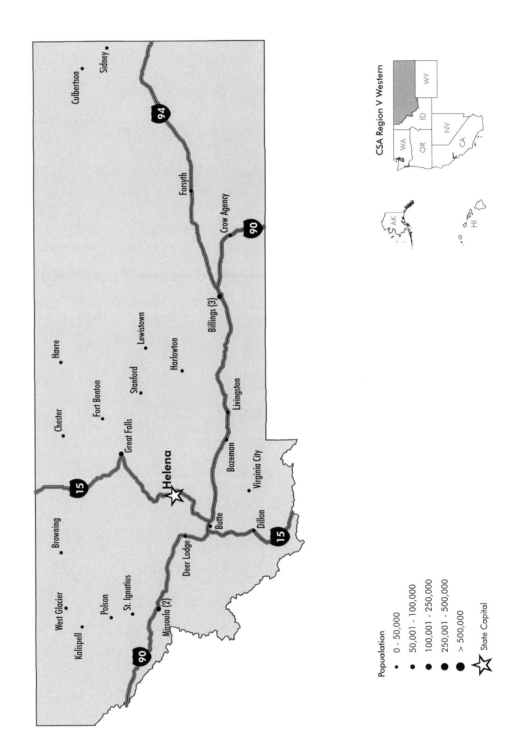

Population

- 0 - 50,000
- 50,001 - 100,000
- 100,001 - 250,000
- 250,001 - 500,000
- > 500,000
☆ State Capital

CSA Region V Western

MONTANA

Moss Mansion Historic House Museum
914 Division Street
Billings, MT 59101
Tel: 406-256-5100 Fax: 406-252-0091
www.mossmansion.com
Hours: Vary by season
Contact: Karen Wegner, Registrar
Institution type: Historic house, city museum
Collection type: Clothing, accessories, uniforms, general textiles, flags
Description: 1850–1914. Original items belonging to P. B. Moss family, including draperies, bedding, clothing and accessories, and uniforms used and worn by the family at the turn of the century.
$ ✍

Peter Yegen Jr. Yellowstone County Museum
1950 Terminal Circle
Billings, MT 59105
Tel: 406-256-6811

Western Heritage Center
2822 Montana Avenue
Billings, MT 59101
Tel: 406-256-6809
www.ywhc.org

Museum of the Rockies
CAROLINE MCGILL TEXTILE AND
HISTORY COLLECTION
600 West Kagy Boulevard
Bozeman, MT 59717

Bolero vest and culottes, saddle-tan leather, circa 1935. Courtesy of Museum of the Rockies.

Tel: 406-994-6622 Fax: 406-994-2682
www.museumoftherockies.org
Hours: Mon–Sat 9–5 pm, Sun 12:30–5 pm (Winter); Mon–Sun 8–8 pm (Summer)
Contact: Margaret Woods, Textile Curator; Amy McKune, Collections Manager
Institution type: History museum, university museum
Collection type: Clothing, accessories, uniforms, costumes, general textiles, quilts
Description: 1850–1960. Collection documents the culture, social life, and economy of early settlement and growth in the northern Rockies. Collection includes men's, women's, children's clothing; military and nursing uniforms; ritual, cowboy, and cowboy-related clothing; tailored,

ready-to-wear, and handmade items; accessories; and household linens, rugs, quilts, and bedspreads. The collection documents the stratification of society with objects from affluent and less affluent households.

$ ✍

Museum of the Plains Indian

Junction of Highway 2 and 89 West
Browning, MT 59417
Tel: 406-338-2230
www.iacb.doi.gov/museums/museum_plains.html

Arts Chateau Museum

321 West Broadway
Butte, MT 59701
Tel: 406-723-7600
www.artschateau.org
http://goldwest.visitmt.com/listings/3143.htm

Liberty County Museum

2nd Street East and Madison
Chester, MT 59522
Tel: 406-759-5256

Little Bighorn Battlefield National Monument

I-90 and Highway 212
Crow Agency, MT 59022-0039
Tel: 406-638-2621
www.nps.gov/libi

Culbertson Museum

Highway 2 East
Culbertson, MT 59218-0095
Tel: 406-787-6320

Grant-Kohrs Ranch National Historic Site

266 Warren Lane
Deer Lodge, MT 59722
Tel: 406-846-2070
www.nps.gov/grko

Beaverhead County Museum

15 South Montana
Dillon, MT 59725-2433
Tel: 406-683-5027

Rosebud County Pioneer Museum

1335 Main Street
Forsyth, MT 59327
Tel: 406-356-7547

Museum of the Northern Great Plains

1205 20th Street
Fort Benton, MT 59442
Tel: 406-622-5316

Cascade County Historical Museum and Society

422 2nd Street South
Great Falls, MT 59405
Tel: 406-452-3462
www.highplainsheritage.org

Upper Musselshell Museum

11 South Central
Harlowton, MT 59036
Tel: 406-632-5519
www.harlowtonmuseum.com

H. Earl Clack Museum

Holiday Village Mall
Havre, MT 59501
Tel: 406-265-4000 Fax: 406-265-5487
Hours: Tue–Sat 10–5 pm (Summer); Tue–Sat 1–5 pm (Winter)
Contact: Emily Mayer Lossing, Manager
Institution type: History museum, county museum
Collection type: Clothing, accessories, uniforms, flags
Description: 1850–present. Victorian clothing and military uniforms.

Montana Historical Society

225 North Roberts
Helena, MT 59620
Tel: 406-444-2694 Fax: 406-444-2696
www.montanahistoricalsociety.org
Hours: Tue–Sat 9–5 pm, Thu 9–8 pm
Contact: George Oberft, Curator of Historical Collections
Institution type: Art museum, history museum, state museum
Collection type: Costumes, general textiles
Description: 1850–present. 3,000 costume related items, all Montana related, dating primarily 1880 through the 1950s. Collection includes items of Euro-American and Chinese American origin.

$ ✍

Beaded buckskin dress, Blackfeet, circa 1880–1890. Courtesy of Montana Historical Society.

Dress, pink linen, circa 1910. Courtesy of Historical Museum at Fort Missoula.

Conrad Mansion Museum

Woodland Avenue, between 3rd and 4th
  Streets
Kalispell, MT 59903
Tel: 406-755-2166 Fax: 406-755-2176
www.conradmansion.com
Hours: Mon–Sun 10–6 pm (May 15–Oct 15)
Contact: Teri Florman, Manager
Institution type: History museum, historic house,
  city museum
Collection type: Clothing
Description: 1850–present.
$

Central Montana Historical Association Museum

408 NE Main Street
Lewistown, MT 59457
Tel: 406-538-5436

Yellowstone Gateway Museum of Park County

118 West Chinook
Livingston, MT 59047
Tel: 406-222-4184
www.livingstonmuseums.org

Historical Museum at Fort Missoula

Building 322 Fort Missoula
Missoula, MT 59804
Tel: 406-728-3476 Fax: 406-543-6277
www.fortmissoulamuseum.org

Hours: Mon–Sat 10–5 pm, Sun 12–5 pm
  (Summer); Tue–Sun 12–5 pm (Winter)
Contact: L. J. Richards, Senior Curator
Institution type: History museum, historic house,
  county museum
Collection type: Clothing, general textiles
Description: 1850–present. More than 2,000
  items, mostly from Montana. Majority of
  clothing is from the 1880s to the 1970s, male
  and female, adults and children. Collection
  includes flat pieces, 1880s–1960s. The 1920s
  are well represented.
$

Missoula Art Museum

335 North Pattee
Missoula, MT 59802
Tel: 406-728-0447 Fax: 406-543-8691
www.missoulaartmuseum.org
Hours: Tue–Fri 10–6 pm, Sat 10–3 pm
Contact: Jennifer Reifsneider, Registrar
Institution type: Art museum
Collection type: General textiles
Description: 1961–present. Collection focuses on
  art that is relevant to the culture of the Amer-
  ican West, with an emphasis on contemporary
  Montana artists. Textiles include the work of
  Hmong immigrant community and artists
  such as Lela Autio, Dana Boussard, Nancy
  Erickson, and Miriam Schapiro.

Quilts, nineteenth and twentieth centuries. Courtesy of Miracle of America Museum.

Miracle of America Museum

58176 U.S. Highway 93
Polson, MT 59860
Tel: 406-883-6804
www.cyberport.net/museum
Hours: Mon–Sun 8–8 pm (Summer); Mon–Sat
8–5 pm, Sun 1–5 pm (non-Summer)
Contact: Joanne Mangels
Institution type: History museum
Collection type: Clothing, accessories, uniforms,
general textiles, flags
Description: 1850–present. Several hundred textile objects, from hand-woven rugs to bonnets;
quilts (44) made from materials as diverse as
flour sacks and silks; and more than 150 items
of clothing, including a late-1800s bustle wedding dress, flapper dresses, sports clothes,
swimsuits, motorcycle gear, children's wear, and
men's clothing from nightshirts to tuxedos.
Accessories include hats, gloves, shoes, and
bags. Native American wear includes buckskin
outfits, dancing regalia, glove bags, and moccasins. Holdings include more than 200 military uniforms.
$ 🖐

Mondak Heritage Center

120 3rd Avenue SE
Sidney, MT 59270
Tel: 406-433-3500

Judith Basin County Museum

19 3rd South
Stanford, MT 59479
Tel: 406-566-2974

Flathead Indian Museum

1 Museum Lane
St. Ignatius, MT 59865
Tel: 406-745-2951

Montana Heritage Commission

STATE OF MONTANA VIRGINIA CITY
COLLECTIONS
300 West Wallace Street
Virginia City, MT 59755
Tel: 406-843-5441 Fax: 406-843-5447
www.montanaheritagecommission.com
Hours: Mon–Sun 8–7 pm (Summer); Mon–Fri
8–5 pm (Winter)
Contact: Janna Hermanson, Curator
Institution type: History museum, historic house,
state museum
Collection type: Clothing, accessories, uniforms,
costumes, general textiles, flags
Description: 1850–1960. Costume, textiles, and
objects of personal adornment are part of a collection of more than 1 million objects housed
in seventy-five historic buildings. Costume
material is representative of fashionable and
adaptive clothing worn in the Rocky Mountain
West. Two-thirds may be original to the Virginia City area with the bulk dating from 1875
to 1940. Early-twentieth-century corsets in
original packaging; store stock (unworn, store
tags still on) men's and boy's suits, coats, and
short pants, circa 1880–1915; store stock
women's and children's thermal underwear,
1880–1920; women's shoes, circa 1920–1935;
and ribbons, buttons, and other notions,
1870–1930, in original packaging.
🖐

Glacier National Park Museum

Glacier National Park
West Glacier, MT 59936
Tel: 406-888-7936

NEBRASKA

Brown County Historical Society
456 Old Highway 7
Ainsworth, NE 69210
Tel: 402-387-2061
Hours: Mon–Thu 11–4 pm
Contact: Carol Larson, Secretary
Institution type: History museum
Collection type: Clothing, accessories, uniforms, general textiles, quilts, flags
Description: 1850–present. Local history collection includes household tools, clothing, and textiles; genealogical files; pioneer objects; and documents.

Knight Museum
908 Yellowstone
Alliance, NE 69301
Tel: 308-762-2384
www.cityofalliance.net

Plainsman Museum
210 16th Street
Aurora, NE 68818
Tel: 402-694-6531
www.plainsmanmuseum.org

Gage County Historical Society and Museum
101 North 2nd
Beatrice, NE 68310
Tel: 402-228-1679
www.beatricene.com/gagecountymuseum

Hours: Tue–Fri 9–12 pm, 1–5 pm, Sat 9–12 pm, Sun 1:30–5 pm (Memorial Day–Labor Day)
Contact: Rita Clawson, Curator
Institution type: History museum
Collection type: Clothing, accessories, uniforms, costumes, general textiles
Description: 1850–present. Clothing relates to the history of Gage County, composed of costumes and textiles collected locally from 1860 to 1960. Strengths are wedding dresses (52), headwear (242), footwear (107), and women's dresses (150). Collection also includes children's items (161), men's items (67), underwear (113), miscellaneous (303), accessories (342), and textiles (176).

Furnas-Gosper Historical Society and Museum
401 Nebraska Avenue
Beaver City, NE 68922
Tel: 308-268-2208

Dundy County Historical Society
522 Arapahoe
Benkelman, NE 69021
Tel: 308-423-2750

Brownville Historical Society Museum
Main Street
Brownville, NE 68321
Tel: 402-825-6001

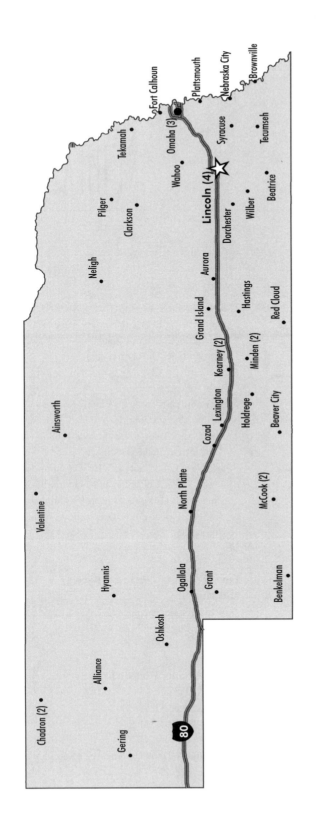

Chadron (2)

Gering

80

Alliance

Hyannis

Valentine

Oshkosh

Ogallala

Grant

Benkelman

North Platte

McCook (2)

Ainsworth

Cozad

Lexington

Holdrege

Beaver City

Kearney (2)

Minden (2)

Grand Island

Hastings

Red Cloud

Neligh

Aurora

Dorchester

Wilber

Beatrice

Pilger

Clarkson

Lincoln (4)

Syracuse

Tecumseh

Tekamah

Wahoo

Omaha (3)

Fort Calhoun

Plattsmouth

Nebraska City

Brownville

Population

· 0 - 50,000

• 50,001 - 100,000

● 100,001 - 250,000

● 250,001 - 500,000

● > 500,000

☆ State Capital

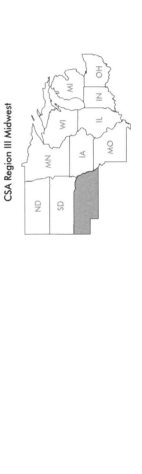

CSA Region III Midwest

Dawes County Historical Museum

341 Country Club Road
Chadron, NE 69337
Tel: 308-432-4999
www.chadron.com/memberpages/dchm
Hours: Mon–Sat 10–4 pm (Memorial Day–Sep)
Contact: Belvadine Lecher
Institution type: History museum
Collection type: Clothing, accessories, uniforms, costumes, general textiles, quilts, flags
Description: 1850–present. Wedding gowns from 1868 to 1961, a Spanish-American War uniform, 6 World War I Army uniforms, 20 World War II uniforms, 10 World War II Navy uniforms, 5 World War II Air Force uniforms, 2 West Point uniforms, hats, bonnets, beaver fur hats, and 45 quilts.

Museum of the Fur Trade

6321 East Highway 20
Chadron, NE 69337
Tel: 308-432-3843
www.furtrade.org
Hours: Mon–Sun 8–5 pm (Memorial Day–Sep)
Contact: Curator
Institution type: History museum
Collection type: Clothing, accessories, general textiles
Description: Pre-1700–1900. Textiles were the single most important class of goods traded to American Indians, and the Museum of the Fur Trade collection is the most comprehensive in existence. Collection includes silver, beads, and other trade goods that tell the story of the trade interaction between the American Indians and explorers, trappers, and traders.

Clarkson Historical Museum

221 Pine Street
Clarkson, NE 68629
Tel: 402-892-3863 Fax: 402-892-3059

The 100th Meridian Museum

206 East 8th
Cozad, NE 69130-0325
Tel: 308-784-1100

Saline County Historical Museum

1445 State Highway 30
Dorchester, NE 68343
Tel: 402-947-2911

Washington County Historical Association

104 North 14th Street
Fort Calhoun, NE 68023
Tel: 402-468-5740
www.newashcohist.org

North Platte Valley Museum

11th and J Streets
Gering, NE 69341
Tel: 308-436-5411
www.npvm.org

Stuhr Museum of the Prairie Pioneer

3113 West Highway 34
Grand Island, NE 68801
Tel: 308-385-5316 Fax: 308-385-5028
www.stuhrmuseum.org
Hours: Mon–Sat 9–5 pm, Sun 12–5 pm
Contact: Leslie Vollnogle, Curator
Institution type: History museum, historic house, county museum
Collection type: Clothing, accessories, uniforms, general textiles, quilts
Description: 1800–1960. Items from circa 1840 to 1930 with a central Nebraska connection. Museum holds more than 9,500 textiles—many items with hand embroidery. Collection includes petticoats, nightgowns, wedding dresses, flapper dresses, World War I uniforms, baby gowns, doilies, table scarves, and a 330-piece quilt collection, which is the second largest in Nebraska.

$ 🖊

Perkins County Historical Society

Central Avenue and 6th
Grant, NE 69140
Tel: 308-352-4019

Hastings Museum

1330 North Burlington
Hastings, NE 68901
Tel: 402-461-2399
www.hastingsmuseum.org

Nebraska Prairie Museum of the Phelps County Historical Society

North Burlington Highway 183
Holdrege, NE 68949
Tel: 308-995-5015
www.nebraskaprairie.org

Grant County Museum and Historic Site

105 East Harrison
Hyannis, NE 69350
Tel: 308-458-2371 Fax: 308-458-2485

Fort Kearney Museum

131 South Central Avenue
Kearney, NE 68847
Tel: 308-234-5200

Museum of Nebraska Art

2401 Central Avenue
Kearney, NE 68847
Tel: 308-865-8559

Dawson County Historical Society Museum

805 North Taft Street
Lexington, NE 68850
Tel: 308-324-5340

Quilt, circa 1888. Courtesy of International Quilt Study Center.

International Quilt Study Center

University of Nebraska–Lincoln
Department of Textiles, Clothing and Design, HE 234
Lincoln, NE 68583
Tel: 402-472-5418
www.quiltstudy.org
Hours: Mon–Fri 9–4:30 pm, Sat–Sun 1–4 pm
Contact: Marin F. Hanson, Assistant Curator
Institution type: University museum
Collection type: Quilts
Description: 1850–present. Center houses one of the largest publicly owned collections,

including the Ardis and Robert James Collection (1,000 antique and cutting edge studio art quilts), Helen Cargo Collection of African American quilts primarily from Alabama, Sara Miller Collection of Midwestern Amish crib quilts, the Jonathan Holstein Quilt Collection (400 quilts), and the Holstein Collection of Archival Materials. Featured quilt is a New York Beauty pattern probably made in Missouri from the James Collection.

The Lentz Center for Asian Culture

1155 Q Street
Lincoln, NE 68588-0252
Tel: 402-472-5841

Museum of Nebraska History, Nebraska State Historical Society

131 Centennial Mall North
Lincoln, NE 68501
Tel: 800-833-6747
www.nebraskahistory.org
Hours: Mon–Fri 9–4:30 pm, Sat–Sun 1–4 pm
Contact: Deborah Arenz
Institution type: State museum
Collection type: Clothing, accessories, general textiles, quilts
Description: 1850–present. Collection of 5,000 items includes clothing and accessories of Nebraskans from the mid-1800s to today. Holdings include a large collection of quilts, coverlets, rugs, and other textiles.

National Museum of Roller Skating

4730 South Street, Suite 2
Lincoln, NE 68506
Tel: 402-483-7551 Fax: 402-483-1465
www.rollerskatingmuseum.com
Hours: Mon–Fri 9–5 pm
Contact: Amanda Ray, Curator
Institution type: History museum
Collection type: Clothing, accessories, uniforms, costumes, flags
Description: 1900–present. Roller skating costumes from early 1900s to present day. Feature items include costumes from Gloria Nord of the Skating Vanities and Tammy Kettermen, Miss Arizona 1989. Collection also includes vaudeville costumes from the early 1900s, rink

Tara Lipinski, 1991. Courtesy of National Museum of Roller Skating.

uniforms, skating T-shirts, banners and flags from around the world, and skating costumes and uniforms.

✍

High Plains Museum
421 Norris Avenue
McCook, NE 69001
Tel: 308-345-3661

Senator George Norris State Historic Site
706 Norris Avenue
McCook, NE 69001
Tel: 308-345-8484
www.nebraskahistory.org/sites/norris/
index.htm

Harold Warp Pioneer Village Foundation
138 East Highway 6
Minden, NE 68959
Tel: 308-832-1181
www.pioneervillage.org

Kearney County Historical Museum
713 South Minden Avenue
Minden, NE 68959
Tel: 308-832-1765

Arbor Lodge State Historical Park
2nd and Centennial Avenues
Nebraska City, NE 68410
Tel: 402-873-7222

Antelope County Historical Museum
509 L Street
Neligh, NE 68756
Tel: 402-887-4999

Lincoln County Historical Society
2403 North Buffalo Bill Avenue
North Platte, NE 69101
Tel: 308-534-5640

Front Street
519 East 1st
Ogallala, NE 69153
Tel: 308-284-6000
www.megavision.net/frontstreet

Durham Western Heritage Museum
801 South 10th Street
Omaha, NE 68108
Tel: 402-444-5071
www.dwhm.org

El Museo Latino
4701 South 25th Street
Omaha, NE 68107
Tel: 402-731-1137
www.elmuseolatino.org

General Crook House Museum and Library
5730 North 30th Street, 11B
Omaha, NE 68111
Tel: 402-455-9990
www.omahahistory.org/museum.htm

Historical Society of Garden County
West 1st and East Street
Oshkosh, NE 69154
Tel: 308-772-3115

Pilger Museum
345 North Main Street
Pilger, NE 68768
Tel: 402-396-3422
www.stanton.net/stantoncountyhistoricalsociety
.htm

Cass County Historical Society Museum
646 Main Street
Plattsmouth, NE 68048
Tel: 402-296-4770

Willa Cather Pioneer Memorial and Educational Foundation
413 North Webster
Red Cloud, NE 68970
Tel: 402-746-2653
www.willacather.org

Otoe County Museum of Memories
366 Poplar
Syracuse, NE 68446
Tel: 402-269-3482

Johnson County Historical Society
3rd and Lincoln Streets
Tecumseh, NE 68450
Tel: 402-335-3258

Burt County Museum
319 North 13th Street
Tekamah, NE 68061
Tel: 402-374-1505

Cherry County Historical Society
Main Street and Highway 20
Valentine, NE 69201
Tel: 402-376-2015

Saunders County Historical Complex
204 North Walnut
Wahoo, NE 68066
Tel: 402-443-3090
www.visitsaunderscounty.org/attractions/museum/index.htm
Hours: Tue–Sat 10–4 pm, Sun 1:30–4:30 pm (Apr–Sep); Tue–Sat 10–4 pm (Oct); Tue–Fri 10–4 pm (Nov–Mar)
Contact: Erin Hauser
Institution type: County museum
Collection type: Clothing, accessories, uniforms, costumes, general textiles, flags
Description: 1850–present. Clothing from everyday wear to wedding dresses and military uniforms.

✍️

Wilber Czech Museum
102 West 3rd
Wilber, NE 68465
Tel: 402-821-2183

NEVADA

Nevada State Museum
MARJORIE RUSSELL CLOTHING AND
TEXTILE RESEARCH CENTER
2351 Arrowhead Drive
Carson City, NV 89701
Tel: 775-687-6173 Fax: 775-684-8315
http://dmla.clan.lib.nv.us/docs/museums/cc/
russell_home.htm
Hours: By appointment
Contact: Jan Loverin
Institution type: State museum
Collection type: Clothing, accessories, uniforms,
costumes, general textiles, quilts, flags
Description: 1700–present. Marjorie Russell
Clothing and Textile Research Center houses
textile artifacts from the Nevada State
Museum, the Nevada Historical Society, and
the Jessie Pope Costume Collection from the
University of Nevada. Strengths are the quilt
collection, hats, children's wear, flags, banners,
military, and men's wear.

Northeastern Nevada Museum
1515 Idaho Street
Elko, NV 89801
Tel: 775-738-3418
www.museum-elko.us

White Pine Public Museum
2000 Aultman Street
Ely, NV 89301
Tel: 775-289-4710
www.idsely.com/~wpmuseum

*Gown of Nevada First Lady Idelle Balzar, 1927. Courtesy
of Nevada State Museum.*

Churchill County Museum and Archives
1050 South Maine Street
Fallon, NV 89406
Tel: 775-423-3677 Fax: 775-423-3662
www.churchillcounty.org/museum
Hours: Mon–Sat 10–5 pm, Sun 12–5 pm
Contact: Donna Cossette, Registrar
Institution type: County museum
Collection type: Clothing, accessories, uniforms,
general textiles, quilts, flags
Description: 1850–present. General clothing from
1850 to the 1960s and over 40 quilts of
varying ages and styles. Focus is on Nevada his-
tory.

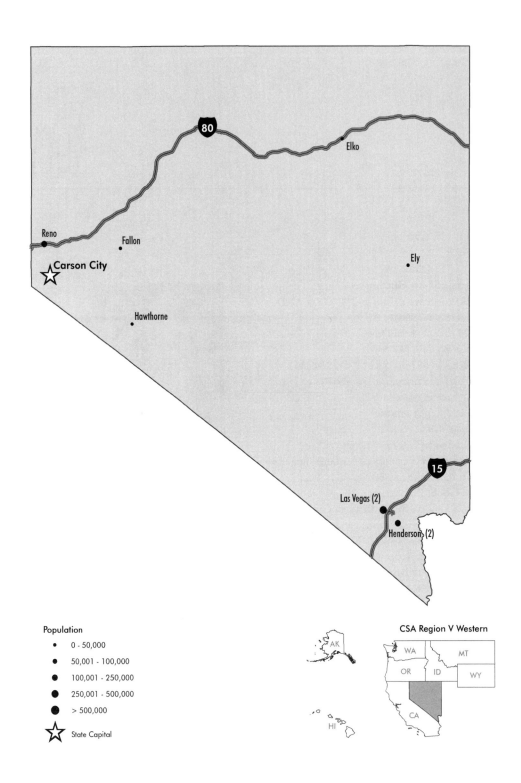

Population

- • 0 - 50,000
- • 50,001 - 100,000
- ● 100,001 - 250,000
- ● 250,001 - 500,000
- ● > 500,000
- ☆ State Capital

CSA Region V Western

Mineral County Museum

400 10th Street
Hawthorne, NV 89415
Tel: 775-945-5142 Fax: 775-945-0706
http://web0.greatbasin.net/~mcmuseum
Hours: Tue–Sat 11–5 pm
Contact: Georgana Mayne
Institution type: History museum, county
    museum
Collection type: Clothing, accessories, uniforms,
    general textiles, quilts, flags
Description: 1850–present. Clothing and textiles
    on display include military uniforms from the
    1860s to the 1970s; women's clothing,
    including 1869 reception gown and undergar-
    ments, 1880s complete riding outfit, a wed-
    ding dress, and other dresses from 1909 to
    1920; children's clothing from the 1930s; tat-
    ting and lace along with quilts and other hand-
    made items; and additional clothing items
    from the 1940s to the 1950s in the archives.

Clark County Museum

1830 South Boulder Highway
Henderson, NV 89015
Tel: 702-455-7955 Fax: 702-455-7948
www.co.clark.nv.us/Parks/Clark_County
    _Museum.htm
Hours: Mon–Sun 9–4:30 pm
Contact: Suzanne Turgeon, Registrar
Institution type: County museum
Collection type: Clothing, accessories
Description: 1850–1960.

Howard W. Cannon Aviation Museum

1830 South Boulder Highway
Henderson, NV 89015
Tel: 702-455-7968 Fax: 702-455-7948
www.co.clark.nv.us/Parks/Clark_County
    _Museum.htm
Hours: Mon–Sun 9–4:30 pm
Contact: Mark P. Hall-Patton, CEO and Director
Institution type: History museum, county
    museum
Collection type: Clothing, accessories, uniforms,
    costumes
Description: 1900–present.

Red, white, and blue hot pants costume. Courtesy of Liberace Museum.

Liberace Museum

1775 East Tropicana
Las Vegas, NV 89119
Tel: 702-798-5595 Fax: 702-798-7386
www.liberace.org
Hours: Mon–Sat 10–5 pm, Sun 12–4 pm
Contact: Jerry Goldberg
Institution type: History museum, city museum
Collection type: Accessories, costumes
Description: 1700–present. 250 costumes and
    accessories of Liberace, 17 pianos, 8 automo-
    biles, 28 pieces of jewelry, and 1,000 pieces of
    fine china and crystal and other antiques and
    artifacts.

$

Nevada State Museum and Historical Society

700 Twin Lakes Drive
Las Vegas, NV 84107
Tel: 702-486-5205 Fax: 702-486-5172
http://dmla.clan.lib.nv.us/docs/museums/lv/
    vegas.htm
Hours: Mon–Sun 9–5 pm
Contact: David Millman, Michelle Lord, Curators
Institution type: History museum, state museum
Collection type: Clothing, accessories, uniforms,
    costumes
Description: 1900–present. Mostly women's
    clothing, with a small amount of casino
    workers' accessories and uniforms.

$

Nevada Historical Society

1650 North Virginia Street
Reno, NV 89503
Tel: 775-688-1190 Fax: 775-688-2917
http://dmla.clan.lib.nv.us/docs/museums/reno/
his-soc.htm

Canterbury Shaker Village

288 Shaker Road
Canterbury, NH 03224
Tel: 603-783-9511
www.shakers.org
Hours: Mon–Sun 10–4 pm (mid-May–Dec)
Contact: Jennifer Carroll-Plante
Institution type: History museum
Collection type: Clothing, accessories, general textiles, flags
Description: 1760–present. Living Shaker settlement from 1792 to 1992 has twenty-five original structures. Guided tours include a specific textile tour. Strengths include a large collection of early toweling, Shaker woven blankets, and items produced for sale such as knit sweaters and Dorothy cloaks. Holdings include a large collection of everyday clothing.

$ ✍

Sandwich Historical Society

4 Maple Street
Center Sandwich, NH 03227
Tel: 603-284-6269
www.sandwichnh.com/history

Old Fort Number 4 Associates

Springfield Road, Route 11
Charlestown, NH 03603
Tel: 603-826-5700
www.fortat4.com

Dress, cotton fabric from Cocheco Mfg. Co., circa 1895. Courtesy of Museum of New Hampshire History.

Museum of New Hampshire History

6 Eagle Square
Concord, NH 03301-4923
Tel: 603-856-0613 Fax: 603-228-6308
www.nhhistory.org/museum.html
Hours: Tue–Sat 9:30–5 pm, Sun 12–5 pm
Contact: Doug Copeley, Registrar
Institution type: History museum
Collection type: Clothing, accessories, uniforms, costumes, general textiles, flags
Description: 1700–present. Clothing, textiles, accessories, uniforms, and costumes made and/or used in New Hampshire.

$ ✍

Franconia

93

Tamworth

Center Sandwich

Meredith

Hanover

Enfield

Laconia

89

Wolfeboro (2)

New London

Salisbury

South Sutton

Canterbury

Charlestown

Concord

Dover

Hopkinton

Durham (2)

Portsmouth (6)

Hillsborough

Walpole

95

Keene

Hancock

Manchester (2)

Hampton

Peterborough

Sandown

93

Population

- • 0 - 50,000
- • 50,001 - 100,000
- ● 100,001 - 250,000
- ● 250,001 - 500,000
- ● > 500,000
- ☆ State Capital

CSA Region I Northeast

ME

VT

MA

CT

RI

Annie E. Woodman Institute

182 Central Avenue
Dover, NH 03821
Tel: 603-742-1038

Durham Historic Association Museum

Newmarket Road and Main Street
Durham, NH 03824
Tel: 603-868-5436

Homespun gown, circa 1800. Courtesy of The Irma Bowen Textile Collection, University of New Hampshire Museum.

University of New Hampshire Museum

THE IRMA BOWEN TEXTILE
COLLECTION
Dimond Library, 18 Library Way
Durham, NH 03824
Tel: 603-862-1081
www.izaak.unh.edu/museum
Hours: Mon–Fri 9–5 pm, Sat 1–5 pm (during semester schedule only)
Contact: Dale Valena, Astrida Schaeffer
Institution type: University museum
Collection type: Clothing, accessories
Description: 1760–1960. Women's clothing and accessories from 1780 to 1930, paisley shawls, and children's clothing. Collection is most noted for its blue-and-white striped, homespun gown, circa 1780, a rare example of everyday clothing. Other special items include a silk quilted petticoat, cardinal, and clogs owned by Temperence Pickering Knight of Newington, New Hampshire (1732–1823); brown cloth shoes; and red and white leather shoes.
$ 🖏

Enfield Shaker Museum

24 Caleb Dyer Lane
Enfield, NH 03748
Tel: 603-632-4346
www.shakermuseum.org

New England Ski Museum

Parkway Exit 34B, next to the Cannon
    Mountain Tramway
Franconia, NH 03580
Tel: 603-823-7177
www.skimuseum.org
Hours: Mon–Sun 12–5 pm (Dec–Mar)
Contact: Jeffrey R. Leich, Executive Director
Institution type: History museum
Collection type: Clothing, accessories
Description: 1915–present.
🖏

Cloak, circa 1770. Courtesy of Tuck Museum.

Tuck Museum

40 Park Avenue
Hampton, NH 03843
Tel: 603-926-2543
www.hamptonhistoricalsociety.org
Hours: Wed, Fri, Sun 1–4 pm, and by appointment
Contact: Betty Moore, Museum Coordinator
Institution type: History museum
Collection type: Clothing, accessories, uniforms, costumes, general textiles, flags
Description: 1760–1914. Women's clothing of the eighteenth and nineteenth centuries.
🖏

Hancock Historical Society
7 Main Street
Hancock, NH 03449
Tel: 603-525-9379

Hood Museum of Art
HENRY B. WILLIAMS COSTUME
COLLEGE
Dartmouth College
6204 Hopkins Center
Hanover, NH 03755
Tel: 603-646-2808
www.dartmouth.edu/~hood/menu.html
Hours: By appointment
Contact: Margaret Spicer
Institution type: Art museum, university museum
Collection type: Clothing, accessories, uniforms
Description: 1760–1960

The Franklin Pierce Homestead
2nd NH Turnpike
Hillsborough, NH 03244
Tel: 603-478-1081
www.conknet.com/~hillsboro/pierce

New Hampshire Antiquarian Society
300 Main Street
Hopkinton, NH 03229
Tel: 603-746-3825

The Wyman Tavern
339 Main Street
Keene, NH 03431
Tel: 603-352-1895

Belknap Mill Society
The Mill Plaza
533 Main Street
Laconia, NH 03426
Tel: 603-524-8813

Lawrence L. Lee Scouting Museum
40 Blondin Road
Manchester, NH 03109
Tel: 603-669-8919 Fax: 603-625-2467
www.scoutingmuseum.org
Hours: Mon–Sun 10–4 pm (Jul–Aug); Sat 10–4
pm (Sep–Jun)
Contact: Edward Rowan, Curator
Institution type: History museum
Collection type: Uniforms

Description: 1900–present. Large collection of
U.S. and international Scouting uniforms for
various youth and adult programs includes
Cub Scouts, Boy Scouts, Air and Sea Scouts,
Explorers, Venturers, and similar programs
from around the world, dating from the
founding of Scouting in 1907 to the present.

Manchester Historic Association
129 Amherst Street
Manchester, NH 03101
Tel: 603-622-7531
www.manchesterhistoric.org

Meredith Historical Society
Main Street
Meredith, NH 03253
Tel: 603-279-8704

New London Historical Society
179 Little Sunapee Road
New London, NH 03257
Tel: 603-526-6564
www.nlhs.net

Peterborough Historical Society
19 Grove Street
Peterborough, NH 03458
Tel: 603-924-3235
www.peterboroughhistory.org

The Children's Museum of Portsmouth
GLOBAL SOLES
280 Marcy Street
Portsmouth, NH 03801
Tel: 603-436-3853 Fax: 603-436-7706
www.childrens-museum.org
Hours: Tue–Sat 10–5 pm, Sun 1–5 pm
Contact: Susan Kaufmann
Institution type: Children's museum
Collection type: Clothing, accessories, costumes
Description: 1961–present. Global Soles is a mul-
ticultural exhibit consisting of six stations, each
representing a world culture—Germany,
Greece, Inuit, Aymara, Morocco, and Japan—
using clothing and accessories to learn about
different cultures.
$

John Paul Jones House Museum

43 Middle Street
Portsmouth, NH 03802-0728
Tel: 603-436-8420
http://seacoastnh.com/touring/jpjhouse.html

Moffatt-Ladd House and Garden

154 Market Street
Portsmouth, NH 03801-3730
Tel: 603-436-8221

Strawbery Banke Museum

Marcy Street
Portsmouth, NH 03802-0300
Tel: 603-433-1100
www.strawberybanke.org

Warner House

150 Daniel Street
Portsmouth, NH 03802-0895
Tel: 603-436-5909
www.warnerhouse.org

Wentworth Gardner and Tobias Lear Houses Association

50 Mechanic Street
Portsmouth, NH 03802-0563
Tel: 603-436-4406

Salisbury Historical Society

94 New Road
Salisbury, NH 03268
Tel: 603-648-2774

Sandown Historical Society and Museum

Route 121-A Depot
Sandown, NH 03873
Tel: 603-887-4520
www.sandown.us/historical%20society/
    historicalhomepage.htm
Hours: Sat–Sun 1–5 pm (May–Oct)
Contact: Bertha Deveau
Institution type: History museum
Collection type: Clothing, accessories, uniforms, costumes
Description: 1800–present. Baby christening gowns, wedding dresses, children's clothing, men's and women's clothing and accessories, and World War I and World War II uniforms.

South Sutton Old Store Museum

12 Meeting House Hill Road
South Sutton, NH 03273
Tel: 603-938-5843

Remick Country Doctor Museum and Farm

58 Cleveland Hill Road
Tamworth, NH 03886
Tel: 603-323-7591 Fax: 603-323-8382
www.remickmuseum.org
Hours: Mon–Fri 10–4 pm (Jul–Oct)
Contact: Gerry Eldridge, Curator; Winnie Mitchell, Assistant Curator
Institution type: History museum, historic house
Collection type: Clothing, accessories, uniforms, general textiles, flags
Description: 1800–present. Clothing from the Remick family from the 1800s to the present. Highlights are wedding apparel from 1842 and a white organdy two-piece dress with pink silk belt and bows. Other items include tan linen three-piece suit, jacket, pants, and vest; black bearskin coat and cap; woolen coat with rabbit lining (worn 1894–1896); small child's clothing (worn 1906–1907) with photos; mourning dresses worn between 1877 and 1911; mink muff; underwear—winter and summer split tail drawers, winter and summer undershirts, and winter and summer petticoats.

Walpole Historical Society

Main Street
Walpole, NH 03608
Tel: 603-756-4861
Hours: Wed, Sat 2–4 pm
Institution type: History museum

Wolfeboro Historical Society

233 South Main Street
Wolfeboro, NH 03894
Tel: 603-569-4997
www.wolfeborohistoricalsociety.org

Wright Museum

77 Center Street, Route 28
Wolfeboro, NH 03894
Tel: 603-569-6326
www.wrightmuseum.org

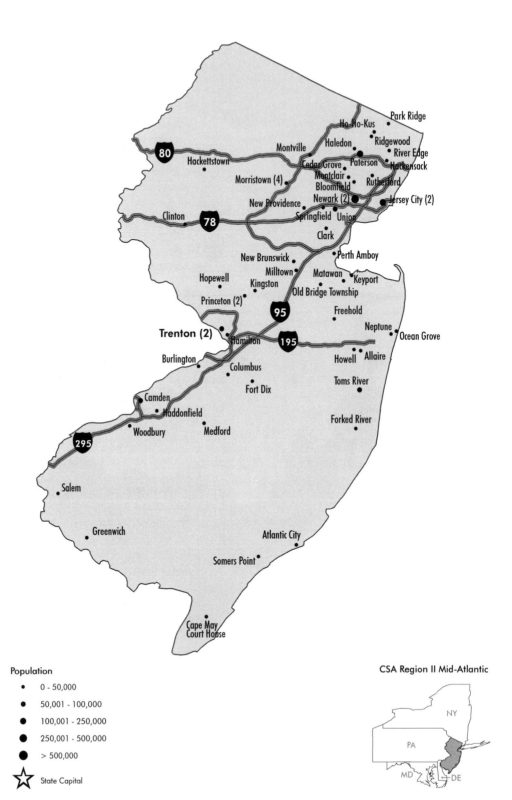

Park Ridge
Ho-Ho-Kus
Montville
Haledon
Ridgewood
River Edge
Hackensack
Hackettstown
Cedar Grove
Paterson
Morristown (4)
Montclair
Rutherford
Bloomfield
New Providence
Newark (2)
Jersey City (2)
Clinton
Springfield
Union
Clark
New Brunswick
Perth Amboy
Hopewell
Milltown
Matawan
Keyport
Kingston
Old Bridge Township
Princeton (2)
Freehold
Neptune
Trenton (2)
Ocean Grove
Hamilton
Burlington
Columbus
Howell
Allaire
Fort Dix
Toms River
Camden
Haddonfield
Woodbury
Medford
Forked River
Salem
Greenwich
Atlantic City
Somers Point
Cape May
Court House

Population

• 0 - 50,000
• 50,001 - 100,000
● 100,001 - 250,000
● 250,001 - 500,000
● > 500,000
☆ State Capital

CSA Region II Mid-Atlantic

NY
PA
MD
DE

NEW JERSEY

Historic Allaire Village
 County Route 524
 Allaire, NJ 07727
 Tel: 732-919-3500 Fax: 732-938-3302
 www.allairevillage.com
 Hours: Wed–Sun 11–5 pm (Memorial Day–Labor
 Day); 10–4 pm (May, Sep, Oct weekends)
 Contact: Laura M. Poll
 Institution type: History museum, historic house
 Collection type: Clothing, accessories, flags
 Description: 1850–1960.
 $ ✍

Atlantic City Historical Museum
 New Jersey Avenue and the Boardwalk
 Atlantic City, NJ 08401
 Tel: 609-347-5839
 www.acmuseum.org

**Historical Society of Bloomfield New
Jersey**
 90 Broad Street
 Bloomfield, NJ 07003
 Tel: 973-566-6220

Burlington County Historical Society
 451 High Street
 Burlington, NJ 08016
 Tel: 609-386-4773
 http://08016.com/bchs.html

Camden County Historical Society
 1900 Park Boulevard
 Camden, NJ 08103
 Tel: 856-964-3333
 www.cchsnj.com

Cape May County Historical Museum
 504 Route 9 North
 Cape May Court House, NJ 08210
 Tel: 609-465-3535

Cedar Grove Historical Society
 903 Pompton Avenue
 Cedar Grove, NJ 07009
 Tel: 973-239-5414

Dr. William Robinson Plantation
 593 Madison Hill Road
 Clark, NJ 07066
 Tel: 732-381-3081

Red Mill Museum Village
 56 Main Street
 Clinton, NJ 08809
 Tel: 908-735-4101
 www.theredmill.org

Mansfield Township Historical Society
 4 Fitzgerald Lane
 Columbus, NJ 08022
 Tel: 609-298-4174

Lacey Historical Society

Route 9
Forked River, NJ 08731
Tel: 609-971-0467

Fort Dix Museum

6501 Pennsylvania Avenue
Fort Dix, NJ 08640
Tel: 609-562-6983

Monmouth County Historical Association

70 Court Street
Freehold, NJ 07728
Tel: 732-462-1466 Fax: 732-462-8346
www.monmouthhistory.org
Hours: Tue–Sat 10–4 pm
Contact: Bernadette M. Rogoff, Curator of Collections
Institution type: Art museum, history museum, historic house
Collection type: Clothing, accessories, uniforms, general textiles, quilts, flags
Description: 1760–present. Items made in Monmouth County or worn by Monmouth County residents, including eighteenth-century garments—shifts, red wool capes, and round gowns; work and formal men's, women's, and children's clothes; 65 quilts; 150 samplers; American Revolution, Civil War, World War I, and World War II uniforms and accessories; and jewelry, combs, handbags, bonnets, hats, shoes, wedding items, sewing, weaving, and knitting tools and accessories.
$ ✍

Cumberland County Historical Society

960 Ye Greate Street
Greenwich, NJ 08323
Tel: 856-455-4055

New Jersey Naval Museum

Corner Court and River Streets
Hackensack, NJ 07601
Tel: 201-342-3268
www.njnm.com

Hackettstown Historical Society Museum and Library

106 Church Street
Hackettstown, NJ 07840
Tel: 908-852-8797

Historical Society of Haddonfield

343 Kings Highway East
Haddonfield, NJ 08033
Tel: 856-429-7375
www.historicalsocietyofhaddonfield.org
Hours: Wed–Fri 1–4 pm, Sun 1–4 pm
Contact: Dianne Snodgrass
Institution type: History museum
Collection type: Clothing, accessories, uniforms, general textiles, quilts, flags
Description: Pre-1700–present. Infants', children's, women's, and men's items and military uniforms, and quilts.
$ ✍

American Labor Museum, Botto House National Landmark

83 Norwood Street
Haledon, NJ 07508
Tel: 973-595-7953 Fax: 973-595-7291
www.geocities.com/labormuseum
Hours: Wed–Sat 1–4 pm
Contact: Angelica M. Santomauro, Director
Institution type: History museum
Collection type: Clothing, accessories, general textiles
Description: 1850–1960. Needlework and clothing of immigrant workers and silk samples from silk mills in Paterson, New Jersey.
$ ✍

John Abbott II House

2200 Kuser Road
Hamilton, NJ 08690
Tel: 609-585-1686

The Friends of the Hermitage

335 North Franklin Turnpike
Ho-Ho-Kus, NJ 07423
Tel: 201-445-8311 Fax: 201-445-0437
www.thehermitage.org
Hours: Wed–Sun 1–4 pm
Contact: Pamela Smith
Institution type: History museum
Collection type: Clothing, accessories, uniforms, general textiles, quilts
Description: 1800–present. Primarily American collection includes lingerie, nightgowns, and corsets, 1800–1960s; dresses, 1800–1970; wedding dresses and gowns, 1850–1965; girls' clothing, 1800–1930; boys' clothing,

1850–1910; and infants' wear, 1800–1920.
Accessories are mostly American, including
fans, 1850–1930s; headwear, 1840–1960;
shoes, 1850–1960s; parasols, 1860s–1930;
handbags with emphasis on beaded bags;
muffs; and gloves, mittens, scarves, and shawls.
Textile collection is primarily American,
including quilts, household pieces, and bedspreads.

$ ✍

Hopewell Museum

28 East Broad Street
Hopewell, NJ 08525
Tel: 609-466-0103

Howell Historical Society and Committee Museum

427 Lakewood-Farmingdale Road
Howell, NJ 07731
Tel: 732-938-2212
www.howellnj.com/historic

Afro-American Historical Society Museum

1841 Kennedy Boulevard
Jersey City, NJ 07305
Tel: 201-547-5262

Jersey City Museum

350 Montgomery Street
Jersey City, NJ 07302
Tel: 201-413-0303
www.jerseycitymuseum.org

Steamboat Dock Museum, Keyport Historical Society

2 Broad Street
Keyport, NJ 07735
Tel: 732-264-6119
Hours: Sun 1–4 pm, Mon 10–12 pm (May–Oct)
Contact: Angel Jeandron
Institution type: History museum
Collection type: Clothing, accessories, uniforms,
   flags
Description: 1850–1960.
✍

Historic Rockingham

County Road 603 (Laurel Avenue)
Kingston, NJ 08528

Tel: 609-683-7132
www.rockingham.net
Hours: Wed–Sat 10–12 pm, 1–4 pm; Sun 1–4 pm
Contact: Margaret Carlsen
Institution type: Historic house, state museum
Collection type: General textiles
Description: 1700–1799. Rockingham is the 1710
   historic house where George and Martha
   Washington were residing when they received
   news that the Treaty of Paris was signed and
   the United States was a free country. Objects in
   the collection include furniture, metals,
   ceramics, woodenware, archival materials, and
   textiles.

Burrowes Mansion Museum

94 Main Street
Matawan, NJ 07747
Tel: 732-566-3817

Air Victory Museum

68 Stacy Haines Road
Medford, NJ 08055
Tel: 609-267-4488
www.airvictorymuseum.org

Eureka Fire Museum

39 Washington Avenue
Milltown, NJ 08850
Tel: 732-828-7207

Montclair Historical Society

108 Orange Road
Montclair, NJ 07042
Tel: 973-744-1796
www.montclairhistorical.org

Montville Township Historical Museum

6 Taylortown Road
Montville, NJ 07045
Tel: 973-334-3665

Macculloch Hall Historical Museum and Gardens

45 Macculloch Avenue
Morristown, NJ 07960
Tel: 973-538-2404
www.macullochhall.org
Hours: Sun, Wed, Thu 1–4 pm
Institution type: History museum, historic house
$ ✍

Morris County Historical Society at Acorn Hall

68 Morris Avenue
Morristown, NJ 07960
Tel: 973-267-3465 Fax: 973-267-8773
www.acornhall.org
Hours: Mon 10–4 pm, Thu 10–4 pm, Sun 1–4 pm
Contact: Debra K. Westmoreland
Institution type: History museum, historic house, county museum
Collection type: Clothing, accessories, uniforms, costumes, general textiles, quilts, flags
Description: 1750–present. Primarily American women's clothing from the Victorian period; children's and men's clothing are also represented. Other items include work dresses to ball gowns; undergarments; accessories, including beaded bags, hair jewelry, shoes, and shawls. One of the oldest pieces is a calash circa 1780. Highlights include Charles Worth 1890s ball gown. Holdings include a wedding dress collection of 55 pieces from 1840 to 1960, with many styles from Quaker style to an 1888 gown hand-embroidered in India to flapper style.

$

The Morris Museum

6 Normandy Heights Road
Morristown, NJ 07960
Tel: 973-971-3700x3703
www.morrismuseum.org

Morristown National Historical Park

30 Washington Place
Morristown, NJ 07960
Tel: 973-539-2016
www.nps.gov/morr

Township of Neptune Historical Museum

25 Neptune Boulevard
Neptune, NJ 07754-1125
Tel: 732-988-5200

Buccleuch Mansion

Buccleuch Park, Easton Avenue
New Brunswick, NJ 08901
Tel: 732-745-5094

New Providence Historical Society

1350 Springfield Avenue
New Providence, NJ 09974
Tel: 908-665-1034
Hours: Tue 10–12 pm, Thu 10–12 pm and 2–5 pm, and by appointment
Contact: Director
Institution type: History museum, historic house
Collection type: Clothing, accessories, costumes
Description: 1800–1914. Collection includes notable Worth gown from Paris.

New Jersey Historical Society

52 Park Place
Newark, NJ 07102
Tel: 973-596-8500 Fax: 973-596-6957
www.jerseyhistory.org
Hours: Tue–Sat 10–5 pm
Contact: Tim Decker, Collections Manager
Institution type: History museum
Collection type: Clothing, accessories, uniforms, costumes, general textiles, quilts, flags
Description: 1760–present. More than 3,700 costumes and accessories. Blankets, quilts, and coverlets (100), flags (100), and samplers (30) form an outstanding collection of New Jersey textiles. Collection of men's, women's, and children's clothing is noted for its representation of everyday life and artifacts from working and middle-class New Jerseyans.

Nigerian Yoruba chief's robe, early-twentieth century. Courtesy of the Newark Museum

The Newark Museum

49 Washington Street
Newark, NJ 07102

Tel: 973-596-6660 Fax: 973-596-6666
www.newarkmuseum.org

Hours: Wed–Sun 12–5 pm, and by appointment

Contact: Valrae Reynolds, Senior Curator

Institution type: Art museum, city museum, historic house

Collection type: Clothing, accessories, uniforms, costumes, general textiles, quilts

Description: Pre-1700–present. Global collection includes costumes, textiles, and accessories related to the everyday life of people all over the world. Collection includes particularly strong holdings in Coptic textiles, pan-Asian holdings with emphasis on Tibet, American quilts, New Jersey textiles, and African textiles.

$ ✍

Historical Society of Ocean Grove

50 Pitman Avenue
Ocean Grove, NJ 07756
Tel: 732-774-1869 Fax: 732-774-1685
www.oceangrovehistory.org

Hours: Mon, Wed, Thu 10–4 pm, Fri–Sat 10–5 pm

Institution type: History museum

✍

Thomas Warne Historical Museum and Library

4216 Route 513
Old Bridge Township, NJ 07747
Tel: 732-566-2108 Fax: 732-566-6943

Hours: Tue 7–9 pm, Wed 9:30–12 pm, 1st Sun 1–4 pm

Contact: Director

Institution type: History museum

Collection type: Clothing, accessories, uniforms, costumes, general textiles, quilts, flags

Description: 1850–1960. Hats, shoes, purses, male and female underwear, coats, dresses, uniforms, quilts, rugs, table linens, capes, skirts, jackets, tops, and wedding dresses.

✍

Pascack Historical Society

19 Ridge Avenue
Park Ridge, NJ 07656
Tel: 201-573-0307

Hours: Wed 10–12 pm, Sun 1–4 pm

Contact: Barbara Burns

Institution type: History museum

Collection type: Clothing, accessories, uniforms,

costumes, general textiles, quilts, flags

Description: 1800–present. 9 coverlets from the early- to mid-nineteenth century; uniforms from Spanish-American War to the present; wedding dresses from the mid-nineteenth century to the 1950s; Victorian garments; hats from the late eighteenth century to the 1960s; handbags from the late eighteenth century to the 1960s; and fans, quilts, shoes, and accessories.

Passaic County Historical Society

Lambert Castle, Valley Road
Paterson, NJ 07503
Tel: 973-247-0085
www.lambertcastle.org

The Kearney Cottage

63 Catalpa Avenue
Perth Amboy, NJ 08861
Tel: 732-826-1826

Historical Society of Princeton

158 Nassau Street
Princeton, NJ 08540
Tel: 609-921-6748
www.princetonhistory.org

Thomas Clarke House–Princeton Battlefield State Park

500 Mercer Road
Princeton, NJ 08540-4810
Tel: 609-921-0074

Schoolhouse Museum of the Ridgewood Historical Society

650 East Glen Avenue
Ridgewood, NJ 07450
Tel: 201-652-4584

Bergen County Historical Society

1201 Main Street
River Edge, NJ 07661
Tel: 201-343-9492
www.bergencountyhistory.org

Meadowlands Museum

91 Crane Avenue
Rutherford, NJ 07070
Tel: 201-935-1175
www.meadowlandsmuseum.org

Salem County Historical Society
79-83 Market Street
Salem, NJ 08079
Tel: 856-935-5004
www.salemcountyhistoricalsociety.com

Atlantic County Historical Society
907 Shore Road
Somers Point, NJ 08244
Tel: 609-927-5218
www.aclink.org/achs

Springfield Historical Society
126 Morris Avenue
Springfield, NJ 07081
Tel: 973-376-4784

Ocean County Historical Museum
26 Hadley Avenue
Toms River, NJ 08754-2191
Tel: 732-341-1880
www.oceancountyhistory.org
Hours: Tue–Thu 1–4:30 pm, 1st Fri 5–9 pm, Sat
10–2 pm, and by appointment

New Jersey State Museum
205 West State Street
Trenton, NJ 08625-0530
Tel: 609-292-6300
www.newjerseystatemuseum.org

Trenton City Museum
Ellarslie in Cadwalader Park
319 East State Street
Trenton, NJ 08618
Tel: 609-989-3632
www.ellarslie.org

Liberty Hall Museum
1003 Morris Avenue
Union, NJ 07083
Tel: 908-527-0400
www.libertyhallnj.org

Gloucester County Historical Society
58 North Broad Street
Woodbury, NJ 08096
Tel: 856-848-8531
www.rootsweb.com/~njglouce/gchs

NEW MEXICO

Albuquerque Museum

2000 Mountain Road NW

Albuquerque, NM 87104

Tel: 505-243-7255

www.cabq.gov/museum

Indian Pueblo Cultural Center

2401 12th Street NW

Albuquerque, NM 87104

Tel: 505-843-7270 Fax: 505-842-6959

www.indianpueblo.org

Hours: Mon–Sun 9–5 pm

Contact: Elizabeth A. Chestnut

Institution type: History museum

Collection type: Clothing, accessories, costumes

Description: 1900–present. Primarily Pueblo
Indian (Southwest area) ceramics, paintings,
and prints. Also Pueblo Indian textiles,
women's, men's, and children's traditional (over
1,500 years of tradition) dresses called mantas,
kilts, sashes, and leggings. Holdings include
approximately 20 Navajo rugs.

$ ✍

Maxwell Museum of Anthropology

University of New Mexico

1 University of New Mexico MSCO1 1050

Albuquerque, NM 87131

Tel: 505-277-4405

Rattlesnake Museum

202 San Felipe NW

Albuquerque, NM 87104-1426

Tel: 505-242-6569 Fax: 505-242-6569

www.rattlesnakes.com

Hours: Vary, see website

Institution type: History museum, natural science
museum

$ ✍

ACCESSORIES AND FLAGS COLLECTION

Contact: Bob Myers

Collection type: Accessories, flags

Description: 1915–present. Reptile related
bracelets, earrings, buckles, cufflinks, belts,
shoes, boots, pins, buttons, rings, tie clasps,
and tie tacs as well as reptile related zoo pennants, reptile exhibit pennants, zoo patches,
police and fire patches, military and scout
patches, reptile related pins, and early American flag reproductions depicting rattlesnakes.

SPORTS UNIFORMS COLLECTION

Contact: Bob Myers

Collection type: Uniforms

Description: 1915–present. American and Canadian uniforms depicting reptilian mascots.
Sports represented are bicycling, soccer,
bowling, football, baseball, hockey, and field
hockey. Collection also includes helmets, caps,
gear, and equipment, 1930–2004. Examples
include Arizona Diamondbacks, Amarillo Rat-
tlers, and others.

TEXTILE COLLECTION

Contact: Bob Myers

Collection type: Clothing, general textiles

Description: 1915–present. Reptile related vests,
dresses, and clothing with reptile prints or reptile skins; reptile related children's Halloween

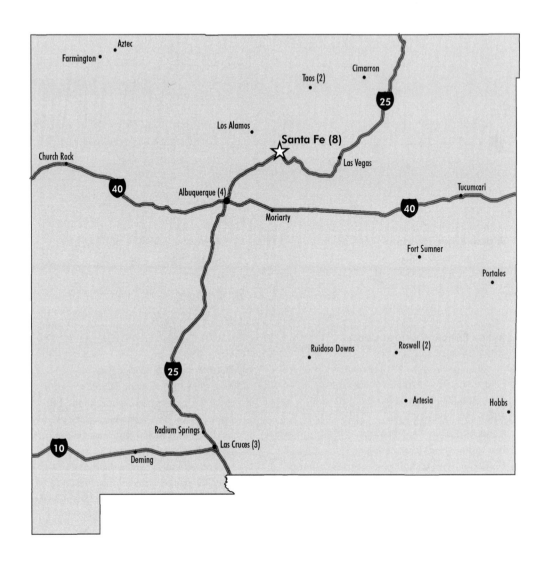

Aztec

Farmington

Taos (2)

Cimarron

Los Alamos

Santa Fe (8)

Las Vegas

Church Rock

Albuquerque (4)

Tucumcari

Moriarty

Fort Sumner

Portales

Ruidoso Downs

Roswell (2)

Artesia

Hobbs

Radium Springs

Las Cruces (3)

Deming

Population

- 0 - 50,000
- 50,001 - 100,000
- 100,001 - 250,000
- 250,001 - 500,000
- > 500,000

☆ State Capital

CSA Region VII Southwest

UT | CO | KS

AZ | | OK

| TX

costumes and masks, 1962–present; and reptile related sewing machines and thimbles.

Artesia Historical Museum and Art Center

505 Richardson Avenue
Artesia, NM 88210
Tel: 505-748-2390

Aztec Museum and Pioneer Village

125 North Main Avenue
Aztec, NM 87410
Tel: 505-334-9829
www.aztecnm.com/museum/museum_index.htm

Red Rock Museum

Red Rock State Park
Churchrock, NM 87311
Tel: 505-863-1337
www.ci.gallup.nm.us/rrsp/00182_redrock.html

Philmont Museums

Philmont Scout Ranch, Route 1
Cimarron, NM 87714
Tel: 505-376-2281
www.nmculture.org/cgi-bin/
instview.cgi?_recordnum=PHIL

Deming Luna Mimbres Museum

301 South Silver Street
Deming, NM 88030
Tel: 505-546-2382
www.cityofdeming.org/museum.html

Farmington Museum

3041 East Main Street
Farmington, NM 87402
Tel: 505-599-1174
www.farmingtonmuseum.org

Billy the Kid Museum

1601 East Sumner
Fort Sumner, NM 88119
Tel: 505-355-2380

Lea County Cowboy Hall of Fame and Western Heritage Center

5317 Lovington Highway, NMJC Campus
Hobbs, NM 88240-9121
Tel: 505-392-1275

Branigan Cultural Center

500 North Water
Las Cruces, NM 88001
Tel: 505-541-2155
www.lascruces-culture.org/html/
cultural_center.html

New Mexico Farm and Ranch Heritage Museum

4100 Dripping Springs Road
Las Cruces, NM 88011
Tel: 505-522-4100
http://spectre.nmsu.edu:16080/frhm

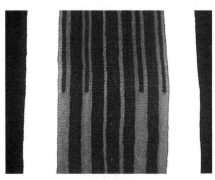

Second phase Navajo chief's blanket, 1862. Courtesy of New Mexico State University Museum.

New Mexico State University Museum

University Avenue and Solano Street
Las Cruces, NM 88003
Tel: 505-646-3739 Fax: 505-646-1419
www.nmsu.edu/~museum
Hours: Tue–Sat 12–4 pm
Contact: Terry R. Reynolds, Curator of Collections
Institution type: University museum
Collection type: Clothing, accessories, uniforms, costumes, general textiles, flags
Description: 1850–present. Navajo and Rio Grande rugs and weavings, 1860–1970; historic clothing, shoes, and hats, 1880–1960; historic military uniforms, 1900–1970; and New World ethnic clothing, shoes, and hats, 1930–1990s.

City of Las Vegas and Rough Riders Memorial Collection
727 Grand Avenue
Las Vegas, NM 87701
Tel: 505-454-1401
http://lasvegasnmcchp.com/tours/douglas/
9roughrider.htm

Los Alamos Historical Museum
1921 Juniper Street
Los Alamos, NM 87544
Tel: 505-662-6272
www.losalamos.com/historicalsociety

Moriarty Historical Society Museum
777 Old U.S. Route 6 SW
Moriarty, NM 87035-1366
Tel: 505-832-4764

Roosevelt County Museum
Eastern New Mexico University
Portales, NM 88130
Tel: 505-562-1011

Fort Selden State Monument
1280 Fort Selden Road
Radium Springs, NM 88054
Tel: 505-526-8911
www.nmculture.org/cgi-bin/
instview.cgi?_recordnum=SELD

The General Douglas L. McBride Museum
101 West College Boulevard
Roswell, NM 88201
Tel: 505-624-8220
www.nmmi.cc.nm.us/museum

Historical Center for Southeast New Mexico
200 North Lea Avenue
Roswell, NM 88201
Tel: 505-622-8333
www.hssnm.net/house.htm

The Hubbard Museum of the American West
841 Highway 70 West
Ruidoso Downs, NM 88346
Tel: 505-378-4142
www.hubbardmuseum.org

Institute of American Indian Arts Museum
108 Cathedral Plaza
Sante Fe, NM 87501
Tel: 505-983-8900
www.iaiancad.org

Museum of Indian Arts and Culture and Laboratory of Anthropology
710 Camino Lejo
Sante Fe, NM 87505
Tel: 505-476-1250
www.miaclab.org

Museum of International Folk Art
Museum Hill off Camino Lejo
Santa Fe, NM 87504
Tel: 505-476-1200 Fax: 505-476-1300
www.moifa.org
Hours: Tue–Sun 10–5 pm
Contact: Bobbie Sumberg
Institution type: State museum
Collection type: Clothing, accessories, costumes, general textiles
Description: 1800–present. 20,000 pieces of textiles and costume from the nineteenth and twentieth centuries, representing one hundred countries. Strengths in Indian embroidery, Swedish rural weaving, Palestinian costume, Mexican and Guatemalan costume and textiles, and Rio Grande textiles. Museum houses the Neutrogena Collection.
$ ✍

Museum of New Mexico
113 Lincoln Avenue
Sante Fe, NM 87501
Tel: 505-476-5060
www.museumofnewmexico.org

Museum of Spanish Colonial Art—Mosca
750 Camino Lejo
Sante Fe, NM 87505
Tel: 505-982-2226
www.spanishcolonial.org

Palace of the Governors
120 Lincoln Avenue
Sante Fe, NM 87504
Tel: 505-476-5028 Fax: 505-476-5104
www.palaceofthegovernors.org
Hours: Tue–Sun 10–5 pm
Contact: Louise Stiver

Fiesta wear, twentieth century. Courtesy of Palace of the Governors.

Institution type: State museum

Collection type: Clothing, accessories, uniforms, costumes, general textiles, quilts, flags

Description: 1850–1960. Items that uniquely reflect the Spanish, Mexican, frontier, and early-twentieth-century influences in the Southwest region. This is a valuable collection that includes a number of historically significant pieces from well-known Europeans and Americans. More than 100 costumes illustrate the fusion of cultures in the American Southwest. Larger collections include Victorian-era clothing and accessories from New Mexico families. Other holdings include regional fiesta clothing from fiesta royalty and fiesta visitors; a small sample of Rio Grande weavings, quilts, and lacework; and flags.

$ 🖎

School of American Research and Indian Arts Research Center

660 Garcia Street
Santa Fe, NM 87505
Tel: 505-954-7205
www.sarweb.org

The Wheelwright Museum of the American Indian

704 Camino Lejo
Santa Fe, NM 87505
Tel: 505-982-4636
www.wheelwright.org

Millicent Rogers Museum of Northern New Mexico

1504 Museum Road
Taos, NM 87571
Tel: 505-758-2462
www.millicentrogers.org

Taos Historic Museums

222 Ledoux Street
Taos, NM 87571
Tel: 505-758-0505
www.taoshistoricmuseums.com

Tucumcari Historical Research Institute

416 South Adams
Tucumcari, NM 88401
Tel: 505-461-4201

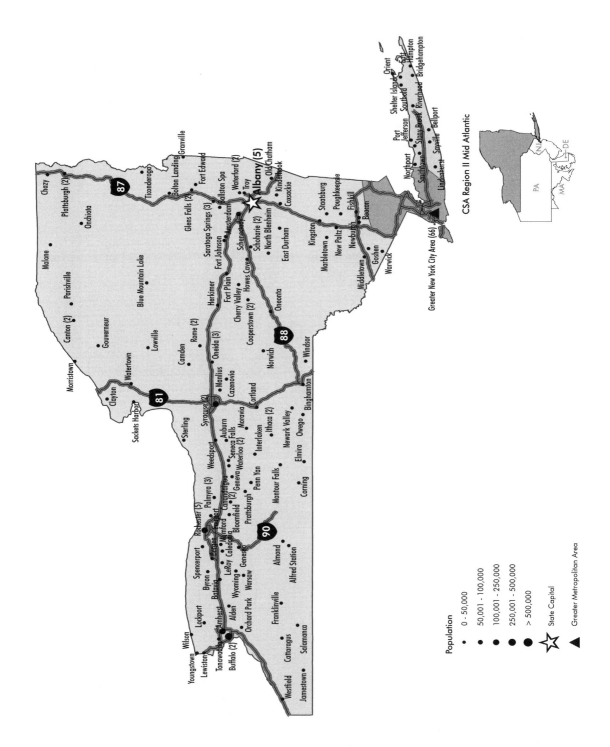

CSA Region II Mid Atlantic

Greater New York City Area (66)

Population

· 0 - 50,000

• 50,001 - 100,000

● 100,001 - 250,000

⬤ 250,001 - 500,000

⬤ > 500,000

☆ State Capital

▲ Greater Metropolitan Area

Youngstown
Wilson
Lewiston
Lockport
Tonawanda
Amherst
Buffalo (2)
Orchard Park
Alden
Wyoming
Warsaw
Franklinville
Cattaraugus
Salamanca
Westfield
Jamestown
Alfred Station
Almond
Spencerport
Byron
Batavia
LeRoy
Caledonia
Geneseo
Rochester (5)
Fairport
Mumford
Bloomfield (2)
Canandaigua
Geneva (2)
Prattsburgh
Palmyra (3)
Penn Yan
Weedsport
Seneca Falls
Waterloo (2)
Auburn
Moravia
Interlaken
Newark Valley
Elmira
Owego
Montour Falls
Corning
Ithaca (2)
Cortland
Cazenovia
Manlius
Syracuse (2)
Sterling
Sackets Harbor
Clayton
Watertown
Morristown
Gouverneur
Canton (2)
Parishville
Malone
Chazy
Ondrota
Plattsburgh (2)
Ticonderoga
Bolton Landing
Granville
Fort Edward
Glens Falls
Saratoga Springs (3)
Ballston Spa
Amsterdam
Fort Johnson
Herkimer
Fort Plain
Rome (2)
Oneida (3)
Camden
Lowville
Blue Mountain Lake
Cherry Valley
Howes Cave
Cooperstown (2)
Oneonta
Norwich
Windsor
Binghamton
Schenectady
Schoharie (2)
North Blenheim
East Durham
Troy
Albany (5)
Waterford (2)
Old Chatham
Kinderhook
Coxsackie
Kingston
Stadsburg
Marbletown
Poughkeepsie
Fishkill
Beacon
New Paltz
Newburgh
Middletown
Goshen
Warwick

Northport
Port Jefferson
Smithtown
Lindenhurst
Shelter Island
Southold
Stony Brook
Sayville
Bellport
Orient
East Hampton
Riverhead
Bridgehampton

PA
NJ
DE
MA

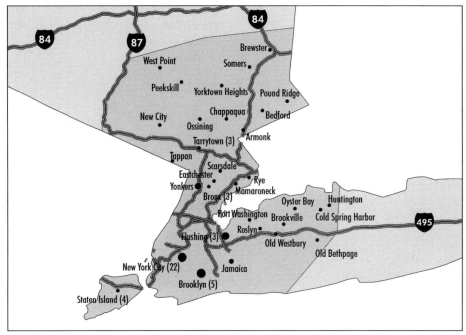

Greater New York City Area (66)

Albany Institute of History and Art

125 Washington Avenue

Albany, NY 12210

Tel: 518-463-4478

www.albanyinstitute.org

Historic Cherry Hill

523 1/2 South Pearl Street

Albany, NY 12202

Tel: 518-434-4791 Fax: 518-434-4806

www.historiccherryhill.org

Hours: Thu–Fri 12–5 pm, Sat 10–5 pm, Sun 1–5

pm (Apr–Jun, Oct–Dec); Tue–Sat 10–5 pm,

Sun 1–5 pm (Jul–Sep)

Contact: Erin Crissman

Institution type: History museum, historic house

Collection type: Clothing, accessories, general textiles

Description: 1760–present. Collection acquired by five generations of the Van Rensselaer-Rankin family between the mid-eighteenth century and 1963. More than 7,000 textiles such as household furnishings, bedding, floor coverings, and needlework. Other items include clothing for men, women, and children (everyday and special occasion wear), patterns, samples, trim, unfinished garments, and accessories.

$ 🔊

New York State Museum
Empire State Plaza, Madison Avenue
Albany, NY 12230
Tel: 518-474-5877
www.nysm.nysed.gov
Hours: Mon–Sun 9:30–5 pm

Shaker Heritage Society
875 Watervliet Shaker Road
Albany, NY 12211-1051
Tel: 518-456-7890
www.crisny.org/not-for-profit/shakerwv

Ten Broeck Mansion
9 Ten Broeck Place
Albany, NY 12210
Tel: 518-436-9826
Hours: Thu–Fri 10–4 pm, Sat–Sun 1–4 pm (May–Dec)

Alden Historical Society
13213 Broadway
Alden, NY 14004
Tel: 716-937-7606

Dress with train and stole, circa 1795–1805. Courtesy of American Costume Studies.

American Costume Studies
592 Main Street, Box 71
Alfred Station, NY 14803
Tel: 607-587-9488 Fax: 607-587-9488
www.costumestudies.com

Hours: By appointment
Contact: Susan Greene
Institution type: Private museum
Collection type: Clothing, accessories
Description: 1760–1899. Apparel for middle-class men, women, children, and infants, including underwear, outerwear, coats, and accessories. Dates range from 1780 to 1880, with concentration from 1800 to 1825. Mostly daily wear and some formal wear. Printed fabrics are a special interest. Subcollections include a group of 90 items from Interlaken, New York, 1790–1860.

$ 🔊

Hagadorn House Museum of the Almond Historical Society
7 North Main Street
Almond, NY 14804
Tel: 607-276-6781

Alligator shoes and matching handbag, circa 1940s. Courtesy of Amherst Museum.

Amherst Museum
3755 Tonawanda Creek Road
Amherst, NY 14226
Tel: 716-689-1440 Fax: 716-689-1409
www.amherstmuseum.org
Hours: Tue–Sun 9:30–4:30 pm (Apr–Sep); Tue–Fri 9:30–4:30 pm (Oct–Mar)
Contact: Kristie Dobbins
Institution type: History museum, historic house, city museum
Collection type: Clothing, accessories, uniforms, costumes, general textiles, quilts, flags
Description: 1760–present. Items worn, used, and acquired by residents of western New York. Holdings include quilt collection, strong twentieth-century costume and accessory col-

lections, and a very extensive nineteenth- and twentieth-century wedding gown collection.

$ 🖎

Walter Elwood Museum
300 Guy Park Avenue
Amsterdam, NY 12010
Tel: 518-843-5151
www.walterelwoodmuseum.com

North Castle Historical Society
440 Bedford Road
Armonk, NY 10504
Tel: 914-273-4510

Seward House
33 South Street
Auburn, NY 13021
Tel: 315-253-3351
www.sewardhouse.org

Wire hoop made at Ballston Spa, circa 1860. Courtesy of Brookside Museum of the Saratoga County Historical Society.

Brookside Museum of the Saratoga County Historical Society
6 Charlton Street
Ballston Spa, NY 12170
Tel: 518-885-4000
www.brooksidemuseum.org
Hours: Tue–Fri 10–4 pm, Sat 10–2 pm
Contact: Linda Gorham
Institution type: History museum, historic house
Collection type: Clothing, accessories, uniforms, general textiles, quilts, flags

Description: 1800–present. Textiles pertaining to Saratoga County history, including affluent textiles and clothing of working class. Collection includes men's, women's, and children's clothing, with greatest strength in Victorian era clothing and accessories. Quilts are of regional interest from regional quilters. Holdings also include collection of hoop skirts and corsets made in Ballston Spa.

$ 🖎

The Holland Land Office Museum
131 West Main Street
Batavia, NY 14020
Tel: 716-343-4727
www.hollandlandoffice.com

The Madam Brett Homestead
50 Van Nydeck Avenue
Beacon, NY 12508
Tel: 845-831-6533

Museum of the Bedford Historical Society
38 Village Green
Bedford, NY 10506
Tel: 914-234-9751
www.bedfordhistoricalsociety.org

Bellport-Brookhaven Historical Society and Museum
31 Bellport Lane
Bellport, NY 11713
Tel: 631-286-0888

Bergen Museum of Local History
7547 Lake Road
Bergen, NY 14416
Tel: 585-494-1121

Roberson Museum and Science Center
30 Front Street
Binghamton, NY 13905
Tel: 607-772-0660
www.roberson.org

Bloomfield Academy Museum
8 South Avenue
Bloomfield, NY 14443
Tel: 585-657-7244

Adirondack Museum

Route 28 North and 30
Blue Mountain Lake, NY 12812
Tel: 518-352-7311x101
www.adkmuseum.org

Marcella Sembrich Opera Museum

4800 Lakeshore Drive
Bolton Landing, NY 12814
Tel: 518-644-2492 Fax: 518-644-2191
www.operamuseum.org
Hours: Mon–Sun 10–12:30 pm, 2–5:30 pm
(Jun–Sep)
Contact: Administrative director
Institution type: Historic house
Collection type: Accessories, costumes, general
textiles, flags
Description: 1850–1914. Couture costumes from
Sembrich's performances in Europe and the
Metropolitan Opera that feature textiles, bead-
work, embroidery, and couture workmanship.

Southeast Museum

67 Main Street
Brewster, NY 10509
Tel: 845-279-7500
www.southeastmuseum.org

Bridge Hampton Historical Society

2368 Main Street and Corwith Avenue
Bridgehampton, NY 11932-0977
Tel: 613-537-1088
www.hamptons.com/bhhs

The Bronx County Historical Society

3309 Bainbridge Avenue
Bronx, NY 10467
Tel: 718-881-8900
www.bronxhistoricalsociety.org

City Island Nautical Museum

190 Fordham Street
Bronx, NY 10464
Tel: 718-885-0008
www.cityislandmuseum.org

Van Cortlandt House Museum

Van Cortlandt Park, Broadway at 246th Street
Bronx, NY 10471
Tel: 718-543-3344
www.vancortlandthouse.org

*Pop-top quilt, Kenya, 1970s. Courtesy of Brooklyn Chil-
dren's Museum.*

Brooklyn Children's Museum

145 Brooklyn Avenue
Brooklyn, NY 11213
Tel: 718-735-4400x17 Fax: 718-735-5664
www.brooklynkids.org
Hours: Wed–Fri 1–6 pm, Sat–Sun 11–6 pm
Contact: Beth Alberty
Institution type: Children's museum
Collection type: Clothing, accessories, uniforms,
costumes, general textiles, flags
Description: 1850–present. Clothing and textiles
make up a portion of the larger collection. Collection contains more than 1,000 costumes,
textiles, and accessories plus 1,000 pieces of
jewelry and other adornment. Costumes are
mostly regional or ethnographic. Other items
include more than 2,000 dolls.
$ ✍

The Brooklyn Historical Society

128 Pierrepont Street, Room 617
Brooklyn, NY 11201
Tel: 718-222-4111
www.brooklynhistory.org

Brooklyn Museum of Art

200 Eastern Parkway
Brooklyn, NY 11238
Tel: 718-638-5000
www.brooklynmuseum.org
Hours: Wed–Fri 10–5 pm, Sat–Sun 11–6 pm
Institution type: Art museum
$ ✍

The Kurdish Museum

144 Underhill Avenue
Brooklyn, NY 11238
Tel: 718-783-7930

The Pieter Claesen Wycoff House Museum

5816 Clarendon Road
Brooklyn, NY 11210
Tel: 718-629-5400
www.wyckoffassociation.org

Hillwood Art Museum

720 Northern Boulevard
Brookville, NY 11548
Tel: 516-299-4073 Fax: 516-299-2787
www.liu.edu/museum
Hours: Mon–Fri 9:30–4:30 pm, Thu 9:30–8 pm,
Sat 11–3 pm
Contact: Director
Institution type: Art museum, university museum
Collection type: Clothing, accessories, costumes,
general textiles
Description: Pre-1700–1950. Pre-Columbian and
colonial era textiles, including headwear, man-
tles, and shoes. Holdings include more than
400 African textiles, colonial through the twen-
tieth century.

Buffalo and Erie County Historical Society

25 Nottingham Court
Buffalo, NY 14216
Tel: 716-873-9644
www.bechs.org

Buffalo and Erie County Naval and Military Park

1 Naval Park Cove
Buffalo, NY 14202
Tel: 716-847-1773
www.buffalonavalpark.org

Byron Historical Museum

6407 Town Line Road
Byron, NY 14422
Tel: 585-548-9008

Big Springs Historical Society Museum

3095 Main Street
Caledonia, NY 14423
Tel: 585-538-9880

Carriage House Museum

2 North Park Street
Camden, NY 13316
Tel: 315-245-4652

The Granger Homestead Society

295 North Main Street
Canandaigua, NY 14424
Tel: 585-394-1472
www.grangerhomestead.org

Ontario County Historical Society

55 North Main Street
Canandaigua, NY 14424
Tel: 585-394-4975
www.ochs.org

Pierrepont Museum

864 State Highway 68
Canton, NY 13617
Tel: 315-386-8311

St. Lawrence County Historical Association

3 East Main Street
Canton, NY 13617
Tel: 315-386-8133 Fax: 315-386-8134
www.slcha.org
Hours: Tue–Thu, Sat 12–4 pm, Fri 12–8 pm
Contact: Sue Longshore, Collections Manager
Institution type: History museum, historic house,
county museum
Collection type: Clothing, accessories, uniforms,
general textiles, quilts, flags
Description: 1800–present. Majority of the collection dates between 1850 and 1950 and
includes men's and women's main garments,
outerwear, underwear, and military uniforms.
Accessories include aprons, scarves, belts, and
collars. Household linens include bedding,
quilts, blankets, throws, and table scarves.

Cattaraugus Area Historical Center

23 Main Street
Cattaraugus, NY 14719
Tel: 716-257-3312

Lorenz State Historic Site

17 Rippleton Road
Cazenovia, NY 13035
Tel: 315-655-3200

Horace Greeley House of New Castle Historical Society

100 King Street
Chappaqua, NY 10514
Tel: 914-238-4666

The Alice T. Miner Colonial Collection
9618 Main Street
Chazy, NY 12921
Tel: 518-846-7336
www.minermuseum.org

Cherry Valley Museum
49 Main Street
Cherry Valley, NY 13320
Tel: 607-264-3303
www.cherryvalleymuseum.org

**The Handweaving Museum and
Arts Center**
314 John Street
Clayton, NY 13624
Tel: 315-686-4123
www.hm-ac.org

**Society for the Preservation of
Long Island Antiquities**
161 Main Street
Cold Spring Harbor, NY 11724
Tel: 631-692-4664
www.splia.org

**The Farmer's Museum and New York
State Historical Association**
State Route 80
Cooperstown, NY 13326
Tel: 607-547-1400
www.nysha.org
Hours: Vary by season

**National Baseball Hall of Fame and
Museum**
25 Main Street
Cooperstown, NY 13326-0590
Tel: 607-547-7200
www.baseballhalloffame.org

**The Benjamin Patterson Inn
Museum Complex**
Corning Painted Post Historical Society
59 West Pultney Street
Corning, NY 14830
Tel: 607-937-5281
http://pattersoninnmuseum.org
Hours: Mon–Fri 10–4 pm
Contact: Carrie Fellows, Curator
Institution type: Historic house

Collection type: Clothing, accessories, uniforms,
general textiles
Description: 1800–present
$ ✍

Cortland County Historical Society
25 Homer Avenue
Cortland, NY 13045
Tel: 607-756-6071

Bronck Museum
90 County Road 42
Coxsackie, NY 12051
Tel: 518-731-6490 Fax: 518-731-7672
www.gchistory.org
Hours: Wed–Fri 12–4 pm, Sat 10–4 pm, Sun 1–4
pm (Memorial Day–Labor Day)
Contact: Shelby Mattice, Site Manager
Institution type: History museum, historic house
Collection type: Clothing, accessories, uniforms,
general textiles, quilts, flags
Description: 1800–1914. Primarily late-
nineteenth-century clothing and domestic
textiles, including quilts. Clothing is predominantly women's and children's. Other items
include full or partial military uniforms from
World War I to Vietnam War and a small collection of late-nineteenth- to early-twentieth-
century American flags.
$ ✍

Durham Center Museum
State Route 145
East Durham, NY 12423
Tel: 518-239-8461

East Hampton Historical Society
101 Main Street
East Hampton, NY 11937
Tel: 631-324-6850
www.easthamptonhistory.org

Eastchester Historical Society
388 California Road
Eastchester, NY 10709
Tel: 914-793-1900
Hours: Wed 10–4 pm, and by appointment
Contact: Saul Radin
Institution type: History museum
Collection type: Clothing, accessories, general tex-
tiles, flags

Description: 1800–1960. Mainly nineteenth-
and twentieth-century objects. Access is limited.

Chemung Valley History Museum
415 East Water Street
Elmira, NY 14901
Tel: 607-734-4167
www.chemungvalleymuseum.org

Fairport Historical Museum
Perinton Historical Society, 18 Perrin Street
Fairport, NY 14450-2122
Tel: 716-223-3989
www.angelfire.com/ny5/fairporthistmuseum

Van Wyck Homestead Museum
504 Route 9
Fishkill, NY 12524-0133
Tel: 845-896-9560

The Godwin-Ternbach Museum
Queens College, 65-30 Kissena Boulevard
Flushing, NY 11367
Tel: 718-997-4747
www.qc.edu/art/gtmus.html

Queens College–CUNY
HISTORIC COSTUME COLLECTION
65-30 Kissena Boulevard
Flushing, NY 11367
Tel: 718-997-4168 Fax: 718-997-4163
Hours: By appointment
Contact: Elizabeth D. Lowe
Institution type: University collection
Collection type: Clothing, accessories, uniforms
Description: 1760–present. Mostly women's
clothing. Oldest item is from the late eigh-
teenth century. Collection is strong in objects
from designers 1980–present.

Queens Historical Society and Kingsland Homestead
Weeping Beech Park, 143-35 37th Avenue
Flushing, NY 11354
Tel: 718-939-0647
www.queenshistoricalsociety.org/index.html

Old Fort House Museum
29 Lower Broadway
Fort Edward, NY 12828
Tel: 518-747-9600
www.ftedward.com

Old Fort Johnson
Route 5
Fort Johnson, NY 12070
Tel: 518-843-0300
www.oldfortjohnson.org

Fort Plain Museum
389 Canal Street
Fort Plain, NY 13339
Tel: 518-993-2527

Ischua Valley Historical Society
9 Pine Street
Franklinville, NY 14737
Tel: 716-676-5651
Hours: Sun 2–5 pm (Memorial Day–Labor Day),
and by appointment
Contact: Gertrude Schnell, President
Institution type: History museum, historic house
Collection type: Clothing, general textiles, quilts
Description: 1850–present. Collection includes
various clothing items and quilts.

Livingston County Historical Society Museum
30 Center Street
Geneseo, NY 14454
Tel: 716-243-2281
www.livingstoncountyhistoricalsociety.org

Geneva Historical Society
543 South Main Street
Geneva, NY 14456
Tel: 315-789-5151 Fax: 315-789-0314
www.genevahistoricalsociety.com
Hours: Tue–Fri 9–5 pm, Sat–Sun 1:30–4:30 pm
(Jul–Aug)
Contact: John Marks
Institution type: History museum, historic house
Collection type: Clothing, accessories, uniforms,
costumes, general textiles, quilts, flags
Description: 1700–present. Clothing and textiles
represent Geneva and Finger Lakes region and
include mostly women's and children's cos-
tumes, with some men's and some military.

Collection also includes locally produced quilts and coverlets. Items of interest include women's suffrage banner, 1800 muslin pelisse, and a select number of interesting fabric examples.

Chapman Historical Museum

348 Glen Street
Glens Falls, NY 12801
Tel: 518-793-2826
www.chapmanmuseum.org

The Hyde Collection

161 Warren Street
Glens Falls, NY 12801
Tel: 518-792-1761 Fax: 518-792-9197
www.hydecollection.org
Hours: Tue–Sat 10–5 pm, Sun 12–5 pm
Contact: Erin Budis Coe
Institution type: Art museum, historic house
Collection type: Clothing, costumes, general textiles
Description: Pre-1700–1960. Period clothing from the nineteenth and twentieth centuries, fifteenth-century to twentieth-century velvets, fifteenth-century French tapestries, copper plate printed toiles, and other textiles and furnishing fabrics.

The Harness Racing Museum and Hall of Fame

240 Main Street
Goshen, NY 10924
Tel: 845-294-6330
www.harnessmuseum.com

Gouverneur Museum

30 Church Street
Gouverneur, NY 13642
Tel: 315-287-0570
Hours: Wed, Sat 1–3 pm
Contact: Joseph Laurenza
Institution type: History museum
Collection type: Clothing, accessories, uniforms
Description: 1800–1960. Collection includes men's and women's clothing.

Slate Valley Museum

17 Water Street
Granville, NY 12832
Tel: 518-642-1417
www.slatevalleymuseum.org

Herkimer County Historical Society

400 North Main Street
Herkimer, NY 13350
Tel: 315-866-6413
www.rootsweb.com/~nyhchs
Hours: Mon–Fri 10–4 pm
Contact: Susan R. Perkins
Institution type: History museum
Collection type: Clothing, accessories, uniforms, general textiles, flags
Description: 1800–1960. A small collection of clothing, 50 U.S. flags, and 1 uniform from World War II. Clothing and textile collection is very limited.

$ 🖊

Iroquois Indian Museum

324 Caverns Road
Howes Cave, NY 12092
Tel: 518-296-8949
www.iroquoismuseum.org

Huntington Historical Society

209 Main Street
Huntington, NY 11743
Tel: 631-427-7045
www.huntingtonhistoricalsociety.org
Hours: Tue–Fri 1–4 pm
Contact: Judith Estes
Institution type: History museum, historic house
Collection type: Clothing, accessories, costumes, general textiles, quilts, flags
Description: 1800–1960. 5 Worth gowns and many lawn dresses, all with Huntington connection. Holdings also include children's clothing; extensive accessories, including parasols and beaded handbags; and quilt collection (50) and samplers (34).

$ 🖊

Interlaken Historical Society

8391 Main Street
Interlaken, NY 14847
Tel: 607-532-8505
www.interlakenhistory.org

Hours: Sat–Sun 10–4 pm (Jul–Sep), and by
appointment
Contact: Diane Nelson, Collections Chair
Institution type: History museum
Collection type: Clothing, uniforms, costumes,
quilts
Description: 1760–present. Clothing and textile
items from 1790s to present, emphasizing the
communities of southern Seneca County, New
York.

✍

Cornell University, Department of Textiles and Apparel

208 Martha Van Rensselaer Hall
Ithaca, NY 14853
Tel: 607-255-8064 Fax: 607-255-1093
http://char.txa.cornell.edu/treasures/index.html
Hours: Mon–Sun 8–6 pm, by appointment only
Contact: Charlotte Jirousek
Institution type: University collection
Collection type: Clothing, accessories, uniforms,
general textiles, quilts
Description: Pre-1700–present. Predominately
Western fashion and accessories from 1800 to
2000. Holdings include a small but significant
collection of ethnographic costumes and tex-
tiles and a significant collection of nineteenth-
century children's wear. Oldest items are
Coptic and pre-Columbian textiles and European textile examples from the fifteenth century.

$ ✍

The History Center in Tompkins County

401 East State Street, Suite 100
Ithaca, NY 14850
Tel: 607-642-8264
www.thehistorycenter.net
Hours: Tue, Thu, Sat 11–5 pm
Institution type: History museum, county
museum, city museum

✍

King Manor Museum

150-03 Jamaica Avenue
Jamaica, NY 11432
Tel: 718-658-7400
www.kingmanor.org/home.asp
Hours: Thu–Fri 12–2 pm, Sat–Sun 1–5 pm
(Feb–Dec)

Institution type: Historic house
$ ✍

Fenton History Center

67 Washington Street
Jamestown, NY 14701
Tel: 716-664-6256
www.fentonhistorycenter.org
Hours: Mon–Sat 10–4 pm
Contact: Phoebe Forbes
Institution type: History museum, historic house,
city museum
Collection type: Clothing, accessories, uniforms,
costumes, general textiles, quilts, flags
Description: 1800–present. Clothing, uniforms,
flags and banners, textiles, quilts, and accessories, all pertaining to the Chautauqua
County, New York, area, including a few items
from the first settlers of 1809. Areas of greater
concentration are Victorian era and
1900–1970. Collection also includes objects
from current era, particularly T-shirts and
items from Jamestown events.

$ ✍

Columbia County Historical Society

5 Albany Avenue
Kinderhook, NY 12106
Tel: 518-758-9265

Senate House State Historical Site

312 Fair Street
Kingston, NY 12401
Tel: 845-338-2786
www.nysparks.state.ny.us/sites/
info.asp?siteID=26

LeRoy Historical Society

23 East Main Street
LeRoy, NY 14482
Tel: 585-768-7433 Fax: 585-768-7579
www.jellomuseum.com
Hours: Mon–Fri 10–4 pm
Contact: Lynne Belluscio
Institution type: History museum, historic house
Collection type: Clothing, accessories, uniforms,
general textiles, flags
Description: 1800–present. Mid- to late-
nineteenth-century clothing and good early-
twentieth-century items, mostly from the
western New York region.

$ ✍

The Lewiston Museum

469 Plain Street
Lewiston, NY 14092
Tel: 716-754-4214
Hours: Wed 1–4 pm, Wed–Sun 1–4 pm
(Jun–Sep)
Contact: Nona McQuay, Curator
Institution type: History museum, historic house
Collection type: Clothing, accessories, uniforms, general textiles
Description: 1850–present. Costumes, dresses, and uniforms of the Niagara Frontier. All decades since 1850 are represented by men's and women's clothing, underclothing, and accessories. Included are Jenny Lind's gloves, left during her visit for the wedding of her servants.

Old Village Hall Museum

215 South Wellwood Avenue
Lindenhurst, NY 11757
Tel: 631-957-4385

Niagara County Historical Society

215 Niagara Street
Lockport, NY 14094-2605
Tel: 716-434-7433 Fax: 716-434-3309
www.niagaracounty.org
Hours: Wed–Sat 1–5 pm (Jan–Jun, Sep–Dec); Mon–Fri 10–5 pm, Sat–Sun 1–5 pm (Jul–Aug)
Contact: Linda B. Covell
Institution type: History museum, historic house, county museum
Collection type: Clothing, accessories, quilts, flags
Description: 1850–1960. Good quilt and coverlet collection, women's clothing, hats, and purses.

$ 🖎

Lewis County Historical Society Museum

7552 South State Street
Lowville, NY 13367
Tel: 315-376-8957

Franklin County Historical and Museum Society and House of History

51 Milwaukee Street
Malone, NY 12953
Tel: 518-483-2750

Larchmont Historical Society

740 West Boston Post Road, Suite 301
Mamaroneck, NY 10538
Tel: 914-381-2239

Town of Manlius Museum and Historical Society

101 Scoville Avenue
Manlius, NY 13104
Tel: 315-682-6660

Ulster County Historical Society

2682 Route 209
Marbletown, NY 12402
Tel: 845-338-5614

Historical Society of Middletown and Wallkill Precinct

25 East Avenue
Middletown, NY 10940
Tel: 914-342-0941

Schuyler County Historical Society

108 North Catherine
Montour Falls, NY 14865
Tel: 607-535-9741

Cayuga-Owasco Lakes Historical Society

14 West Cayuga
Moravia, NY 13118
Tel: 315-497-3906

Red Barn Museum

518 River Road
Morristown, NY 13669
Tel: 315-375-6390

Genesee Country Village and Museum

1410 Flint Hill Road
Mumford, NY 14511
Tel: 585-538-6822
www.gcv.org

Bement-Billings Farmstead

9142 Route 38
Newark Valley, NY 13811
Tel: 607-642-9516

David Crawford House

189 Montgomery Street
Newburgh, NY 12550
Tel: 845-561-2585
www.newburghhistoricalsociety.com/
museum.html

Historical Society of Rockland County

20 Zukor Road
New City, NY 10956
Tel: 845-634-9629
www.rocklandhistory.org

Huguenot Historical Society

18 Broadhead Avenue
New Paltz, NY 12561
Tel: 845-255-1660 Fax: 845-255-0376
www.hhs-newpaltz.org
Hours: By appointment
Contact: Leslie LeFevre Stratton
Institution type: History museum, historic house
Collection type: Clothing, accessories, uniforms, costumes, general textiles, quilts
Description: 1760–1960. Primarily women's and children's clothing and accessories focus on nineteenth-century items from New York State. Holdings also include a large collection of domestic and bedding textiles, including quilts, woven coverlets, bed and table linens, and floor coverings, with local history from Ulster County/Lower Hudson Valley. Small collection of American and European lace.
$ ✍

American Jewish Historical Society

15 West 16th Street
New York, NY 10011
Tel: 212-294-6160
www.ajhs.org

Chancellor Robert R. Livingston Masonic Library and Museum

71 West 23rd Street
New York, NY 10010-4171
Tel: 212-337-6620
www.nymasoniclibrary.org

Cooper-Hewitt National Design Museum, Smithsonian Institution

2 East 91st Street
New York, NY 10128
Tel: 212-849-8300
www.si.edu/ndm

Dyckman Farmhouse Museum and Park

4881 Broadway at 204th Street
New York, NY 10034
Tel: 212-304-9422
www.dyckmanfarmhouse.org

El Museo Del Barrio

1230 5th Avenue
New York, NY 10029
Tel: 212-831-7272
www.elmuseo.org

Fraunces Tavern Museum

54 Pearl Street
New York, NY 10004
Tel: 212-425-1778 Fax: 212-509-3467
www.frauncestavernmuseum.org
Hours: Tue–Fri 12–5 pm, Sat 10–5 pm
Contact: Nadezhda Williams
Institution type: History museum, historic house
Collection type: Clothing, accessories, general textiles
Description: 1700–1899. 3 military hats circa 1812, 2 small eighteenth-century samplers, commemorative ribbons, eighteenth-century man's jacket and breeches, 2 eighteenth-century men's vests, and 1 pair eighteenth-century woman's stays.
$ ✍

The George Gustav Heye Center

Alexander Hamilton U.S. Custom House
One Bowling Green
New York, NY 10004
Tel: 212-514-3700
www.americanindian.si.edu
Hours: Mon–Sun 10–5 pm, Thu 10–8 pm
Institution type: Federal museum
Collection type: Costumes, general textiles
Description: Pre-1700–present. For current exhibitions, visit the website.
✍

The Glove Museum

15 West 28th Street, Suite 401
New York, NY 10001
Tel: 212-803-1600 Fax: 212-683-9099
www.wegloveyou.com
Hours: By appointment
Contact: Jay G. Ruckel
Institution type: History museum
Collection type: Accessories, costumes

Description: Pre-1700–present. Collections dating from circa 1600 to the present include all types of hand wear (both fashionable and utilitarian), glove stretchers, glove boxes, glove button-hooks, patents' trade cards, billyheads, advertisements, designer sketches, textiles, glove novelties, glove bygones, old tools of the glove-makers, and other related items.

$ ✍🏻

The Hispanic Society of America
613 West 155th Street and Broadway
New York, NY 10032
Tel: 212-926-2234
www.hispanicsociety.org

Japan Society Gallery
333 East 47th Street
New York, NY 10017
Tel: 212-715-1233
www.japansociety.org

The Jewish Museum
1109 5th Avenue
New York, NY 10128
Tel: 212-423-3200
www.thejewishmuseum.org

Robe à la française, English, circa 1750. Courtesy of Metropolitan Museum of Art, Costume Institute.

Metropolitan Museum of Art
THE COSTUME INSTITUTE
1000 Fifth Avenue
New York, NY 10028
Tel: 212-570-3908
www.metmuseum.org
Hours: Tue–Sun 9:30–5 pm
Contact: Harold Koda, Curator

Institution type: Art museum
Collection type: Clothing, accessories, costumes
Description: Pre-1700–present. More than 80,000 costumes and accessories spanning five continents and just as many centuries. Possessing the greatest collection of costume in the world is taken as a responsibility of exhibition, interpretation, and research. State-of-the-art costume conservation laboratory is adjacent to the collection and study-storage facilities are accessible by appointment to designers, students, and academics.

$ ✍🏻

Mount Vernon Hotel Museum and Garden
421 East 61st Street
New York, NY 10021
Tel: 212-838-6878
www.mvhm.org
Hours: Tue–Sun 11–4 pm
Contact: Lisa Bedell
Institution type: Historic house
Collection type: Clothing, accessories, costumes, quilts
Description: 1760–1960. Small collection of objects donated to the museum by members of the Colonial Dames of America, the museum's parent organization. In the textile collection there are 12 quilts, and in the costume collection there is a pair of slippers, a child's dress, and assorted personal objects.

$ ✍🏻

The Museum at Fashion Institute of Technology
Fashion Institute of Technology
Seventh Avenue at 27th Street
New York, NY 10001
Tel: 212-217-5701
www.fitnyc.edu/museum
Hours: Tue–Fri 12–8 pm, Sat 10–5 pm
Institution type: University museum
✍🏻
COSTUME COLLECTION
Contact: Ellen Shanley
Collection type: Clothing, accessories
Description: 1700–present. More than 50,000 objects from the mid-eighteenth century to the present. Strengths are in twentieth-century holdings and particularly in couture and ready-to-wear women's clothing. Designers include Armani, Balenciaga, Beene, Blass, Chanel,

Evening dress by Frederick Worth, circa 1883. Courtesy of the Museum at Fashion Institiute of Technology.

Millennium Woman, catsuit designed by Charmaine Spice for Miss Trinidad and Tobago, 1998. Courtesy of Museum of the City of New York.

Dior, Galanos, Gaultier, Halston, James, McCardell, Miyake, Moschino, Poiret, and Schiaparelli. More than 20,000 accessories, including shoes, hats, bags, belts, and hosiery in addition to smaller collections of costume jewelry and eyeglasses.

TEXTILE COLLECTION

Contact: Lynn Felsher

Collection type: General textiles

Description: Pre-1700–present. More than 30,000 textiles from the fifteenth century to the present illustrate a broad variety of textile techniques and traditions from around the world. Collection contains 1,300 fabric sample books from the mid-nineteenth century to the 1960s and 14,000 jacquard point papers and painted textile designs. In addition to the permanent collection, 250,000 textile swatches dating from the nineteenth century have been grouped thematically for visual reference.

Museum of Chinese in the Americas

70 Mulberry Street, 2nd Floor
New York, NY 10013
Tel: 212-619-4785 Fax: 212-619-4720
www.moca-nyc.org
Hours: Mon–Sun 12–6 pm
Institution type: History museum
$ ✍

The Museum of Television and Radio

25 West 52nd Street
New York, NY 10019
Tel: 212-621-6600
www.mtr.org

Museum of the City of New York

1220 5th Avenue
New York, NY 10029
Tel: 212-534-1672 Fax: 212-534-5974
www.mcny.org
Hours: Wed–Sun 10–5 pm
Contact: Phyllis Magdison
Institution type: History museum, city museum
Collection type: Clothing, accessories, uniforms, costumes, general textiles
Description: 1700–present. Celebrated and unparalleled for their splendor, documentation, and extraordinary degree of preservation, the 27,000 objects document the stylist evolution of our nation's fashion capital and chronicle the social history of its constituency as well. This living archive of New York City's attire embraces the twenty-first-century holdings with as much enthusiasm as the eighteenth-century holdings. 129 couture designs by the pre-eminent couture house of Worth/Paris; fashions of contemporary New Yorkers, as exemplified by the Millenium Woman catsuit worn in a recent Brooklyn 1998 Miss Trinidad and Tobago competition; and an array of Afro-centric wedding designs.
$ ✍

New York Historical Society

170 Central Park West
New York, NY 10024
Tel: 212-873-3400
www.nyhistory.org
Hours: Mon–Sat 10–6 pm
Contact: Margi Hofer

Institution type: Art museum, history museum

Collection type: Clothing, accessories, uniforms, general textiles, quilts, flags

Description: 1700–1899. Includes strong holdings in military uniforms and accoutrements. Collection also contains textiles, samplers, flags, and quilts and moderate holdings of personal and costume related accessories and jewelry.

$ ✍

The New York Public Library for the Performing Arts

40 Lincoln Center Plaza

New York, NY 10023

Tel: 212-970-1830

www.nypl.org/research/lpa/lpa.html

The Studio Museum in Harlem

144 West 125th Street

New York, NY 10027

Tel: 212-864-4500

www.studiomuseuminharlem.org

The Ukrainian Museum

203 2nd Avenue

New York, NY 10003

Tel: 212-228-0110

www.ukrainianmuseum.org

Yeshiva University Museum

15 West 16th Street

New York, NY 10011

Tel: 212-294-8330x8815 Fax: 212-294-8335

www.yumuseum.org

Hours: Sun, Tue–Thu 11–5 pm

Contact: Bonni-Dara Michaels

Institution type: Art museum, history museum, university museum

Collection type: Clothing, accessories, uniforms, general textiles

Description: Pre-1700–present. Ceremonial and domestic textiles. Ceremonial textiles include wimpels (Torah wrappers), including one from 1643, Torah Ark curtains, Torah mantles, and lectern covers. Domestic textiles are from Yugoslavia, Russia, Germany, and United States. Clothing and accessories number 573 items, including Ottoman, North African, central and western European, central Asian, Palestinian, and American ceremonial and bridal dresses and accessories.

$ ✍

Lansing Manor House Museum

NY State Route 30

North Blenheim, NY 12131

Tel: 518-827-6121

www.nypa.gov/vc/blengil.htm

Northport Historical Society Museum

215 Main Street

Northport, NY 11768

Tel: 631-757-9859

www.northporthistorical.org

Chenango County Historical Society Museum

45 Rexford Street

Norwich, NY 13815

Tel: 607-334-9227

www.chenangocounty.org/chencohistso

Old Bethpage Village Restoration

1303 Round Swamp Road

Old Bethpage, NY 11804

Tel: 516-572-8401 Fax: 516-572-8413

www.oldbethpage.org

The Shaker Museum and Library

88 Shaker Museum Road

Old Chatham, NY 12136

Tel: 518-794-9100x201

www.smandl.org

Old Westbury Gardens

71 Old Westbury Road

Old Westbury, NY 11568

Tel: 516-333-0048

www.oldwestburygardens.org

Six Nations Indian Museum

1462 County Route 60

Onchiota, NY 12989

Tel: 518-891-2299

Madison County Historical Society

435 Main Street

Oneida, NY 13421-0415

Tel: 315-363-4136

www.dreamscape.com/mchs1900

Hours: Mon–Fri 9–4 pm

Contact: Michael Flanagan, Collections Manager

Institution type: History museum

Collection type: Clothing, accessories, uniforms, costumes, general textiles, flags

Description: 1760–present. Strengths are in late-nineteenth-century to early-twentieth-century clothing, especially dresses.

$

Oneida Community Mansion House

170 Kenwood Avenue
Oneida, NY 13421
Tel: 315-363-0745
www.oneidacommunity.org

Shakowi Cultural Center

Oneida Indian Nation, 5 Territory Road
Oneida, NY 13421-9304
Tel: 315-363-1424
www.oneida-nation.net/shakowi

The National Soccer Hall of Fame

18 Stadium Circle
Oneonta, NY 13820
Tel: 607-432-3351
www.soccerhall.org

Orchard Park Historical Society

4287 South Buffalo Street
Orchard Park, NY 14127
Tel: 716-662-2185

Oysterponds Historical Society

Village Lane
Orient, NY 11957-0263
Tel: 631-323-2480
Hours: Thu, Sat, Sun 2–5 pm (Summer), call for hours
Contact: Amy Folk
Institution type: Art museum, history museum, historic house
Collection type: Clothing, accessories, uniforms, costumes, general textiles, quilts, flags
Description: 1700–1960. Items from Orient and East Marion villages of eastern Long Island from the mid-nineteenth century through the early twentieth century. Men's, women's, and children's clothing (outerwear and underwear), hats, shoes, handbags, uniforms, household linens, quilts, coverlets, parasols, fans, samplers, and flags.

$

Ossining Historical Society Museum

196 Croton Avenue
Ossining, NY 10562
Tel: 914-941-0001
www.ossininghistorical.org

Tioga County Historical Society

110 Front Street
Owego, NY 13827
Tel: 607-687-2460 Fax: 607-687-7788
www.tiogahistory.org
Hours: Tue–Sat 10–4 pm
Contact: Gwenyth Goodnight
Institution type: History museum, county museum
Collection type: Clothing, accessories, uniforms, costumes, general textiles, quilts, flags
Description: 1850–1960. Mostly mid- to late-nineteenth-century items. Highlights include a quilt made by a local tailor for his daughter using scraps of suiting material from his tailoring shop, circa 1900, and samplers from the late eighteenth century.

Raynham Hall Museum

20 West Main Street
Oyster Bay, NY 11771
Tel: 516-922-6808
www.raynhamhallmuseum.org

Alling Coverlet Museum

122 William Street
Palmyra, NY 14522
Tel: 315-597-6981
www.palmyrany.com/historicpal/index.htm

Historic Palmyra Museum

132 Market Street
Palmyra, NY 14522
Tel: 315-597-6981
www.palmyrany.com/historicpal/index.htm

Joseph Smith Historical Farm—Museum of Church History and Art

603 Route 21 South
Palmyra, NY 14522
Tel: 801-240-0297

Parishville Museum
Main Street
Parishville, NY 13672
Tel: 315-265-7619

The Peekskill Museum
124 Union Avenue
Peekskill, NY 10566
Tel: 914-736-0473
www.peekskillmuseum.com

Oliver House Museum and Yates County Genealogical and Historical Society
200 Main Street
Penn Yan, NY 14527
Tel: 315-536-7318
www.yatespast.com

Clinton County Historical Association and Museum
3 Cumberland Avenue
Plattsburgh, NY 12901
Tel: 518-561-0340

Kent-Delord House Museum
17 Cumberland Avenue
Plattsburgh, NY 12901
Tel: 518-561-1035

Historical Society of Greater Port Jefferson
115 Prospect Street
Port Jefferson, NY 11777
Tel: 631-473-2665
www.portjeffhistorical.org

Cow Neck Peninsula Historical Society and Sands-Willets House
336 Port Washington Boulevard
Port Washington, NY 11050
Tel: 516-365-9074
www.cowneck.org

Locust Grove
YOUNG FAMILY COLLECTION
2683 South Road
Poughkeepsie, NY 12601
Tel: 845-454-4500 Fax: 845-485-7122
www.morsehistoricsite.org
Hours: Mon–Fri 9–5 pm
Contact: Curator
Institution type: Historic house

Collection type: Clothing, accessories, general textiles
Description: 1875–1975. Clothing and accessories purchased for use at the Locust Grove estate in New York's Hudson Valley region. Formal and everyday clothes (250 pieces), household textiles (1,000 pieces), and accessories (500 pieces), including hats, fans, shoes, and undergarments. Collection survives intact in its original setting and includes fine art and furniture in a historic house museum as well as personal possessions, including the Young family archives.
$ ✍

Pound Ridge Society and Museum
255 Westchester Avenue
Pound Ridge, NY 10576
Tel: 914-764-4333

Narcissa Prentiss House
7226 Mill Pond Road
Prattsburgh, NY 14873
Tel: 607-522-4537

Suffolk County Historical Society
300 West Main Street
Riverhead, NY 11901
Tel: 631-727-2881

Baker-Cederberg Museum and Archives
Rochester General Hospital
1425 Portland Avenue
Rochester, NY 14621
Tel: 585-922-3521
www.viahealth.org/body_rochester.cfm?id=506

Rochester Historical Society
485 East Avenue
Rochester, NY 14607
Tel: 585-271-2705 Fax: 585-271-9089
www.rochesterhistory.org
Hours: Mon–Fri 8:30–4:30 pm
Institution type: History museum, historic house
$ ✍
CLOTHING COLLECTION
Contact: Lizabeth Dailey
Collection type: Clothing, accessories, uniforms, costumes
Description: 1700–1960. Spans 180 years and includes 1820s day dresses, 1850s maternity dresses, 1970s hot pants, nineteenth-century

men's drop front breeches, and 1940s children's winter leggings. Highlights include Susan B. Anthony's gown worn for state occasions and an evening dress worn by First Lady Mrs. William McKinley. Men's collection has national significance as Rochester was a major production center for men's clothing, particularly Hickey-Freeman suits.

TEXTILE COLLECTION

Contact: Lizabeth Dailey

Collection type: General textiles, quilts

Description: 1800–1960. Bed linens, quilts, coverlets, blankets, rugs, tablecloths, napkins, towels, doilies, lambrequins, curtains, wall hangings, samplers (1780s–1820s), and embroidered pictures. Other items include lace collection with 700 items and embroidered wall hangings and pictures, including a silk-on-silk picture of Abraham and Isaac and a large needlepoint portrait of George Washington.

Rochester Museum and Science Center

657 East Avenue
Rochester, NY 14607-2177
Tel: 585-271-4320 Fax: 585-271-0492
www.rmsc.org

Hours: Mon–Sat 9–5 pm, Sun 12–5 pm

Institution type: History museum

$ ✍

CLOTHING, COSTUMES, AND ACCESSORIES

Contact: Brian L. Nagel

Collection type: Clothing, accessories, costumes

Description: 1700–present. Regional collections from 1800 through the 1960s include boxed collections of undergarments, collars, wraps, and accessories. Collection is rich in 1870–1910s, including items from local dressmakers and retailers and manufacturers from New York and Paris. Other items include hats, shoes, and buttons made in Rochester and elsewhere. Accessories include more than 900 women's fans.

FLAGS

Contact: Brian L. Nagel

Collection type: Flags

Description: 1760–present. Primarily U.S. flags, from an early thirteen-star homespun flag circa 1796 through fifty-star flags. Other items include numerous flags and banners from foreign countries.

GENERAL TEXTILES

Contact: Brian L. Nagel

Collection type: General textiles, quilts

Description: 1700–1960. Historical objects with strengths in household furnishings, especially quilts, coverlets, and early handweaving, including 170 coverlets, mostly regional, dating from 1833 to 1876; 120 samplers dating from 1726 to 1880, most with documentation; and a representative lace collection.

MILITARY UNIFORMS

Contact: Brian L. Nagel

Collection type: Uniforms

Description: 1760–present. Regional in scope, the collection includes primarily men's and women's uniforms or uniform elements worn by local individuals during Civil War, World War I, and World War II. Collection includes at least 1 coat and sash reportedly worn during the Revolutionary War and uniforms from the War of 1812, Mexican-American War, Spanish-American War, Korean War, and Vietnam War, many with associated accoutrements.

Collection type: Quilts

Contact: Brian L. Nagel

Description: 1760–1960. Quilts that were made and/or owned in the Genesee Valley region (80 percent) and quilts from areas that supplied immigrants to Rochester, including other parts of New York State, New England, and Pennsylvania (20 percent). The geographic focus and documentation makes this quilt collection one of the largest and significant regional collections with all types and techniques represented.

The Strong Museum, Children and Family History Museum

1 Manhattan Square
Rochester, NY 14607
Tel: 585-263-2701 x241 Fax: 585-263-2493
www.strongmuseum.org

Hours: Mon–Thu 10–5 pm, Fri 10–8 pm, Sat 10–5 pm, Sun 12–5 pm

Contact: Nicolas Ricketts

Institution type: History museum

Collection type: Clothing

Description: 1850–present. Collection is generally representative of middle-class life for children and adults in the Northeast.

$ ✍

Susan B. Anthony House

17 Madison Street
Rochester, NY 14608
Tel: 585-235-6124
www.susanbanthonyhouse.org

Erie Canal Village

5789 New London Road
Rome, NY 13440
Tel: 888-374-3226
www.eriecanalvillage.net

Rome Historical Society Museum

200 Church Street
Rome, NY 13440
Tel: 315-336-5870

Van Nostrand-Starkins House

221 Main Street
Roslyn, NY 11576
Tel: 516-625-4363

The Rye Historical Society and Square House Museum

1 Purchase Street
Rye, NY 10580
Tel: 914-967-7588
www.ryehistoricalsociety.org

Sackets Harbor Battlefield State Historic Site

505 West Washington Street
Sackets Harbor, NY 13685
Tel: 315-646-3634
http://sacketsharborny.com/battlefield.html

Seneca-Iroquois National Museum

814 Broad Street
Salamanca, NY 14779
Tel: 716-945-1738
www.senecamuseum.org

Historical Society of Saratoga Springs

The Casino, Congress Park
Saratoga Springs, NY 12866
Tel: 518-584-6920
www.saratogahistory.org/history

National Museum of Dance

99 South Broadway
Saratoga Springs, NY 12866

Tel: 518-584-2225x3001
www.dancemuseum.org
Hours: By appointment
Contact: Dolores E. Corrign, Volunteer Coordinator
Institution type: Private museum
Collection type: Accessories, costumes
Description: 1915–present. Dance costumes and related objects.
$ ✍

National Museum of Racing and Hall of Fame

191 Union Avenue
Saratoga Springs, NY 12866
Tel: 518-584-0400 Fax: 518-584-4574
www.racingmuseum.org
Hours: Mon–Sun 9–5 pm (Jul–Aug during Saratoga Race Meet); Mon–Sat 10–4 pm, Sun 12–4 pm
Contact: Lori Fisher, Curator of Collections
Institution type: Art museum, history museum
Collection type: Clothing, accessories, uniforms, general textiles
Description: 1900–present. Thoroughbred racing jockey apparel, including silks and caps, boots, dickies, breeches, helmets, underwear, goggles, and whips. Other objects include a small number of trainer accessories (hats, canes), popular culture items (neckties featuring famous thoroughbreds), horse blankets with documented provenance, saddlecloths, and commemorative scarves.
$ ✍

Sayville Historical Society

Edwards Street and Collins Avenue
Sayville, NY 11782
Tel: 631-563-0186

Scarsdale Historical Society

937 Post Road
Scarsdale, NY 10583
Tel: 914-723-1744 Fax: 914-723-2185
Hours: Mon–Fri 9–4 pm, weekends by appointment
Contact: Mimi Sherman, Consulting Curator
Institution type: Historic house
Collection type: Clothing, uniforms, general textiles, flags
Description: 1850–1914
$ ✍

Schenectady Museum

MARJORIE BRADT FOOTE COSTUME
COLLECTION
15 Nott Terrace Heights
Schenectady, NY 12308
Tel: 518-382-7890 Fax: 518-382-7893
www.schenectadymuseum.org
Hours: Tue–Fri 10–4:30 pm, Sat–Sun 12–5 pm
Contact: Bridget Kelly Stein
Institution type: History museum
Collection type: Clothing, accessories, costumes
Description: 1800–present. Primarily upper-class
  women's fashion from circa 1850 through the
  1960s, including under- and outerwear,
  dresses, wedding gowns, contemporary
  designers, and accessories—hats, shoes, fans,
  beaded handbags, and make-up compacts.
  Most objects are from the Greater Capital
  Region of New York and New England.
  $ ✍

Old Stone Fort Museum Complex

145 Fort Road
Schoharie, NY 12157
Tel: 518-295-7192
www.schohariehistory.net/OSF.htm

Schoharie Colonial Heritage Association

1743 Palatine House, Spring Street
Schoharie, NY 12157
Tel: 518-295-7505
www.midtel.net/~scha

Seneca Falls Historical Society

55 Cayuga Street
Seneca Falls, NY 13148
Tel: 315-568-8412
www.sfhistoricalsociety.org

Shelter Island Historical Society

16 South Ferry Road
Shelter Island, NY 11964
Tel: 516-749-0025
www.shelterislandhistsoc.org

Smithtown Historical Society

5 North Country Road
Smithtown, NY 11787
Tel: 631-265-6768
www.smithtownhistorical.org

Somers Historical Society Museum and Museum of the Early American Circus

Elephant Hotel, Route 100
Somers, NY 10589
Tel: 914-277-4977

Southold Historical Society and Museum

54325 Main Road
Southold, NY 11971
Tel: 631-765-5500 Fax: 631-765-5500
www.southoldhistoricalsociety.org
Hours: Mon–Fri 9–3 pm
Contact: Geoffrey Fleming, Director
Institution type: Art museum, history museum,
  historic house
Collection type: Clothing, accessories, uniforms,
  costumes, general textiles, flags
Description: 1700–1960. Textiles, clothing, acces-
  sories, photographs, furniture, and other deco-
  rative arts.
  $ ✍

Ogden Historical Society

568 Colby Street
Spencerport, NY 14559
Tel: 716-352-0660

*Livery uniform,
circa 1895–1920.
Courtesy of Staats-
burgh State His-
toric Site.*

Staatsburgh State Historic Site

Old Post Road
Staatsburg, NY 12580
Tel: 845-889-8851 Fax: 845-889-8843
www.staatsburgh.org
Hours: Sun 11–4 pm (Jan–Mar); Tue–Sat 10–5
  pm (Apr–Oct); Wed–Sun 12–5 pm (Dec)
Contact: Susan B. Walker

Institution type: Historic house, state museum

Collection type: Clothing, uniforms, general textiles

Description: Pre-1700–1960. Minimal clothing as part of larger collection of objects, including 2 footman's uniforms and some circa 1900 linens. Textile strengths are late-nineteenth-century French silk damask and brocade bed hangings, curtains, and upholstery. Other items include late-seventeenth- and early-eighteenth-century tapestries (Flemish) and original and late-nineteenth-century tapestry upholstery.

$ ✍️

Garibaldi and Meucci Museum of the Order Sons of Italy in America

420 Tompkins Avenue
Staten Island, NY 10305
Tel: 718-442-1608

Historic Richmond Town and Staten Island Historical Society

441 Clarke Avenue
Staten Island, NY 10306
Tel: 718-351-1611
www.historicrichmondtown.org

Jacques Marchais Museum of Tibetan Art

338 Lighthouse Avenue
Staten Island, NY 10306
Tel: 718-987-3500 Fax: 718-351-0402
www.tibetanmuseum.org
Hours: Wed–Sat 1–5 pm
Contact: Sarah Johnson
Institution type: Art museum
Collection type: Clothing, general textiles
Description: Pre-1700–present. Tibetan Buddhist art from Tibet, Mongolia, and Northern China from the fifteenth century through the early twentieth century. Holdings include objects from Japan, Nepal, and Thailand.

$ ✍️

Staten Island Institute of Arts and Sciences

75 Stuyvesant Place
Staten Island, NY 10301
Tel: 718-727-1135
www.statenislandmuseum.org

Sterling Historical Society

Route 104A
Sterling, NY 13156
Tel: 315-564-6189
www.lakeontario.net/sterlinghistory
Hours: Mon–Sun 2–5 pm
Contact: Volunteer staff
Institution type: History museum, historic house
Collection type: Clothing, uniforms, general textiles, flags
Description: 1850–1960.

$ ✍️

The Long Island Museum of American Art, History, and Carriages

1200 Route 25A
Stony Brook, NY 11790
Tel: 631-751-0066 Fax: 631-751-0353
www.longislandmuseum.org
Hours: Wed–Sat 10–5 pm, Sun 12–5 pm
Contact: Joshua Ruff
Institution type: Art museum, history museum
Collection type: Clothing, accessories, uniforms, costumes, general textiles, quilts, flags
Description: 1760–present. Men's, women's, and children's clothing from the 1790s to the 1980s as well as accessories, quilts, coverlets, samplers, and other textiles. Strengths include handmade and home-sewn nineteenth-century dresses, many of Long Island origin; wedding dress and mourning outfits; Ann Woodward collection of designer and couture clothing; and quilts and samplers of aesthetic and historic importance.

$ ✍️

Erie Canal Museum

318 Erie Boulevard East
Syracuse, NY 13202
Tel: 315-471-0593
www.eriecanalmuseum.org

Onondaga Historical Association Museum and Research Center

311 Montgomery Street
Syracuse, NY 13202
Tel: 315-428-1864
www.cynhistory.org

Tappantown Historical Society

PO Box 71
Tappan, NY 10983

Historic Hudson Valley

150 White Plains Road
Tarrytown, NY 10591
Tel: 914-631-8200 Fax: 914-631-0089
www.hudsonvalley.org
Hours: Vary by historic site
Contact: Kathleen Eagen Johnson, Curator
Institution type: History museum, historic house
Collection type: Clothing, accessories, costumes
Description: 1800–1900. 200 garments and accessories dating from the eighteenth century through the nineteenth century, most having a direct connection to the individuals who lived and worked at Sunnyside, Montgomery Place, or VanCortlandt Manor—three of the six historic properties. Highlights include diplomatic uniforms worn by Washington Irving, livery worn by Livingston family servants, dresses belonging to the VanCortlandt family, a banyan with a New York history of ownership, and "Rip Van Winkle" theatrical costume worn by noted actor Joseph Jefferson.
$ ✍

The Historical Society of Tarrytown

1 Grove Street
Tarrytown, NY 10591
Tel: 914-631-8374

Lyndhurst

635 South Broadway
Tarrytown, NY 10591
Tel: 914-631-4481 Fax: 914-631-5634
www.lyndhurst.org
Hours: Tue–Sun 10–5 pm (mid-Apr–Oct)
Contact: Cathryn Anders
Institution type: Historic house
Collection type: Clothing, accessories, uniforms, general textiles
Description: 1850–1960. Primarily clothing of Anna Gould, Duchess of Talleywood, 1940–1959. Other items include servants' uniforms, domestic linens, rugs, bearskins, and items relating to Lyndhurst Sewing School.
$ ✍

Fort Ticonderoga Museum

30 Fort Road
Ticonderoga, NY 12883
Tel: 518-585-2821
www.fort-ticonderoga.org

Historical Society of the Tonawandas

113 Main Street
Tonawanda, NY 14150-2129
Tel: 716-694-7406

Rensselaer County Historical Society

57 2nd Street
Troy, NY 12180
Tel: 518-272-7232 Fax: 518-273-1264
www.rchsonline.org
Hours: Tue–Sat 12–5 pm
Contact: Stacy P. Draper
Institution type: History museum
Collection type: Clothing, accessories, uniforms, costumes, general textiles
Description: 1760–1960. Men's, women's, and children's clothing with accessories and military uniforms. Collection places special emphasis on 1830s–1890s items relating to people who lived in Rensselaer County, New York.
$ ✍

Warsaw Historical Museum

15 Perry Avenue
Warsaw, NY 14569
Tel: 716-786-5240

Historical Society of the Town of Warwick

Forester Avenue
Warwick, NY 10990
Tel: 845-986-3236
www.warwickhistoricalsociety.org

New York State Bureau of Historic Sites

SITE SPECIFIC COLLECTIONS AT
TWENTY-THREE HISTORIC PROPERTIES
Peebles Island
Waterford, NY 12188
Tel: 518-237-8643
www.nysparks.com
Hours: Vary by site and by season
Contact: Robin Campbell, Associate Curator
Institution type: History museum, historic house, state museum
Collection type: Clothing, accessories, uniforms, costumes, general textiles, flags
Description: 1760–1960. Collections vary depending on historic site. Some of the historic houses have collections that relate directly to the families that lived there while other sites' collections are not historically connected to the

house, site, or family. Most items are American, some specifically New York State. At Olana State Historic Site, the collection is of late-nineteenth-century Mid-Eastern garments collected by Frederic Church, a Hudson River landscape painter.

$ ✍

Waterford Historical Museum and Cultural Center
2 Museum Lane
Waterford, NY 12188
Tel: 518-238-0809
www.timesunion.com/communities/whm

Peter Whitmer Historical Farm—Museum of Church History and Art
1451 Aunkst Road
Waterloo, NY 13165
Tel: 801-240-0297

Terwilliger Museum
31 East Williams Street
Waterloo, NY 13165
Tel: 315-539-0533 Fax: 315-539-7798
Hours: Tue–Fri 1–4 pm
Contact: James T. Hughes
Institution type: History museum
Collection type: Clothing, accessories, uniforms, general textiles, flags
Description: 1800–1960.
$ ✍

Jefferson County Historical Society
228 Washington Street
Watertown, NY 13601
Tel: 315-782-3491

Old Brutus Historical Society
8943 North Seneca Street
Weedsport, NY 13166
Tel: 315-834-9243
Hours: Mon–Tue 9–12 pm, Sun 1–4 pm (Memorial Day–Labor Day)
Contact: Jeanne L. Baker
Institution type: History museum
Collection type: Clothing, accessories, uniforms, general textiles, quilts, flags
Description: 1800–present. Clothing of residents of Weedsport, New York, area as well as quilts,

coverlets, wedding dresses, and uniforms from World War I through Iraq.

✍

West Point Museum
U.S. Military Academy, Building 2110
West Point, NY 10996
Tel: 845-938-2203
www.usma.edu/museum

Chautauqua County Historical Society
Main and Portage Streets
Center of Village Park
Westfield, NY 14787
Tel: 716-326-2977

Wilson Historical Museum
645 Lake Street
Wilson, NY 14172
Tel: 716-751-9886

Old Stone House Museum
22 Chestnut Street
Windsor, NY 13865
Tel: 607-655-1491

Middlebury Historical Society
22 South Academy Street
Wyoming, NY 14591
Tel: 716-495-6582

The Hudson River Museum
511 Warburton Avenue
Yonkers, NY 10701
Tel: 914-963-4550x236
www.hrm.org

Town of Yorktown Museum
1974 Commerce Street
Yorktown Heights, NY 10598
Tel: 914-962-4379
www.yorktownmuseum.org

Old Fort Niagara
Fort Niagara State Park
Youngstown, NY 14174
Tel: 716-745-7611
www.oldfortniagara.org

NORTH CAROLINA

Stanly County Historic Preservation Commission and Museum

245 East Main Street
Albemarle, NC 28001
Tel: 704-986-3777
www.co.stanly.nc.us/departments/hpc

Biltmore Estate

1 North Pack Square
Asheville, NC 28801
Tel: 828-225-6321 Fax: 828-225-6383
www.biltmore.com
Hours: Mon–Sun 9–5 pm
Contact: Darren Poupore
Institution type: Historic house
Collection type: Clothing, uniforms, general textiles
Description: 1760–1960. Collection of George W. Vanderbilt and his descendants ranges from exquisite household linens to servants' livery of the late nineteenth century. Vast collection of upholstery textiles dates from the mid-1800s to the early twentieth century, including more than 300 carpets and a fabulous collection of sixteenth-century tapestries.
$ ✍

Smith-McDowell House Museum

283 Victoria Road
Asheville, NC 28801
Tel: 828-253-9231 Fax: 828-253-5518
www.wnchistory.org
Hours: Tue–Sat 10–4 pm, Sun 1–4 pm
Contact: Rebecca Lamb

Institution type: Historic house
Collection type: Clothing, accessories, costumes, general textiles
Description: 1800–present. Collection includes women's clothing and aprons.
$ ✍

Thomas Wolfe Memorial

52 North Market Street
Asheville, NC 28801
Tel: 828-253-8304
www.wolfememorial.com

The Country Doctor Museum

6642 Peele Road
Bailey, NC 27807
Tel: 252-235-4165 Fax: 252-235-2372
www.countrydoctormuseum.org
Hours: Tue–Sat 10–4 pm
Contact: Anne Anderson
Institution type: History museum
Collection type: Clothing, uniforms
Description: 1900–present. Artifacts of historical significance used by country doctors of the nineteenth century and early twentieth century. Nursing school uniforms, World War II nursing uniforms, caps, and capes.
$ ✍

Beaufort Historical Association

130 Turner Street
Beaufort, NC 28516
Tel: 252-728-5225 Fax: 252-728-4966
www.beaufort-nc.com/bha

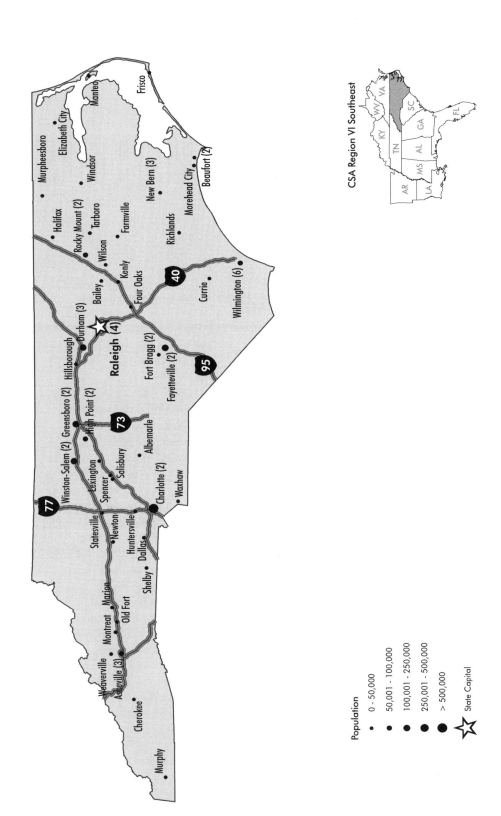

CSA Region VI Southeast

Frisco

Manteo

Murpheesboro

Elizabeth City

Windsor

New Bern (3)

Beaufort (2)

Morehead City

Halifax

Rocky Mount (2)

Tarboro

Farmville

Richlands

Wilson

Kenly

Bailey

Four Oaks

40

Currie

Wilmington (6)

Durham (3)

Raleigh (4)

Hillsborough

Fort Bragg (2)

95

Greensboro (2)

High Point (2)

Fayetteville (2)

Winston-Salem (2)

73

Albemarle

Lexington

Salisbury

Spencer

Charlotte (2)

77

Waxhaw

Statesville

Newton

Huntersville

Dallas

Shelby

Marion

Montreat

Old Fort

Weaverville

Asheville (3)

Cherokee

Murphy

Population

- 0 - 50,000
- 50,001 - 100,000
- 100,001 - 250,000
- 250,001 - 500,000
- > 500,000
☆ State Capital

Flag, hand-woven and hand-sewn, circa 1790s. Courtesy of Beaufort Historical Association.

Hours: Mon–Sat 9–5 pm
Contact: Tanesha Langhorne
Institution type: History museum, historic house
Collection type: Clothing, general textiles, quilts, flags
Description: 1760–1899. 6 house tour buildings; period textiles, mainly quilts and clothing and an original thirteen-star flag; and interesting samplers.
$ 🖎

North Carolina Maritime Museum

315 Front Street
Beaufort, NC 28516
Tel: 252-728-7317 Fax: 252-728-2108
www.ah.dcr.state.nc.us/sections/maritime/
default.htm
Hours: Mon–Fri 9–5 pm
Contact: Connie Mason
Institution type: State museum
Collection type: Clothing, accessories, uniforms, general textiles, flags
Description: 1915–present. Maritime related items, including Naval Services uniforms, portions of uniforms, sails, and accessories and steamship, international, and marine fishing flags.
🖎

Charlotte Museum of History and Hezekiah Alexander Homestead

3500 Shamrock Drive
Charlotte, NC 28215
Tel: 704-568-1774 Fax: 704-566-1817
www.charlottemuseum.org
Hours: Tue–Sat 10–5pm, Sun 1–7pm
Contact: Kris Carmichael
Institution type: History museum, historic house

Collection type: Clothing, accessories, uniforms, costumes, general textiles, quilts, flags
Description: 1750–present. Collection focuses on Charlotte and the surrounding NC/SC Piedmont region. Quilts, coverlets, and clothing items including military uniforms (primarily World War II), 1920's era dresses, and a wide variety of accessories.

Gentleman's waistcoat and coat (left), circa 1780-1790, gentleman's suit (right), circa 1770. Courtesy of The Mint Museum of Art.

The Mint Museum of Art

2730 Randolph Road
Charlotte, NC 28207
Tel: 704-337-2001 Fax: 704-337-2101
www.mintmuseum.org
Hours: Wed–Sat 10–5 pm, Tue 10–10 pm, Sun 12–5 pm
Contact: Charles L. Mo
Institution type: Art museum
Collection type: Clothing, accessories, uniforms, costumes
Description: 1700–present. 7,500 items spanning the eighteenth century through the twenty-first century. Primarily women's fashions and accessories from the early eighteenth century through contemporary haute couture, representative examples of men's and children's fashions and accessories, and vintage women's shoes numbering 1,000 pairs.
$ 🖎

Museum of the Cherokee Indian

589 Tsali Boulevard
Cherokee, NC 28719
Tel: 828-497-3481
www.cherokeemuseum.org

Moores Creek National Battlefield

40 Patriots Hall Drive
Currie, NC 28435
Tel: 910-283-5591
www.nps.gov/mocr

Gaston County Museum of Art and History

131 West Main Street
Dallas, NC 28034-0429
Tel: 704-922-7681
www.gastoncountymuseum.org

Bennett Place State Historic Site

4409 Bennett Memorial Road
Durham, NC 27705
Tel: 919-383-4345
www.ah.dcr.state.nc.us/sections/hs/bennett/
    bennett.htm

Duke Homestead State Historic Site

2828 Duke Homestead Road
Durham, NC 27705
Tel: 919-477-5498 Fax: 919-479-7092
www.dukehomestead.nchistoricsites.org
Hours: Tue–Sat 10–4 pm
Contact: Dale Coats
Institution type: History museum, state museum
Collection type: Clothing, accessories, costumes
Description: 1850–1899.

Nasher Museum of Art at Duke University

Duke University Road and Anderson Street
Durham, NC 27708-0732
Tel: 919-684-5135
http://nasher.duke.edu

Museum of the Albemarle

501 South Water Street
Elizabeth City, NC 27909-4863
Tel: 252-335-1453 Fax: 252-335-0637
www.museumofthealbemarle.com
Hours: Tue–Sat 9–5 pm, Sun 2–5 pm
Contact: Tom Butchko
Institution type: History museum, state museum
Collection type: Clothing, accessories, uniforms, costumes, general textiles, quilts, flags
Description: 1760–present. Quilts, especially nineteenth-century with Alamance plaid backing and twentieth-century patterns and fabrics. Collection is especially strong in women's clothing. Other items include twen-

tieth-century military uniforms, including U.S. Coast Guard.

May Museum and Farmville Heritage Center

213 South Main Street
Farmville, NC 27828
Tel: 252-753-5814

Airborne and Special Operations Museum

100 Bragg Boulevard
Fayetteville, NC 28301
Tel: 910-483-3003 Fax: 910-483-8232
www.asomf.org
Hours: Tue–Sat 10–5 pm, Sun 12–5 pm
Contact: John S. Duvall or Mary Dennings
Institution type: History museum, federal museum
Collection type: Clothing, accessories, uniforms, flags
Description: 1915–present. World War II, Airborne and Special Operations uniforms, equipment, weapons, and accessories. Holdings also include an excellent collection of World War II jump uniforms and paratrooper weapons.

$

Museum of the Cape Fear Historical Complex

801 Arsenal Avenue
Fayetteville, NC 28305
Tel: 910-486-1330 Fax: 910-486-1585
www.ncmuseumofhistory.org/osm/mcf.html

82nd Airborne Division War Memorial Museum

Gela and Ardennes Streets
Fort Bragg, NC 28310
Tel: 910-432-3443 Fax: 910-432-1642
www.bragg.army.mil/18abn/museums.htm
Hours: Tue–Sat 10–4:30 pm
Contact: John W. Aarsen
Institution type: History museum, federal museum
Collection type: Clothing, uniforms, flags
Description: 1915–present. U.S. Army uniforms from 1917 to the present, including some captured uniforms from World War II to the present. Other items include a U.S. Army unit flag from the 82nd Division.

JFK Special Warfare Museum

Ardennes and Marion Streets
Building D-2502
Fort Bragg, NC 28307
Tel: 910-432-1533
www.soc.mil/swcs/museum/museum.shtml

Bentonville Battleground State Historic Site

5466 Harper House Road
Four Oaks, NC 27524
Tel: 910-594-0789
www.ah.dcr.state.nc.us/sections/hs/bentonvi/
bentonvi.htm

Frisco Native American Museum and Natural History Center

53536 Highway 12
Frisco, NC 27936
Tel: 252-995-4440
www.nativeamericanmuseum.org

Greensboro Historical Museum

130 Summit Avenue
Greensboro, NC 27401-3016
Tel: 336-373-2043
www.greensborohistory.org

Guilford Courthouse National Military Park

2332 New Garden Road
Greensboro, NC 27410-2355
Tel: 336-288-1776
www.nps.gov/guco

Historic Halifax State Historic Site

St. David and Dobb Streets
Halifax, NC 27839
Tel: 252-583-7191
www.ah.dcr.state.nc.us/sections/hs/halifax/
halifax.htm

High Point Museum and Historical Park

1859 East Lexington Avenue
High Point, NC 27262
Tel: 336-885-1859
www.highpointmuseum.org

Springfield Museum of Old Domestic Life

555 East Springfield Road
High Point, NC 27263
Tel: 336-882-3054

Orange County Historical Museum

201 North Churton Street
Hillsborough, NC 27278
Tel: 919-732-2201
www.orangecountymuseum.org

Latta Plantation

5225 Sample Road
Huntersville, NC 28078
Tel: 704-875-2312 Fax: 704-875-1724
www.lattaplantation.org
Hours: Tue–Sat 10–5 pm, Sun 1–5 pm
Contact: Kristin Toler
Institution type: Historic house
Collection type: Clothing, costumes, quilts
Description: 1760–1960. Quilts and clothing, with an exceptional 1828 dress in good condition.
$ ✍

Tobacco Farm Life Museum

Highway 301 North, 709 Church Street
Kenly, NC 27542
Tel: 919-284-3431
www.tobaccofarmlifemuseum.org

Davidson County Historical Museum

2 South Main Street
Lexington, NC 27292
Tel: 336-242-2035 Fax: 336-242-2871
www.co.davidson.nc.us/museum
Hours: Tue–Fri 10–4 pm, 1st Sun 2–4 pm
Contact: Catherine Hoffmann
Institution type: History museum, county museum
Collection type: Clothing, accessories, uniforms, general textiles
Description: 1850–1960. This is a local history collection with most items from circa 1900.
✍

Roanoke Island Festival Park, Homeport of the Elizabeth II

1 Festival Park
Manteo, NC 27954
Tel: 252-475-1500 Fax: 252-475-1507
www.roanokeisland.com
Hours: Vary seasonally
Contact: Scott Stroh, Executive Director
Institution type: Art museum, history museum, theater museum, state museum
Collection type: Clothing, accessories, uniforms, general textiles, quilts, flags

Description: 1850–present. Quilts are strength as are general textiles, uniforms, and accessories relating to local maritime history.

$ ✍️

Historic Carson House

1805 U.S. Highway 70 West
Marion, NC 28752
Tel: 704-724-4948

Presbyterian Historical Society

318 Georgia Terrace
Montreat, NC 28757
Tel: 828-669-7061
www.history.pcusa.org

The History Place

1008 Arendell Street
Morehead City, NC 28557
Tel: 252-247-7533

Murfreesboro Historical Association

116 East Main Street
Murfreesboro, NC 27855
Tel: 252-398-3099 Fax: 252-398-5871
Hours: Mon–Fri 8–5 pm
Contact: Dale Neighbors, Executive Director
Institution type: History museum, historic house
Collection type: Clothing, accessories, uniforms, costumes, quilts, flags
Description: 1800–1960. Small numbers of period clothing, U.S. flags, country store items of clothing and accessories, and some quilts and coverlets.

$ ✍️

Cherokee County Historical Museum

87 Peachtree Street
Murphy, NC 28906
Tel: 828-837-6792
www.tib.com/cchm

Attmore-Oliver House

510 Pollock Street
New Bern, NC 28560
Tel: 252-638-8558
www.newbernhistorical.org

Friends of Fireman's Museum

408 Hancock Street
New Bern, NC 28560
Tel: 252-636-4087

Tryon Palace Historic Sites and Gardens

610 Pollock Street
New Bern, NC 28562
Tel: 252-514-4900
www.tryonpalace.org

Catawba County Museum of History

One Courthouse Square
Newton, NC 28658
Tel: 828-465-0383
www.catawbahistory.org

Mountain Gateway Museum

102 Water Street
Old Fort, NC 28762
Tel: 828-668-9259

Mordecai Historic Park

1 Mimosa Street
Raleigh, NC 27604
Tel: 919-833-6404

Inaugural ball gown for First Lady Dorothy McAulay Martin, 1985. Courtesy of North Carolina Museum of History.

North Carolina Museum of History

5 East Edenton Street
Raleigh, NC 27601-1011
Tel: 919-715-0200 Fax: 919-733-8655
www.ncmuseumofhistory.org
Hours: Tue–Sat 9–5 pm, Sun 12–5 pm
Institution type: History museum, state museum
✍️
CLOTHING AND TEXTILES
COLLECTION
Contact: Louise Benner
Collection type: Clothing, accessories, uniforms, general textiles, quilts

Description: 1760–present. More than 18,000 items of civilian clothing and accessories. Approximately 60 percent is women's clothing, 25 percent men's, and 15 percent children's. Flat textiles include more than 150 full-sized quilts, 21 samplers, 100 (approximately) coverlets, carriage robes, table and bed linens, and decorative needlework.

THE MILITARY COLLECTION

Contact: Tom Belton

Collection type: Accessories, uniforms

Description: 1850–present. More than 1,000 uniforms and accessories ranging from pre–Civil War to Operation Iraqi Freedom.

North Carolina State University Gallery of Art and Design

2610 Cates Avenue, Room 3302
Raleigh, NC 27695-7306
Tel: 919-515-3102
http://gad.ncsu.edu
Hours: Wed–Fri 12–8 pm, Sat–Sun 2–8 pm
Contact: Gregory Tyler
Institution type: University museum
Collection type: Clothing, accessories, uniforms, general textiles, quilts
Description: Pre-1700–present. Western clothing and accessories from the eighteenth century to 1980 as well as costumes and textiles from Guatemala, Peru, Bolivia, Japan, China, India, Indonesia, Africa, Europe, and North America; Asian rugs; and nineteenth- and twentieth-century printed and woven swatches.

Raleigh City Museum

220 Fayetteville Street Mall
Raleigh, NC 27601-1310
Tel: 919-832-3775
www.raleighcitymuseum.org

Onslow County Museum

301 South Wilmington Street
Richlands, NC 28574
Tel: 910-324-5008
www.co.onslow.nc.us/museum

Rocky Mount Arts Center

225 South Church Street
Rocky Mount, NC 27803
Tel: 252-972-1163
www.ci.rocky-mount.nc.us/artscenter

Stonewall House

1331 Stonewall Lane
Rocky Mount, NC 27804
Tel: 252-443-4148

Rowan Museum, Old Stone House 1766 and Utzman-Chambers House 1815

202 North Main Street
Salisbury, NC 28147
Tel: 704-633-5946 Fax: 704-633-9858
Hours: Thu–Sun 1–4 pm
Contact: Mary Jane Fowler
Institution type: History museum, historic house
Collection type: Clothing, accessories
Description: 1760–present. Collection includes southern fashions and accessories.
$ ✐

Cleveland County Historical Museum

Courthouse Square
Shelby, NC 28150-1333
Tel: 704-482-8186

North Carolina Transportation Museum

411 South Salisbury Avenue
Spencer, NC 28159
Tel: 704-636-2889
www.nctrans.org

Iredell Museum of Arts and Heritage

1335 Museum Road
Statesville, NC 28625
Tel: 704-873-4734 Fax: 704-873-4407
www.iredellmuseum.org
Hours: Mon–Sun 9–5 pm
Contact: Henry A. Poore
Institution type: Art museum, history museum, county museum, city museum
Collection type: Clothing, accessories, uniforms, general textiles, quilts, flags
Description: 1800–present. Items range from a tablecloth used in the Chester A. Arthur White House to a growing World War I and World War II collection to handmade quilts to modern clothing of the 1980s.
$ ✐

Blount-Bridgers House, Hobson Pittman Memorial Gallery

130 Bridgers Street
Tarboro, NC 27886
Tel: 252-823-4159
www.edgecombearts.org

Museum of the Waxhaws and Andrew Jackson Memorial

8125 Waxhaw Highway, 75 East
Waxhaw, NC 28173
Tel: 704-843-1832
www.perigee.net/~mwaxhaw

Zebulon B. Vance Birthplace State Historic Site

911 Reems Creek Road
Weaverville, NC 28787
Tel: 828-645-6706
www.ah.dcr.state.nc.us/sections/hs/vance/vance
.htm

Battleship North Carolina

Battleship Drive, Eagles Island
Wilmington, NC 28402-0480
Tel: 910-251-5797
www.battleshipnc.com
Hours: Mon–Sun 8–5 pm (Winter); Mon–Sun
8–8 pm (Summer)
Contact: Mary Ames B. Sheret
Institution type: History museum, state museum
Collection type: Uniforms, general textiles, flags
Description: 1900–1960. World War II-era U.S.
Navy and U.S. Marine Corps uniforms and
gear for enlisted men and officers; World War
II flags, cloth navigational charts, pennants,
commissioning pennants, sweetheart pillow-
cases, and Japanese flags; U.S. Navy uniforms
from 1908 to 1921; and a few examples of
World War II aviators' and divers' clothing.
$ ✍

Bellamy Mansion Museum of History and Design Arts

503 Market Street
Wilmington, NC 28401
Tel: 910-251-3700
www.bellamymansion.org

The Burgwin-Wright Museum House and Gardens

224 Market Street
Wilmington, NC 28401
Tel: 910-762-0570
www.geocities.com/PicketFence/Garden/4354

Cape Fear Museum

814 Market Street
Wilmington, NC 28411
Tel: 910-341-4350 Fax: 910-341-4037
www.CapeFearMuseum.com
Hours: Tue–Sat 9–5 pm, Sun 1–5 pm (Winter);
Mon–Sat 9–5 pm, Sun 1–5 pm (Summer)
Contact: Barbara L. Rowe
Institution type: History museum, county
museum
Collection type: Clothing, accessories, uniforms,
costumes, general textiles, flags
Description: 1850–present. Textiles and costumes
relating to the history of the Lower Cape Fear
region of southeast North Carolina. Collection
is strongest in twentieth-century clothing and
military.
$ ✍

Lower Cape Fear Historical Society

126 South 3rd Street
Wilmington, NC 28401
Tel: 910-762-0492
www.latimerhouse.org
Hours: Mon–Fri 10–4 pm, Sat–Sun 12–5 pm
Contact: Candace McGreevy, Executive Director
Institution type: History museum, historic house
Collection type: Clothing, accessories, general tex-
tiles
Description: 1760–1960.
$ ✍

Wilmington Railroad Museum

501 Nutt Street
Wilmington, NC 28401
Tel: 910-763-2634
www.wrrm.org

Freeman Round House Museum

1202 Nash Street
Wilson, NC 27893
Tel: 252-296-3056
www.freemanroundhouse.com

Historic Hope Plantation

132 Hope House Road
Windsor, NC 27983
Tel: 252-794-3140 Fax: 252-794-5583
www.hopeplantation.org
Hours: Mon–Sat 10–5 pm, Sun 1–5 pm, 10–4
pm (Nov–Mar)

Beaded cap, circa 1810. Courtesy of Historic Hope Plantation.

Velvet cape, 1921–1924. Courtesy of Reynolda House Museum of American Art.

Contact: Glenn Perkins
Institution type: Historic house
Collection type: Clothing, general textiles, quilts, flags
Description: 1760–1899. Emphasis is on functional textiles—quilts and coverlets. Collection includes some clothing items from the late eighteenth century and early nineteenth century and 6 early-nineteenth-century needlework samplers.

$ ✍🏻

Old Salem and Museum of Early Southern Decorative Arts (MESDA)

600 South Main Street
Winston-Salem, NC 27101
Tel: 336-721-7300 Fax: 336-721-7367
www.mesda.org
Hours: Mon–Sat 9:30–5 pm, Sun 1–5 pm
Contact: Johanna M. Brown
Institution type: History museum, art museum
Collection type: Costumes, general textiles
Description: 1700–1900. Approximately 1,500 pieces in textile collection with emphasis on southern origin or Moravian provenance. Collection consists of 7 percent needlework pieces or samplers, 3 percent rugs, 45 percent costumes, 27 percent household textiles (sheets, towels, tablecovers, household linens), and 18 percent bedcovers.

$ ✍🏻

Reynolda House Museum of American Art

2250 Reynolda Road
Winston-Salem, NC 27106
Tel: 336-758-5476 Fax: 336-758-5704
www.reynoldahouse.org
Hours: Tue–Sun 9:30–4:30 pm
Contact: Ruth B. Mullen
Institution type: Art museum, historic house
Collection type: Clothing, accessories, costumes, general textiles
Description: 1850–1960. 650 items of clothes worn by Reynolds family, circa 1890–1960. Collection includes mostly women's clothes and accessories and a few men's garments.

$ ✍🏻

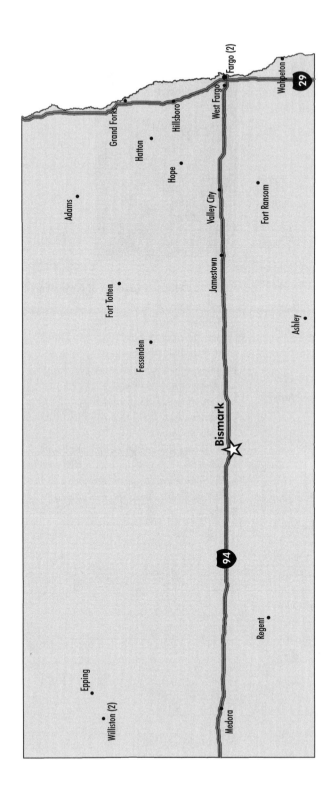

CSA Region III Midwest

Population

- 0 - 50,000
- 50,001 - 100,000
- 100,001 - 250,000
- 250,001 - 500,000
- > 500,000

☆ State Capital

NORTH DAKOTA

Adams Log Cabin
Adams Park
Adams, ND 58210
Tel: 701-944-2792

McIntosh County Historical Society
107 3rd Avenue NE
Ashley, ND 58413
Tel: 701-288-3388

State Historical Society of North Dakota
612 East Boulevard Avenue
Bismarck, ND 58501-0830
Tel: 701-328-2666 Fax: 701-328-3710
www.state.nd.us/hist
Hours: Mon–Fri 8–5 pm, Sat 9–5 pm, Sun 11–5 pm
Contact: Jenny Yearous
Institution type: History museum, state museum
Collection type: Clothing, accessories, uniforms, costumes, general textiles, quilts, flags
Description: 1850–present. 6,500 items of clothing, accessories, and household textiles, including Native American clothing and related items from tribes of North Dakota and the Northern Great Plains; ethnic clothing, textiles, and textile related tools from various northern European immigrant groups that settled in North Dakota; Euro-American fashion, everyday and special occasion clothing, and military uniforms; and quilts, tablecloths, and other household textiles.

Buffalo Trails Museum
Main Street
Epping, ND 58843
Tel: 701-859-4361
www.epping.govoffice.com

North Dakota State University
EMILY P. REYNOLDS HISTORIC COSTUME COLLECTION
1201 North University Drive
Fargo, ND 58105
Tel: 701-231-7367 Fax: 701-231-7174
www.ndsu.nodak.edu/ercc
Hours: By appointment
Contact: Ann Braaten, Sara Sunderlin
Institution type: University collection
Collection type: Clothing, accessories, general textiles
Description: 1760–present. More than 4,000 items, including the Textile and Clothing Collection of the NDSU Libraries' Germans from Russia Heritage Collection and examples of historic clothing for students to study. The collection mission was broadened to preserve the North Dakota cultural heritage and surrounding region through textiles, clothing, and related items.

Plains Art Museum
704 1st Avenue North
Fargo, ND 58108-2338
Tel: 701-232-3821
www.plainsart.org

Wells County Museum
305 1st Street South
Fessenden, ND 58438
Tel: 701-547-3100

Ransom County Historical Society
101 Mill Road SE
Fort Ransom, ND 58033
Tel: 701-678-2045
www.members.tripod.com/rchsmuseum
Hours: Fri–Sun 1–5 pm (Summer)
$ ✍🏛

Fort Totten State Historic Site
Building 14
Fort Totten, ND 58335
Tel: 701-766-4441
www.state.nd.us/hist/totten/totten.htm

North Dakota Museum of Art
CONTEMPORARY FIBER ART
261 Centennial Drive
Grand Forks, ND 58202
Tel: 701-777-4195 Fax: 701-777-4425
www.ndmoa.com
Hours: Mon–Fri 9–5 pm, Sat–Sun 7–9 pm
Collection type: General textiles
Institution type: Art museum
Description: 1961–present. Collection includes
   contemporary fiber art since 1980.
$ ✍🏛

Hatton-Eielson Museum
405 Eielson Street
Hatton, ND 58240
Tel: 701-543-3726
www.eielson.org

Traill County Historical Society
306 West Caledonia Avenue
Hillsboro, ND 58045
Tel: 701-636-5571
www.hillsborond.com/museum.html
Hours: Sat–Mon 2–5 pm (Jun–Aug)

Steele County Historical Society
301 Steele Avenue
Hope, ND 58046
Tel: 701-945-2394
www.steelecomuseum.com
Hours: Tue–Fri 9–5 pm, Sun 2–5 pm (Memorial
   Day–Labor Day)
$ ✍🏛

Stutsman County Memorial Museum
321 3rd Avenue SE
Jamestown, ND 58402-1002
Tel: 701-252-6741

Chateau De Mores State Historic Site
I 94, Exit 27
Medora, ND 58645
Tel: 701-623-4355
www.state.nd.us/hist/chateau/chateau.htm

Hettinger County Historical Society
336 Pacific Street
Regent, ND 58650
Tel: 701-563-4631
www.hettingercounty.org/tourism/museum.asp

Barnes County Historical Museum
315 Central Avenue North
Valley City, ND 58072
Tel: 701-845-0966
www.ohwy.com/nd/b/bacohimu.htm
Hours: Mon–Sat 10–4 pm
✍🏛

Richland County Historical Museum
11 7th Avenue North
Wahpeton, ND 58075
Tel: 701-642-3075
www.wahpetonbreckenridgechamber.com/
   visitor_museum.htm
Hours: Tue, Thu, Sat–Sun 1–4 pm (Spring,
   Summer, Fall)

**Cass County History Museum at
Bonanzaville**
1351 West Main Avenue
West Fargo, ND 58078
Tel: 701-282-2822
www.bonanzaville.com

Fort Buford State Historic Site
15349 39th Lane NW
Williston, ND 58801
Tel: 701-572-9034
www.discovernd.com/hist/buford/buford.htm

Frontier Museum
6330 2nd Avenue West
Williston, ND 58801
Tel: 701-572-9751

Stan Hywet Hall and Garden

714 North Portage Path
Akron, OH 44303
Tel: 330-836-5533
www.stanhywet.org

Detail, Rose of Sharon quilt, circa 1850–1870.
Courtesy of Sauder Village.

Sauder Village

22611 State Route 2
Archbold, OH 43502
Tel: 419-446-2541 Fax: 419-445-5251
www.saudervillage.org
Hours: Tue–Sat 10–5 pm, Sun 1–5 pm
Contact: Sara Feldbauer, Curator of Collections
Institution type: History museum
Collection type: Clothing, accessories, uniforms, general textiles, quilts, flags
Description: 1850–1960. Women's, men's, and children's clothing, including dresses, suits,

shirts, waists, undergarments, hats, and accessories; 68 quilts or coverlets from the late 1800s to 1949; and 23 art quilts.
$ 🔊

Ashland County Historical Society

420 Center Street
Ashland, OH 44805
Tel: 419-289-3111 Fax: 419-207-8153
Hours: Mon–Fri 10–4 pm
Contact: Margery McBurney
Institution type: History museum, county museum
Collection type: Clothing, general textiles, quilts
Description: 1850–present. Collection includes clothing and textiles from local people or individuals with a connection to Ashland.
🔊

Aurora Historical Society

Aurora Memorial Library Building
115 East Pioneer Trail
Aurora, OH 44202
Tel: 330-562-6502

Gay 90s Mansion Museum

532 North Chestnut Street
Barnesville, OH 43713
Tel: 740-425-3505

Rose Hill Museum

27715 Lake Road
Bay Village, OH 44140
Tel: 440-871-7338
www.bayhistorical.com

CSA Region III Midwest

Bedford Historical Society Museum and Library

30 South Park Street
Bedford, OH 44146
Tel: 440-232-0796
www.bedfordohiohistory.org
Hours: Mon–Wed 7:30–10 pm, Thu 10–4 pm,
2nd Sun 2–5 pm
Contact: Janet Caldwell
Institution type: History museum, historic house
Collection type: Clothing, accessories, uniforms,
costumes, general textiles, quilts, flags
Description: 1850–1960. Clothing and textiles
related to people from Bedford, Ohio.
✍

Historic Lyme Village Association

5001 State Route 4
Bellevue, OH 44811
Tel: 419-483-6052
www.lymevillage.com
Hours: Mon–Sun 11–4 pm (Jun–Aug)
Contact: Alvina Schaeffer
Institution type: History museum, historic house
Collection type: Clothing, accessories, uniforms,
costumes, general textiles, quilts, flags
Description: 1850–1960.
$ ✍

Wood County Historical Museum and Center

13660 County Home Road
Bowling Green, OH 43402
Tel: 419-352-0967
www.woodcountyhistory.org
Hours: Mon–Sun 9:30–4:30 pm (Apr 15–Oct,
Dec)
Contact: Randy Brown
Institution type: History museum, historic house,
county museum
Collection type: Clothing, accessories, uniforms,
costumes, general textiles
Description: 1850–present. Clothing, accessories,
and household textiles.
✍

Brooklyn Historical Society

4442 Ridge Road
Brooklyn, OH 44144
Tel: 216-941-0160

Century Village Museum

14653 East Park Street
Burton, OH 44021-0153
Tel: 440-834-1492
www.geaugahistorical.org

Guernsey County Museum

218 North 8th Street
Cambridge, OH 43725
Tel: 740-439-5884

Canal Fulton Heritage Society

103 Tuscarawas Street
Canal Fulton, OH 44614
Tel: 330-854-3808

Canton Classic Car Museum

Market Avenue and 6th Street SW
Canton, OH 44702
Tel: 330-455-3603
www.cantonclassiccar.org

National Football Museum

2121 George Halas Drive NW
Canton, OH 44708
Tel: 330-456-8207 Fax: 330-456-9080
www.profootballhof.com
Hours: Mon–Sun 9–5 pm
Contact: Jason Aikens, Curator
Institution type: History museum
Collection type: Clothing, accessories, uniforms,
costumes, general textiles, flags
Description: 1850–present. Items associated with
the history of professional American football,
including uniforms from players and other tex-
tiles.
$ ✍

William McKinley Presidential Library Museum

FIRST LADY IDA MCKINLEY
COLLECTION
800 McKinley Monument Drive NW
Canton, OH 44708
Tel: 330-455-7043 Fax: 330-455-1137
www.mckinleymuseum.org
Hours: Mon–Sat 9–5 pm, Sun 12–5 pm
Contact: Kimberly A. Kenney
Institution type: History museum
Collection type: Clothing, accessories, uniforms,
general textiles

Description: 1850–present. First Lady Ida Saxton McKinley's dresses and gowns. Strengths include shoes, hats, and purses. Other holdings include general textile collection of Stark County, 1840–1980.

$ 🖎

The McCook House Civil War Museum
Public Square
Carrollton, OH 44615
Tel: 330-627-3345
www.ohiohistory.org/places/mcookhse

Mercer County Historical Museum, The Riley House
130 East Market
Celina, OH 45822
Tel: 419-586-6065

Centerville-Washington Township Historical Society
26 North Main Street
Centerville, OH 45459
Tel: 937-312-0040 Fax: 937-312-0015
www.mvcc.net/Centerville/histsoc
Hours: Tue–Fri 12–4 pm
Institution type: History museum, historic house
🖎

Chagrin Falls Historical Society
21 Walnut Street
Chagrin Falls, OH 44022
Tel: 440-247-4695

Ross County Historical Society
45 West 5th Street
Chillicothe, OH 45601
Tel: 740-772-1936
www.rosscountyhistorical.org

Betts House Research Center
416 Clark Street
Cincinnati, OH 45203
Tel: 513-651-0734 Fax: 513-651-2143
www.bettshouse.org
Hours: Tue–Sat 11–3 pm, and by appointment
Contact: Beth Sullebarger, Sullebarger and Associates
Institution type: Historic house
Collection type: Clothing, general textiles
Description: 1800–present
$ 🖎

Dress, circa 1860s. Courtesy of Betts House Research Center.

Cary Cottage
7000 Hamilton Avenue
Cincinnati, OH 45231
Tel: 513-522-3860
www.clovernook.org/carycottage.html

Minaret dress by Issey Miyake, 1995. Courtesy of Cincinnati Art Museum.

Cincinnati Art Museum
953 Eden Park Drive
Cincinnati, OH 45202
Tel: 513-639-2943 Fax: 513-639-2996
www.cincinnatiartmuseum.org
Hours: Tue–Sun 11–5 pm
Contact: Cynthia Amneus
Institution type: Art museum

Collection type: Clothing, accessories, costumes, general textiles

Description: 1760–present. Women's, men's, and children's dress, including ethnic dress. Strength is women's nineteenth-century dress. Objects are not limited to being made or worn in Cincinnati. Holdings include significant collection of hair jewelry and second largest collection of Elizabeth Hawes designs. Textiles date from 1750 to 1960s, all types, including ethnic.

Cincinnati Fire Museum
315 West Court Street
Cincinnati, OH 45202
Tel: 513-621-5553
www.cincyfiremuseum.com

Cincinnati Museum Center
1301 Western Avenue
Cincinnati, OH 45203
Tel: 513-287-7000
www.cincymuseum.org

Heritage Village Museum
11450 Lebanon Pike, Route 42
Cincinnati, OH 45262
Tel: 513-563-9484 Fax: 513-563-0914
www.heritagevillagecincinnati.org
Hours: Tue–Sat 12–4 pm, Sun 1–5 pm
Contact: Kathleen Luhn
Institution type: History museum, historic house
Collection type: Clothing, accessories, general textiles
Description: 1800–1914. Collection supports the museum mission to interpret nineteenth-century life in southwest Ohio. Items represent a broad spectrum of life from rural farm life to high society city living in downtown Cincinnati, from 1850 and later.

$

Jewish Institute of Religion Skirball Museum
3101 Clifton Avenue, Hebrew Union College
Cincinnati, OH 45220
Tel: 513-221-1875
www.huc.edu/museums

Kemper Log House Museum
11450 Lebanon Pike Route 42
Cincinnati, OH 45262
Tel: 513-563-9484 Fax: 513-563-0914
www.heritagevillagecincinnati.org
Hours: Tue–Sat 12–4 pm, Sun 1–5 pm
Contact: Kathleen Luhn
Institution type: History museum
Collection type: Clothing
Description: 1800–1899. Specific collection is connected to the James Kemper family of Cincinnati, Ohio. Reverend Kemper was the first Presbyterian minister north of the Ohio River. Family moved into this log house on June 4, 1804.

$

The Taft Museum
316 Pike Street
Cincinnati, OH 45202-4293
Tel: 513-241-0343
www.taftmuseum.org

Icon of the Virgin, sixth century. Courtesy of Cleveland Museum of Art.

Cleveland Museum of Art
11150 East Boulevard
Cleveland, OH 44106
Tel: 216-707-2258
www.clemusart.com
Hours: Tue–Sun 10–5 pm, Wed and Fri 10–9 pm
Contact: Louise W. Mackie, Curator
Institution type: Art museum
Collection type: Accessories, costumes, general textiles

Description: Pre-1700–present. International textile collection reflects the Cleveland Museum of Art's emphasis on high artistic quality. Collection contains approximately 4,500 textiles from sixty-two countries, with strengths in textiles from pre-Columbian Peru, Italy, France, Islamic countries, central Asia, and medieval China. Museum also holds a few other Asian costumes.

$ 🖎

Cleveland Police Museum

1300 Ontario Street
Cleveland, OH 44113-1600
Tel: 216-623-5055
www.clevelandpolicemuseum.org

International Women's Air and Space Museum

1501 North Marginal Road, Room 165
Cleveland, OH 44114
Tel: 216-623-1111
www.iwasm.org/index.php

Rock and Roll Hall of Fame

1 Key Plaza
Cleveland, OH 44114-1022
Tel: 216-781-7625
www.rockhall.com

Evening dress, Chanel, circa 1926. Courtesy of the Collection of the Western Reserve Historical Society.

Western Reserve Historical Society

10825 East Boulevard
Cleveland, OH 44106
Tel: 216-721-5722 Fax: 216-721-1681
www.wrhs.org

Hours: Mon–Sat 10–5 pm, Sun 12–5 pm
Contact: Megan Spagnolo, Curator of Costumes and Textiles
Institution type: History museum, historic house
Collection type: Clothing, accessories, uniforms, costumes, general textiles, flags
Description: 1700–present. Men's, women's, and children's clothing from the mid-eighteenth century to the present. Strengths include early-twentieth-century women's clothing, maternity clothing, Shaker and Quaker clothing, paisley shawls, and beaded purses.

$ 🖎

Log House Museum of the Historical Society of Columbiana-Fairfield Town

10 East Park Avenue
Columbiana, OH 44408
Tel: 330-482-2983

Kelton House Museum and Garden

586 East Town Street
Columbus, OH 43215-4888
Tel: 614-464-2022 Fax: 614-464-3346
www.keltonhouse.com
Hours: Mon–Fri 10–5 pm, Sun 1–4 pm, and by appointment
Contact: Georgeanne Reuter, Lisa Smith
Institution type: History museum, historic house
Collection type: Clothing, accessories, general textiles
Description: 1850–1960. Extensive collection of textiles includes map embroidery, tablecloths, dresser scarves, doilies, bed linens, pillowcases, towels, Berlin work, napkins, antimacassers, and samplers. Clothing includes dresses, petticoats, corsets, and collars.

$ 🖎

Ohio Historical Society

1982 Velma Avenue
Columbus, OH 43211
Tel: 614-297-2300
www.ohiohistory.org
Hours: Tue–Sat 9–5 pm, Sun 12–5 pm
Contact: Michael Harsh, Acting Chief, Collections and Curatorial
Institution type: History museum
Collection type: Clothing, accessories, uniforms, costumes, general textiles, quilts, flags
Description: 1760–present. Governors' wives'

dresses, more than 400 documented Ohio quilts, and Shaker and Zoar (communal living groups) collections, 1840–1910.

$ ✍

Costume worn by chanteuse Canta Maya, circa 1930. Courtesy of Ohio State University Historic Costume and Textiles Collection.

Ohio State University
HISTORIC COSTUME AND TEXTILES COLLECTION
1787 Neil Avenue, Room 175
Columbus, OH 43210
Tel: 614-292-3090 Fax: 614-688-8133
http://costume.osu.edu/
Hours: Wed–Sat 11–4 pm
Contact: Gayle Strege
Institution type: University collection
Collection type: Clothing, accessories, uniforms, costumes, general textiles, flags
Description: 1700–present. Men's, women's, and children's European and North American clothing and accessories, 1740–present. Strengths include women's nineteenth- and twentieth-century designers. Significant pieces include a Charles Frederick Worth ballgown circa 1887 and Charles James's first abstract gown in 1953. Other items include large collection of ethnographic clothing and textiles with significant holdings from Indonesia and Thailand. Extensive button collection of Mrs. Ann Rudolph is housed within the collection.

✍

Johnson-Humrickhouse Museum
300 North Whitewoman Steet
Coshocton, OH 43812
Tel: 740-622-8710
www.jhmuseum.org/

Dayton Art Institute
456 Belmonte Park North
Dayton, OH 45405
Tel: 937-223-5277
www.daytonartinstitute.org

Montgomery County Historical Society
224 North St. Clair Street
Dayton, OH 45402-1230
Tel: 937-228-6271
www.daytonhistory.org

Au Glaize Village
12296 Krouse Road
Defiance, OH 43512
Tel: 419-784-0107
www.defiance-online.com/auglaize

J. E. Reeves Home and Museum
325 East Iron Avenue
Dover, OH 44622
Tel: 330-343-7040
www.doverhistory.org

Croatian Heritage Museum and Library
34900 Lakeshore Boulevard
Eastlake, OH 44095
Tel: 440-946-2044

Hickories Museum of the Lorain County Historical Society
509 Washington Avenue
Elyria, OH 44035
Tel: 440-322-3341

Hancock Historical Museum
FLAG CITY FLAG COLLECTION
422 West Sandusky Street
Findlay, OH 45840
Tel: 419-423-4433 Fax: 419-423-2154
www.hancockhistoricalmuseum.org
Hours: Wed–Fri 12:30–4:30 pm, Sun 1–4 pm
Contact: Paulette J. Weiser
Institution type: History museum, historic house

Collection type: Clothing, accessories, uniforms, costumes, general textiles, quilts, flags

Description: 1800–present. Predominantly women's clothing and accessories from the mid-nineteenth century to the mid-twentieth century. Other items include men's and children's clothing. The museum also holds large uniform collection, primarily World War II; quilt and coverlet collection; and fairly large flag collection, primarily United States, 1840–present.

$ 🖊

Harding Museum
302 Park Avenue
Franklin, OH 45005
Tel: 513-746-8295

Rutherford B. Hayes Presidential Center
Spiegel Grove
Fremont, OH 43420
Tel: 419-332-2081 Fax: 419-332-4952
www.rbhayes.org/hayes
Hours: Mon–Sat 9–5 pm, Sun 12–5 pm
Institution type: History museum, historic house, state museum

$ 🖊

Ashtabula County Historical Society
5685 Lake Road
Geneva-on-the-Lake, OH 44041
Tel: 440-466-7337

Granville Historical Museum
115 East Broadway
Granville, OH 43023
Tel: 740-587-3951

Garst Museum
205 North Broadway
Greenville, OH 45331
Tel: 937-548-5250
www.garstmuseum.org

Motts Military Museum
5075 South Hamilton Road
Groveport, OH 43125
Tel: 614-836-1500
www.mottsmilitarymuseum.org

Butler County Museum
327 North 2nd Street
Hamilton, OH 45011

Tel: 513-896-9930
www.home.fuse.net/butlercountymuseum

Johnson Historic Home—Museum of Church History and Art
6203 Pioneer Trail Road
Hiram, OH 44234
Tel: 801-240-0297

Hudson Library and Historical Society
96 Library Street
Hudson, OH 44236
Tel: 330-653-6658 Fax: 330-650-4693
www.hudsonlibrary.org
Hours: Mon–Thu 9–9 pm, Fri–Sat 9–5 pm, Sun 12–5 pm
Contact: E. Leslie Polott, Curator; Gwen Mayer, Archivist
Institution type: History museum
Collection type: Clothing, accessories, uniforms, general textiles
Description: 1800–present. Local history objects, with strengths from 1800 to 1900.

🖊

Lawrence County Gray House Museum
506 South 6th Street
Ironton, OH 45638
Tel: 740-532-1222

Clothing and accessories, eighteenth–twentieth centuries. Courtesy of Kent State University Museum.

Kent State University Museum
Rockwell Hall at Kent State University
Kent, OH 44242
Tel: 330-672-3450 Fax: 330-672-3218
www.kent.edu/museum
Hours: Wed, Fri–Sat 10–4:45 pm, Thu 10–8:45 pm, Sun 12–4:45 pm

Contact: Jean L. Druesedow, Director; Anne Bissonnette, Curator

Institution type: University museum

Collection type: Clothing, accessories, uniforms, costumes, general textiles

Description: Pre-1700–present. One of the great private collections now in a public institution, holdings include excellent collection of eighteenth-century contemporary Western urban fashion; a large collection of Far Eastern costumes from China, India, and Japan; and Western European folk costumes.

$ 🖎

Kirtland Historical Site—Museum of Church History and Art

7800 Kirtland-Chardon Road
Kirtland, OH 44904
Tel: 801-240-0297

Lake County Historical Society

8610 Mentor Road
Kirtland Hills, OH 44060
Tel: 440-255-8979
www.lakehistory.org

Virginia Marti College of Art and Design

11724 Detroit Avenue
Lakewood, OH 44107
Tel: 216-221-8584 Fax: 216-221-2311
www.virginiamarticollege.com

Hours: Mon–Fri 9–5 pm

Institution type: University collection

$ 🖎

The Georgian House

105 East Wheeling Street
Lancaster, OH 43130
Tel: 740-654-9923
www.fairfieldheritage.org

The Sherman House

137 East Main Street
Lancaster, OH 43130
Tel: 740-787-5891
www.shermanhouse.org

Richland County Historical Society Museum

51 West Church Street
Lexington, OH 44904
Tel: 419-884-0277

Allen County Historical Society

620 West Market Street
Lima, OH 45801
Tel: 419-222-9426 Fax: 419-222-0649
www.allencountymuseum.org

Hours: Tue–Sun 1–5 pm

Contact: John Carnes

Institution type: History museum, historic house, county museum

Collection type: Clothing, accessories, general textiles, quilts, flags

Description: 1760–present. Strengths include 1860–1910 women's costumes. Collection contains 300 flags, quilts, and coverlets. Geographic scope is predominately Ohio and the Midwest.

Black River Historical Society of Lorain

309 West 5th
Lorain, OH 44052
Tel: 440-245-2563
www.loraincityhistory.org

Greater Loveland Historical Society Museum

201 Riverside Drive
Loveland, OH 45140
Tel: 513-683-5692
www.lovelandmuseum.org

The Castle

418 4th Street
Marietta, OH 45750
Tel: 740-373-4180
www.mariettacastle.org

The Marion County Historical Society

169 East Church Street
Marion, OH 43302
Tel: 740-387-4255
www.historymarion.org

Massillon Museum

121 Lincoln Way East
Massillon, OH 44646
Tel: 330-833-4061 Fax: 330-833-2925
www.massillonmuseum.org

Hours: Tue–Sat 9:30–5 pm, Sun 2–5 pm, and by appointment

Contact: Alex Nicholis

Dress, ivory silk taffeta and lace evening gown, circa 1910. Courtesy of Massillon Museum.

Institution type: Art museum, history museum

Collection type: Clothing, accessories, uniforms, costumes, general textiles, quilts, flags

Description: 1760–present. Women's, children's, and men's clothing and accessories; military, occupational, and sports uniforms; circus performers' costumes; and a large collection of quilts, flags, and other textiles.

Wolcott House Museum Complex

1031 River Road
Maumee, OH 43537
Tel: 419-893-9602
www.maumee.org/recreation/wolcott.htm

Promont House Museum

GREATER MILFORD AREA HISTORICAL SOCIETY COLLECTION
906 Main Street
Milford, OH 45150
Tel: 513-248-0324 Fax: 513-248-2304
http://promonthouse.org

Bodice detail, gown, 1879. Courtesy of Promont House Museum.

Hours: Fri–Sun 1:30–4:30 pm, and by appointment

Contact: Jean Johnson Shaw

Institution type: History museum

Collection type: Clothing, accessories, uniforms, general textiles, quilts, flags

Description: 1850–present. Clothing from 1850 to 1950. Premier piece is a 1879 gown worn by the bride of John M. Pattison, the forty-third governor of Ohio. Other items include linens, furs, and quilts from 1870 to 1920, flags, and accessories.

$ ✍

Mount Pleasant Historical Society

342 Union Street
Mount Pleasant, OH 43939
Tel: 740-769-2893

The Sherwood-Davidson House

Veterans' Park, 6th Street
Newark, OH 43058
Tel: 740-345-4898
www.lchsohio.org

Hours: Tue–Sat 1–4 pm

Contact: Emily Larson

Institution type: Historic house

Collection type: Clothing, accessories, uniforms, general textiles, flags

Description: 1850–1960. Clothing, accessories, and textiles. Clothing and accessory displays are changed seasonally and for special events.

✍

Temperance Tavern

221 West Canal Street
Newcomerstown, OH 43832
Tel: 614-498-7735

Hoover Historical Center

1875 East Maple Street
North Canton, OH 44720-3331
Tel: 330-499-0287 Fax: 330-494-4725
www.walsh.edu/content.php?sid=2979&cid=13

Hours: Wed–Sat 1–4 pm

Contact: Ann Haines, Operations Coordinator

Institution type: History museum, historic house, university collection

Collection type: Clothing, accessories, uniforms, flags

Description: 1850–present. Hoover family furnishings. Late-1800s and early-1900s manual vacuum cleaners, women's fashions, Hoover family decorative arts, household linens, table runners and doilies, and war memorabilia.

$ ✍

Firelands Historical Society Museum
4 Case Avenue
Norwalk, OH 44857
Tel: 419-668-6038

Oberlin Heritage Center—Oberlin Historical and Improvement Organization (OHIO)
73 South Professor Street
Oberlin, OH 44074
Tel: 440-774-1700 Fax: 440-774-8061
www.oberlinheritage.org
Hours: Tue–Sat 10–3 pm
Contact: Prue Richards, Collections Assistant
Institution type: History museum, historic house
Collection type: Clothing, accessories, uniforms, costumes, general textiles
Description: 1800–1960. Large number of children's and doll clothes. Collection is well rounded in terms of sewing techniques, traditions, and textiles.

$ ✍

Motorcycle Hall of Fame Museum
13515 Yarmouth Drive
Pickerington, OH 43147
Tel: 614-856-2222x1234
www.motorcyclemuseum.org

Reading Historical Society Museum
22 West Benson Street
Reading, OH 45215
Tel: 513-761-8535

Salem Historical Society and Museum
208 South Broadway Avenue
Salem, OH 44460
Tel: 330-337-8514
www.salemohio.com/historicalsociety

103rd Ohio Volunteer Infantry Memorial Foundation
5501 East Lake Road
Sheffield Lake, OH 44054
Tel: 440-949-2790

Jefferson County Historical Association
426 Franklin Avenue
Steubenville, OH 43952
Tel: 740-283-1133
www.rootsweb.com/~ohjcha

Strongsville Historical Society
13305 Pearl Road
Strongsville, OH 44136
Tel: 440-572-0057
Hours: Wed, Sat–Sun 10–4 pm (May–Oct)
Institution type: Historic house
✍

Seneca County Museum
28 Clay Street
Tiffin, OH 44883
Tel: 419-447-5955

Twinsburg Historical Society
8996 Darrow Road
Twinsburg, OH 44087
Tel: 216-487-5565
www.twinsburg.com/historicalsociety

National Afro-American Museum and Cultural Center
1350 Brush Row Road
Wilberforce, OH 45384
Tel: 937-376-4944
www.ohiohistory.org/places/afroam

Clinton County Historical Society
149 East Locust Street
Wilmington, OH 45177
Tel: 937-382-4684 Fax: 937-382-5634
www.clintoncountyhistory.org
Hours: Wed–Fri 1–4 pm
Contact: Kay Fisher
Institution type: History museum, historic house, county museum
Collection type: Clothing, accessories, uniforms, general textiles, flags
Description: 1800–1960. Clinton County clothing, with majority dating between 1870 and 1930. Strengths include Quaker clothing. Other items include hats, purses, shoes, and military uniforms.
✍

Wayne County Historical Society
546 East Bowman Street
Wooster, OH 44691
Tel: 330-264-8856
www.waynehistorical.org

Flight jacket, worn by Jackie Coogan, 1940s.
Courtesy of National Museum of the United
States Air Force.

**National Museum of the United States
Air Force**
1100 Spaatz Street
Wright-Patterson Air Force Base, OH 45433-
7102
Tel: 937-255-7204 Fax: 937-255-3910
www.wpafb.af.mil/museum
Hours: Mon–Sun 9–5 pm
Contact: Terry Aitken, Senior Curator
Institution type: Federal museum
Collection type: Accessories, uniforms, flags
Description: 1900–present. Emphasis is on air
service such as Army Air Corps, Army Air
Forces, and Air Force, duty and flight uni-
forms, flight equipment, and accoutrements.
🖊

Greene County Historical Society
74 West Church Street
Xenia, OH 45385
Tel: 937-372-4606 Fax: 937-372-5660
Hours: Tue–Fri 9–12 pm, 1–3:30 pm, call for
weekend hours
Contact: John Balmer, President
Institution type: County museum
Collection type: Clothing, accessories, uniforms,
general textiles, quilts, flags
Description: 1800–present. Quilts, coverlets,
clothing, shoes, bags, hosiery, jewelry, hats, and
uniforms. Highlights include a large collection
of Cosley woven coverlets, 1846–1870.
🖊

**Pioneer and Historical Society of
Muskingum County**
115 Jefferson Street
Zanesville, OH 43701
Tel: 740-454-9500 Fax: 740-454-9500
Hours: Tue–Fri 12–4 pm, and by appointment
Contact: Linda Smucker
Institution type: History museum, historic house,
county museum
Collection type: Clothing, accessories, uniforms
Description: 1800–present. Women's, men's, and
children's clothing and accessories, with the
major portion being women's clothing.
$ 🖊

Zoar State Memorial
198 Main Street
Zoar, OH 44697
Tel: 330-874-3011
www.ohiohistory.org/places/zoar

OKLAHOMA

The Anadarko Philomathic Museum
311 East Main Street
Anadarko, OK 73005
Tel: 405-247-3240

Indian City Museum
Indian City USA
Anadarko, OK 73005
Tel: 405-247-5661
www.indiancityusa.com/museum.asp

Southern Plains Indian Museum
715 East Central
Anadarko, OK 73005
Tel: 405-247-6221

Woolaroc Museum
State Highway 123
Bartlesville, OK 74003
Tel: 918-336-0307
www.woolaroc.org

Top of Oklahoma Historical Museum
303 South Main Street
Blackwell, OK 74631
Tel: 580-363-0209

Black Kettle Museum
101 South L.L. Males
Cheyenne, OK 73628
Tel: 405-497-3929

Tom Mix Museum
712 North Delaware
Dewey, OK 74029
Tel: 918-534-1555

Chisholm Trail Heritage Center
1000 Chisholm Trail Parkway
Duncan, OK 73533
Tel: 580-252-6692 Fax: 580-252-6567
www.onthechisholmtrail.com/Muse.htm
Hours: Tue–Sat 10–5 pm, Sun 1–5 pm
Contact: Cova Williams
Institution type: History museum
Collection type: Clothing, uniforms
Description: 1851–1899. Small collection
    includes 1 mannequin dressed in cowboy
    ensemble: hat, shirt, scarf, leather wrist cuffs,
    jeans, chaps, and boots.
$ ✍

**Stephens County Historical Society
and Museum**
Highway 81 and Beech, Fuqua Park
Duncan, OK 73533
Tel: 580-252-0717

Canadian County Historical Museum
300 South Grand
El Reno, OK 73036
Tel: 405-262-5121

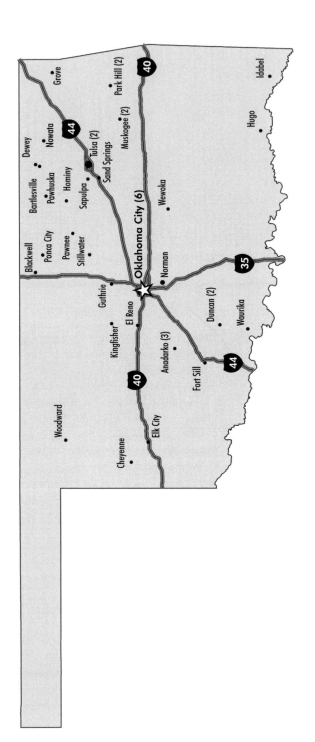

Grove

Park Hill (2)

Idabel

40

Nowata

Dewey

44

Muskogee (2)

Hugo

Tulsa (2)

Sand Springs

Bartlesville

Pawhuska

Hominy

Sapulpa

Wewoka

Blackwell

Ponca City

Pawnee

Stillwater

Oklahoma City (6)

Norman

35

Guthrie

El Reno

Duncan (2)

Waurika

Kingfisher

Anadarko (3)

Fort Sill

44

40

Woodward

Elk City

Cheyenne

Population

• 0 - 50,000

● 50,001 - 100,000

● 100,001 - 250,000

● 250,001 - 500,000

● > 500,000

☆ State Capital

CSA Region VII Southwest

UT CO KS

AZ NM TX

National Route 66 Museum and Old Town Complex

2717 West Highway 66
Elk City, OK 73644
Tel: 405-225-6266

Fort Sill National Historical Landmark

437 Quanah Road
Fort Sill, OK 73503-5100
Tel: 580-442-5123
http://sill-www.army.mil/Museum/
HOME%20PAGE.htm

Har-Ber Village Museum

4404 West 20th Street
Grove, OK 74344
Tel: 918-786-3488 Fax: 918-787-6213
www.har-bervillage.com
Hours: Mon–Sat 9–6 pm, Sun 12:30–6 pm
(Mar–Nov 15)
Contact: Jan Norman
Institution type: Historic house
Collection type: Clothing, accessories, uniforms,
costumes, general textiles
Description: 1800–present. Village of early 1800s
includes 114 buildings and 5 streets on self-
guided tours. Mannequins in each building are
dressed as interpretive tools.
$ ✍

Oklahoma Territorial Museum

402 East Oklahoma Avenue
Guthrie, OK 73044
Tel: 405-282-1889

Drummond Home

305 North Price
Hominy, OK 74035
Tel: 918-885-2374

Choctaw County Historical Society

309 North B Street
Hugo, OK 74743
Tel: 580-326-6630

Museum of the Red River

812 East Lincoln Road
Idabel, OK 74745
Tel: 508-286-3616
www.museumoftheredriver.org

Governor Seay Mansion

605 Zellers Avenue
Kingfisher, OK 73750
Tel: 405-375-5176
www.ok-history.mus.ok.us

Ataloa Lodge Museum

2299 Old Bacone Road
Muskogee, OK 74403
Tel: 918-683-4581

The Five Civilized Tribes Museum

1109 Honor Heights Drive
Muskogee, OK 74401
Tel: 918-683-1701
www.fivetribes.com

Cleveland County Historical Museum and Historical Society

508 North Peters
Norman, OK 73069
Tel: 405-321-0156
www.normanhistorichouse.org
Hours: Tue–Sat 10–4 pm
Contact: Jaime Evans
Institution type: Historic house, county museum,
city museum
Collection type: Clothing, accessories, costumes
Description: 1850–1914. Primarily Victorian era
costumes from the post–Civil War 1800s to the
early 1900s, mainly American with one or two
pieces from Europe. Most items originated in
Oklahoma. Strengths are mourning costumes,
wedding dress, baby and children's clothes, and
undergarments.

Nowata County Historical Society Museum

121 South Pine Street
Nowata, OK 74048
Tel: 918-273-1191

45th Infantry Division Museum

2145 NE 36th
Oklahoma City, OK 73111
Tel: 405-424-5313
www.45thdivisionmuseum.com

ASA National Softball Hall of Fame and Museum Complex

2801 NE 50th
Oklahoma City, OK 73111
Tel: 405-424-5266
www.asasoftball.com

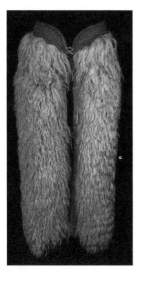

Angora chaps, circa 1920. Courtesy of National Cowboy and Western Heritage Museum.

National Cowboy and Western Heritage Museum

1700 NE 63rd Street
Oklahoma City, OK 73111
Tel: 405-478-2250
www.nationalcowboymuseum.org
Hours: Mon–Sun 9–5 pm
Contact: Curator of Collections
Institution type: History museum
Collection type: Clothing, accessories
Description: 1850–present. Founded in 1955 in Oklahoma City, Oklahoma, the National Cowboy and Western Heritage Museum has a mission to preserve and interpret the heritage of the American West for the enrichment of the public. Among the museum's holdings are more than 100,000 historic photographs, documents, and objects relating to ranching, rodeo, and the Hollywood cowboy figure, including clothing and accoutrements.
$ ✍

Oklahoma Firefighters Museum

2716 NE 50th Street
Oklahoma City, OK 73111
Tel: 405-424-3440
www.osfa.info/muse.html

Oklahoma Museum of History

2100 North Lincoln Boulevard
Oklahoma City, OK 73044
Tel: 405-522-5248 Fax: 405-522-5402
www.ok-history.mus.ok.us
Hours: Mon–Sat 9–4:30 pm
Contact: Jeff Briley
Institution type: History museum, state museum
Collection type: Clothing, accessories, uniforms, general textiles, quilts
Description: 1850–1960. More than 10,000 artifacts, including clothing, quilts, rugs, and accessories.

Overholser Mansion

405 NW 15th
Oklahoma City, OK 73103
Tel: 405-528-8485

Cherokee National Museum

21192 South Keeler Drive
Park Hill, OK 74451
Tel: 918-456-6007
www.cherokeeheritage.org/Default.aspx?tabid=247

Murrell Home

19479 East Murrell Home Road
Park Hill, OK 74451
Tel: 918-456-2751 Fax: 918-456-2751
www.ok-history.mus.ok.us/mus-sites/masnum12.htm
Hours: Sat 10–5 pm, Sun 1–5 pm (Nov–Feb); Wed–Sat 10–5 pm, Sun 1–5 pm (Mar–Oct)
Contact: Shirley Pettengill
Institution type: Historic house
Collection type: Clothing, accessories, costumes
Description: 1850–1899. Textiles belonging to Murrell and Ross family members, 1860s–1900, including baby clothing, dresses, gloves, shoes, and Masonic materials.
✍

Osage County Historical Society Museum

700 North Lynn Avenue
Pawhuska, OK 74056
Tel: 918-287-9924

Pawnee Bill Ranch

1141 Pawnee Bill Road
Pawnee, OK 74058
Tel: 918-762-2513

Pioneer Woman Museum

701 Monument
Ponca City, OK 74604
Tel: 580-765-6108
www.pioneerwomanmuseum.com
Hours: Tue–Sat 9–5 pm, Sun 1–5 pm
Contact: Rebecca Larsen Brave
Institution type: History museum, state museum
Collection type: Clothing, general textiles
Description: 1850–present. General collection includes clothing and textiles.
$ ✍

Sand Springs Cultural and Historical Museum

6 East Broadway
Sand Springs, OK 74063
Tel: 918-246-2509
www.sandspringsok.org/shell.asp?pg=30

Sapulpa Historical Museum

100 East Lee
Sapulpa, OK 74066
Tel: 918-224-4871

National Wrestling Hall of Fame

405 West Hall of Fame Avenue
Stillwater, OK 74075
Tel: 405-377-5243
www.wrestlinghalloffame.org

Gilcrease Museum

1400 North Gilcrease Museum Road
Tulsa, OK 74127-2100
Tel: 918-596-2700
www.gilcrease.org

The Philbrook Museum of Art

2727 South Rockford Road
Tulsa, OK 74114-4104
Tel: 918-748-5300
www.philbrook.org

Chisholm Trail Historical Museum

614 Monroe
Waurika, OK 73573
Tel: 580-228-2166

Seminole Nation Museum

524 South Wewoka Avenue
Wewoka, OK 74884
Tel: 405-257-5580

Plains Indians and Pioneers Museum

2009 Williams Avenue
Woodward, OK 73801
Tel: 580-256-6136

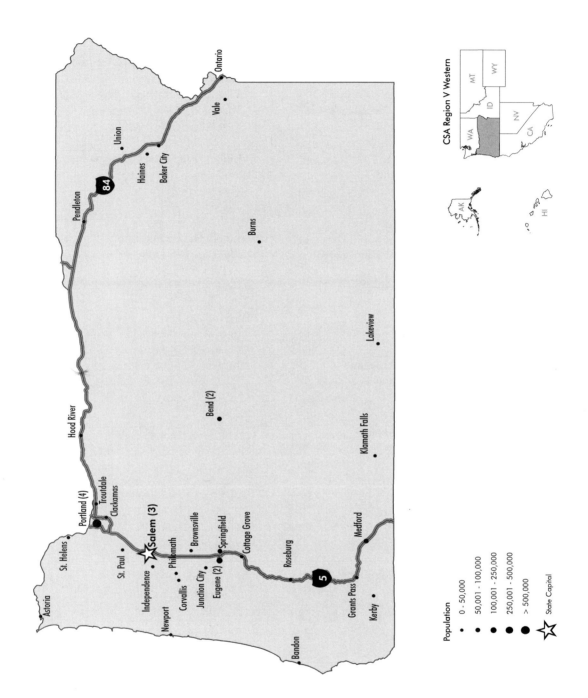

CSA Region V Western

Population

· 0 - 50,000
• 50,001 - 100,000
● 100,001 - 250,000
⬤ 250,001 - 500,000
⬤ > 500,000

☆ State Capital

Astoria
St. Helens
Newport
Corvallis
Junction City
Eugene (2)
Independence
Philomath
St. Paul
Brownsville
Springfield
Cottage Grove
Salem (3)
Clackamas
Troutdale
Portland (4)
Hood River
Pendleton
Union
Haines
Baker City
Vale
Ontario
Burns
Lakeview
Bend (2)
Klamath Falls
Medford
Roseburg
Grants Pass
Kerby
Bandon

OREGON

Heritage Museum

1618 Exchange Street
Astoria, OR 97103
Tel: 503-338-4849 Fax: 503-325-7727
www.clatsophistoricalsociety.org
Hours: Mon–Sun 10–5 pm (Summer); Tue–Fri
11–4 pm (Winter)
Contact: Lisa Studts, Curator
Institution type: County museum
Collection type: Clothing, accessories, uniforms,
general textiles, flags
Description: 1850–1960. Victorian clothing, pri-
marily, and women's regatta dresses.
$ 🖎

National Historic Oregon Trail
Interpretive Center

22267 Oregon Highway 86
Baker City, OR 97814
Tel: 541-523-1843 Fax: 541-523-1834
www.blm.gov/nhp/spotlight/state_info/
highlights/or/nhotic
Hours: Mon–Sun 9–6 pm (Apr–Oct); 9–4 pm
(Nov–Mar)
Contact: Sarah Lecompte
Institution type: Federal museum
Collection type: Clothing
Description: 1800–1899. Items from the Oregon
Trail era, circa 1830–1870, and items related to
American westward migration, frontier, and
gold mining.
$ 🖎

Bandon Historical Society Museum

270 Fillmore Avenue
Bandon, OR 97411
Tel: 541-347-2164
http://bandonhistoricalmuseum.org

Deschutes County Historical Society

129 NW Idaho Avenue
Bend, OR 97701
Tel: 541-389-1813

The High Desert Museum

59800 South Highway 97
Bend, OR 97702-7963
Tel: 541-382-4754 Fax: 541-382-5256
www.highdesertmuseum.org

Linn County Historical Museum
and Moyer House

101 Park Avenue
Brownsville, OR 97327
Tel: 541-466-3390 Fax: 541-466-3390
www.co.linn.or.us/museum
Hours: Mon–Sat 11–4 pm, Sun 1–5 pm
Contact: Della Klinkebiel
Institution type: County museum
Collection type: Clothing, accessories, uniforms,
costumes, general textiles, quilts, flags
Description: 1850–1960. Blankets from B'Ville
Woolen Mill, precursor to Pendleton Mills;
quilts and various handiwork from as early as
1865; clothing from various prominent citizens
of the area; and uniforms from World War I.

Harney County Historical Museum

18 West D Street
Burns, OR 97720
Tel: 541-573-1461
www.burnsmuseum.com

Oregon Military Museum

Camp Withycombe
10101 SE Clackamas Road
Clackamas, OR 97015
Tel: 503-557-5359

Oregon State University, Department of Design and Human Environment

DHE, 224 Milam
Corvallis, OR 97331
Tel: 541-737-0984 Fax: 541-737-0993
www.hhs.oregonstate.edu/dhe/facilities/apparel
-design-studio.html
Hours: Student access only
Contact: Elaine Pedersen
Institution type: University collection
Collection type: Clothing, accessories, uniforms, costumes, general textiles
Description: Pre-1700–present. Euro-American and other ethnic and cultural groups' clothing and accessories. Strength is in its breadth of objects, with textiles and dress objects from most inhabited continents.

Cottage Grove Museum and Annex

147 H Street and Birch Avenue
Cottage Grove, OR 97424
Tel: 541-942-3963

Jordan Schnitzer Museum of Art

1430 Johnson Lane
Eugene, OR 97403
Tel: 541-346-3027
http://uoma.uoregon.edu/

Oregon Air and Space Museum

90377 Boeing Drive
Eugene, OR 97402
Tel: 541-461-1101

Schmidt House Museum and Research Library

508 SW 5th Street
Grants Pass, OR 97526
Tel: 541-479-7827
www.webtrail.com/jchs/schmidt.html

Eastern Oregon Museum on the Old Oregon Trail

3rd and Wilcox
Haines, OR 97833
Tel: 541-856-3233
www.hainesoregon.com/eomuseum.html

Hood River County Historical Museum

300 East Port Marina Drive
Hood River, OR 97031
Tel: 541-386-6772
www.co.hood-river.or.us/museum
Hours: Mon–Sat 10–4 pm, Sun 12–4 pm (Apr–Aug); Mon–Fri 12–4 pm (Sep–Oct)
Contact: Connie Nice, Museum Coordinator
Institution type: County museum
Collection type: Clothing, accessories, uniforms, costumes, general textiles, quilts, flags
Description: 1800–present.

Independence Heritage Museum

FORSYTHE COLLECTION
112 South 3rd Street
Independence, OR 97351
Tel: 503-838-4989 Fax: 503-606-3282
www.open.org/herimusm
Hours: Wed, Sat 1–5 pm, Thu–Fri 1–4 pm
Contact: Peggy Schorsch
Institution type: History museum
Collection type: Quilts
Description: 1915–1960. Quilts from Polk County, Washington, and Marion County, Oregon; 1930s quilts including Flower Basket, Sun Bonnet, and Wedding Ring quilts; and a Sun Bonnet quilt made by the Ladies Aide Society of Salem, Oregon, and Wenatchee, Washington.

$

Junction City Historical Society

655 Holly Street
Junction City, OR 97448
Tel: 541-998-2924
www.junctioncity.com/history
Hours: Thu 3–5 pm, last Sat 1–4 pm
Contact: Kitty Goodin
Institution type: History museum, historic house
Collection type: Clothing, accessories, quilts
Description: 1850–1914. Dresses of local people from the 1870s to the 1890s, Scandinavian and

Danish dresses, undergarments from Denmark, and quilts from 1860 to 1915.

Kerbyville Museum
24195 Redwood Highway
Kerby, OR 97531
Tel: 541-592-5252
www.kerbyvillemuseum.com

Favell Museum of Indian Artifacts and Western Art
125 West Main Street
Klamath Falls, OR 97601
Tel: 541-882-9996
Hours: Mon–Sat 9:30–5:30 pm
Contact: Patsy H. McMillan, CEO
Institution type: Art museum, history museum
Collection type: Clothing
Description: 1800–1849. Collection includes Native American beaded dresses and shirts.

$

Schminck Memorial Museum
128 South E Street
Lakeview, OR 97630
Tel: 541-947-3134

Southern Oregon Historical Society
106 North Central Avenue
Medford, OR 97501
Tel: 541-773-6536
www.sohs.org
Hours: Wed–Sun 10–5 pm
Contact: Steve Wyatt, Curator of Collections
Institution type: History museum
Collection type: Clothing, accessories, uniforms, general textiles, quilts
Description: 1850–1960. More than 3,000 items of dress and appearance, including day and evening wear, military uniforms, children's clothing, quilts, coverlets, and other household items.

$

Oregon Coast History Center
545 SW 9th
Newport, OR 97365
Tel: 541-265-7509
www.newportnet.com/coasthistory/home.htm

Four Rivers Cultural Center and Museum
676 SW 5th Avenue
Ontario, OR 97914
Tel: 541-889-8191

Heritage Station, Umatilla County Historical Society Museum
108 SW Frazer
Pendleton, OR 97801
Tel: 541-276-0012
www.umatillahistory.org

Benton County Historical Society and Museum
1101 Main Street
Philomath, OR 97370
Tel: 541-929-6230 Fax: 541-929-6261
www.bentoncountymuseum.org
Hours: Tue–Sat 10–4:30 pm
Contact: Mary K. Gallagher, Collections Manager
Institution type: Art museum, history museum
Collection type: General textiles
Description: 1850–present. General textile collection emphasizes objects related to the history of Benton County, Oregon.

Dress. Courtesy of Oregon Historical Society.

Oregon Historical Society
1200 SW Park Avenue
Portland, OR 97205
Tel: 503-222-1741
www.ohs.org
Hours: Mon–Sat 10–5 pm, Sun 12–5 pm
Contact: Marsha Matthews, Director of Artifact Collections and Exhibits

Institution type: History museum

Collection type: Clothing, accessories, uniforms, general textiles, flags

Description: 1850–present. Items from regional clothing manufacturers and Oregon Trail era clothing.

$ ✍☐

Oregon Sports Hall of Fame and Museum

321 SW Salmon
Portland, OR 97204
Tel: 503-227-7466
www.oregonsportshall.org

Pittock Mansion

3229 NW Pittock Drive
Portland, OR 97210
Tel: 503-823-3623
www.pittockmansion.com

Washington County Historical Society

17677 NW Springville Road
Portland, OR 97229
Tel: 503-645-5353
www.washingtoncountymuseum.org

Douglas County Museum of History and Natural History

123 Museum Drive
Roseburg, OR 97470
Tel: 541-957-7007 Fax: 541-957-7017
www.co.douglas.or.us/museum

Hours: Mon–Fri 9–5 pm, Sat 10–5 pm, Sun 12–5 pm

Contact: Jena Mitchell, Karen Bratton, Dennis Ruley

Institution type: History museum, county museum

Collection type: Clothing, accessories, uniforms, general textiles, quilts

Description: 1850–present. Wedding gowns; Victorian dresses, petticoats, shoes, and hats; Native American outerwear; and military uniforms from both World Wars. Quilt and coverlet collection includes the "Peony with Flying Geese Border" quilt by Susannah Weaver Hall, one of the first settlers in the area.

$ ✍☐

Robert Newell House, DAR Museum

8089 Champoeg Road NE
St. Paul, OR 97137
Tel: 503-266-3944

Bush House Museum

600 Mission Street SE
Salem, OR 97302
Tel: 503-581-2228
www.salemart.org/bush/index.htm

Hours: Tue–Sun 2–5 pm

Contact: Program coordinator

Institution type: Historic house

Collection type: Clothing, accessories, general textiles, flags

Description: 1850–1914.

$ ✍☐

Historic Deepwood Estate Museum

1116 Mission Street SE
Salem, OR 97302
Tel: 503-363-1825
www.deepwood.org

Mission Mill Museum

1313 Mill Street SE
Salem, OR 97301
Tel: 503-585-7012 Fax: 503-588-9902
www.missionmill.org

Hours: Mon–Sat 10–5 pm

Contact: Kuri Gill

Institution type: History museum, historic house

Collection type: Clothing, general textiles, quilts

Description: 1800–1960. Furnishings and household items of 1830–1860; machinery and artifacts related to the Northwest woolen industry; handmade textiles, particularly coverlets; and quilts of Oregon Trail period or later.

$ ✍☐

Springfield Museum

590 Main Street
Springfield, OR 97477
Tel: 541-726-3677
www.springfieldmuseum.com

Columbia County Historical Society Museum

Old County Courthouse
St. Helens, OR 97051
Tel: 503-397-3868 Fax: 503-397-7257

Troutdale Historical Society
   726 East Historic Columbia River Highway
   Troutdale, OR 97060
   Tel: 503-661-2164

Union County Museum
   311 South Main Street
   Union, OR 97883
   Tel: 541-562-6003

Stonehouse Museum—Malheur Historical Project
   255 Main Street
   Vale, OR 97918
   Tel: 541-473-2070

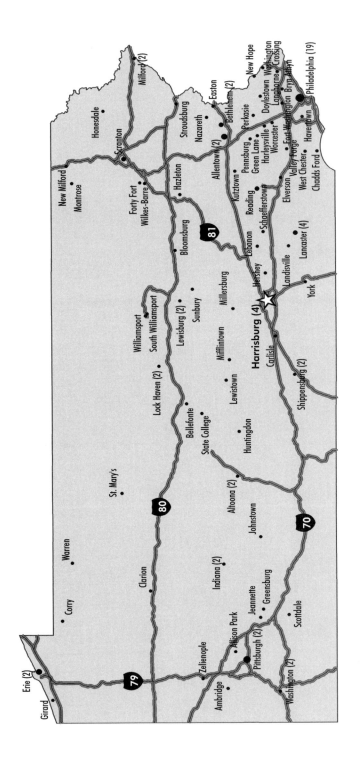

Population

· 0 - 50,000
• 50,001 - 100,000
● 100,001 - 250,000
● 250,001 - 500,000
● > 500,000
☆ State Capital

CSA Region II Mid-Atlantic

Milford (2)
Honesdale
New Hope
Washington Crossing
Easton
Bethlehem (2)
Perkasie
Doylestown
Langhorne
Washington Crossing
Bryn Athyn
Philadelphia (19)
Stroudsburg
Nazareth
Allentown (2)
Pennsburg
Green Lane
Harleysville
Worcester
Fort Washington
Havertown
Scranton
Kutztown
Elverson
Valley Forge
West Chester
Chadds Ford
New Milford
Montrose
Hazleton
Reading
Schaefferstown
Forty Fort
Wilkes-Barre
Bloomsburg
Lebanon
Landisville
Lancaster (4)
York
Williamsport
South Williamsport
Lewisburg (2)
Sunbury
Millersburg
Hershey
Mifflintown
Harrisburg (4)
Carlisle
Lock Haven (2)
Lewistown
Shippensburg (2)
Bellefonte
State College
Huntingdon
St. Mary's
Altoona (2)
Johnstown
Warren
Clarion
Indiana (2)
Jeannette
Greensburg
Scottdale
Corry
Zelienople
Allison Park
Pittsburgh (2)
Washington (2)
Ambridge
Erie (2)
Girard

278 ■ **Pennsylvania**

PENNSYLVANIA

Allentown Art Museum

5th and Court Streets
Allentown, PA 18105
Tel: 610-432-4333
www.allentownmuseum.org

Lehigh County Historical Society

Old Court House
501 Hamilton Street
Allentown, PA 18105
Tel: 610-435-1074

Depreciation Lands Museum

4743 South Pioneer Road
Allison Park, PA 15101
Tel: 412-486-0563

Blair County Historical Society

3419 Oak Lane
Altoona, PA 16602
Tel: 814-942-3916 Fax: 814-942-7078
www.blaircohistory.org
Hours: Tue–Sun 1–4:30 pm; research hours: Tue,
Fri 9–4:30 pm
Contact: Margaret L. Fields
Institution type: History museum, historic house
Collection type: Clothing, accessories, uniforms,
general textiles, flags
Description: 1800–present. Founded in 1846, col-
lection contains items from Blair County,
including clothing and accessories, mostly
1870 to 1970, and other textiles, 1840s to the
present.

$

Railroaders Memorial Museum

1300 9th Avenue
Altoona, PA 16602
Tel: 814-946-0834
www.railroadcity.com

Old Economy Village

270 16th Street
Ambridge, PA 15003
Tel: 724-266-4500x206 Fax: 724-266-7506
www.oldeconomyvillage.org
Hours: Tue–Sat 9–5 pm, Sun 12–5 pm
Contact: Sarah J. Buffington
Institution type: History museum, historic house,
state museum
Collection type: Clothing, accessories, general textiles, flags
Description: 1800–1914. Collection originated
with the Harmony Society, a German-
American religious communal society from
Wurttemberg, Germany, who lived in Harmony, Pennsylvania; New Harmony, Indiana;
and Economy, Pennsylvania, from 1804 until
1905. Highlights include Harmonist-made silk
fabrics and ribbons as well as Harmonist
clothing and accessories.

$ ✍

Centre County Library and Historical Museum

203 North Allegheny Street
Bellefonte, PA 16823
Tel: 814-355-1516

Kemerer Museum of Decorative Arts

427 North New Street
Bethlehem, PA 18018
Tel: 610-868-6868
www.historicbethlehem.org/decorative.jsp

Moravian Museum of Bethlehem

66 West Church Street
Bethlehem, PA 18018
Tel: 610-867-0173
www.historicbethlehem.org/museum

Columbia County Historical and Genealogical Society

225 Market Street
Bloomsburg, PA 17815-0360
Tel: 570-784-1600
www.colcohist-gensoc.org

Glencairn Museum

1001 Cathedral Road
Bryn Athyn, PA 19009
Tel: 215-914-2982 Fax: 215-914-2986
www.glencairnmuseum.org
Hours: Mon–Fri 9–5 pm, Sat 11–1 pm; tours by
    appointment only
Contact: Bret Bostock, Collections Manager
Institution type: Art museum, history museum,
    historic house, university museum
Collection type: Clothing, costumes, general tex-
    tiles
Description: 1800–present.
$ ✍

Cumberland County Historical Society

21 North Pitt Street
Carlisle, PA 17013
Tel: 717-249-7610
www.historicalsociety.com

Brandywine Battlefield Park

U.S. Route 1
Chadds Ford, PA 19317
Tel: 610-459-3342
www.ushistory.org/brandywine

The Sutton-Ditz House Museum

18 Grant Street
Clarion, PA 16214-1501
Tel: 814-226-4450

Corry Area Historical Society

937 Mead Avenue
Corry, PA 16407
Tel: 814-664-4749

Mercer Museum and Fonthill Museum of the Bucks County Historical Society

84 South Pine Street
Doylestown, PA 18901
Tel: 215-345-0210 Fax: 215-230-0823
www.mercermuseum.org
Hours: Mon–Sat 10–5 pm, Tue 10–9 pm, Sun
    12–5 pm
Contact: Cory M. Amsler, Curator
Institution type: History museum, historic house,
    county museum
Collection type: Clothing, general textiles, quilts
Description: Pre-1700–present. 50,000 tools and
    products of early handcrafts, artifacts of
    everyday living, Pennsylvania German material
    culture, folk art, and local history.
$ ✍

Northampton County Historical and Genealogical Society

107 South 4th Street
Easton, PA 18042
Tel: 610-253-1222
www.northamptonctymuseum.org

Hopewell Furnace National Historic Site

2 Mark Bird Lane
Elverson, PA 19520
Tel: 610-582-8773
www.nps.gov/hofu

Erie County Historical Society

419 State Street
Erie, PA 16501
Tel: 814-454-1813
www.eriecountyhistory.org
Hours: Change seasonally
Contact: Stephanie Taylor
Institution type: History museum, historic house,
    county museum
Collection type: Clothing, accessories, uniforms,
    costumes, general textiles, flags
Description: 1760–present.
$ ✍

Watson-Curtze Mansion

356 West 6th Street

Erie, PA 16507

Tel: 814-871-5790

www.eriecountyhistory.org

Historical Society of Fort Washington

473 Bethlehem Pike

Fort Washington, PA 19034

Tel: 215-646-6065

Nathan Denison House

35 Denison Street

Forty Fort, PA 18704

Tel: 570-288-5531

Battles Museum of Rural Life

436 Walnut Street

Girard, PA 16917-1650

Tel: 814-774-4788

www.eriecountyhistory.org

Goschenhoppen Historians—Folklife Library and Museum

Route 29, Red Men's Hall

Green Lane, PA 18054

Tel: 215-234-8953

www.goschenhoppen.org

Hours: Sun 1:30–4 pm (Apr–Oct)

Contact: Alan Keyser, Historian and Curator

Institution type: Historic house

Collection type: Clothing, general textiles

Description: 1760–1960. Collections focus on Pennsylvania's German folklife and locally used or made items.

✍🏻

Westmoreland County Historical Society

41 West Otterman Street

Suite 310

Greensburg, PA 15601

Tel: 724-836-1800

www.starofthewest.org

Mennonite Heritage Center

565 Yoder Road

Harleysville, PA 19438

Tel: 215-256-3020

www.mhep.org

Fort Hunter Mansion and Park

5300 North Front Street

Harrisburg, PA 17110

Tel: 717-599-5751

www.forthunter.org

Hours: Tue–Sun 10–4:30 pm (May–Dec)

Contact: Carl Dickson

Institution type: History museum, historic house, county museum

Collection type: Clothing, accessories

Description: 1850–1914. Clothing owned by the last occupant of the mansion, Helen Boas Reily (1862–1932), ranging from ball gowns to suits, as well as underwear, fans, and hats. Collection also features additional dresses from the 1860s.

$ ✍🏻

The John Harris/Simon Cameron Mansion

The Historical Society of Dauphin County

219 South Front Street

Harrisburg, PA 17104

Tel: 717-233-3462

www.dauphincountyhistoricalsociety.org

Pennsylvania Historical and Museum Commission

300 North Street

Harrisburg, PA 17120

Tel: 717-787-3362 Fax: 717-783-9924

www.phmc.state.pa.us

Hours: Vary by museum and site

Contacts: Vary by museum and site

Institution type: Art museum, history museum, historic house, state museum

Collection type: Clothing, accessories, uniforms, costumes, general textiles, flags

Description: Pre-1700–present. Collections represent history and pre-history of Pennsylvania. Clothing and textiles are represented at each of the twenty-five sites around the state.

$ ✍🏻

The State Museum of Pennsylvania

300 North Street

Harrisburg, PA 17108

Tel: 717-787-4980

www.statemuseumpa.org

Haverford Township Historical Society

Karakung Drive

Powder Mill Valley Park

Havertown, PA 19083

Tel: 610-789-5169

www.haverfordhistoricalsociety.org

Greater Hazelton Historical Society
55 North Wyoming Street
Hazelton, PA 18021
Tel: 570-455-8576

Hershey Museum
170 West Hersheypark Drive
Hershey, PA 17033
Tel: 717-520-5722
www.hersheymuseum.org

Wayne County Historical Society
810 Main
Honesdale, PA 18431
Tel: 570-253-3240
www.waynehistorypa.org

Huntingdon County Historical Society
106 4th Street
Huntingdon, PA 16652
Tel: 814-643-5449
www.huntingdonhistory.org

Historical and Genealogical Society of Indiana County
200 South 6th Street
Indiana, PA 15701-2999
Tel: 724-463-9600
www.rootsweb.com/~paicgs

The Jimmy Stewart Museum
845 Philadelphia Street
Indiana, PA 15701
Tel: 724-349-6112
www.jimmy.org

Bushy Run Battlefield
Route 993
Jeannette, PA 15644
Tel: 724-527-5584
www.bushyrunbattlefield.com

Johnstown Area Heritage Association
304 Washington Street
Johnstown, PA 15907
Tel: 814-539-1889
www.jaha.org

Pennsylvania German Cultural Heritage Center at Kutztown University
Luckenbill Road
Kutztown, PA 19530
Tel: 610-683-1589
www.kutztown.edu/news/german_heritage.shtml

Heritage Center of Lancaster County
13 West King Street
Lancaster, PA 17603
Tel: 717-299-6440
www.lancasterheritage.com

James Buchanan Foundation for the Preservation of Wheatland
1120 Marietta Avenue
Lancaster, PA 17603
Tel: 717-392-8721 Fax: 717-295-8827
www.wheatland.org
Hours: Mon–Sun 9–4:30 pm
Institution type: Historic house
$ 🖎

Lancaster County Historical Society
230 North President Avenue
Lancaster, PA 17603
Tel: 717-392-4633
www.lancasterhistory.org

Landis Valley Museum
2451 Kissel Hill Road
Lancaster, PA 17601
Tel: 717-569-0401
www.landisvalleymuseum.org

Amos Herr House Foundation and Historic Society
1756 Nissley Road
Landisville, PA 17538
Tel: 717-898-8822

Historic Langhorne Association
160 West Maple Avenue
Langhorne, PA 19047
Tel: 215-757-1888
http://hla.buxcom.net
Hours: Wed 10–12 pm, 7–9 pm, Sat 10–12 pm, and by appointment
Contact: Evelyn Aicher, Chair
Institution type: History museum
Collection type: Clothing, accessories, uniforms, costumes, general textiles, flags

Description: 1850–present. Quaker bonnets, women's hats, wedding dresses, men's top hats and derbys, gowns from the 1930s and 1940s, and children's clothes and shoes.

The Lebanon County Historical Society
924 Cumberland Street
Lebanon, PA 17042
Tel: 717-272-1473
www.lebanonhistory.org

Packwood House Museum
15 North Water Street
Lewisburg, PA 17837
Tel: 570-524-0323 Fax: 570-524-0548
www.packwoodhousemuseum.com
Hours: Tue–Sat 10–5 pm
Contact: Sara Phinney Kelley
Institution type: Art museum, history museum, historic house
Collection type: Clothing, accessories, general textiles, quilts
Description: 1800–present. Clothing from 1910 to 1960; an extensive hat collection, many made in Pennsylvania; more than 300 Pennsylvania quilts and coverlets; and miscellaneous textiles.

$

Slifer House
Riverwoods, 1 River Road
Lewisburg, PA 17837
Tel: 570-524-2245

McCoy House
17 North Main Street
Lewistown, PA 17044
Tel: 711-242-1022
www.mccoyhouse.com

Heisey Museum and Clinton County Historical Society
362 East Water Street
Lock Haven, PA 17745
Tel: 570-748-7254
www.clintoncountyhistory.com

Piper Aviation Museum Foundation
1 Piper Way
Lock Haven, PA 17745

Tel: 570-748-8283
www.pipermuseum.com

Juniata County Historical Society
498 Jefferson Street, Suite B
Mifflintown, PA 17059
Tel: 717-436-5152
www.rootsweb.com/~pajchs

The Columns Museum
608 Broad Street
Milford, PA 18337
Tel: 570-296-8126 Fax: 570-296-6106
www.pikehistory.org
Hours: Wed, Sat–Sun 1–4 pm
Contact: Elizabeth Cotteril, Vaughne Hansen
Institution type: History museum, historic house, county museum
Collection type: Clothing, accessories, uniforms, costumes, general textiles, flags
Description: 1800–present. Vintage wedding gowns, dresses, and uniforms dating back to 1800s. Highlights include costumes worn by actress Jeannie Gourlay, witness to Lincoln assassination.

$

Pike County Historical Society
608 Broad Street
Milford, PA 18337
Tel: 570-296-8126

Historical Society of Millersburg and Upper Paxton Township Museum
330 Center Street
Millersburg, PA 17061
Tel: 717-692-4084

Susquehanna County Historical Society and Free Library Association
2 Monument Square
Montrose, PA 18801
Tel: 570-278-1881
www.susqcohistsoc.org

Moravian Historical Society
214 East Center Street
Nazareth, PA 18064
Tel: 610-759-5070 Fax: 610-759-2461
www.moravianhistoricalsociety.org
Hours: Mon–Fri 1–4 pm
Contact: Mark A. Turdo, Curator

Institution type: History museum

Collection type: Clothing, accessories, uniforms, costumes, general textiles, flags

Description: 1700–present. Collection covers six centuries of history on six continents. Specific textile items are from various periods of Moravian Church culture and history, with the most items from Nazareth Hall Military Academy (uniforms, flags).

$ 🖉

The Parry Mansion Museum

45 South Main Street
New Hope, PA 18938
Tel: 215-862-5652
www.parrymansion.org/parrymansion.htm

Old Mill Village Museum

Route 848
New Milford, PA 18834
Tel: 570-465-3448 Fax: 570-465-9508
www.oldmillvillage.com
Hours: Sun 12–5 pm (May–Oct)
Institution type: State museum
$ 🖉

Schwenkfelder Library and Heritage Center

105 Seminary Street
Pennsburg, PA 18073
Tel: 215-679-3103 Fax: 215-679-8175
www.schwenkfelder.com
Hours: Tue–Wed and Fri 9–4 pm, Thu 9–8 pm, Sat 10–3 pm, Sun 1–4 pm
Contact: Candace Perry
Institution type: History museum
Collection type: Clothing, accessories, uniforms, costumes, general textiles, quilts, flags
Description: 1760–1960. Samplers, needlework pictures, quilts, and sewing accessories, including pincushions; clothing circa 1790–1920, including significant handspun linen examples of shortgowns, aprons, and kerchiefs; personal accessories, including Queen's and Irish stitch eighteenth-century pocketbooks; military uniforms, circa 1861–1945; and other uniforms, including local bands and Boy Scouts, circa 1870–1940.

🖉

Pearl S. Buck House and Historic Site

520 Dublin Road
Perkasie, PA 18944

Tel: 215-249-0100 Fax: 215-249-9657
www.pearl-s-buck.org/psbi/PSBHouse/
visiting.asp
Hours: Tue–Sat 10–4 pm, Sun 12-4 pm (Mar–Dec)
Contact: Kristen Froehlich
Institution type: Historic house
Collection type: Clothing, general textiles
Description: 1900–present. Pearl S. Buck's clothing, hats, shoes, handbags, and household textiles—Asian and American.
$ 🖉

The African American Museum in Philadelphia

701 Arch Street
Philadelphia, PA 19106
Tel: 215-574-0380
www.aampmuseum.org

American Swedish Historical Foundation and Museum

1900 Pattison Avenue
Philadelphia, PA 19145
Tel: 215-389-1776
www.americanswedish.org

Walking dress, circa 1900. Courtesy of Atwater Kent Museum of Philadelphia.

Atwater Kent Museum of Philadelphia

15 South 7th Street
Philadelphia, PA 19106
Tel: 215-685-4839 Fax: 215-685-4837
www.philadelphiahistory.org
Hours: Wed–Mon 10–5 pm
Institution type: History museum, city museum
$ 🖉

ATWATER KENT COLLECTION

Contact: Susan G. Drinan

Collection type: Clothing, accessories, uniforms, costumes, general textiles, quilts, flags

Description: 1700–present. The museum's three collections contain over 3,000 objects from the Philadelphia region dating from the mid-eighteenth century to the 1990s and together are a strong representation of material culture in the Philadelphia region. Atwater Kent Collection includes clothing, accessories, and uniforms ranging from eighteenth-century men's clothing to dresses from a local department store that closed in 1990. Textiles are mainly bedding, including nineteenth-century quilts, coverlets, and samplers from 1750 to 1950.

FRIENDS HISTORICAL ASSOCIATION COLLECTION

Contact: Susan G. Drinan

Collection type: Clothing, accessories, general textiles

Description: 1700–1960. The Friends Historical Association Collection was gathered by the Quaker community and transferred to AKMP in 1987. Majority is women's and children's clothing from the nineteenth century. Collection includes a large selection of Quaker bonnets and caps, a variety of accessories, some outerwear, and a few items of men's eighteenth-century clothing and nineteenth-century hats. Collection also features samplers, caps, and accessories of Rebecca Jones, a well-known Quaker preacher who lived in Philadelphia from 1739 to 1818.

HISTORICAL SOCIETY OF PENNSYLVANIA ART AND ARTIFACT COLLECTION

Contact: Susan G. Drinan

Collection type: Clothing, accessories, uniforms, costumes, general textiles, quilts, flags

Description: 1760–1960. The Historical Society of Pennsylvania was created in 1824 and stewardship of the Art and Artifact Collection came to AKMP in 2001. Majority of clothing and textiles in this collection are from the nineteenth century. Collection is stored off-site and is available on a limited basis.

Bartram's Garden

54th Street and Lindbergh Boulevard
Philadelphia, PA 19143

Tel: 215-729-5281
www.bartramsgarden.org
Hours: House: Tue–Sun 12–4 pm (Mar–Dec 15); Gardens: Tue–Sun 10–5 pm
Contact: Joel T. Fry

Civil War and Underground Railroad Museum of Philadelphia

1805 Pine Street
Philadelphia, PA 19103
Tel: 215-735-8196
www.netreach.net/~cwlm
Hours: Thu–Sat 11–4:30 pm
Contact: Beth Tischler
Institution type: History museum
Collection type: Clothing, uniforms
Description: 1850–1899.

$ ✍

Japanese or Chinese fan, circa 1870–90. Courtesy of The Design Center at Philadelphia University.

The Design Center at Philadelphia University

4200 Henry Avenue
Philadelphia, PA 19144
Tel: 215-951-2860 Fax: 215-951-2615
www.philau.edu/designcenter
Hours: Vary
Contact: Nancy Packer
Institution type: University collection
Collection type: Clothing, accessories, costumes, general textiles
Description: Pre-1700–1960. Collection ranges from Coptic and pre-Columbian artifacts, paisley shawls, and beaded bags to Chinese imperial court attire and fashions by Worth, Callot Soeurs, Hattie Carnegie, and Adrian. Collection includes American and European garments and accessories from the late eighteenth century through the twentieth century, many with Philadelphia provenances, and tra-

ditional costumes from around the world. Collection documents the history of Philadelphia's textile industry through textiles, swatches, and manufacturing tools.

Charles James, circa 1950. Courtesy of Drexel University, College of Media Arts and Design.

Drexel University, College of Media Arts and Design

DREXEL HISTORIC COSTUME
COLLECTION

33rd and Market Streets
Philadelphia, PA 19104
Tel: 215-895-4941 Fax: 215-895-1779
http://digimuse.cis.drexel.edu
Hours: By appointment with curator
Contact: Bella Veksler
Institution type: University collection
Collection type: Clothing, accessories, costumes
Description: 1850–present. Teaching collection, mostly women's wear from 1875 to the present. time. Extensive collection of lace, lingerie, and accessories. Drexel family donations and a variety of objects.

The Fabric Workshop and Museum

1315 Cherry Street, 5th Floor
Philadelphia, PA 19107
Tel: 800-713-1315
www.fabricworkshopandmuseum.org

Germantown Historical Society

5501 Germantown Avenue
Philadelphia, PA 19144
Tel: 215-844-1683 Fax: 215-844-2831
www.libertynet.org/ghs
Hours: Mon–Fri 9–5 pm, Sun 1–5 pm
Contact: Mary K. Dabney
Institution type: History museum
Collection type: Clothing, accessories, uniforms, costumes, general textiles, quilts
Description: 1700–present. Clothing, textiles, and accessories made or used in northwest Philadelphia from the eighteenth century through the twentieth century, including Quaker clothing; Civil War uniforms; quilts; samplers; children's clothing; wedding dresses; and Germantown stockings, hats, and shoes.

$

Independence Seaport Museum

211 South Columbus Boulevard
Philadelphia, PA 19106
Tel: 215-925-5439
www.phillyseaport.org

Lemon Hill Mansion

Lemon Hill and Sedgelay Drives, East Park
Philadelphia, PA 19130
Tel: 215-646-7084
www.lemonhill.org

Loudoun Mansion

4650 Germantown Avenue
Philadelphia, PA 19144
Tel: 215-686-2067

The Masonic Library and Museum of Pennsylvania

1 North Broad Street
Philadelphia, PA 19107
Tel: 215-988-1485 Fax: 215-988-1972
www.pagrandlodge.org/mlam/index.html
Hours: Tue–Fri 9–5 pm, Sat 9–12 pm
Contact: Laura Libert
Institution type: History museum
Collection type: Accessories

Description: 1760–present. Textiles and Masonic regalia, including aprons, sashes, and banners, focusing specifically on items manufactured or used in the state of Pennsylvania. Notable artifacts include the embroidered silk apron of Brother and President George Washington, given to him by Brother Marquis de Lafayette; French sash reputed to have belonged to Brother Benjamin Franklin; the apron and cuffs of Brother Edward VII, Prince of Wales; and a hand-painted banner carried in the Revolutionary War and the War of 1812.

Philadelphia Mummers Museum

1100 South 2nd Street
Philadelphia, PA 19147
Tel: 215-336-3050
www.mummers.com

Evening dresses, Elsa Schiaparelli Summer 1939 Collection. Courtesy of Philadelphia Museum of Art.

Philadephia Museum of Art

DEPARTMENT OF COSTUME AND TEXTILES
26th Street and Benjamin Franklin Parkway
Philadelphia, PA 19130
Tel: 215-684-7570 Fax: 215-236-4330
www.philamuseum.org
Hours: Tue–Sun 10–5 pm, Fri 10–8:45 pm
Contact: Dilys Blum, Curator; Kristina Haugland, Associate Curator

Institution type: Art museum
Collection type: Clothing, accessories, uniforms, general textiles, quilts
Description: Pre-1700–present. Art museum collections contain cloth, clothing, and accessories begun for the 1876 Philadelphia Centennial Exposition. Strengths include twentieth-century millinery, Victorian fashion dolls with extensive wardrobes, American appliqué quilts, lace, eighteenth- and nineteenth-century European and American printed textiles, and eighteenth- through twentieth-century American dress and accessories. Most popular item of clothing is Princess Grace of Monaco's (Grace Kelly) wedding dress. Holdings also include extensive collection of Elsa Schiaparelli's costumes and accessories; folk textiles; and Chinese, Japanese, Indian, Persian, and Southeast Asian costumes and textiles.

$

Please Touch Museum

210 North 21st Street
Philadelphia, PA 19103
Tel: 215-963-0667 Fax: 215-963-0424
www.pleasetouchmuseum.org
Hours: Mon–Sun 9–4:30 pm
Contact: Stacey A. Swigart
Institution type: Children's museum
Collection type: Clothing, accessories, uniforms, costumes, general textiles
Description: 1850–present. General collection includes variety of styles and types—primarily clothing worn by children—and features Philadelphia, Pennsylvania, regional uniforms and clothing and a variety of ethnic and multicultural textiles.

$ 🖊

Rosenbach Museum and Library

2010 DeLancey Place
Philadelphia, PA 19103
Tel: 215-732-1600
www.rosenbach.org

Stenton

4601 North 18th Street
Philadelphia, PA 19140
Tel: 215-329-7312 Fax: 215-329-7312
www.stenton.org
Hours: Tue–Sat 1–4 pm (Apr–Dec), and by appointment

Contact: Laura Stutman

Institution type: Historic house

Collection type: Clothing, accessories, costumes, general textiles

Description: 1700–1960. Historic house, clothing, accessories, and furnishing textiles; 5 whole-cloth quilts with Logan and Norris family provenances; linen and cotton American blue furniture check double festoon drapery panels; Logan family bedding and table linens; Logan family clothes; baby and children's clothes, including an early-eighteenth-century printed dress and needlework baby caps; needlework wallet made by Hannah Logan for John Smith; and assorted bonnets, shoes, and bed hangings not related to the Logan family, including a palimpore and purple toile bed-hangings.

$ 🖊

Woodmere Art Museum

9201 Germantown Avenue
Philadelphia, PA 19118
Tel: 215-247-0476
www.woodmereartmuseum.org

Clayton, the Henry Clay Frick Estate

7227 Reynolds Street
Pittsburgh, PA 15208-2923
Tel: 412-371-0600
www.frickart.org

Senator John Heinz Pittsburgh History Center

1212 Smallman Street
Pittsburgh, PA 15222
Tel: 412-454-6340 Fax: 412-454-6029
www.pghhistory.org

Hours: Mon–Sun 10–5 pm

Contact: Kathleen Wendell, Collections Manager

Institution type: History museum

Collection type: Clothing, accessories, uniforms, costumes, general textiles, quilts

Description: 1800–present. Workers' clothing such as heat resistant clothing for steel industry; A & P Grocery store uniform; construction clothing (work belts and boots); ethnic clothing from Slavik countries; clothing relating to Italian, Irish, and Jewish heritage; circa 1900 gowns from elite families; boys' dresses, circa 1815; Oscar de la Renta bikini;

Heat suit used at the Edgar Thompson Works, U.S. Steel Corporation, circa 1970. Courtesy of Senator John Heinz Pittsburgh History Center.

and clothing using aluminum fibers designed for Alcoa Aluminum Co. Flat textiles include ethnic banners and quilts from 1790 to the present.

$ 🖊

Historical Society of Berks County

940 Centre Avenue
Reading, PA 19601
Tel: 610-375-4375
www.berksweb.com/histsoc

Hours: Tue–Sat 9–4 pm

Contact: Vicky Heffner

Institution type: Art museum, history museum, county museum

Collection type: Clothing, accessories, uniforms, costumes, general textiles, flags

Description: 1750–present. More than 3,000 objects of clothing, with the earliest pieces dating from 1790.

$ 🖊

Historic Schaefferstown

BRENDLE MUSEUM COLLECTION
111 North Market Street
Schaefferstown, PA 17088-0307
Tel: 717-949-2244
www.hsimuseum.org

Hours: Tue–Fri 1–4 pm, Sat 10–12 pm

Contact: Sue E. Small

Institution type: History museum

Collection type: Clothing, accessories, uniforms, costumes, general textiles, flags

Description: 1850–present. Primarily late-nineteenth- and early-twentieth-century

women's clothing, town band uniforms, and
1963 Schaefferstown bicentennial celebration
costumes.

West Overton Museums

West Overton Village
Scottdale, PA 15683-1168
Tel: 724-887-7910 Fax: 724-887-5010
Hours: Tue–Sat 10–4 pm, Sun 12–5 pm
(May–Oct)
Contact: Mary Ann Mogus
Institution type: History museum, historic house
Collection type: Clothing, accessories, uniforms,
costumes
Description: 1850–1960. Clothing dating from
1860 to the 1940s, including military uniforms
through the Korean War, gowns, coats,
bodices, hats, shoes, and men's and children's
clothing.

The Catlin House Museum of the Lackawanna Historical Society

232 Monroe Avenue
Scranton, PA 18510
Tel: 717-344-3841

Shippensburg Historical Society Museum

52 West King Street
Shippensburg, PA 17257
Tel: 717-532-6727

Shippensburg University Fashion Archives

PENNSYLVANIA COLLECTION
1871 Old Main Drive
Shippensburg, PA 17257
Tel: 717-477-1239
www.ship.edu/~fasharch
Hours: Mon–Thu 12–4 pm, and by appointment
Contact: Katherine Cooker
Institution type: University collection
Collection type: Clothing, accessories
Description: 1850–1960. Clothing manufactured
in Pennsylvania and related to the history of its
garment industry.

Peter J. McGovern Little League Baseball Museum

Route 15
South Williamsport, PA 17701
Tel: 570-326-3607
www.littleleague.org/museum/index.asp

Centre County Historical Society

1001 East College Avenue
State College, PA 16801
Tel: 814-234-4779
www.centrecountyhistory.org

Historical Society of St. Marys and Benzinger Township

99 Erie Avenue
St. Marys, PA 15857
Tel: 814-834-6525
Hours: Tue 10–4 pm, Thu 1–4 pm and 6–8 pm
Contact: Alice Beimel
Institution type: City museum
Collection type: Clothing, accessories, uniforms,
costumes, general textiles, flags
Description: 1850–1899. Household items,
clothing, farm items, photographs, church
records, and genealogy records.

Monroe County Historical Association

900 Main Street
Stroudsburg, PA 18360
Tel: 570-421-7703
www.mcha-pa.org
Hours: Tue–Fri 9–4 pm, Sun 1–4 pm
Contact: Amy Leiser
Institution type: History museum
Collection type: Clothing, accessories, general tex-
tiles
Description: 1760–1960.
$

The Hunter House

1150 North Front Street
Sunbury, PA 17801
Tel: 570-286-4083

Valley Forge National Historical Park

North Gulph Road
Valley Forge, PA 19482
Tel: 610-783-1000
www.nps.gov/vafo

Warren County Historical Society Museum

210 4th Avenue
Warren, PA 16365
Tel: 814-723-1795

David Bradford House

175 South Main Street
Washington, PA 15301
Tel: 724-222-3604
www.bradfordhouse.org

Washington County Historical Society

LeMoyne House, 49 East Maiden Street
Washington, PA 15301
Tel: 724-225-6740
www.wchspa.org

Washington Crossing Historic Park

1112 River Road
Washington Crossing, PA 18977
Tel: 215-493-4076

Quaker dress and bonnet, circa 1840–1860. Courtesy of Chester County Historical Society.

Chester County Historical Society

HEAD TO TOE
225 North High Street
West Chester, PA 19380
Tel: 610-692-4800 Fax: 610-692-4357
www.chestercohistorical.org
Hours: Mon–Sat 9:30–4:30 pm, Wed 9:30–8 pm, Library 1–8 pm
Contact: Ellen Endslow
Institution type: History museum, county museum
Collection type: Clothing, accessories, uniforms, quilts

Description: 1700–present. Chester County and region are areas of focus. Clothing and many accessories worn by women in the 1800s; the largest known collection of 1700s shortgowns; Quaker clothing, including dresses, bonnets, caps, and shawls; children's clothing; undergarments of adults; and men's clothing, including military uniforms and suits.

$ 🖎

Luzerne County Historical Society

69 South Franklin Street
Wilkes-Barre, PA 18701
Tel: 570-823-6244
www.luzernecountyhistory.com

The Thomas T. Taber Museum

858 West 4th Street
Williamsport, PA 17701
Tel: 570-326-3326
www.lycoming.org/lchsmuseum

Peter Wentz Farmstead

Shearer Road
Worcester, PA 19490
Tel: 610-584-5104
www.montcopa.org/historicsites/
    peter%20wentz%20narrative.htm

York County Heritage Trust, Museum and Library

250 East Market Street
York, PA 17403
Tel: 717-848-1587
www.yorkheritage.org

Zelienople Historical Society

243 South Main Street
Zelienople, PA 16063
Tel: 724-452-9457 Fax: 724-452-4244
www.fyi.net/~zhs
Hours: Mon–Fri 9–3 pm
Contact: Joyce M. Bessor
Institution type: History museum, historic house
Collection type: Clothing, accessories, uniforms
Description: 1800–present. Clothing and accessories, including nineteenth-century women's dresses, skirts, blouses, underwear, and shoes; men's suits, coats, and hats; and children's clothes and uniforms, 1916–2000.

$ 🖎

RHODE ISLAND

Blithewold Mansion, Gardens, and Arboretum

101 Ferry Road, Route 114
Bristol, RI 02809
Tel: 401-253-2707
www.blithewold.org

Haffenreffer Museum of Anthropology, Brown University

300 Tower Street
Bristol, RI 02809-4071
Tel: 401-253-8388
www.haffenreffermuseum.org

Western Rhode Island Civic Historical Society

7 Station Street
Coventry, RI 02816
Tel: 401-821-4095

Pettaquamscutt Historical Society

2636 Kingstown Road
Kingston, RI 02881
Tel: 401-783-1328

University of Rhode Island Historic Textile and Costume Collection

55 Lower College Road, Suite 3
Kingston, RI 02881
Tel: 401-874-4574 Fax: 401-874-2581
www.uri.edu/hss/tmd/Collection.htm
Hours: Mon–Fri 8:30–4:30 pm
Contact: Margaret T. Ordonez, Director

Boy's suit worn by William Utter Arnold, 1770–80. Courtesy of University of Rhode Island Historic Textile and Costume Collection.

Institution type: University collection
Collection type: Clothing, accessories, general textiles, quilts
Description: 1700–present. Strengths of collection are nineteenth-century apparel, accessories, and textiles of men, women, and children. Ethnographic textiles and costumes, southern New England costumes and textiles from the eighteenth century through the twentieth century, and early-twentieth-century apparel fabrics. Geographic scope of the collection is worldwide.

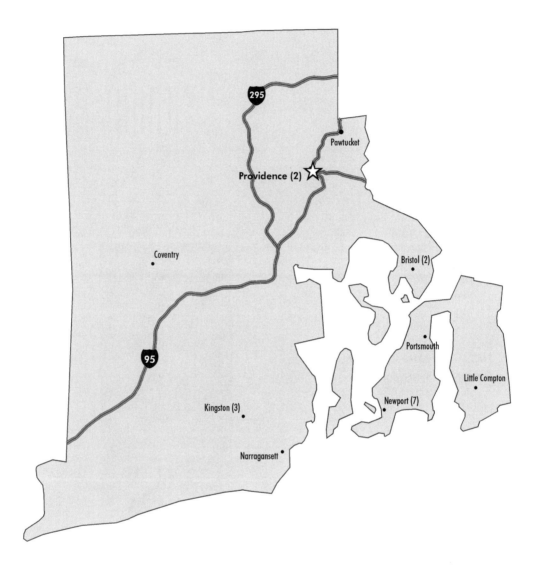

Pawtucket

Providence (2) ☆

Coventry

Bristol (2)

Portsmouth

Little Compton

Kingston (3)

Newport (7)

Narragansett

Population

●   0 - 50,000

●   50,001 - 100,000

●   100,001 - 250,000

●   250,001 - 500,000

●   > 500,000

☆   State Capital

CSA Region I Northeast

Paper pattern, 1928. Courtesy of Commercial Pattern Archive, University of Rhode Island Library Special Collections.

University of Rhode Island Library Special Collections
Betty Williams, URI Theatre, and Joy S. Emery Collections

COMMERCIAL PATTERN ARCHIVE

15 Lippett Road

Kingston, RI 02881

Tel: 401-874-2713 Fax: 401-874-4608

www.uri.edu/library/special_collections/copa

Hours: Mon–Fri 9–4:30 pm

Contact: Joy Emery

Institution type: University collection

Collection type: Patterns

Description: 1800–present. Commercially produced paper patterns for home sewers dating from 1864 to the 1990s, primarily by U.S. pattern companies. More than 20,000 patterns plus supplemental fashion periodicals, journals, tailoring journals, trade catalogs, and books relating to clothing and home sewing.

The Little Compton Historical Society

548 West Main Road

Little Compton, RI 02837

Tel: 401-635-4035 Fax: 401-635-4035

www.littlecompton.org

Hours: Thu–Mon 9–5 pm (Jun–Oct); Mon–Fri 9–5 pm (Nov–May)

Contact: Laura Anderson, Site Manager

Institution type: History museum, historic house

Collection type: Clothing, accessories, uniforms, costumes, general textiles, quilts

Description: 1760–1960. New England quilts, linens, clothing, accessories, and samplers primarily from the late eighteenth century through the early twentieth century. Dresses and quilts are the strengths of collection. The earliest dress is a circa 1800 Quaker dress.

$ ✍

South County Museum

Strathmore Street

Narragansett, RI 02882

Tel: 401-783-5400 Fax: 401-783-0506

www.southcountymuseum.org

Hours: Vary throughout the year

Contact: Pat Weeden

Institution type: History museum

Collection type: Clothing, accessories, uniforms, costumes, general textiles, flags

Description: 1700–1960. Museum was established in 1933, and items are local in origin, although some cover a wider geographic region. Dresses, flags, Civil War uniforms and accessories, hats, and a significant collection of Quaker clothing, including wedding clothes dating from the mid- to late nineteenth century.

$ ✍

Artillery Company of Newport Military Museum

23 Clarke Street

Newport, RI 02840

Tel: 401-846-8488

www.newportartillery.org

Belcourt Castle

657 Bellevue Avenue

Newport, RI 02840-4288

Tel: 401-849-1566

www.belcourtcastle.com

Hours: Vary by season

Contact: Harle H. Tinney, Executive Director

Institution type: Historic house

Collection type: Uniforms, costumes, general textiles, flags

Description: Pre-1700–present. European church vestments; clothing from eighteenth-century Europe and twentieth-century America; uniforms and accessories; a few costumes; tapestries from the sixteenth and seventeenth centuries, as well as table covers and embroideries from the seventeenth through the twentieth centuries; 5 flags or banners of distinction of nineteenth- or twentieth-century European origin; and draperies and upholstery fabrics as early as the mid-1600s.

$ ✍

International Tennis Hall of Fame and Museum

TED TINLING COLLECTION

194 Bellevue Avenue
Newport, RI 02840
Tel: 401-849-3990 Fax: 401-849-3780
www.tennisfame.com

Hours: Mon–Sun 9:30–5 pm
Contact: Nicole Markham, Curator of Collections
Institution type: History museum
Collection type: Clothing, accessories, uniforms
Description: 1850–present. Clothing and accessories worn while playing the sport of tennis, 1874–present. Largest sub-collection is the Ted Tinling Collection (British designer, 1910–1990), featuring tennis costumes from the 1940s to the 1980s. The museum also collects player-worn tennis clothing (e.g., Serena Williams's "Catsuit"). Highlights include British cavalry uniform worn by Major Walter Clopton Wingfield, innovator of modern game of tennis.

$ 🖾

Museum of Yachting

Fort Adams State Park
Newport, RI 02840
Tel: 401-847-1018
www.moy.org

Naval War College Museum

686 Cushing Road, Coasters Harbor Island
Newport, RI 02841-1207
Tel: 401-841-4052
www.nwc.navy.mil/museum

Newport Historical Society and the Museum of Newport History

127 Thames Street
Newport, RI 02840
Tel: 401-846-0813
www.newporthistorical.org

The Preservation Society of Newport County

TEXTILE AND FASHION ARTS COLLECTION

424 Bellevue Avenue
Newport, RI 02840
Tel: 401-847-1000
www.newportmansions.org

Wedding dress of Gertrude Vanderbilt, 1896. Courtesy of The Preservation Society of Newport County.

Hours: Mon–Sun 10–5 pm (Summer), vary by site (Fall, Winter, Spring)
Contact: Rebecca Kelly
Institution type: Historic house
Collection type: Clothing, accessories, costumes, general textiles
Description: 1800–present. Society maintains 11 house museums spanning 250 years of American history and displayed with fine and decorative arts. Annually from April to October a selection of fashions is exhibited at Rosecliff from its collection of approximately 5,000 items. Overall collection consists of costumes and related accessories, primarily of Newport provenance, dating from the eighteenth century through the present day with a concentration on couture clothing from 1890 through the 1920s.

$ 🖾

Slater Mill Historic Site

67 Roosevelt Avenue
Pawtucket, RI 02862-0696
Tel: 401-725-8638
www.slatermill.org

Hours: Mon–Sun 10–5 pm (May–Oct), and by appointment
Contact: Andrian Paquette
Institution type: History museum
Collection type: Clothing, accessories, costumes, general textiles, flags
Description: 1800–present. Handwoven and household goods, clothing, and lace and cloth samples produced in local textile mills. Artifacts are from the New England region, dating

Lace sample from Seenock Lace Company, date unknown. Courtesy of Slater Mill Historic Site.

Chinese Imperial robe, circa 1736–1796. Courtesy of Museum of Art, Rhode Island School of Design.

from the nineteenth century, with a focus on both industrial and pre-industrial methods of textile production. Textile related tools and books.

$ ✎⌂

Portsmouth Historical Society

870 East Main Road and Union Street
Portsmouth, RI 02871
Tel: 401-683-9178

Museum of Art, Rhode Island School of Design

224 Benefit Street
Providence, RI 02903
Tel: 401-454-6502
www.risd.edu/museum.cfm
Hours: Tue–Sun 10–5 pm, 3rd Thu 10–9 pm
Contact: Madelyn Shaw, Associate Curator
Institution type: Art museum, university collection
Collection type: Clothing, accessories, general textiles
Description: Pre-1700–present. Encyclopedic collection of worldwide costume and textiles includes European textiles from the fifteenth century and American and European textiles and costumes from the seventeenth century into the twenty-first century. Collection highlights include pre-contact Andean, Coptic, Islamic, and Native American items and important Asian textiles and costumes from Turkey, Persia, India, central Asia, mainland and insular Southeast Asia, China, and Japan. Collection also contains 300 early-twentieth-century textiles and garments and eighteen cubic feet of records from Providence's Tirocchi Dressmakers' Shop (1915–1947).

$ ✎⌂

Rhode Island Historical Society

110 Benevolent Street
Providence, RI 02906
Tel: 401-331-8575
www.rihs.org

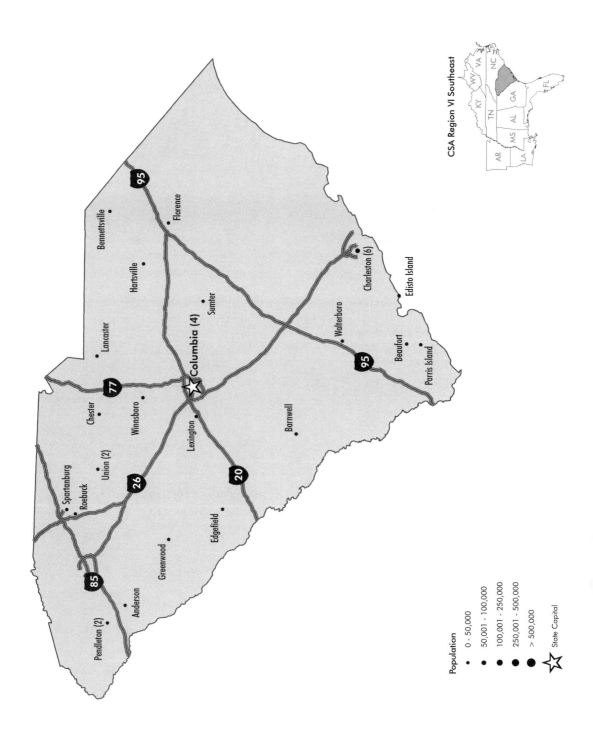

CSA Region VI Southeast

Population

- 0 - 50,000
• 50,001 - 100,000
● 100,001 - 250,000
⬤ 250,001 - 500,000
⬤ > 500,000
☆ State Capital

Bennettsville
Florence
Hartsville
Charleston (6)
Edisto Island
Sumter
Walterboro
Columbia (4)
Lancaster
Beaufort
Parris Island
Chester
Winnsboro
Barnwell
Lexington
Spartanburg
Union (2)
Roebuck
Edgefield
Greenwood
Anderson
Pendleton (2)

95
95
77
26
20
85

SOUTH CAROLINA

Anderson County Museum
202 East Greenville Street
Anderson, SC 29621
Tel: 864-260-4000
www.andersoncountysc.org/museum.htm

Barnwell County Museum
Hagood and Marlboro Avenue
Barnwell, SC 29812
Tel: 803-259-1916

Beaufort Museum
713 Craven Street
Beaufort, SC 29902
Tel: 843-525-7077

Jennings-Brown House Female Academy
123 South Marlboro Street
Bennettsville, SC 29512
Tel: 843-479-5624

American Military Museum
44 John Street
Charleston, SC 29403
Tel: 843-723-9620

The Charleston Museum
360 Meeting Street
Charleston, SC 29403
Tel: 843-722-2996x251 Fax: 843-722-1784
www.charlestonmuseum.org
Hours: Mon–Sat 9–5 pm, Sun 1–5 pm
Contact: Jan Heister, Curator

Eliza Lucas Pinckney shoes, circa 1770. Courtesy of The Charleston Museum.

Dress, silk taffeta, worn by Frances Ann Hardcastle of Savannah, who married William Henley Smith on April 14, 1861, circa 1861. Courtesy of The Charleston Museum.

Institution type: History museum, historic house
Collection type: Clothing, accessories, uniforms, general textiles, quilts, flags
Description: 1700–present. Men's, women's, and children's clothing and accessories; household textiles; samplers and embroideries; and uni-

forms and flags primarily relating to South Carolina Low Country.

$

The Citadel Archives and Museum

171 Moultrie Street
Charleston, SC 29409
Tel: 843-953-6846
www.citadel.edu/archivesandmuseum

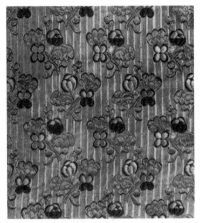

Fabric detail, Henry Middleton's gold brocade, circa 1765–1770. Courtesy of Middleton Place.

Middleton Place

4300 Ashley River Road
Charleston, SC 29407
Tel: 800-782-3608 Fax: 843-766-4460
www.middletonplace.org
Hours: Sun–Sat 9–5 pm
Contact: Mary Edna Sullivan
Institution type: History museum, historic house
Collection type: Clothing
Description: 1700–present. Middleton Place holds a superb collection of eighteenth-century men's clothing and extensive family archives from the eighteenth century to the twenty-first century.

$

National Society of the Colonial Dames of America in South Carolina

89 Cumberland Street
Charleston, SC 29401
Tel: 843-722-3767 Fax: 843-722-9350
Hours: Vary
Contact: Mrs. Louis T. Parker Jr.
Institution type: History museum

Collection type: Clothing, accessories, costumes, general textiles
Description: 1700–1960. Objects in collection include clothing, firearms, glasses, china, furniture, fine art, silver, tea set, and samplers.

Old Exchange and Provost Dungeon

122 East Bay Street
Charleston, SC 29401
Tel: 843-727-2165
www.oldexchange.com

Chester County Historical Society Museum

107 McAliley Street
Chester, SC 29706
Tel: 803-385-2330

Columbia Fire Department Museum

1800 Laurel Street
Columbia, SC 29201
Tel: 803-733-8350

Columbia Museum of Art

Corner of Main and Hampton Streets
Columbia, SC 29202
Tel: 803-799-2810
www.columbiamuseum.org

South Carolina Confederate Relic Room and Museum

301 Gervais Street
Columbia, SC 29201
Tel: 803-737-8094 Fax: 803-799-8099
www.crr.sc.gov
Hours: Tue–Fri 10–5 pm
Contact: Sarah Wooton, Registrar
Institution type: State museum
Collection type: Clothing, accessories, uniforms, flags
Description: 1750–present. Textile collection primarily focuses on South Carolina's military history from the American Revolution through the present. Earliest textile is the vest of John Huger, first secretary of state of South Carolina, circa 1776. Numerous Civil War uniforms and flags as well as homespun textiles and knitted goods.

$

South Carolina State Museum

301 Gervais Street
Columbia, SC 29202
Tel: 803-898-4921 Fax: 803-898-4988
www.museum.state.sc.us
Hours: Mon–Sat 10–5 pm, Sun 1–5 pm
Contact: Elaine Nichols, Curator
Institution type: State museum
Collection type: Clothing, accessories
Description: 1700–present. 2,000 items, including bed linens and South Carolina related items. Earliest piece is a 1740 silk outer petticoat. Strengths of collection are the inaugural clothes of South Carolina governors, First Ladies, and family members.

$ ✑

Oakley Park, UDC Shrine

300 Columbia Road
Edgefield, SC 29824
Tel: 803-637-4027

Edisto Island Historic Preservation Society Museum

8123 Chisolm Plantation Road
Edisto Island, SC 29438
Tel: 843-869-1954

Florence Museum of Art, Science, and History

558 Spruce Street
Florence, SC 29501
Tel: 843-662-3351

The Museum

106 Main Street
Greenwood, SC 29648
Tel: 864-229-7093

Hartsville Museum

222 North 5th Street
Hartsville, SC 29550
Tel: 843-383-3005
www.hartsvillemuseum.org

Andrew Jackson State Park

196 Andrew Jackson Park Road
Lancaster, SC 29720
Tel: 803-285-3344 Fax: 803-285-3344
www.southcarolinaparks.com/stateparks/parkdetail.asp?PID=1797

Hours: Mon–Sun 8–6 pm EST, Mon–Sun 9–9 pm EDT
Contact: Laura Ledford
Institution type: History museum, state museum
Collection type: Clothing, accessories, costumes, general textiles, flags
Description: 1750–1849. Items related to the Carolina Backcountry, including a late 1700s loom that still functions.

$ ✑

Lexington County Museum

231 Fox Street
Lexington, SC 29072
Tel: 803-359-8369

M1912 marine uniform hat, 1918. Courtesy of Parris Island Museum and Historical Society.

Parris Island Museum and Historical Society

Building 111, MCRD
Parris Island, SC 29905
Tel: 843-228-2951 Fax: 843-228-3065
www.pimuseum.us
Hours: Mon–Sun 10–4:30 pm
Contact: Bryan P. Howard
Institution type: History museum, federal museum
Collection type: Accessories, uniforms
Description: 1850–present. Variety of United States Marine Corps uniforms and accessories.

✑

Pendleton District Historical, Recreational, and Tourism Commission

125 East Queen Street
Pendleton, SC 29670
Tel: 864-646-3782

Woodburn Plantation

130 History Lane
Pendleton, SC 29670
Tel: 864-646-7249

Walnut Grove Plantation

1200 Otts Shoals Road
Roebuck, SC 29376
Tel: 864-576-6546
www.sparklenet.com/historicalassociation

The Regional Museum of History of Spartanburg County

100 East Main Street
Spartanburg, SC 29306
Tel: 864-596-3501
www.spartanarts.org/history/
    Historical_Association/Index.htm

Detail, U.S. Air Force uniform, 1954. Courtesy of Sumter County Museum.

Sumter County Museum

122 North Washington Street
Sumter, SC 29150
Tel: 803-775-0908 Fax: 803-436-5820
www.sumtercountymuseum.org
Hours: Tue–Sat 10–5 pm, Sun 2–5 pm
Contact: Rickie Good
Institution type: History museum, historic house
Collection type: Clothing, accessories, uniforms
Description: 1760–present. More than 1,500 items pertinent to the history of Sumter County.

Rose Hill Plantation State Historic Site

2677 Sardis Road
Union, SC 29379
Tel: 864-427-5966
www.southcarolinaparks.com/stateparks
    /parkdetail.asp?PID=540

Union County Historical Foundation Museum

127 West Main Street
Union, SC 29379
Tel: 864-429-5081
Hours: Tue, Thu, Fri 10–3 pm, Sat–Sun 2–5 pm
Contact: Oea Jean Kelly
Institution type: County museum
Collection type: Clothing, accessories, uniforms, costumes, general textiles, quilts, flags
Description: 1800–present. Children's and adults' clothing, 1860–1940; hats, purses, and shoes, 1875–1940; doll clothes, 1850–1920; costumes, including kilt, Austrian lederhosen, Japanese kimono and obi, and Moroccan coat and fez; fraternal organization regalia, 1910–1950; quilts, bedspreads, coverlets, and table linens, 1850–1938; flags, including 1861 Pea Ridge battle flag, 1861–1865 Johnson Rifles battle flag; and uniforms from the Civil War through World War II.

Colleton Museum

239 North Jefferies Boulevard
Walterboro, SC 29488
Tel: 803-549-2303

Fairfield County Museum

231 South Congress Street
Winnsboro, SC 29180
Tel: 803-635-9811 Fax: 803-635-9811
www.fairfieldchamber.org/history.html
Hours: Tue–Sat 10–5 pm
Contact: Janice Miller, Pelham Lyles
Institution type: History museum, historic house, county museum
Collection type: Clothing, accessories, uniforms, general textiles, quilts, flags
Description: 1850–1960. Large number of quilts, military uniforms, Victorian era clothing, and accessories.

Dacotah Prairie Museum

21 South Main Street
Aberdeen, SD 57402-0395
Tel: 605-626-7117 Fax: 605-626-4026
www.dacotahprairiemuseum.com
Hours: Tue–Fri 9–5 pm, Sat–Sun 1–4 pm
Contact: Jackie Ormand
Institution type: History museum, county
    museum
Collection type: Clothing, accessories, uniforms,
    general textiles, flags
Description: 1850–1960. Pre-1950 vintage
    clothing and accessories and vintage hand-
    crafts.

Douglas County Museum Complex

Courthouse Grounds
Armour, SD 57313
Tel: 605-724-2129

South Dakota State University, College of Family and Consumer Sciences

ADALINE SNELLMAN HSIA HISTORIC
AND DECORATIVE ARTS COLLECTIONS
    NFA Building #229
    Brookings, SD 57007
Tel: 605-688-5196 Fax: 605-688-4439
    www3.sdstate.edu/Academics/CollegeOfFamily
        AndConsumerSciences/ApparelMerchandis
        ingandInteriorDesign/Index.cfm
Hours: By appointment
Contact: Jane Hegland
Institution type: University collection

Gown, House of Worth, 1896. Courtesy of South Dakota State University, College of Family and Consumer Sciences.

Collection type: Clothing, accessories, uniforms,
    general textiles, quilts
Description: 1800–present. Primarily used by stu-
    dents and faculty for research, discovery, and
    exhibitions. The 5,000-piece collection spans
    from the mid-1800s to the present and
    includes dress and textiles from around the
    world with an excellent representation of South
    Dakotan material culture.

Beauvais Heritage Center

North Idaho Street
Clark, SD 57225
Tel: 605-532-3722

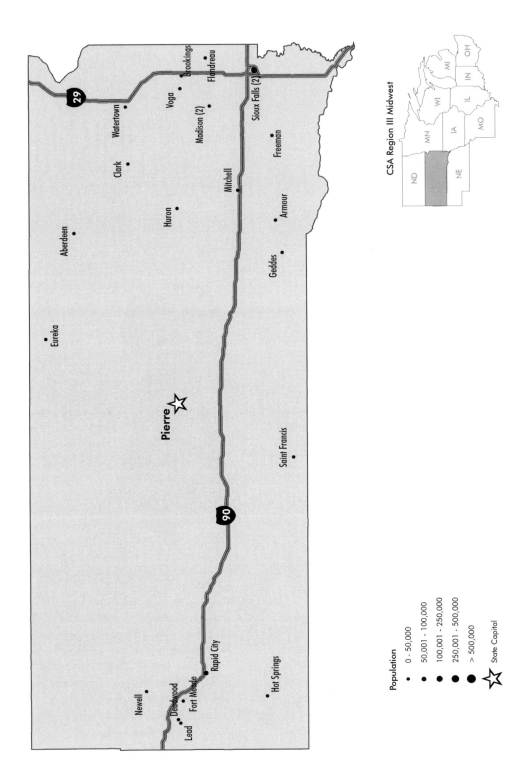

Population

- 0 - 50,000
- 50,001 - 100,000
- 100,001 - 250,000
- 250,001 - 500,000
- > 500,000
☆ State Capital

CSA Region III Midwest

Adams Museum and House
54 Sherman
Deadwood, SD 57732
Tel: 605-578-1094 Fax: 605-578-1194
www.adamsmuseumandhouse.org
Hours: Mon–Sat 9–7 pm, Sun 12–5 pm
(Summer); Mon–Sat 10–4 pm (Winter)
Contact: Arlette Hansen
Institution type: History museum, historic house,
city museum
Collection type: Clothing, accessories, uniforms,
general textiles, flags
Description: 1800–present. Women's, men's, and
children's clothing and accessories; military and
band uniforms and accessories; wedding
gowns; and household linens and handwork.
$ ✏️

Eureka Pioneer Museum of McPherson County
1610 J Avenue
Eureka, SD 57437
Tel: 605-284-2987

Moody County Museum
706 East Pipestone Avenue
Flandreau, SD 57028
Tel: 605-997-3191

Old Fort Meade Museum and Historic Research Association
Building 55
Fort Meade, SD 57741
Tel: 605-347-9822
www.fortmeademuseum.org

Heritage Hall Museum and Archives
748 Main Street
Freeman, SD 57029
Tel: 605-925-4237

Geddes Historic District Village
South End of Main Street
Geddes, SD 57342
Tel: 605-337-2501 Fax: 605-337-3935
www.geddessd.org/papineau
Hours: Mon–Sun 8–7 pm (Summer)
Contact: Ron Dufek
Institution type: History museum, historic house
Collection type: Clothing, accessories, uniforms,
flags

Description: 1800–1914. Rural school items,
1857 log cabin items, 1918 local politician's
home items, and Lewis and Clark items and
keel boat.

Fall River Pioneer Historical Museum
300 North Chicago Street
Hot Springs, SD 57747
Tel: 605-745-5147 (Apr–Oct)

Dakotaland Museum
South Dakota State Fair Grounds and 3rd
Street
Huron, SD 57350
Tel: 605-352-2633
Hours: Mon–Sun 9:30–11:30 am, 1–4 pm,
6:30–8:30 pm (Memorial Day–Labor Day)
Contact: Ruby Johannsen
Institution type: History museum, county
museum, city museum
Collection type: Clothing, accessories, uniforms,
general textiles, flags
Description: 1800–present. Men's and women's
clothing from local area of South Dakota, pri-
marily early twentieth century. Wedding
dresses, baptismal dresses, accessories, shoes,
jewelry, and household linens, including tablecloths, doilies, and dresser scarves.
$ ✏️

Black Hills Mining Museum
323 West Main
Lead, SD 57754
Tel: 605-584-1605
www.mining-museum.blackhills.com

Prairie Village
West Highway 34
Madison, SD 57402
Tel: 605-256-3644
www.prairievillage.org

Smith-Zimmermann Heritage Museum
221 NE 8th Street
Madison, SD 57042
Tel: 605-256-5308
www.smith-zimmermann.dsu.edu

French fashion bride. Courtesy of Enchanted World Doll Museum.

Enchanted World Doll Museum

615 North Main
Mitchell, SD 57301
Tel: 605-996-9896 Fax: 605-996-0210
Hours: Mon–Sun 10–4 pm (Mar–Dec)
Contact: Valerie LaBreche
Institution type: History museum
Collection type: Clothing, accessories
Description: Pre-1700–present. More than 4,800 antique and collectible dolls in period costumes, starting with a doll from 1400 to the present day, set in scenes with appropriate accessories and toys.

$ ✍

Newell Museum

108 3rd Street
Newell, SD 57760
Tel: 605-456-1310

Museum of the South Dakota State Historical Society

900 Governors Drive
Pierre, SD 57501
Tel: 605-773-3458 Fax: 605-773-6041
www.sdhistory.org
Hours: Mon–Fri 9–4:30 pm, Sat–Sun 1–4:30 pm
Contact: Heather Bigeck, Curator of Collections
Institution type: History museum, state museum
Collection type: Clothing, accessories, uniforms, costumes, general textiles, quilts, flags
Description: 1700–present. Native American arti-facts, early pioneer and homesteading materials, and items relating to immigration to South Dakota. Clothing ranges from farm wear to military uniforms to Powwow regalia.

$ ✍

Minnilusa Pioneer Museum

222 New York Street
Rapid City, SD 57701
Tel: 605-394-6099 Fax: 605-394-6940
www.journeymuseum.org
Hours: Mon–Sun 9–5 pm
Contact: Reid L. Riner
Institution type: History museum
Collection type: Clothing, uniforms, general textiles, quilts
Description: 1850–1960. Pioneer clothing from the 1880s, quilts, military uniforms, and Sioux clothing and accessories.

$ ✍

The Center for Western Studies

Augustana College, 2201 South Summit
Sioux Falls, SD 57197
Tel: 605-367-7141

Sioux Empire Medical Museum

1305 West 18th Street
Sioux Falls, SD 57117
Tel: 605-333-6397 Fax: 605-333-1962
Hours: Mon–Fri 11–4 pm
Contact: Thenetta Nerlo or Carol Ann Turgeon, Co-Chairs
Institution type: History museum
Collection type: Clothing, accessories, uniforms
Description: 1850–present. Medical objects, including uniforms and instruments. Museum rooms include nurses' station, patient's care room, and nursery.

✍

Buechel Memorial Lakota Museum

St. Francis Indian Mission
350 South Oak Street
St. Francis, SD 57572
Tel: 605-747-2745
www.sfmission.org/museum

Brookings County Historical Society Museum
215 Samara Avenue
Volga, SD 57071
Tel: 605-627-9149

Mellette House
421 5th Avenue NW
Watertown, SD 57201
Tel: 605-822-4724

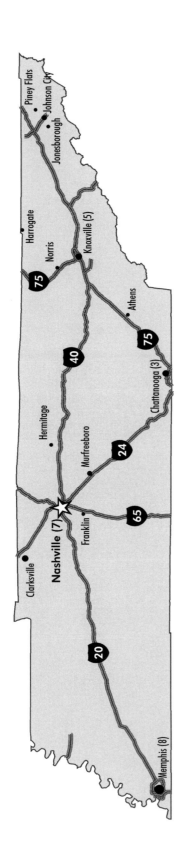

CSA Region VI Southeast

Population

- 0 - 50,000
- 50,001 - 100,000
- 100,001 - 250,000
- 250,001 - 500,000
- > 500,000
☆ State Capital

TENNESSEE

McMinn County Living Heritage Museum

522 West Madison Avenue
Athens, TN 37303
Tel: 423-745-0329
www.usit.com/livher

Chattanooga African Museum and Bessie Smith Hall

200 East Martin Luther King Boulevard
Chattanooga, TN 37403
Tel: 423-266-8658
www.caamhistory.com

Chattanooga Regional History Museum

400 Chestnut Street
Chattanooga, TN 37402
Tel: 423-265-3247
www.chattanoogahistory.com

Medal of Honor Museum of Military History

400 Georgia Avenue
Chattanooga, TN 37401
Tel: 423-267-1737

Customs House Museum and Cultural Center

200 South Second Street
Clarksville, TN 37040
Tel: 931-648-5780 Fax: 931-553-5179
www.customshousemuseum.org
Hours: Tue–Sat 10–5 pm, Sun 1–5 pm
Contact: Amy Andersen

Wedding dress, circa 1873. Courtesy of Customs House Museum and Cultural Center.

Institution type: Art museum, history museum, county museum
Collection type: Clothing, accessories, uniforms, costumes, general textiles, flags
Description: 1800–present. Textiles and clothing primarily from Montgomery County, Tennessee, and secondarily from other parts of the state and southern Kentucky. 1,673 artifacts in clothing and accessories category and 325 artifacts in textile categories with bedding, flags, banners, and remnants.
$ ✍

The Carter House Association

1140 Columbia Avenue
Franklin, TN 37065
Tel: 615-791-1861
www.carter-house.org

Abraham Lincoln Library and Museum

US Highway 25E

Harrogate, TN 37752

Tel: 423-869-6422 Fax: 423-869-6350

www.lmunet.edu/museum

Hours: Mon–Fri 9–4 pm, Sat 11–4 pm, Sun 1–4 pm

Contact: Steven M. Wilson

Institution type: History museum, university collection

Collection type: Clothing, accessories, general textiles

Description: 1850–1899. Clothing and textile objects from Civil War era.

$ ✍

The Hermitage—Home of President Andrew Jackson

4580 Rachel's Lane

Hermitage, TN 37206

Tel: 615-889-2941 Fax: 615-889-9909

www.thehermitage.com

Hours: Mon–Sun 9–5 pm

Contact: Chief Curator

Institution type: History museum, historic house

Collection type: Clothing, accessories, quilts

Description: 1850–1899. Clothing items owned by President Andrew Jackson. Highlights include coverlets, quilts, and bedding, including samples of original Jackson bedding.

$ ✍

Carroll Reece Museum

East Tennessee State University

Gilbreath Drive

Johnson City, TN 37614

Tel: 423-439-4392

www.etsu.edu/reece

Jonesborough-Washington County History Museum

117 Boone Street

Jonesborough, TN 37659

Tel: 423-753-1015

Blount Mansion

200 West Hill Avenue

Knoxville, TN 37902

Tel: 865-525-2375

www.blountmansion.org

Confederate Memorial Hall—Bleak House

3148 Kingston Pike SW

Knoxville, TN 37919

Tel: 865-522-2371

Costume, nineteenth century. Courtesy of the Frank H. McClung Museum, University of Tennessee.

Frank H. McClung Museum

University of Tennessee

1327 Circle Park Drive

Knoxville, TN 37996

Tel: 865-974-2144 Fax: 865-974-3827

http://mcclungmuseum.utk.edu

Hours: Mon–Sat 9–5 pm, Sun 1–5 pm

Contact: Elaine A. Evans, Curator; Robert Pennington, Registrar

Institution type: State museum, university museum

Collection type: Clothing, accessories, uniforms, costumes, general textiles, flags

Description: 1800–1960. Strength is in American costumes and uniforms. Objects in other general categories such as rugs and tapestries; baby, men's, and women's clothes; and an assortment of laces and ribbons.

✍

Mabry-Hazen House

1711 Dandridge Avenue

Knoxville, TN 37915

Tel: 865-522-8661

Ramsey House Museum Plantation

2614 Thorngrove Pike

Knoxville, TN 37914

Tel: 865-546-0745

www.ramseyhouse.org

Art Museum of the University of Memphis
3750 Norriswood Avenue, CFA Building
Memphis, TN 38152
Tel: 901-678-2224
www.amum.org

Fire Museum of Memphis
118 Adams Avenue
Memphis, TN 38103
Tel: 901-320-5650
www.firemuseum.com

Graceland
3764 Elvis Presley Boulevard
Memphis, TN 38116
Tel: 901-332-3322
www.elvis.com

Magevney House
198 Adams
Memphis, TN 38103
Tel: 901-526-4464

Mississippi River Museum
125 North Front Street
Memphis, TN 38103
Tel: 901-576-7230
www.mudisland.com

National Civil Rights Museum
450 Mulberry Street
Memphis, TN 38103
Tel: 901-521-9699
www.civilrightsmuseum.org

Stax Museum of American Soul Music
926 East McLemore Avenue
Memphis, TN 38106
Tel: 901-942-7685 Fax: 901-507-1463
www.soulsvilleusa.com
Hours: Mon–Sat 10–4 pm, Sun 1–4 pm
Contact: Curator of Collections
Institution type: History museum
Collection type: Clothing, accessories, costumes
Description: 1915–present
$ ✍

Woodruff-Fontaine House Museum
680 Adams Avenue
Memphis, TN 38105
Tel: 901-526-1469
www.woodruff-fontaine.com

Hours: Thu–Sat 10–4 pm, Sun 1–4 pm
Contact: Karen Ralston
Institution type: Historic house
Collection type: Clothing, costumes, general textiles, quilts
Description: 1850–1960. Victorian and Edwardian clothing through 1929. Clothing, underwear, and accessories are displayed on mannequins throughout the house. Displays are changed two to three times per year. Also featured are bed linens from the time period.
$ ✍

Oaklands Historic House Museum
900 North Maney Avenue
Murfreesboro, TN 37130
Tel: 615-893-0022 Fax: 615-893-0513
www.oaklandsmuseum.org
Hours: Tue–Sat 10–4 pm, Sun 1–4 pm
Contact: William C. Ledbetter Jr., President
Institution type: Historic house
Collection type: Clothing, accessories, general textiles
Description: 1800–1899.
$ ✍

Association for the Preservation of Tennessee Antiquities
110 Leake Avenue
Nashville, TN 37205
Tel: 615-352-8247

Belle Meade Plantation
5025 Harding Road
Nashville, TN 37205
Tel: 615-356-0501 Fax: 615-356-2336
www.bellemeadeplantation.com
Hours: Mon–Sat 9–5 pm, Sun 11–5 pm
Contact: Stina Fitch, Assistant Curator of Textiles
Institution type: Historic house
Collection type: Clothing, accessories
Description: 1800–1914. Clothing and accessories ranging from the early 1800s to the turn of the century.

Country Music Hall of Fame and Museum
222 5th Avenue
Nashville, TN 37203
Tel: 615-416-2026 Fax: 615-255-2245
www.countrymusichalloffame.com
Hours: Mon–Sun 9–5 pm
Contact: Lauren Bufferd, Vice President, Museum Services

Institution type: History museum

Collection type: Clothing, accessories, costumes, quilts

Description: 1900–present. Costumes and clothing worn by country music artists and musicians, including stage suits by Rodeo Ben, Nathan Turk, Nudie and Rodeo Tailor, Manuel, and a host of other designers. Other items include cowboy boots, hats, and other clothing accessories and quilts and other textiles. Most items are twentieth century and American-made.

$ ✍

Cultural Museum at Scarritt-Bennett Center

1104 19th Avenue South
Nashville, TN 37212
Tel: 615-340-7481
www.scarrittbennett.org/museum/default.aspx

David Lipscomb University

3901 Granny White Pike
Nashville, TN 37204
Tel: 615-269-1000
www.lipscomb.edu

Tennessee State Museum

505 Deaderick Street
Nashville, TN 37243
Tel: 615-741-2692 Fax: 615-741-7231
www.tnmuseum.org

Hours: Tue–Sat 10–5 pm, Sun 1–5 pm

Institution type: Art museum, history museum, state museum

✍

CULTURAL HISTORY COLLECTION

Contact: Mike Bell, Curator

Collection type: Clothing, accessories, uniforms, costumes, general textiles, flags

Description: 1760–present. Items made in Tennessee, used by Tennesseans, or related to Tennesseans. Strengths are in clothing and performance and movie costumes of Tennessee musicians, including the Cash family and Dolly Parton.

FASHION AND TEXTILES COLLECTION

Contact: Candace J. Adelson, Senior Curator

Collection type: Clothing, accessories, uniforms, costumes, general textiles, quilts, flags

Description: 1760–present. Items made in Tennessee, used by Tennesseans, or related to Tennesseans. Strengths are in flags, quilts, coverlets, and clothing.

MILITARY HISTORY COLLECTION

Contact: William C. Baker, Senior Curator; Ron Westphal, Registrar

Collection type: Clothing, accessories, uniforms, general textiles

Description: 1760–present. Items made in Tennessee, used by Tennesseans, or related to Tennesseans. Strengths are in Battle of King's Mountain (Revolutionary War), War of 1812, Mexican War, Civil War, Spanish American War, World War I, and World War II.

NATIVE AMERICAN COLLECTION

Contact: Stephen Cox, Senior Curator and Fabrications Manager

Collection type: Clothing, accessories, costumes, general textiles

Description: 1800–present. Items made in Tennessee, used by Tennesseans, or related to Tennesseans. Strengths are in clothing and accessories, including one Trail of Tears period jacket and a group of recent Choctaw costumes, clothing, and accessories.

Quilt, Rose of Sharon, hand-sewn by slaves on Vine Bower Plantation, circa 1860. Courtesy of Travellers Rest Plantation and Museum.

Travellers Rest Plantation and Museum

636 Farrell Parkway
Nashville, TN 37143
Tel: 615-832-8197 Fax: 615-832-8169
www.travellersrestplantation.org

Hours: Tue–Sat 10–4 pm, Sun 1–4 pm

Contact: Rob DeHart

Institution type: History museum, historic house

Collection type: Clothing, accessories, general textiles, quilts, flags

Description: 1800–1960. Textile collection primarily consists of items that represent Tennessee history and culture in the 1800–1830 time period. Collection is particularly strong in nineteenth-century Tennessee quilts.

$ ✍

Museum of Appalachia

Highway 61
Norris, TN 37828
Tel: 865-494-7680
www.museumofappalachia.com

Rocky Mount Museum

Rocky Mount Parkway
Piney Flats, TN 37686
Tel: 423-538-7396
www.rockymountmuseum.com

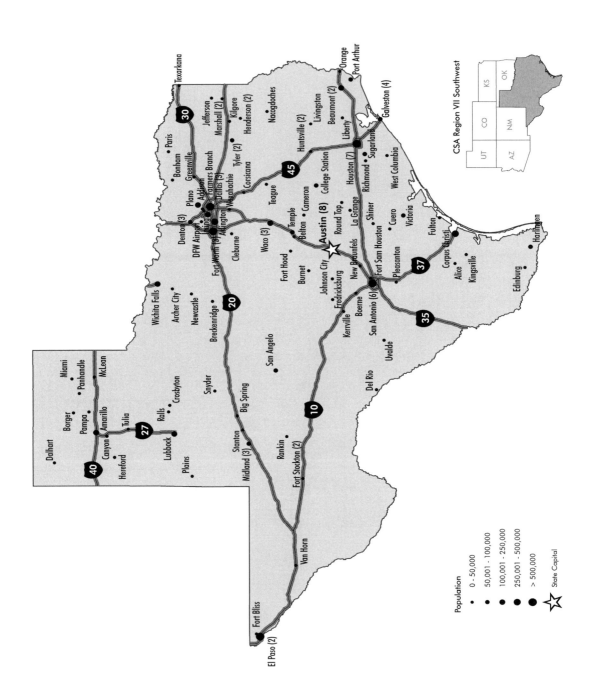

CSA Region VII Southwest

UT CO KS
AZ NM OK

Texarkana

30

Jefferson
Marshall (2)
Kilgore
Henderson (2)
Nacogdoches
Paris
Bonham
Greenville
Farmers Branch
Plano
Addison
Dallas (3)
Tyler (2)
Corsicana
Waxahachie
Teague
45
Huntsville (2)
Livingston
Beaumont (2)
Liberty
Orange
Port Arthur
Galveston (4)
College Station
Houston (7)
Richmond
Sugarland
West Columbia
Denton (3)
Irving
DFW Airport
Fort Worth (6)
Arlington
Cleburne
Waco (3)
Temple
Belton
Cameron
Round Top
La Grange
Shiner
Cuero
Victoria
Fulton
Fort Hood
Burnet
Austin (8)
New Braunfels
Fort Sam Houston
Pleasanton
Corpus Christi
37
Harlingen
Wichita Falls
Archer City
Newcastle
Breckenridge
San Angelo
Johnson City
Fredricksburg
Boerne
Kerrville
San Antonio (6)
Uvalde
Alice
Kingsville
Edinburg
35
20
Del Rio
Miami
McLean
Panhandle
Borger
Pampa
Amarillo
Crosbyton
Ralls
Snyder
Big Spring
Canyon
Hereford
Lubbock
Plains
Stanton
Rankin
Midland (3)
Fort Stockton (2)
10
Van Horn
Dalhart
Tulia
27
40
Fort Bliss
El Paso (2)

Population

• 0 - 50,000
• 50,001 - 100,000
● 100,001 - 250,000
● 250,001 - 500,000
● > 500,000
☆ State Capital

TEXAS

Directors' suits, 1990s. Courtesy of Mary Kay Museum.

Mary Kay Museum

MARY KAY COSMETICS AND MARY KAY
ASH COLLECTION
16251 North Dallas Parkway
Addison, TX 75001
Tel: 972-687-5889
www.marykay.com
Hours: Mon–Fri 8:30–5 pm
Contact: Jennifer Cook
Institution type: History museum
Collection type: Clothing
Description: 1961–present. Evening gowns and
business suits of Mary Kay Ash and career
apparel for independent sales force.

South Texas Museum

66 South Wright Street
Alice, TX 78333
Tel: 512-668-8891

Amarillo Museum of Art

2200 South Van Buren
Amarillo, TX 79109
Tel: 806-371-5050
www.amarilloart.org

Archer County Museum

Old County Jail
Archer City, TX 76351
Tel: 979-864-1208

Legends of the Game Baseball Museum and Learning Center

1000 Ballpark Way, Suite 400
Arlington, TX 76001
Tel: 817-273-5059
www.texasrangers.com

Lyndon B. Johnson Library and Museum

2313 Red River Street
Austin, TX 78705-5702
Tel: 512-916-5170
www.lbjlib.utexas.edu

Mexic-Arte Museum

419 Congress
Austin, TX 78701
Tel: 512-480-9373
www.main.org/mexic-arte
www.mexic-artemuseum.org

Neill-Cochran Museum House

2310 San Gabriel Street
Austin, TX 78705

Tel: 512-478-2335
www.neill-cochranmuseum.org

Pioneer Farms

11418 Sprinkle Cut Off Road
Austin, TX 78754
Tel: 512-837-1215 Fax: 512-837-4503
www.heritagesocietyaustin.org/
pioneerfarms.html
Hours: Wed 9:30–1 pm, Sun 1–5 pm
Contact: Norman Van Brockhoeven
Institution type: History museum
Collection type: Clothing, accessories, costumes,
general textiles
Description: 1850–1899. Objects pertaining to
agrarian life in the Glochlands Prairie of central
Texas during the period 1850–1890.

$

Texas Memorial Museum of Science and History

2400 Trinity
Austin, TX 78705
Tel: 512-232-5504
www.utexas.edu/tmm

Texas Military Forces Museum

2200 West 35th Street
Austin, TX 78763
Tel: 512-782-5659
http://kwanah.com/txmilmus

University of Texas at Austin

HISTORIC CLOTHING COLLECTION
Department of Theatre and Dance
Austin, TX 78713
Tel: 512-471-0641
Hours: By appointment only
Contact: Joseph E. Adams
Institution type: University collection
Collection type: Clothing, accessories, uniforms,
costumes
Description: 1760–present. More than 900 items
ranging from 1770 to the present with the
greatest representation in the early 1900s, rep-
resenting all social strata. Children's clothing,
hats, purses, shoes, fans, undergarments, and
hoops. Small portion of ethnic garments are
also included.

University of Texas Center for American History

TEXAS CLOTHING COLLECTION
SRH 2.101, 1 University Station D1100
Austin, TX 78712
Tel: 512-495-4515 Fax: 512-495-4542
www.cah.utexas.edu
Hours: Mon–Sat 9–5 pm
Contact: Curator
Institution type: History museum, historic house,
university collection
Collection type: Clothing, accessories, costumes,
general textiles, flags
Description: 1800–present. Clothing and acces-
sories of Texas men, women, and children from
the 1820s to the 1990s. Items are primarily
late-nineteenth-century to early-twentieth-
century women's clothing and accessories.
Notable collections of women's hats and of
men's canes.

Fire Museum of Texas

400 Walnut at Mulberry
Beaumont, TX 77704
Tel: 409-880-3927
www.firemuseumoftexas.org

Spindletop—Gladys City Boomtown Museum

Highway 69 at University Drive
Beaumont, TX 77710
Tel: 409-835-0823
www.spindletop.org

Bell County Museum

201 North Main Street
Belton, TX 76513
Tel: 254-933-5243
www.bellcountytx.com/Museum

Heritage Museum and Potton House

510 Scurry
Big Spring, TX 79720
Tel: 915-267-8255

Kuhlmann King Historical House and Museum

402 East Blanco
Boerne, TX 78006
Tel: 830-249-2030
www.rootsweb.com/~txkendal/bahps.htm

Sam Rayburn House Museum

890 West Highway 56
Bonham, TX 75418
Tel: 903-583-5558
www.thc.state.tx.us/samrayhouse/
    srhdefault.html
Hours: Tue–Fri 8–4:30 pm, Sat 9–4:30 pm
Contact: Anne Carlson
Institution type: Historic house, state museum
Collection type: Clothing, accessories, general textiles
Description: 1900–present

Hutchinson County Museum

618 North Main
Borger, TX 79007
Tel: 806-273-0130

Swenson Memorial Museum of Stephens County

116 West Walker
Breckenridge, TX 76424
Tel: 254-559-8471

Fort Croghan Museum

703 Buchanan Drive
Burnet, TX 78611
Tel: 512-756-8281
www.fortcroghan.org

Milam County Historical Museum

201 East Main Street
Cameron, TX 76520
Tel: 254-697-4770
www.geocities.com/milamco/milam-006.htm

Panhandle-Plains Historical Museum

2503 Fourth Avenue
Canyon, TX 79015
Tel: 806-651-2244 Fax: 806-651-2250
www.panhandleplains.org
Hours: Mon–Sat 9–5 pm, Sun 1–6 pm
Contact: Susan G. Denney
Institution type: State museum
Collection type: Clothing, accessories, uniforms, costumes, general textiles, quilts, flags
Description: 1850–present. Museum collects, researches, and exhibits materials that represent the historical, artistic, and scientific heritage of the Texas Panhandle and related areas of the American Southwest. Clothing and Textile

Quilt, reverse appliquéd, 1809. Courtesy of Panhandle-Plains Historical Museum.

Collection ranges in date from circa 1850 to the 1980s. Quilt collection includes over 175 items. Earliest quilt dates from 1809 and was made from cotton grown, spun, woven, and appliquéd into the quilt.

$ 🖋

Layland Museum

201 North Caddo
Cleburne, TX 76031
Tel: 817-645-0940 Fax: 817-641-4161
Hours: Mon–Fri 9–5 pm, 2nd and 4th Sat 10–4 pm
Contact: Julie P. Baker
Institution type: History museum, historic house, city museum
Collection type: Clothing, accessories, uniforms, general textiles, quilts, flags
Description: 1800–1960. Uniforms from Civil War to Vietnam War. Women's and children's clothing predominate. Women's shoes, twentieth-century quilts, and a nineteenth-century textile swatch collection.

🖋

George Bush Presidential Library and Museum

1000 George Bush Drive West
College Station, TX 77845
Tel: 979-260-9552
http://bushlibrary.tamu.edu

Asian Cultures Museum and Educational Center

1809 North Chaparral Street
Corpus Christi, TX 78401

Tel: 361-882-2641
www.geocities.com/asiancm

Navarro County Historical Society, Pioneer Village

912 West Park Avenue
Corsicana, TX 75110
Tel: 903-654-4846

Crosby County Pioneer Memorial Museum

101 West Main Street
Crosbyton, TX 79322
Tel: 806-675-2331
www.crosbycountymuseum.com

DeWitt County Historical Museum

312 East Broadway
Cuero, TX 77954-2806
Tel: 361-275-6322
www.cuero.org/thingstodo.shtml

Dallam-Hartley Museum

108 East 5th Street
Dalhart, TX 79022
Tel: 806-244-4838

Dallas Heritage Village at Old City Park

1717 Gano Street
Dallas, TX 75215
Tel: 214-421-5141 Fax: 214-428-6351
www.oldcitypark.org
Hours: Tue–Sat 10–4 pm, Sun 12–4 pm
Contact: Hal Simon, Chief Curator
Institution type: History museum, historic house

Fan front day dress, 1855. Courtesy of Dallas Heritage Village at Old City Park.

Collection type: Clothing, accessories, uniforms, general textiles, quilts
Description: 1800–1915. 25,000 artifacts dating between 1840 and 1910 in thirty-eight relocated and restored structures in a village setting. Holdings include 2,000 textile items, cultural and domestic artifacts, documentary artifacts, and quilts and coverlets.

$ ✍

Vest of Antonio Lopez de Santa Anna, president/dictator of Mexico, circa 1830–40. Courtesy of Dallas Historical Society.

Dallas Historical Society

3939 Grand Avenue, Hall of State
Dallas, TX 75210
Tel: 214-421-4500 Fax: 214-421-7500
www.dallashistory.org
Hours: Tue–Sat 9–5 pm, Sun 1–5 pm
Contact: Alan Olson, Melanie Sanford
Institution type: History museum
Collection type: Clothing, accessories, uniforms, costumes, general textiles, quilts, flags
Description: 1800–present
✍

Dallas Museum of Art

1717 North Harwood Street
Dallas, TX 75201
Tel: 214-922-1200
www.dallasmuseumofart.org

Whitehead Memorial Museum

1308 South Main Street
Del Rio, TX 78840
Tel: 830-774-7568
www.whitehead-museum.com

Denton County Historical Museum and Texas Heritage Center

5800 North I-35
Denton, TX 76201
Tel: 940-380-0877

Victorian-inspired wedding dress by Victor Costa, 1993. Courtesy of Texas Fashion Collection.

Texas Fashion Collection

University of North Texas Fine Arts
  Department
Denton, TX 76203
Tel: 940-565-2732 Fax: 940-565-4717
www.art.unt.edu/tfc
Hours: Mon–Fri 9–5 pm, and by appointment
Contact: Myra Walker
Institution type: University collection
Collection type: Clothing, accessories, general textiles
Description: 1800–present. Nineteenth- and twentieth-century couture, high fashion, and principal ready-to-wear designs by American and international designers who have designed under their own name or in conjunction with the fashion industry. Significant holdings of Balenciaga, Givenchy, Norman Norell, and Oscar de la Renta along with numerous other twentieth-century designers.

Texas First Ladies Historic Costume Collection, Texas Woman's University

Administration Conference Tower
Second Floor
Denton, TX 76204
Tel: 940-898-3644 Fax: 940-898-3556
www.twu.edu/firstladies/intro–about.htm

Inaugural gown worn by Texas First Lady Laura Bush, 1995. Courtesy of Texas First Ladies Historic Costume Collection, Texas Woman's University.

Hours: Mon–Fri 8–5 pm, or by appointment
Contact: Anyah Martinez
Institution type: University collection
Collection type: Clothing, accessories, costumes
Description: 1800–present. Established in 1940 by the Texas Society of the Daughters of the American Revolution (DAR) and presented to Texas Woman's University (TWU). Texas Woman's University, with ongoing assistance from the DAR and with the generous gifts of the governors' wives, has maintained and added to this collection. Latest acquisition was the inaugural gown worn by Governor Perry's wife, Anita.

American Airlines C. R. Smith Museum

4601 Highway 360 at FAA Road
DFW Airport, TX 75261
Tel: 817-967-5905
www.crsmithmuseum.org

Museum of South Texas History

121 East McIntyre
Edinburg, TX 78541
Tel: 956-383-6911 Fax: 956-381-8518
www.mosthistory.org/index.html
Hours: Tue–Sat 10–5 pm, Sun 1–5 pm
Contact: Tom Fort
Institution type: History museum
Collection type: Clothing, accessories, uniforms
Description: 1900–1960. General local history collection contains primarily late-nineteenth-

and early-twentieth-century items, including women's clothing and military uniforms.

$ 🖐

El Paso Museum of History
12901 Gateway West
El Paso, TX 79928
Tel: 915-858-1928
www.elpasotexas.gov/history

Magoffin Home State Historic Site
1120 Magoffin Avenue
El Paso, TX 79901
Tel: 915-533-5147
www.tpwd.state.tx.us/spdest/findadest/
     parks/magoffin_home

Farmers Branch Historical Park
2540 Farmers Branch Lane
Farmers Branch, TX 75381-9010
Tel: 972-406-0184
www.ci.farmers-branch.tx.us/ParksRec/
     HistoricalPark.html

Fort Bliss Museum
Building 5000, Pleasonton Road
Fort Bliss, TX 79916
Tel: 915-568-6940

1st Cavalry Division Museum
56th and 761st Tank Battalion Avenue,
     Building 2218
Fort Hood, TX 76545
Tel: 254-287-3626 Fax: 254-287-6423
www.hood.army.mil/1CD_Museum
Hours: Mon–Fri 9–4 pm, Sat–Sun 12–4 pm
Contact: Steven Draper
Institution type: Federal museum
Collection type: Clothing, accessories, uniforms, general textiles, flags
Description: 1850–present

🖐

Fort Sam Houston Museum
1210 Stanley Road
Fort Sam Houston, TX 78234-5002
Tel: 210-221-1886
http://ameddregiment.amedd.army.mil/
     fshmuse/fshmuse.htm

Annie Riggs Memorial Museum
301 South Main Street
Fort Stockton, TX 79735
Tel: 915-336-2167

Historic Fort Stockton
300 East 3rd
Fort Stockton, TX 79735
Tel: 915-336-2400

Cattle Raisers Museum
1301 West 7th Street
Fort Worth, TX 76102
Tel: 817-332-8551
www.cattleraisersmuseum.org

Log Cabin Village
2100 Log Cabin Village Lane
Fort Worth, TX 76109
Tel: 817-926-5881 Fax: 817-922-0246
www.logcabinvillage.org
Hours: Tue–Fri 9–4 pm, Sat–Sun 1–5 pm
Contact: Ivette Ray
Institution type: History museum, city museum
Collection type: General textiles, quilts
Description: 1800–1899. Collection includes nineteenth-century quilts and coverlets that range from simple, utilitarian quilts to very intricate ones.

$ 🖐

National Cowgirl Museum and Hall of Fame
1720 Gendy Street
Fort Worth, TX 76107
Tel: 817-336-4475 Fax: 817-336-2470
www.cowgirl.net

Cowgirl outfit of Fern Sawyer, circa 1950. Courtesy of National Cowgirl Museum and Hall of Fame.

Hours: Tue–Sat 10–5 pm, Sun 12–5 pm

Contact: Curator of Collections

Institution type: History museum

Collection type: Clothing, accessories, costumes, general textiles

Description: 1900–present. Clothing worn by female performers in rodeos and Wild West shows and clothing worn by working ranch women. Bulk of the collection is from 1940 to 1980 with a strong emphasis on hats and boots. Items include popular culture objects showing the image of the American cowgirl, such as Dale Evans' costumes.

$ ✍

Admiral Nimitz Museum and Historical Center

340 East Main Street

Fredericksburg, TX 78624

Tel: 830-997-4379 Fax: 830-997-8220

www.nimitz-museum.org

Hours: Mon–Sun 10–5 pm

Contact: Jeffrey William Hunt

Institution type: History museum, state museum

Collection type: Clothing, accessories, uniforms, general textiles, flags

Description: 1915–1960. Uniforms and accessories of Allied and Axis armed forces during World War II and pre- and post-war uniforms. Civilian clothing as well as wartime civilian clothing.

✍

Fulton Mansion State Historic Site

316 South Fulton Beach Road

Fulton, TX 78358

Tel: 361-729-0386

www.tpwd.state.tx.us/spdest/findadest/parks/fulton_mansion

Hours: Wed–Sun 9–4 pm (guided tours only)

Contact: Alison Giesen

Institution type: Historic house, state museum

Collection type: Clothing, accessories, costumes, general textiles

Description: 1851–1915. High-style Victorian suburban villa, includes a small selection of costumes, textiles, and accessories in its displays.

$ ✍

Galveston County Historical Museum

2219 Market Street

Galveston, TX 77550

Tel: 409-766-2340

www.galvestonhistory.org

Lone Star Flight Museum and Texas Aviation Hall of Fame

2002 Terminal Drive

Galveston, TX 77552-0099

Tel: 409-740-7722 Fax: 409-740-7612

www.lsfm.org

Hours: Mon–Sun 9–5 pm

Institution type: History museum

$ ✍

The Moody Mansion Museum

2618 Broadway

Galveston, TX 77550

Tel: 409-762-7668

www.moodymansion.org

Hours: Mon–Sat 10–4 pm, Sun 12–4 pm

Contact: Curator of Collections

Institution type: Historic house

Collection type: Clothing, accessories, costumes, general textiles, flags

Description: 1800–present. Collection is strong in twentieth-century dress and appearance with a few items from the mid- to late-nineteenth century. Garments (mostly women's) and day wear, evening wear, sleepwear, underclothes, hats, purses, shoes, gloves, curtains, bed linens, flags, pennants, table linens, and Eastern rugs.

$ ✍

Rosenberg Library

2310 Sealy

Galveston, TX 77550

Tel: 409-763-8854

Hours: Mon–Sat 9–5 pm

Contact: Lise Darst

Institution type: History museum

Collection type: Clothing, accessories, uniforms, costumes, general textiles

Description: 1850–present. Artifacts that document the history of Galveston and early Texas. Military uniforms from World War I and World War II; wedding dresses from 1859 to 1956; Galveston Mardi Gras costumes; and women's clothing and children's christening dresses from 1856 to 1912.

$

American Cotton Museum

600 I-30
Greenville, TX 75403
Tel: 903-450-4502
www.cottonmuseum.com

Rio Grande Valley Museum

Boxwood at Raintree
Harlingen, TX 78550
Tel: 956-430-8500

Depot Museum

514 North High Street
Henderson, TX 75652
Tel: 903-657-4303 Fax: 903-657-2679
www.depotmuseum.com
Hours: Mon–Fri 9–5 pm, Sat 9–1 pm
Contact: Susan Weaver
Institution type: History museum, county museum
Collection type: Clothing, accessories, general textiles, quilts, flags
Description: 1800–1960. Collection of clothing 1870–1940 includes quilts and textile household items. Museum offers workshops in textile production, and flax team demonstrates processing flax into linen for groups and festivals.

$

Howard-Dickinson House Museum

501 South Main Street
Henderson, TX 75653
Tel: 903-657-6925

Deaf Smith County Museum

400 Sampson
Hereford, TX 79045
Tel: 806-363-7070

The Heritage Society

1100 Bagby
Houston, TX 77002
Tel: 713-655-1912
www.heritagesociety.org
Hours: Tue–Sat 10–4 pm, Sun 12–4 pm
Contact: Wallace Sage
Institution type: History museum, historic house

Collection type: Clothing, accessories
Description: 1850–1960.

$

Holocaust Museum Houston

5401 Caroline Street
Houston, TX 77004
Tel: 713-942-8000x100
www.hmh.org

Chanel couture dresses and jackets, 1973. Courtesy of Houston Community College Fashion Collection.

Houston Community College

FASHION COLLECTION
1300 Holman SJAC 325A
Houston, TX 77266-7517
Tel: 713-718-6152 Fax: 713-718-6188
www.hccs.edu
Hours: Vary
Contact: Kay King
Institution type: University collection
Collection type: Clothing, accessories, costumes
Description: 1900–present. Collection focuses on twentieth- and twenty-first-century designer clothing and accessories for women with strengths from 1960 to the 1980s. Significant hats, shoes, and wedding dresses. Holdings include an ethnic clothing collection of traditional costumes from many of the countries represented in the college's student population of ninety different national origins. An exhibition is mounted annually, but the collection is primarily used as a study collection.

Houston Police Museum

17000 Aldine Westfield Road
Houston, TX 77073
Tel: 281-230-2360

The Museum of Fine Arts, Houston

1001 Bissonnet
Houston, TX 77265-6826
Tel: 713-639-7300
www.mfah.org
Hours: Tue–Wed 10–5 pm, Thu 10–9 pm,
Fri–Sat 10–7 pm, Sun 12:15–7 pm
Contact: Curator of Collections
Institution type: Art museum
Collection type: Clothing, accessories, general textiles, costumes
Description: 1900–present. Wide ranging collection of clothing and accessories with major focus on European and American designers of the twentieth century, including Claire McCardell, Zandra Rhodes, Geoffrey Beene, Jeanne Lanvin, Madame Gres, Issey Miyake, and Mary McFadden.
$ ✍

National Museum of Funeral History

415 Barren Springs Drive
Houston, TX 77090
Tel: 281-876-2063
www.nmfh.org

Space Center Houston

1601 NASA Road 1
Houston, TX 77058
Tel: 281-244-2105
www.spacecenter.org

Sam Houston Memorial Museum

1402 19th Street
Huntsville, TX 77341
Tel: 936-294-1832
www.samhouston.org

Sam Houston State University

20TH CENTURY COSTUME
COLLECTION
Department of Family and Consumer Sciences
Huntsville, TX 77341
Tel: 936-294-1184 Fax: 936-294-4204
www.shsu.edu/~hec_www
Hours: Call for appointment
Contact: Janice White

Institution type: University collection
Collection type: Clothing, accessories
Description: 1900–present. Study collection for use by students. Items vary from turn-of-the-century wedding gown to designer garments and accessories from 1980s and 1990s.
✍

National Scouting Museum

1329 West Walnut Hill Lane
Irving, TX 75038
Tel: 972-580-2100 Fax: 972-580-2020
www.bsamuseum.org
Hours: Mon–Tue, Thu–Sat 10–5 pm, Sun 1–5 pm
Contact: Elizabeth Brantley
Institution type: Art museum, history museum
Collection type: Clothing, accessories, quilts, flags
Description: 1900–present. Boy Scout uniforms, flags, International Scout uniforms, patches, and quilts.
$ ✍

Jefferson Historical Society and Museum

233 West Austin
Jefferson, TX 75657
Tel: 903-665-2775

Lyndon B. Johnson National Historical Park

100 Lady Bird Lane
Johnson City, TX 78636
Tel: 830-868-7128
www.nps.gov/lyjo

The Hill Country Museum

226 Earl Garrett Street
Kerrville, TX 78028
Tel: 830-896-8633

Rangerette Showcase, Kilgore College

1100 Broadway Boulevard
Kilgore, TX 75662
Tel: 903-983-8273 Fax: 903-988-7511
www.rangerette.com

King Ranch Museum

405 North 6th Street
Kingsville, TX 78363
Tel: 361-595-1881
www.king-ranch.com/museum.htm

Fayette Heritage Museum and Archives

855 South Jefferson
La Grange, TX 78945
Tel: 979-968-6418
http://lagrange.fais.net/museum

Sam Houston Regional Library and Research Center

650 FM1011
Liberty, TX 77575-0310
Tel: 936-336-8821
www.tsl.state.tx.us/shc
Hours: Mon–Fri 8–5 pm, Sat 9–4 pm
Contact: Lisa Meisch
Institution type: History museum, historic house, state museum
Collection type: Clothing, accessories, uniforms, general textiles, quilts, flags
Description: 1800–present. Clothing, accessories, and other textiles that document the history of southeast Texas. Majority of items are men's, women's, and children's everyday and special occasion clothing ranging from 1850 to 1950 from southeast Texas families and individuals. Collection of quilts and quilt tops from 1850 to the 1930s.

Polk County Memorial Museum

514 West Mill Street
Livingston, TX 77351
Tel: 936-327-8192
www.livingston.net/museum
Hours: Mon–Fri 9–5 pm
Contact: Wanda L. Bobinger
Institution type: History museum, county museum
Collection type: Clothing
Description: 1800–1899. Civil War–1890s clothing and accessories, mostly women's clothing, walking suits, and children's clothes.

Museum of Texas Tech University

4th Street and Indiana Avenue
Lubbock, TX 79409-3191
Tel: 806-742-2442 Fax: 806-742-1136
www.depts.ttu.edu/museumttu
Hours: Tue–Sat 10–5 pm, Sun 1–5 pm

Wedding dresses, (left to right) 1876, 1890, 1887. Courtesy of Museum of Texas Tech University.

Contact: Mei Campbell, Curator
Institution type: History museum, university museum
Collection type: Clothing, accessories, general textiles, quilts
Description: 1800–present. More than 50,000 items, including men's, women's, and children's clothing and accessories primarily from Texas and surrounding states. 1800s pioneer and frontier women's clothing collection.

Harrison County Historical Museum

707 North Washington
Marshall, TX 75671
Tel: 903-938-2680
www.marshall_chamber.com/pages/museum.php

Starr Family Home State Historic Site

407 West Travis Street
Marshall, TX 75670
Tel: 903-935-3044
www.tpwd.state.tx.us/spdest/findadest/parks/starr_family
Hours: Fri–Sat 10–4 pm, Sun 1–5 pm, and by appointment
Contact: John Thomas
Institution type: Historic house, state museum
Collection type: Clothing
Description: 1850–1960. Costume collection of 300 items dates from the 1850s through the

1930s. Women's and children's clothing (the Starr family had six daughters, no sons). Children's clothing collection from the 1920s to the 1930s includes French and New York designer sets.

$ ✍

McLean-Alanreed Area Museum

116 Main Street
McLean, TX 79057
Tel: 806-779-2731

Roberts County Museum

Route 1 Highway 60
Miami, TX 79059
Tel: 806-868-3291
www.rootsweb.com/~txrobert

American Airpower Heritage Museum and Confederate Air Force

9600 Wright Drive
Midland, TX 79711
Tel: 915-563-1000
www.airpowermuseum.org

Museum of the Southwest

1705 West Missouri Avenue
Midland, TX 79701
Tel: 915-683-2882
www.museumsw.org

Z. Taylor Brown-Sarah Dorsey House

213 North Weatherford
Midland, TX 79701
Tel: 915-682-2931

Stone Fort Museum

Alumni and Griffith Boulevards
Stephen F. Austin State University
Nacogdoches, TX 75962
Tel: 936-468-2408

Sophienburg Museum and Archives

401 West College Street
New Braunfels, TX 78130
Tel: 830-629-1572
www.nbtx.com/sophienburg
Hours: Mon–Sat 8–5 pm, Sun 1–5 pm
Contact: Bonne Burton
Institution type: History museum
Collection type: Clothing, accessories, uniforms, general textiles, flags

Description: 1800–present. Large collection of period clothing from 1850 to the present reflects life of pioneers and development of the community.

$ ✍

Fort Belknap Museum and Archives

FM Road, 2 miles south of Newcastle
Newcastle, TX 76372
Tel: 940-549-1856

Heritage House of Orange County Association

905 West Division
Orange, TX 77630
Tel: 409-886-5385
www.heritagehouseoforange.org

White Deer Land Museum

112-116 South Cuyler
Pampa, TX 79065
Tel: 806-669-8041
www.museuminpampa.org

Carson County Square House Museum

503 Elsie
Panhandle, TX 79068
Tel: 806-537-3524 Fax: 806-537-5628
www.squarehousemuseum.org
Hours: Mon–Sat 9–5 pm, Sun 1–5 pm
Contact: Roy Maldonado
Institution type: History museum, historic house
Collection type: Clothing, accessories, uniforms, costumes, general textiles, quilts, flags
Description: 1760–present. Broad collection of clothing includes infants', children's, men's, women's, and military items. Household items include quilts and bed and table linens. Skins and live mounts of animals.

✍

Sam Bell Maxey House State Historic Site

812 South Church Street
Paris, TX 75460
Tel: 903-785-5716
www.tpwd.state.tx.us/spdest/findadest/
parks/sam_bell_maxey_house
Hours: Fri 1–5 pm, Sat 8–5 pm, Sun 1–5 pm, and by appointment

Contact: Judy Brummett
Institution type: Historic house, state museum
Collection type: Clothing, accessories
Description: 1850–present. Collection of about
650 objects includes clothing worn by the
Maxeys and their extended family from the
1860s to the 1960s.

$ ✍️

Tsa Mo Ga Memorial Museum

1109 Avenue H
Plains, TX 79355
Tel: 806-456-8855

Heritage Farmstead Museum

1900 West 15th Street
Plano, TX 75075
Tel: 972-881-0140 Fax: 972-422-6481
www.heritagefarmstead.org
Hours: Mon–Fri 10–4 pm, Sat–Sun 1–5 pm
Institution type: History museum, historic house
$ ✍️

Longhorn Museum

1959 Highway 97 East
Pleasanton, TX 78064
Tel: 830-569-6313

Museum of the Gulf Coast

700 Procter Street
Port Arthur, TX 77640
Tel: 409-982-7000
www.museum.lamarpa.edu

Ralls Historical Museum

801 Main Street
Ralls, TX 79357
Tel: 806-253-2425

Rankin Museum

101 West Main Street
Rankin, TX 79778
Tel: 915-693-2758

Fort Bend Museum Association

500 Houston
Richmond, TX 77406
Tel: 281-342-6478
www.fortbendmuseum.org

The University of Texas at Austin Center for American History

WINEDALE HISTORICAL CENTER
FM Road 2714
Round Top, TX 78954
Tel: 979-278-3530
www.cah.utexas.edu/divisions/Winedale.html
Hours: Sat 10–6 pm, Sun 12–6 pm (May–Oct);
Sat 9–5 pm, Sun 12–5 pm (Nov–Apr);
Mon–Fri, by appointment
Contact: Harmon Howze, Collections Manager
Institution type: Historic house
Collection type: Clothing, accessories, general textiles, quilts
Description: 1800–1899. Historic quilts (80),
coverlets, rugs, and show towels.
✍️

Miss Hattie's Bordello Museum

18 1/2 East Concho Avenue
San Angelo, TX 76903
Tel: 325-653-0112 Fax: 326-655-2616
www.misshatties.com
Hours: Mon–Wed 4–5 pm, Thu–Sat 1–4 pm
Contact: Mark Priest
Institution type: History museum
Collection type: Clothing
Description: 1900–1970. Clothing and accessories
found in Miss Hattie's Bordello.
✍️

The Alamo

300 Alamo Plaza
San Antonio, TX 78299
Tel: 210-225-1391
www.thealamo.org

Buckhorn Saloon and Museum

318 East Houston Street
San Antonio, TX 78205
Tel: 210-247-4002
www.buckhornmuseum.com

Pioneers, Trail Drivers, and Texas Rangers Memorial Museum

3805 Broadway
San Antonio, TX 78209
Tel: 210-661-4238

Texas Air Museum

8406 Cadmus
San Antonio, TX 78214
Tel: 210-977-9885
www.texasairmuseum.com

The University of Texas at San Antonio Institute of Texan Cultures

801 South Bowie
San Antonio, TX 78205
Tel: 210-458-2297 Fax: 210-458-2218
www.texancultures.utsa.edu
Hours: Tue–Wed 10–6 pm, Thu–Sat 10–8 pm, Sun 12–5 pm
Contact: Meg Gibson
Institution type: History museum, state museum, university collection
Collection type: Clothing, accessories, uniforms, costumes, general textiles, quilts, flags
Description: 1760–present. Items from the different ethnic groups who settled Texas and includes quilts, Native costumes, flags, uniforms, and textile production artifacts.
$ ✍

Witte Museum

3801 Broadway
San Antonio, TX 78209
Tel: 210-357-1861 Fax: 210-357-1882
www.wittemuseum.org
Hours: Mon, Wed–Sat 10–5 pm, Sun 12–5 pm, Tue 10–8 pm
Contact: Michaele Haynes

Appliquéd quilt with Mexican eagle, circa 1875. Courtesy of Witte Museum.

Institution type: History museum
Collection type: Clothing, accessories, uniforms, costumes, general textiles, quilts, flags
Description: 1760–present. Collection is best known for the formal dresses and trains worn during Fiesta San Antonio. Holdings also include Euro-American nineteenth- and twentieth-century clothing and accessories and ethnographic materials ranging from American Indian weavings and beadwork to Chinese court robes; nineteenth- and early-twentieth-century quilts, bedcovers, and linens; and samplers from 1781 to the 1850s. Museum has a significant collection of nineteenth-century Mexican or Tejano textiles, including samplers, table runners, colchas, and a reboza, and a collection of circus costumes, including those worn in las carpas (Mexican American tent circuses).
$

Edwin Wolters Memorial Museum

306 South Avenue I
Shiner, TX 77984
Tel: 512-594-3774

Scurry County Museum

Western Texas College, 6200 College Avenue
Snyder, TX 79549
Tel: 915-573-6107

Martin County Historical Museum

207 East Broadway
Stanton, TX 79782
Tel: 915-756-2722

The Museum of Southern History

14080 Southwest Freeway
Sugarland, TX 77487
Tel: 281-269-7171

Burlington-Rock Island Railroad Museum

208 South 3rd Avenue
Teague, TX 75860
Tel: 254-739-3551
www.therailroadmuseum.com

Railroad and Heritage Museum

315 West Avenue B
Temple, TX 76501
Tel: 254-298-5172 Fax: 254-298-5171
www.rrhm.org

Hours: Tue–Sat 10–4 pm, Sun 12–4 pm

Contact: Mary Lynn Irving

Institution type: History museum

Collection type: Clothing, accessories, uniforms, costumes, general textiles, quilts

Description: 1850–present. Collection includes items pertaining to railroading, military, and daily life from the 1880s to the 1950s. Also includes hand-woven blankets, quilts, and crocheted and knitted clothing accessories.

$ ✍

Bustle dress, circa 1883. Courtesy of Texarkana Museums System.

Texarkana Museums System

219 North State Line Avenue
Texarkana, TX 75504
Tel: 903-793-4831 Fax: 903-793-4831
www.texarkanamuseums.org

Hours: Tue–Sat 10–4 pm

Institution type: History museum, historic house, county museum

$ ✍

CLOTHING AND TEXTILE COLLECTION

Contact: J. A. Simmons

Collection type: Clothing, accessories, uniforms, costumes, general textiles, quilts, flags

Description: 1800–present. Clothing and textiles dating from 1820 to the present; quilts, 1840–1930; men's, women's, and children's clothing, circa 1830–1980; hats, shoes, and other accessories, circa 1820–1985; Oriental rugs, 1895–1940; and other textiles, circa 1850–1950.

OLIVIA SMITH MOORE SHOE COLLECTION

Contact: J.A. Simmons

Collection type: Accessories

Description: 1915–present. More than 500 pairs of shoes dated 1920 to 1985 owned by the late Olivia Smith Moore. Women's house slippers, casual, dress, orthopedic, and work shoes, mostly purchased from Neiman-Marcus.

Swisher County Archives and Museum Association

127 SW 2nd
Tulia, TX 79088
Tel: 806-995-2819

Goodman Museum

624 North Broadway
Tyler, TX 75702
Tel: 903-531-1286

Smith County Historical Society

125 South College Avenue
Tyler, TX 75702
Tel: 903-592-5561
www.smithcountyhistory.org

John Nance Garner Memorial Museum

333 North Park Street
Uvalde, TX 78801
Tel: 830-278-5018
www.cah.utexas.edu/divisions/Garner.html

Hours: Tue–Sat 9–5 pm

Contact: P. Cox, Director

Institution type: Historic house

Collection type: Clothing, accessories, quilts

Description: 1915–1960. Dress clothing belonging to John Nance Garner and his wife Ettie during his tenure as vice president to President Franklin Roosevelt (1933–1941) as well as clothing worn during earlier congressional career (1902–1933). Items include numerous hats, a Garner trademark; a quilt made by supporters of "Garner for President" in the 1932 presidential campaign; and 19 men's dress collars.

✍

Culberson County Historical Museum

12 West Broadway
Van Horn, TX 79855
Tel: 915-283-8028

McNamara House Museum

502 North Liberty
Victoria, TX 77901
Tel: 361-575-8227
www.viptx.net/museum

Historic Waco Foundation

810 South 4th Street
Waco, TX 76706
Tel: 254-753-5166
www.historicwaco.org

Texas Ranger Hall of Fame and Museum

100 Texas Ranger Trail
Waco, TX 76706
Tel: 254-750-8631 Fax: 254-750-8629
www.texasranger.org
Hours: Mon–Sun 9–5 pm
Contact: Tracie Evans, Collections Manager
Institution type: History museum, state museum, city museum
Collection type: Clothing, accessories, uniforms, general textiles, flags
Description: 1800–present. Professional and personal items relating to the officers of the legendary law enforcement agency known as the Texas Rangers and materials relating to other associated law enforcement agencies, officers, criminals, Texas history, and the Hollywood popular culture image of the Texas Rangers.
$ ✍️

Texas Sports Hall of Fame

1108 South University Parks Drive
Waco, TX 76706
Tel: 254-756-1633
www.tshof.org

Ellis County Museum

201 South College
Waxachachie, TX 75168
Tel: 972-937-0681
www.rootsweb.com/~txecm

Varner-Hogg Plantation State Historic Site

MISS IMA HOGG DECORATIVE ARTS COLLECTION
1702 North 13th Street
West Columbia, TX 77486
Tel: 979-345-4656 Fax: 979-345-4412
www.tpwd.state.tx.us/spdest/findadest/
    parks/varner_hogg_plantation
Hours: Tue–Sat 9–4 pm
Contact: Robert Cook, Executive Director
Institution type: History museum, historic house, state museum
Collection type: Clothing, accessories, uniforms, general textiles, quilts
Description: 1800–1900. Nineteenth-century American quilts and other decorative arts.
$ ✍️

Kell House Museum

900 Bluff Street
Wichita Falls, TX 76301
Tel: 940-723-2712
www.wichitaheritage.org

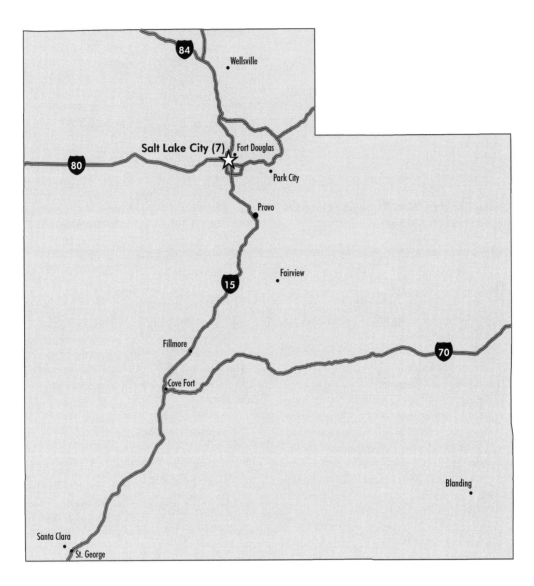

Wellsville

Salt Lake City (7) Fort Douglas

Park City

Provo

Fairview

Fillmore

Cove Fort

Blanding

Santa Clara

St. George

Population

- 0 - 50,000
- 50,001 - 100,000
- 100,001 - 250,000
- 250,001 - 500,000
- > 500,000
☆ State Capital

CSA Region VII Southwestern

UTAH

Edge of the Cedars State Park Museum
660 West 400 North
Blanding, UT 84511
Tel: 435-678-2238
www.stateparks.utah.gov/park_pages/edge.htm

Cove Fort—Museum of Church History and Art
Cove Fort, UT 84713
Tel: 801-240-0297

Fairview Museum of History and Art
85 North 100 East
Fairview, UT 84629
Tel: 435-427-9216
www.byways.org/browse/byways/13831/places/14554

Territorial Statehouse State Park and Museum
50 West Capitol Avenue
Fillmore, UT 84631
Tel: 435-743-5316

Fort Douglas Military Museum
32 Potter Street
Fort Douglas, UT 84113
Tel: 801-581-1710

Park City Historical Society and Museum
528 Main Street
Park City, UT 84060
Tel: 435-649-7457
www.parkcityhistory.org

Hours: Mon–Sat 11–5 pm
Contact: Sandra Morrison
Institution type: History museum
Collection type: Clothing, general textiles, flags
Description: 1900–present. Assortment of Park City memorabilia, including high school sports and music uniforms, dresses worn by Park City's richest woman in the 1900s, flags made by the Croatian Lodge, and children's clothing from the 1920s.

Brigham Young University
DIVISION OF DESIGN AND PRODUCTION COSTUME SHOP
D-101 Harris Fine Arts Center
Provo, UT 84602
Tel: 801-422-7168 Fax: 801-422-0654
Hours: Mon–Fri 8–5 pm
Contact: Deanne E. DeWitt
Institution type: University collection
Collection type: Clothing, accessories, uniforms, costumes, general textiles
Description: 1850–present. A vintage clothing collection of more than 700 pieces used for research for theatrical productions.

Beehive House—Museum of Church History and Art
67 East South Temple Street
Salt Lake City, UT 84111
Tel: 801-240-0297
Hours: Mon–Fri 9:30–6:30 pm (Jun–Aug);

Mon–Sat 9:30–4:30 pm, Sun 10–1 pm
(Sep–May)
Institution type: Historic house

Chase Home Museum of Utah Folk Arts
Liberty Park, 600 East 1100 South
Salt Lake City, UT 84102
Tel: 801-533-5760
www.folkartsmuseum.org

Lion House—Museum of Church History and Art
63 East South Temple Street
Salt Lake City, UT 84111
Tel: 801-240-0297

Museum of Church History and Art
45 North West Temple Street
Salt Lake City, UT 84105
Tel: 801-240-4615 Fax: 801-240-5342
www.lds.org/churchhistory/museum
Hours: Mon–Fri 9–9 pm, Sat–Sun 10–7 pm
Contact: Jennifer Feik
Institution type: History museum, art museum
Collection type: Clothing, accessories, uniforms, costumes, general textiles, quilts, flags
Description: 1800–present. Objects from the founding of the Church of Jesus Christ of Latter Day Saints in 1830 through the present day. Garments and textiles, including many quilts, that were used in the eastern United States and were brought to Utah; items worn or used in Utah; textile fragments, yarns, and silk cocoons from early attempts at sericulture and other textile industries in Utah; and historic and contemporary textiles and apparel from various countries. Highlights include a tapa cloth collection of 211 pieces and contemporary textile art and commemorative textile pieces.
$ ✍

Pioneer Memorial Museum
300 North Main Street
Salt Lake City, UT 84103-1699
Tel: 801-532-6479
www.dupinternational.org
Hours: Mon–Sun 9–5 pm
Contact: Edith Menna
Institution type: History museum
Collection type: Clothing, accessories, uniforms, costumes, general textiles, flags
Description: 1760–1960. Objects owned, used, or created by pioneers of Utah; commemorative memorabilia of pioneer holidays. Period room displays include stage coaches, wagons, and a fire engine.
$ ✍

This Is the Place Heritage Park
2601 Sunnyside Avenue
Salt Lake City, UT 84108
Tel: 801-582-1847
www.thisistheplace.org

Utah State Historical Society
300 Rio Grande Street
Salt Lake City, UT 84101-1182
Tel: 801-533-3500
http://history.utah.gov

Jacob Hamblin Home—Museum of Church History and Art
Santa Clara Boulevard and Hamblin Drive
Santa Clara, UT 84765
Tel: 801-240-0297

Brigham Young Winter Home—Museum of Church History and Art
67 West 200 North
St. George, UT 84770
Tel: 801-240-0297

American West Heritage Center
4025 South Highway 89 and Highway 91
Wellsville, UT 84339
Tel: 435-245-6050
www.americanwestcenter.org

DAR John Strong Mansion Museum

6656 Vermont Route 17 West
Addison, VT 05491
Tel: 802-888-7335
www.northshirecomputer.com/VTDAR
Hours: Sat–Sun 10–5 pm (Memorial Day–Labor
Day)
Contact: Maureen Labenski
Institution type: Historic house
Collection type: Costumes, general textiles
Description: 1760–1914. Bed furnishings, food
service and cleaning linens, samplers, hand-
woven goods, and mid- to late-nineteenth-
century costumes.

$ ✍

Vermont Historical Society

60 Washington Street
Barre, VT 05641-4209
Tel: 802-479-8500
www.vermonthistory.org

Rockingham Free Public Library and Museum

65 Westminster Street
Bellows Falls, VT 05101
Tel: 802-463-4270
www.rockingham.lib.vt.us
Hours: Vary, call ahead for hours
Contact: Christine Burchstead
Institution type: History museum
Collection type: Clothing, accessories, uniforms,
quilts

Wedding dress worn by four generations of the same family, circa 1880. Courtesy of Rockingham Free Public Library and Museum.

Description: 1800–1960. Public library has a
small museum of local history on top floor.
Grand Army of the Republic (GAR) uniform,
various accessories such as hats, shoes, gloves,
quilts, a wedding dress circa 1900, post–Civil
War dresses, and men's wool jackets.

✍

Mount Holly Community Historical Museum

Tarbelville Road
Belmont, VT 05730
Tel: 802-259-3722
www.mounthollyvtmuseum.org

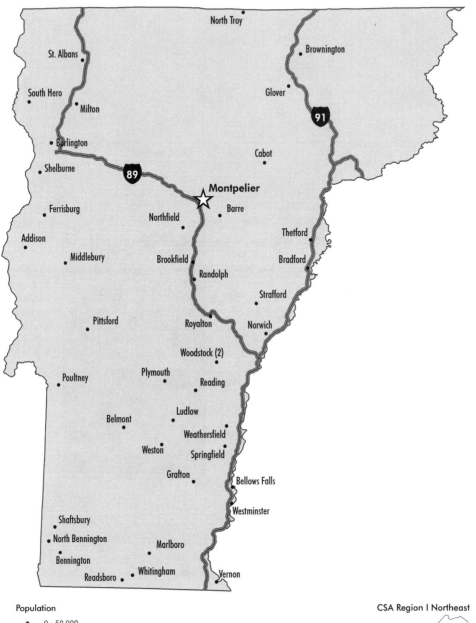

North Troy

Brownington

St. Albans

South Hero

Glover

Milton

91

Cabot

Burlington

Shelburne

89

★ **Montpelier**

Barre

Ferrisburg

Northfield

Thetford

Addison

Brookfield

Bradford

Middlebury

Randolph

Strafford

Pittsford

Royalton

Norwich

Woodstock (2)

Poultney

Plymouth

Reading

Ludlow

Belmont

Weathersfield

Weston

Springfield

Grafton

Bellows Falls

Westminster

Shaftsbury

North Bennington

Marlboro

Bennington

Readsboro

Whitingham

Vernon

Population

- 0 - 50,000
- 50,001 - 100,000
- 100,001 - 250,000
- 250,001 - 500,000
- > 500,000

★ State Capital

CSA Region I Northeast

The Bennington Museum

75 Main Street
Bennington, VT 05201
Tel: 802-447-1571
www.benningtonmuseum.org

Bradford Historical Society

172 North Main Street
Bradford, VT 05033
Tel: 802-222-4727

Historical Society of Brookfield

1133 Ridge Road
Brookfield, VT 05036
Tel: 802-276-3959
Hours: Sun 2–5 pm (Jul–Aug)
Contact: Jacalin W. Wilder
Institution type: History museum, historic house
Collection type: Clothing, accessories, uniforms, costumes, general textiles, flags
Description: 1800–1960. Garments from 1850 to 1930 with strengths in 1860–1890 clothing and accessories in historic house, circa 1835.
$ ✍

Orleans County Historical Society and Old Stone House Museum

109 Old Stone House Road
Brownington, VT 05860
Tel: 802-754-2022
www.oldstonehousemuseum.org

The Robert Hull Fleming Museum

61 Colchester Avenue
Burlington, VT 05405
Tel: 802-656-0750 Fax: 802-656-8059
www.flemingmuseum.org
Hours: Tue–Fri 9–4 pm, Sat–Sun 1–5 pm
Institution type: Art museum, university museum
$ ✍

Cabot Historical Society

193 McKinistry
Cabot, VT 05647
Tel: 802-563-2547

Rokeby Museum

4334 Route 7
Ferrisburgh, VT 05456
Tel: 802-877-3406
www.rokeby.org

Bread and Puppet Museum

753 Heights Road, Route 122
Glover, VT 05839
Tel: 802-525-3031

Grafton Historical Society

147 Main Street
Grafton, VT 05146
Tel: 802-843-1010

Black River Academy Museum

14 High Street
Ludlow, VT 05149
Tel: 802-228-5050

Marlboro Historical Society

364 South Road
Marlboro, VT 05344
Tel: 802-464-0329
www.marlboro.vt.us/historical.htm

The Henry Sheldon Museum of Vermont History

1 Park Street
Middlebury, VT 05753
Tel: 802-388-2117
www.henrysheldonmuseum.org
Hours: Tue–Sat 10–5 pm
Institution type: Art museum, history museum, historic house, county museum
$ ✍

Milton Historical Museum

13 School Street
Milton, VT 05468
Tel: 802-893-2340

Vermont State House

STATE OF VERMONT FLAG COLLECTION
115 State Street
Montpelier, VT 05633
Tel: 802-828-5657 Fax: 802-828-3533
Hours: Mon–Fri 7:30–4:30 pm, Sat 11–3 pm (Jul–Oct)
Contact: David Schutz
Institution type: State museum
Collection type: Flags
Description: 1850–present. More than 100 flags carried by Vermonters in wars from the Mexican to Vietnam conflicts; 68 of these banners

5th Regimental Flag, 1864. Courtesy of Vermont State House.

are regimental and U.S. flags from the Civil War, many painted on silk.

✐

The Park-McCullough House
Corner of Park and West Streets
North Bennington, VT 05257
Tel: 802-442-5441
www.parkmccullough.org

Missisquoi Valley Historical Society
Main Street
North Troy, VT 05859
Tel: 802-988-4701

Norwich University Museum
White Chapel, Norwich University
Northfield, VT 05663
Tel: 802-485-2360

Norwich Historical Society
277 Main Street
Norwich, VT 05055
Tel: 802-649-0124

Pittsford Historical Society Museum
3399 U.S. Route 7
Pittsford, VT 05763
Tel: 802-483-2040
www.pittsford-historical.org

Vermont Division for Historic Preservation
President Calvin Coolidge State Historic Site
Plymouth, VT 05056
Tel: 802-672-3773 Fax: 802-672-3337
www.historicvermont.org

Hours: Mon–Sun 9:30–5 pm (late May–mid-Oct)
Contact: William Jenney
Institution type: History museum, historic house, state museum
Collection type: Clothing, accessories, general textiles
Description: 1850–1960. Clothing and personal accessories that belonged to President Calvin Coolidge and his wife Grace. Other textiles include quilts, coverlets, and woven blankets that were made by the Coolidge family and their Plymouth Notch, Vermont, neighbors.
$ ✐

Poultney Historical Society Museum
On The Green
Poultney, VT 05764
Tel: 802-287-4042

Randolph Historical Society
Salisbury Street
Randolph, VT 05060
Tel: 802-728-6677
Hours: By appointment
Institution type: History museum
$ ✐

Reading Historical Society
Main Street, Route 106
Reading, VT 05062
Tel: 802-484-5005

Readsboro Historical Society
7009 Main Street
Readsboro, VT 05350
Tel: 802-423-5432

Royalton Historical Society
4184 Route 14
Royalton, VT 05068
Tel: 802-828-3051

Shaftsbury Historical Society
Historic 7A
Shaftsbury, VT 05262
Tel: 802-447-7488

Shelburne Museum
U.S. Route 7
Shelburne, VT 05482
Tel: 802-985-3346 Fax: 802-985-2331
www.shelburnemuseum.org

Album quilt, circa 1873. Courtesy of Shelburne Museum.

Hours: Mon–Sun 9–5 pm (May–Oct)
Contact: Jean Burks
Institution type: Art museum, history museum
Collection type: Clothing, accessories, general textiles, quilts
Description: 1750–1960. More than 800 men's, women's, and children's clothing items and accessories from the late seventeenth century to the early twentieth century. Strengths are in women's nineteenth-century pieces and approximately 200 wedding dresses. Collection is primarily American. 400 quilts, many from the New England region, and a large collection of hooked rugs from 1800 to 1960. Rughooking was particularly popular in New England, and most pieces are from the region.
$

South Hero Bicentennial Museum

2 Hill Road
South Hero, VT 05486
Tel: 802-372-6615
Hours: Mon–Thu 1:30–3:30 pm (Jun–Aug)
Contact: Barbara Winch, Curator
Institution type: History museum
Collection type: Clothing, accessories, uniforms, general textiles, quilts, flags
Description: 1760–1960. Clothing, shoes, quilts, flags, hats, and other accessories as well as household textiles, including dresser scarves and linen sheets.

Springfield Art and Historical Society

9 Elm Hill
Springfield, VT 05156
Tel: 802-885-2415
www.vmga.org/windsor/springfieldart.html

St. Albans Historical Museum

9 Church Street
St. Albans, VT 05478
Tel: 802-527-7933
www.stalbansmuseum.org
Hours: Mon–Fri 9–4 pm (Jun–Oct), and by appointment
Contact: Donald J. Miner, Director
Institution type: History museum
Collection type: Clothing, accessories
Description: 1850–1914. Clothing from the Smith and Brainard families. The Smiths, both father and son, were governors of Vermont during the Civil War and Spanish American War. Mrs. J. Gregory (Anna Elisa Brainard) Smith and her daughters were very well dressed and bought clothing worldwide. Holdings include dresses from an entire wedding party at the turn of the nineteenth century, 1920s children's clothing, body linen for all ages, and many accessories.

Justin Smith Morrill Homestead

214 Justin Morrill Memorial Highway
Strafford, VT 05072
Tel: 802-828-3051
www.historicvermont.org/morrill

Thetford Historical Society Library and Museum

16 Library Road
Thetford, VT 05074
Tel: 802-785-2068

Vernon Historical Museum

4201 Fort Bridgman Road
Vernon, VT 05354
Tel: 802-257-0292

Reverend Dan Foster House, Museum of the Weathersfield Historical Society

2656 Weathersfield Center Road
Weathersfield, VT 05156
Tel: 802-263-5230
www.weathersfield.org/pages/histsoc.htm

Westminster Historical Society
3651 U.S. Route 5
Westminster, VT 05158
Tel: 802-387-5778

Farrar-Mansur House and Old Mill Museum
Main Street
Weston, VT 05161
Tel: 802-824-5294

Whitingham Historical Museum
Stimpson Hill
Whitingham, VT 05361
Tel: 802-368-2448

Billings Farm and Museum
River Road and Route 12
Woodstock, VT 05091
Tel: 802-457-2355
www.billingsfarm.org

Woodstock Historical Society
26 Elm Street
Woodstock, VT 05091
Tel: 802-457-1822
www.woodstockhistsoc.org

Boy's dress, circa 1899. Courtesy of William King Regional Arts Center.

William King Regional Arts Center

CULTURAL HERITAGE COLLECTION

415 Academy Drive

Abingdon, VA 24210

Tel: 276-628-5005 Fax: 276-628-3922

www.wkrac.org

Hours: Tue–Fri 10–5 pm, Sat–Sun 1–5 pm

Contact: Trisha Blesser

Institution type: Art museum, history museum, historic house

Collection type: Clothing, accessories, costumes, general textiles, quilts, flags

Description: 1800–1960. The Cultural Heritage Project and related collection document and present the artistic legacy of fifteen counties in southwest Virginia and northeast Tennessee. The Fields-Penn 1860 Historic House Museum displays the Cultural Heritage Pro-

ject's permanent collection of decorative and folk arts, including costumes, quilts, and coverlets from 1860 to 1900.

Fort Ward Museum

FRANCIS LORD COLLECTION

4301 West Braddock Road

Alexandria, VA 22304

Tel: 703-838-4848

www.fortward.org

Hours: Tue–Sat 9–5 pm, Sun 12–5 pm

Contact: Wally Owen

Institution type: History museum

Collection type: Accessories, uniforms, flags

Description: 1850–1900. Civil War period (1861–1864) uniforms, arms, and equipment.

$ 🖉

Gadsby's Tavern Museum

134 North Royal Street

Alexandria, VA 22314

Tel: 703-838-4242 Fax: 703-838-4270

www.gadsbystavern.org

Hours: Tue–Sun 10–5 pm, Sun–Mon 1–5 pm (Apr–Oct); seasonal hours at other times

Contact: Gretchen Bulova

Institution type: Historic house

Collection type: Accessories, costumes, general textiles

Description: 1760–present. Collection relates to travel and accommodations between 1749 and 1810 and includes period bedding textiles and clothing accessories. Colonial revival costumes and accessories worn to tavern events between

CSA Region VI Southeast

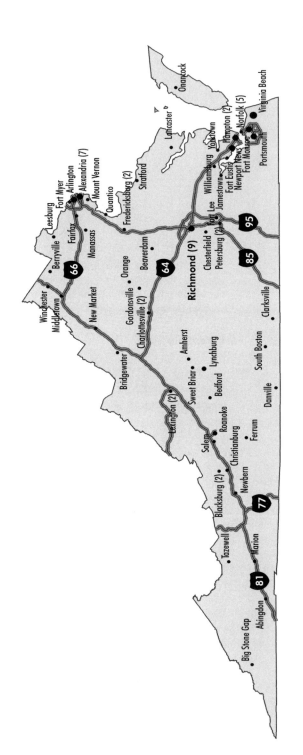

Population

· 0 - 50,000

• 50,001 - 100,000

● 100,001 - 250,000

⬤ 250,001 - 500,000

⬤ > 500,000

☆ State Capital

1929 and 2000. Other items include textiles used for period room displays during the American Legion Post 24 management of the museum (1929–1974).

$ ✍

George Washington Masonic National Memorial

GEORGE WASHINGTON MUSEUM
101 Callahan Drive
Alexandria, VA 22301
Tel: 703-683-2007
www.gwmemorial.org
Hours: Mon–Sun 9–5 pm
Contact: Dustin B. Smith
Institution type: History museum
Collection type: Clothing, accessories, general textiles
Description: 1760–1849. Historical artifacts and information pertaining to George Washington. Washingtonia from Anne Madison and Pattie Willis Washington comprise the core of the collection. Major areas of research and interpretation include Washington the Freemason, early Virginia Freemasonry, the life of Washington in Virginia, the commemoration of Washington after his death, and the Bushrod Washington and John Augustine Washington families.

✍

Lee-Fendall House

614 Oronoco Street
Alexandria, VA 22314
Tel: 703-548-1789
www.leefendallhouse.org

Lyceum, Alexandria's History Museum

1201 South Washington Street
Alexandria, VA 22314
Tel: 703-838-4994
www.alexandriahistory.org
Hours: Mon–Sat 10–5 pm, Sun 1–5 pm
Contact: Jim Mackay, Director
Institution type: History museum
Collection type: Clothing, accessories, general textiles, quilts
Description: 1750–present. Clothing, textiles, and accessories, including several everyday garments from nineteenth-century middle-class Alexandria women.

✍

U.S. Patent and Trademark Office— Museum

600 Dulany Street
Alexandria, VA 22313
Tel: 703-305-8341
www.uspto.gov

Woodlawn Plantation and Frank Lloyd Wright's Pope-Leighey House

9000 Richmond Highway
Alexandria, VA 22309
Tel: 703-780-4000 Fax: 703-780-8509
www.woodlawn1805.org
Hours: Tue–Sun 10–5 pm (Mar–Dec)
Contact: Bruce Whitmarsh, Associate Director of Programs and Interpretation
Institution type: Historic house
Collection type: Clothing, general textiles, quilts
Description: 1760–1960. Flat textiles and bed coverings composed primarily of objects with Woodlawn Plantation provenance, 1800–1839, including various pieces executed by Nellie Custis Lewis, first mistress of Woodlawn. Other items include undyed wool blankets with silk bindings and wool embroidered designs made at Mount Vernon; nineteenth-century pieced and appliquéd quilts; overshot and double weave coverlets; paisley cloths; an ivory silk gown belonging to Nellie Lewis; nineteenth-century infant garments and crib quilts; and a black silk and beaded mantua.

$ ✍

Amherst Museum and Historical Society

154 South Main Street
Amherst, VA 24521
Tel: 804-946-9068
www.members.aol.com/achmuseum/ achmhis.htm

Marymount University in Virginia

2807 North Glebe Road
Arlington, VA 22207
Tel: 703-284-1564 Fax: 703-284-3859
www.marymount.edu
Hours: By appointment
Contact: Sally Garen
Institution type: University collection
Collection type: Clothing, accessories, general textiles
Description: 1760–present. Study collection for students began with a gift from Mrs. Stanley

C. Lewis of articles from the eighteenth and nineteenth centuries. Couture collections have been added.

Scotchtown, Association for the Preservation of Virginia Antiquities

16120 Chiswell Lane
Beaverdam, VA 23015
Tel: 804-227-3500
www.apva.org/scotchtown
Hours: Tue–Sat 10–4:30 pm, Sun 1:30–4:30 pm (Apr–Oct)
Contact: Site Administrator
Institution type: Historic house
Collection type: General textiles, quilts
Description: 1760–1849. Quilts and coverlets for use in the interpretation of late-eighteenth-century Virginian life.

Bedford City and County Museum

201 East Main Street
Bedford, VA 24523
Tel: 540-586-4520
www.bedfordvamuseum.org
Hours: Mon–Sat 10–5 pm
Contact: Director of Collections
Institution type: Historic house
Collection type: Clothing, accessories, uniforms, costumes
Description: 1850–present. Approximately 15 wedding gowns, 1850–1970; 30 military uniforms from 1812 through Desert Storm; and local school and community band uniforms from Bedford County.

$

Clarke County Historical Association

32 East Main Street
Berryville, VA 22611
Tel: 540-955-2600
www.clarkehistory.org

Southwest Virginia Museum Historical State Park

10 West 1st Street North
Big Stone Gap, VA 24219
Tel: 276-523-1322
www.dcr.virginia.gov/parks/swvamus.htm

Historic Smithfield, Association for the Preservation of Virginia Antiquities

1000 Smithfield Plantation Road
Blacksburg, VA 24060
Tel: 540-231-3947
www.apva.org/apva/smithfield_plantation.php
Hours: Thu–Sun 1–4:30 pm (Apr–1st weekend in Dec)
Contact: Terry Nicholson, Site Administrator
Institution type: Historic house
Collection type: General textiles
Description: 1760–1899. Quilts and coverlets used in interpreting life in Blacksburg, Virginia, during the late-eighteenth century and nineteenth century.

Virginia Tech

CHRIS GLISSON HISTORIC COSTUME AND TEXTILE COLLECTION
101 Wallace Hall
Blacksburg, VA 24061
Tel: 540-231-6781 Fax: 540-231-1697
www.ahrm.vt.edu/ct/costumes/index.html
Hours: Mon–Fri 8–4:30 pm
Contact: Sherry Schofield-Tomschin
Institution type: University collection
Collection type: Clothing, accessories, general textiles, quilts
Description: 1800–present. Women's apparel, including designer garments, wedding gowns, and clothing from working to elite social classes and outerwear, lingerie, and accessories from each decade since 1840. Historic textiles consist of laces, coverlets, quilts, and household items. Historic books, patterns, and other items.

Reuel B. Pritchett Museum

Bridgewater College, East College Street
Bridgewater, VA 22812
Tel: 540-828-5462
www.bridgewater.edu

Monticello

Route 53, Thomas Jefferson Parkway
Charlottesville, VA 22902
Tel: 434-984-9832 Fax: 434-977-7757
www.monticello.org
Hours: Mon–Sun 8–5 pm (Mar–Oct); Mon–Sun 9–4:30 pm (Nov–Feb)

Contact: Carrie Taylor
Institution type: Historic house
Collection type: Clothing, accessories, costumes
Description: 1760–1849. Monticello houses the premier collection for the comprehensive study of Thomas Jefferson and the Monticello community. The costumes and accessories collection consists primarily of objects used by Thomas Jefferson and his family, who resided at Monticello until 1826.

$ ✍

University of Virginia Department of Drama
THE COLLECTION OF HISTORIC DRESS
109 Culbreth Road
Charlottesville, VA 22903
Tel: 434-924-8965 Fax: 434-924-1447
www.virginia.edu
Hours: By appointment
Contact: Gweneth West
Institution type: Theater museum, university collection
Collection type: Clothing, accessories
Description: 1760–present. Greatest strength is 1890–1940. Oldest garment is a man's wool coat and breeches, circa 1795. 1830s dresses and bodices, a complete silk 1860s crinoline gown, a slave dress, 1880s bustle gowns, 1900 Edwardian laces, and World War I era "Suffragette" and World War II era "utility" dresses.

✍

Chesterfield Historical Society of Virginia
10201 Iron Bridge Road
Chesterfield, VA 23832
Tel: 804-777-9663
www.chesterfieldhistory.com

Montgomery Museum and Lewis Miller Regional Art Center
300 South Pepper Street
Christianburg, VA 24072
Tel: 540-382-5644
www.montgomerymuseum.org

Prestwould Foundation
U.S. Highway 15
Clarksville, VA 23927
Tel: 804-373-8672

Danville Museum of Fine Arts and History
975 Main Street
Danville, VA 24541
Tel: 804-792-5644
www.danvillemuseum.org

Fairfax County Park Authority
12055 Government Center Parkway, Suite 927
Fairfax, VA 22035
Tel: 703-631-1429 Fax: 703-631-8319
www.co.fairfax.va.us/parks/collections/index.htm
Hours: by appointment
Contact: Jeanne Niccolls
Institution type: History museum, historic house, county museum
Collection type: Clothing, accessories, general textiles
Description: 1800–present

✍

Blue Ridge Institute and Museum
Route 40, Ferrum College
Ferrum, VA 24088
Tel: 540-365-4416
www.ferrum.edu

U.S. Army Transportation Museum
Besson Hall, Building 300
Fort Eustis, VA 23604
Tel: 757-878-1115
www.transchool.eustis.army.mil/museum/museum.html

The United States Army Quartermasters Museum
Building 5218, A Avenue
Fort Lee, VA 23801
Tel: 804-734-4203
www.qmmuseum.lee.army.mil

Casemate Museum
20 Bernard Road
Fort Monroe, VA 23651
Tel: 757-788-3391
www-tradoc.army.mil/museum

The Old Guard Museum
3rd Infantry (The Old Guard)
204 Lee Avenue
Fort Myer, VA 22211-1199

Army dress blue uniform, first female Tomb of the Unknown Soldier sentinel, 1996. Courtesy of The Old Guard Museum.

Tel: 703-696-6670 Fax: 703-696-4256
www.mdw.army.mil/oldguard
Hours: Mon–Sat 9–4 pm, Sun 1–4 pm
Contact: Kirk Heflin
Institution type: History museum, federal museum
Collection type: Clothing, uniforms, flags
Description: 1850–present. U.S. Army uniforms and flags of the 3rd Infantry (The Old Guard), the Army's official ceremonial unit, and generic examples from the Civil War to the present with an emphasis on the twentieth century.

✍

George Washington's Fredericksburg Foundation

1201 Washington Avenue
Fredericksburg, VA 22401
Tel: 540-373-3381x15 Fax: 540-371-6066
www.kenmore.org
Hours: Mon–Sun 10–5 pm, hours change seasonally
Contact: David Voelkel
Institution type: Historic house
Collection type: Clothing, accessories, general textiles
Description: 1700–present. Clothing and accessory collection contains items from 1770 to 1780, when Betty Washington Lewis (sister of George Washington) and Fielding Lewis lived at Kenmore, the finest plantation in Fredericks-

burg. Items include a rare stay with period alterations, Lewis's pocketbook and earrings, and other Washington family jewelry. Various household textiles, including bed hangings, curtains, case covers, and bed linens. Textile study collection of eighteenth- and early-nineteenth-century fabric includes pieces from plain to fancy.

$ ✍

James Monroe Museum and Memorial Library

908 Charles Street
Fredericksburg, VA 22401
Tel: 540-654-1043
www.umw.edu/jamesmonroemuseum

The Exchange Hotel Civil War Museum

400 South Main Street
Gordonsville, VA 22942
Tel: 540-832-2944
www.hgiexchange.org

Hampton History Center

600 Settlers Landing Road
Hampton, VA 23669
Tel: 757-727-0900
Hours: Mon–Wed 10–5 pm, Thu–Sun 10–7 pm (Memorial Day–Labor Day); Mon–Sat 10–5 pm, Sun 12–5 pm (Labor Day–Memorial Day)

$ ✍

Hampton University Museum

Hampton University
Hampton, VA 23668
Tel: 757-727-5308
www.hampton.edu/museum

Stay, circa 1760. Courtesy of George Washington's Fredericksburg Foundation.

Jamestown-Yorktown Foundation

Route 31 South
Jamestown, VA 23187
Tel: 757-253-4838
www.jamestown-yorktown.state.va.us
Hours: Mon–Sun 9–5 pm
$ ✍

Mary Ball Washington Museum

8346 Mary Ball Road
Lancaster, VA 22503
Tel: 804-462-7280
www.mbwm.org

Loudoun Museum

16 Loudoun Street SW
Leesburg, VA 20175
Tel: 703-777-7427 Fax: 703-777-8873
www.loudounmuseum.org
Hours: Mon–Sat 10–5 pm, Sun 1–5 pm
Contact: Eric Larson
Institution type: History museum
Collection type: Clothing, accessories, uniforms, general textiles, quilts
Description: 1700–present. Largest collection of northern Virginia quilts and samplers in Virginia includes assortment of clothing and accessories. Collection is strong in mid-nineteenth century.
$ ✍

Rockbridge Historical Society

101 East Washington Street
Lexington, VA 24450
Tel: 540-464-1858
www.rockhist.org

Virginia Military Institute Museum

Jackson Memorial Hall
Lexington, VA 24450
Tel: 540-464-7334
www4.vmi.edu/museum

Lynchburg Museum System

901 Court Street
Lynchburg, VA 24504
Tel: 434-847-1459
www.lynchburgmuseum.org

Manassas Museum System

9101 Prince William Street
Manassas, VA 20110
Tel: 703-368-1873
www.manassasmuseum.org

Smyth County Museum

105 East Strother Street
Marion, VA 24354
Tel: 540-783-7067

Belle Grove Plantation

BELLE GROVE AND NATIONAL TRUST
COLLECTIONS AND HITE FAMILY
WEDDING DRESSES
336 Belle Grove Road
Middletown, VA 22645
Tel: 540-869-2028 Fax: 540-869-9638
www.bellegrove.org
Hours: Mon–Sun 10–4 pm (late Mar–Oct)
Institution type: Historic house
Collection type: Clothing, accessories, general textiles, quilts
Description: 1760–1899. Six 1860s quilts with Virginia provenance; Shenandoah Valley woven coverlets dating from 1783 to the 1860s; 1820s–1830s wedding and second-day dresses; and various embroidered textiles.
$ ✍

George Washington's Mount Vernon Estate and Gardens

South End of George Washington Parkway
Mount Vernon, VA 22121
Tel: 703-780-2000
www.mountvernon.org
Hours: Mon–Sun, hours vary seasonally

Wedding shoes of Martha Washington, 1759. Courtesy of Mount Vernon Ladies Association.

Contact: Carol Borchert Cadou, Curator
Institution type: History museum, historic house
Collection type: Clothing, accessories, uniforms, costumes, general textiles
Description: 1700–present. Clothing, textiles, and accessories related to George and Martha Custis Washington and Washington descendants. Highlights include Martha Custis's wedding shoes from 1759.

$ ✍

New Market Battlefield State Historical Park
8895 Collins Drive
New Market, VA 22844
Tel: 540-740-3101
www4.vmi.edu/museum/nm

Wilderness Road Regional Museum
5240 Wilderness Road
Newbern, VA 24126
Tel: 540-674-4835 Fax: 540-674-1266
Hours: Mon–Sat 10:30–4:30 pm, Sun 1:30–4:30 pm
Contact: Sara C. Zimmerman
Institution type: History museum, historic house
Collection type: Clothing, accessories, uniforms, costumes, general textiles, quilts, flags
Description: 1800–1960. Collection includes clothing of children and adults, quilts, and coverlets.

$ ✍

The Virginia War Museum
9285 Warwick Boulevard
Newport News, VA 23607
Tel: 757-247-8523 Fax: 757-247-8627
www.warmuseum.org
Hours: Mon–Sat 9–5 pm, Sun 1–5 pm
$ ✍

Adam Thoroughgood House
820 East Virginia Beach Boulevard
Norfolk, VA 23504
Tel: 757-664-6200
www.virginiabeachhistory.org/
    thoroughgoodhouse.html

Hampton Roads Naval Museum
1 Waterside Drive, Suite 248
Norfolk, VA 23510
Tel: 757-322-2987
www.hrnm.navy.mil

Moses Myers House
331 Bank Street
Norfolk, VA 23510
Tel: 757-664-6283
www.chrysler.org/Myers_house.asp

Norfolk Historical Society
810 Front Street
Norfolk, VA 23510
Tel: 757-625-1720
www.norfolkhistorical.org

Ohef Sholom Temple Archives
530 Raleigh Avenue
Norfolk, VA 23507
Tel: 757-625-4295
www.ohefsholom.org

Kerr Place
69 Market Street
Onancock, VA 23417
Tel: 757-787-8012
www.kerrplace.org

The James Madison Museum
129 Caroline Street
Orange, VA 22960
Tel: 540-672-1776
www.jamesmadisonmus.org

Pamplin Historical Park and the National Museum of the Civil War Soldier
6125 Boydton Plank Road
Petersburg, VA 23803
Tel: 804-861-2408
www.pamplinpark.org
Hours: Mon–Sun 9–5 pm
Contact: Randy Klemm, Curator of Collections
Institution type: History museum
Collection type: Accessories, uniforms, flags
Description: 1850–1899. Objects used and worn during the Civil War by the common soldier and items specifically related to the Petersburg Campaign of 1864–1865.

$ ✍

Ball gown, worn by Otelia Mahone, wife of Confederate general and U.S. senator William Mahone, 1884. Courtesy of Petersburg Museums.

Petersburg Museums

15 West Bank Street
Petersburg, VA 23803
Tel: 804-733-2427 Fax: 804-863-0837
www.petersburg-va.org/tourism
Hours: Mon–Sun 10–5 pm
Contact: Laura Willoughby
Institution type: History museum, historic house, city museum
Collection type: Clothing, accessories, uniforms, costumes, general textiles, quilts, flags
Description: 1800–1960. Textile collection features quilts, costumes, accessories, flags, and other textile items associated with the Petersburg area's three-hundred-year history. Strengths of the collection are mid-nineteenth- to early-twentieth-century quilts, late-nineteenth-century clothing, and a variety of accessories, including fans, purses, hats, and shawls from the late nineteenth century to the early twentieth century.
$ 🖊️

Portsmouth Naval Shipyard Museum

420 High Street
Portsmouth, VA 23704
Tel: 757-393-8591 Fax: 757-393-5244
www.portsnavalmuseums.com
Hours: Tue–Sat 10–5 pm, Sun 1–5 pm
Contact: Alice Hanes, Curator; Corey Thornton, Curatorial Assistant
Institution type: History museum, city museum
Collection type: Clothing, accessories, uniforms, general textiles, flags

Description: 1850–present. Collection consists primarily of historic military uniforms ranging from the Civil War to World War II. Small collection of American naval flags and Korean and German flags.
$ 🖊️

United States Marine Corps Air-Ground Museum

2014 Anderson Avenue
Quantico, VA 22134
Tel: 703-784-2606
www.marineheritage.org/Store/MCHF/index.asp

Spectacles, early nineteenth century. Courtesy of Association for the Preservation of Virginia Antiquities.

Association for the Preservation of Virginia Antiquities (APVA)

204 West Franklin Street
Richmond, VA 23221
Tel: 804-648-1889
www.apva.org
Contact: Katherine Dean, Curator

Henrico County Historic Preservation and Museum Services

8600 Nixon Powers Drive
Richmond, VA 23228
Tel: 804-501-5736
www.co.henrico.va.us/rec/
    HistoricPreservation.htm

John Marshall House, Association for the Preservation of Virginia Antiquities

818 East Marshall Street
Richmond, VA 23219
Tel: 804-648-7998 Fax: 804-648-5880
www.apva.org/marshall
Hours: Tue–Sat 10–5 pm

Contact: Pat Archer, Site Administrator

Institution type: Historic house

Collection type: Clothing, accessories, uniforms, costumes, general textiles

Description: 1800–1849. Clothing and textiles owned by the Marshall family or appropriate for display in John Marshall's home interpreted to circa 1815. Highlights include Polly Marshall's wedding dress and sampler and John Marshall's judicial robe.

Maggie L. Walker National Historic Site

602 North 2nd Street
Richmond, VA 23219
Tel: 804-771-2017
www.nps.gov/malw

Flag of the 4th Virginia Infantry, Co. K, later 27th Virginia Infantry, Co. H, Rockbridge Rifles, circa 1860. Courtesy of Museum of the Confederacy.

Museum of the Confederacy

1201 East Clay Street
Richmond, VA 23219
Tel: 804-649-1861
www.moc.org

Hours: Mon–Sat 10–5 pm, Sun 12–5 pm

Contact: Robert Hancock, Curator

Institution type: History museum, historic house

Collection type: Accessories, uniforms, flags

Description: 1850–1900. Site encompasses two buildings: the White House of the Confederacy restored to its 1861–1865 appearance as Jefferson Davis's executive mansion and a modern museum that houses 510 Confederate flags and more than 250 Confederate uniforms and uniform items.

$ 🖊

Deerskin jacket, circa 1785–1806. Courtesy of Valentine Richmond History Center.

Valentine Richmond History Center

VIRGINIA COSTUME AND TEXTILE INSTITUTE

1015 East Clay Street
Richmond, VA 23227
Tel: 804-649-0711 Fax: 804-643-3510
www.richmondhistorycenter.com/collections/costumes/index.asp

Hours: Tue–Sat 10–5 pm, Sun 1–5 pm

Contact: Suzanne Savery

Institution type: Historic house, city museum

Collection type: Clothing, accessories, uniforms, general textiles, quilts, flags

Description: Pre-1700–present. Objects related to Richmond but also a broader focus, including items worn, used, made, or sold in Virginia from the 1600s to the present. Collection also includes clothing and accessories worn by Virginians of diverse social groups and ages, for private and public occasions. A particular strength is its date range, from a 1668 christening dress to items worn in 2005, eighteenth- and nineteenth-century quilts and samplers, as well as a wide range of household textiles.

$ 🖊

Virginia Commonwealth University

DEPARTMENT OF THEATRE COLLECTION

Department of Theatre
922 Park Avenue

Richmond, VA 23284
Tel: 804-828-6025 Fax: 804-828-6741
Hours: Mon–Fri 10–5 pm
Contact: Elizabeth Hopper
Institution type: University collection
Collection type: Clothing
Description: 1850–1960. Study collection for students in costume design and construction includes primarily women's, twentieth-century, Richmond clothing.

Virginia Museum of Fine Arts
200 North Boulevard
Richmond, VA 23221-2466
Tel: 804-340-1600 Fax: 804-340-1548
www.vmfa.state.va.us
Hours: Wed–Sun 11–5 pm
Contact: Dr. Joseph M. Dye, Curatorial Chairman
Institution type: Art museum, state museum
Collection type: Clothing, general textiles
Description: Pre-1700–1960. This fine arts museum houses an encyclopedic collection. Clothing is mostly non-European. Notable items include a nineteenth-century jeweled royal turban, a nineteenth-century African royal beaded crown, and an Indian talismanic shirt circa 1500 with the text of the entire Qur'an written on it.

Wilton House Museum
215 South Wilton Road
Richmond, VA 23226
Tel: 804-282-5906 Fax: 804-288-9805
www.wiltonhousemuseum.org
Hours: Tue–Sat 10–4 pm
Contact: Dana Hand Evans
Institution type: History museum, historic house
Collection type: Clothing, accessories, general textiles, quilts
Description: 1700–1849. Wide array of textiles, quilts, clothing, shoes, and accessories, including mourning jewelry and eyeglasses. Collection also includes furniture and other decorative arts.

$

Virginia Museum of Transportation
303 Norfolk Avenue SW
Roanoke, VA 24016
Tel: 540-342-5670
www.vmt.org

The Salem Museum
801 East Main Street
Salem, VA 24153
Tel: 540-389-6760
www.salemmuseum.org

South Boston-Halifax County Museum of Fine Arts and History
1540 Wilborn Avenue
South Boston, VA 24592
Tel: 804-572-9200
www.cstone.net/~sbhcm

Stratford, Robert E. Lee Memorial Association
485 Great House Road
Stratford, VA 22558
Tel: 804-493-8038
www.stratfordhall.org

Sweet Briar Museum
Sweet Briar College
Sweet Briar, VA 24595
Tel: 804-381-6102
www.museum.sbc.edu

Historic Crab Orchard Museum and Pioneer Park
Route 19 and 460 at Crab Orchard Road
Tazewell, VA 24651
Tel: 276-988-6755
www.craborchardmuseum.com

Virginia Beach Maritime Museum and the Old Coast Guard Station
24th Street and Broadway
Virginia Beach, VA 23451
Tel: 757-422-1587
www.oldcoastguardstation.com

Colonial Williamsburg Foundation
DeWitt Wallace Decorative Arts Museum
325 Francis Street
Williamsburg, VA 23185
Tel: 757-220-7508 Fax: 757-565-8594
www.colonialwilliamsburg.com

Jacket and petticoat, circa 1775. Courtesy of Colonial Williamsburg Foundation.

Hours: Mon–Sun, hours vary by building and season

Contact: Linda Baumgarten, Kim Ivey

Institution type: Art museum, history museum

Collection type: Clothing, accessories, costumes, general textiles, quilts

Description: 1700–1899. Eighteenth-century men's, women's and children's clothing, mostly English and American; some seventeenth- and nineteenth-century garments; and quilts and coverlets from the seventeenth through the twenty-first century.

$ 🖊

Winchester-Frederick County Historical Society

1340 South Pleasant Valley Road
Winchester, VA 22601
Tel: 540-662-6550 Fax: 540-662-6991
www.winchesterhistory.org

Hours: Mon–Sat 10–4 pm, Sun 12–4 pm (Apr–Oct), and by appointment

Contact: Robert F. Boxley, CEO and President

Institution type: History museum, city museum

Collection type: Clothing, accessories, uniforms, general textiles, quilts, flags

Description: 1760–1960. Clothing and textiles are exhibited on a rotating basis. Earliest object is a 1753 man's waistcoat. Most objects are 1875–1940, primarily women's dress. World War I and World War II uniforms typical of historical society and Quaker wedding dresses and bonnets.

Yorktown: Colonial National Historical Park

Colonial Parkway and Route 238
Yorktown, VA 23690
Tel: 757-898-3400
www.nps.gov/colo

WASHINGTON

Anacortes Museum

1305 8th Street
Anacortes, WA 98221
Tel: 360-293-1915
www.anacorteshistorymuseum.org

Eastside Heritage Center

2102 Bellevue Way SE
Bellevue, WA 98015
Tel: 425-450-1049
www.eastsideheritagecenter.org

Whatcom Museum of History and Art

121 Prospect Street
Bellingham, WA 98225
Tel: 360-676-6981
www.whatcommuseum.org

Kitsap County Historical Society Museum

280 4th Street
Bremerton, WA 98337
Tel: 360-479-6226 Fax: 360-415-9294
www.waynes.net/kchsm
Hours: Tue–Sat 9–5 pm
Contact: Gail Campbell-Ferguson
Institution type: History museum, county
museum
Collection type: Clothing, accessories, uniforms,
costumes, general textiles, flags
Description: 1850–present. Clothing and artifacts
from 1850 to the present that are representa-
tive of what was (or is) worn in Kitsap County.

Women's clothing and accessories comprise the
largest number of items.

Island County Historical Society Museum

908 NW Alexander Street
Coupeville, WA 98239
Tel: 360-678-3310
www.islandhistory.org

Fort Spokane Visitor Center and Museum

44303 State Route 25 North
Davenport, WA 99122
Tel: 509-725-2715
www.nps.gov/laro/home.htm

Lincoln County Historical Museum

Park and 7th Street
Davenport, WA 99122
Tel: 509-725-6711
Hours: Mon–Sat 9–5 pm (May and Sep);
Mon–Sat 9–5 pm, Sun 1–4 pm (Jun–Aug)

Edmonds Art Festival Museum

700 Main Street
Edmonds, WA 98020
Tel: 425-771-6412

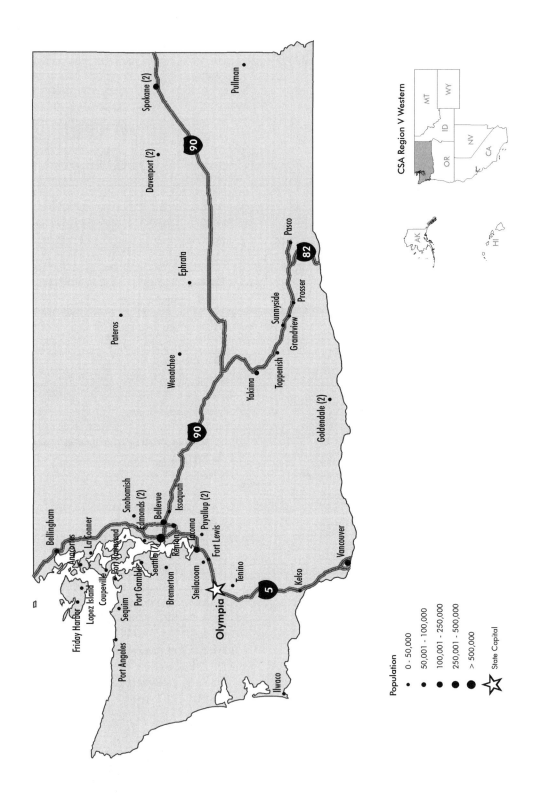

CSA Region V Western

Population
· 0 - 50,000
• 50,001 - 100,000
● 100,001 - 250,000
● 250,001 - 500,000
● > 500,000
☆ State Capital

Edmonds South Snohomish County Historical Society

118 5th Avenue North
Edmonds, WA 98020
Tel: 425-774-0900
www.historicedmonds.org

Grant County Historical Museum

742 Basin Street NW
Ephrata, WA 98823
Tel: 509-754-3334

Fort Lewis Military Museum

Building 4320
Fort Lewis, WA 98433-1001
Tel: 253-967-7206
www.lewis.army.mil/DPTMS/POMFI/
museum.htm

San Juan Historical Society

405 Price Street
Friday Harbor, WA 98250
Tel: 360-378-3949
www.sjmuseum.org

Klickitat County Historical Society

127 West Broadway
Goldendale, WA 98620-0086
Tel: 509-773-4303

Maryhill Museum of Art

35 Maryhill Museum Drive
Goldendale, WA 98620
Tel: 509-773-3733 Fax: 509-773-6138
www.maryhillmuseum.org
Hours: Mon–Sun 9–5 pm (Mar 15–Nov 15)
Institution type: Art museum, historic house
$ 🖾📷
ECCLESIASTICAL COLLECTION
Contact: Betty Long-Schleif
Collection type: General textiles
Description: 1700–1849. Greek Orthodox
Church vestments from Armenia, including
embroidered collars, miters, altar cloths, and
chalice covers.
ROUMANIAN FOLK COSTUME
COLLECTION
Contact: Betty Long-Schleif
Collection type: Clothing, accessories, costumes,
general textiles
Description: 1800–present. First pieces were
donated by Marie, Queen of Roumania, in

1926, consisting of finely embroidered skirts
and dresses of hand-woven linens, headscarves,
and belts of hammered metal. Since that time
additional folk costumes and accessories have
been donated from other Roumanian immigrants. Most of the articles are pre–World War
II, with a distinctive collection worn by
greeters in the Roumanian Pavilion at the 1939
New York World's Fair.
THEATRE DE LA MODE—HAUTE
COUTURE FRENCH FASHION
MANNEQUINS
Contact: Betty Long-Schleif
Collection type: Clothing, accessories
Description: 1940–1950. Twenty-nine-inch wire
mannequins dressed by the famous Parisian
couture fashion houses of 1945–1946. This
miniature collection was established to show
the persistence of French fashion despite four
grueling years of German occupation during
World War II. Designers such as Balenciaga,
Jaques Fath, Madame Gres, and fifty-two
others are placed in nine life-sized theater
decors designed by Cocteau, Christian Berard,
and others.

Ray E. Powell Museum

313 South Division
Grandview, WA 98930
Tel: 509-882-2070

Ilwaco Heritage Museum

115 SE Lake Street
Ilwaco, WA 98624
Tel: 360-642-3446
www.ilwacoheritagemuseum.org

*Roumanian cos-
tume from Oltenia
region, twentieth
century. Courtesy
of Maryhill
Museum of Art.*

Issaquah History Museums

165 SE Andrews and 50 Rainier
    Boulevard North
Issaquah, WA 98027
Tel: 425-392-3500
www.issaquahhistory.org

Cowlitz County Historical Museum

405 Allen Street
Kelso, WA 98626
Tel: 360-577-3119
www.co.cowlitz.wa.us/museum

Skagit County Historical Museum

501 South 4th Street
La Conner, WA 98257-0818
Tel: 360-466-3365
www.skagitcounty.net/museum

Lopez Island Historical Museum

28 Washburn Place, Lopez Village
Lopez Island, WA 98261
Tel: 360-468-3447
www.rockisland.com/~lopezmuseum

Bigelow House Museum

918 Glass Avenue NE
Olympia, WA 98507
Tel: 360-357-6099
www.bigelowhouse.org

Franklin County Historical Museum

305 North 4th Avenue
Pasco, WA 99301
Tel: 509-547-3714

Fort Okanogan Interpretive Center

1B Otto Road
Pateros, WA 98846
Tel: 509-923-2473
www.parks.wa.gov

Clallam County Historical Society

223 East 4th Street
Port Angeles, WA 98362
Tel: 360-452-2662

Port Gamble Historic Museum

3 Rainier Avenue
Port Gamble, WA 98364
Tel: 360-297-8074
www.portgamble.com

Jefferson County Historical Society Museum

540 Water Street
Port Townsend, WA 98368
Tel: 360-385-1003
www.jchsmuseum.org

Benton County Historical Museum

1000 Paterson
Prosser, WA 99350
Tel: 509-786-3842

Washington State University

51 Kruegel Hall
Pullman, WA 99164
Tel: 509-335-7890 Fax: 509-335-7299
http://amdt.wsu.edu
Hours: By appointment
Institution type: University collection

DRUCKER COLLECTION
Contact: Linda Arthur
Collection type: Costumes, general textiles
Description: 1760–present. Minnie Barstow
Drucker Memorial Collection of Oriental Art
consists of 2,300 pieces of Asian textiles, cos-
tume, art, furniture, and accessories dating
2,000 years. Chinese, Korean, and Japanese
artifacts were collected during the years the
Druckers made the Orient their home.

HISTORIC COSTUME AND TEXTILES
COLLECTION
Contact: Linda Arthur
Collection type: Clothing, accessories, costumes,
general textiles, quilts
Description: 1800–present. More than 3,000
items of American textiles and historic
women's, children's, and men's clothing and
accessories from 1835 to the present. Quilts
and woven coverlets and a limited number
(about 200) of ethnic textiles and costumes
from around the world.

Ezra Meeker Mansion

312 Spring Street
Puyallup, WA 98371
Tel: 253-848-1770
www.meekermansion.org

Paul H. Karshner Memorial Museum

309 4th Street NE
Puyallup, WA 98372
Tel: 253-841-8748

Renton Historical Society and Museum

235 Mill Avenue South
Renton, WA 98055-2133
Tel: 425-255-2330
www.rentonhistory.org

Henry Art Gallery

15th Avenue NE and NE 41st Street
University of Washington
Seattle, WA 98195-1410
Tel: 206-543-1739
www.henryart.org

Hours: Tue–Sun 11–5 pm, Thu 11–8 pm

Institution type: Art museum, university collection

$ ✍

ETHNIC COSTUMES AND TEXTILES
COLLECTION

Contact: Judy Sourakli

Collection type: Clothing, costumes, general textiles

Description: Pre-1700–present. Nineteenth- to mid-twentieth-century hand-woven, resist-dyed textiles and hand-printed textiles from India; folk costumes and embroideries from eastern Europe; embroideries, silks, and resist-dyed textiles and garments from East and Southeast Asia; costumes, embroideries, hangings, and rugs from the Middle East and central Asia; hand-woven costumes from Peru, Bolivia, Mexico, and Guatemala; and pre-Columbian textiles.

WESTERN DRESS AND TEXTILES
COLLECTION

Contact: Judy Sourakli

Collection type: Clothing, accessories, costumes, general textiles

Description: Pre-1700–present. Costumes, late eighteenth century to the present; women's, children's, and men's clothing; twentieth-century designer fashions; ecclesiastical vestments and textiles, sixteenth century to nineteenth century; seventeenth- and eighteenth-century Belgian tapestries; lace, including handmade and machine-made examples. Historic costume and fashion collections include Irenee Joshi, Blanche Payne, Guendolen Plestcheeff, and the University of Washington School of Drama Collection.

Memory Lane Museum at Seattle Goodwill

1400 South Lane Street
Seattle, WA 98144
Tel: 206-329-1000
www.seattlegoodwill.org

Hat, TWA flight attendant, circa 1955–59. Courtesy of The Museum of Flight.

The Museum of Flight

9404 East Marginal Way South
Seattle, WA 98108
Tel: 206-764-5700 Fax: 206-764-5707
www.museumofflight.org

Hours: Mon–Sun 10–5 pm

Contact: Dennis Parks, Senior Curator

Institution type: History museum

Collection type: Clothing, accessories, uniforms, flags

Description: 1915–present. U.S. Air Force, Navy, and Army military uniforms from World War I, World War II, and later; accessories such as flight goggles and life jackets; airline uniforms, including flight attendants and pilots from the 1940s until present day from over forty airlines; airline pins, ribbons, and insignia; and a smaller collection of general flight clothing from the 1930s and later.

$ ✍

Museum of History & Industry

2700 24th Avenue East
Seattle, WA 98112
Tel: 206-324-1126 Fax: 206-324-1346
www.seattlehistory.org

Hours: Mon–Sun 10–5 pm

Contact: Mary Montgomery, Curator/Librarian

Institution type: History museum

Collection type: Clothing, accessories, uniforms, costumes, general textiles, flags

Red Cross uniform, circa 1942–45. Courtesy of Museum of History & Industry.

Description: 1850–present. Clothing and textiles used by families in the Pacific Northwest or brought to the area.

$ ✍

Nordic Heritage Museum
3014 NW 67th Street
Seattle, WA 98117
Tel: 206-789-5707
www.nordicmuseum.org

Seattle Art Museum and Asian Art Museum
100 University Street
Seattle, WA 98122-9700
Tel: 206-625-8900
www.seattleartmuseum.org

Wing Luke Asian Museum
407 7th Avenue South
Seattle, WA 98104
Tel: 206-623-5124
www.wingluke.org

Museum and Arts Center in the Sequim Dungeness Valley
175 West Cedar
Sequim, WA 98382
Tel: 360-683-8110
www.sequimmuseum.org

Blackman Museum
118 Avenue B
Snohomish, WA 98290
Tel: 360-568-5235
www.snohomishhistoricalsociety.com/museum.htm
Hours: Sat–Sun 11–3 pm
Institution type: History museum, historic house
✍

Jundt Art Museum
Corner of Pearl Street and Cataldo
Spokane, WA 99258-0001
Tel: 509-323-6611
www.gonzaga.edu

Northwest Museum of Arts and Culture
2316 West 1st Avenue
Spokane, WA 99204
Tel: 509-363-5301 Fax: 509-363-5303
www.northwestmuseum.org
Hours: Tue–Sat 11–5 pm, Sun 12–5 pm
Contact: Laura Thayer, Curator of Collections
Institution type: Art museum, history museum, historic house, state museum
Collection type: Clothing, accessories, uniforms, costumes, general textiles, quilts, flags
Description: 1700–present. Extensive collection of clothing and accessories, primarily for women. North American Indian collection of 2,644 items, primarily from the Pacific Northwest Plateau cultures. Military, nursing, Scouting, Odd Fellow, and Ku Klux Klan uniforms; quilts; coverlets; and flags.
$ ✍

Steilacoom Historical Museum Association
112 Main Street
Steilacoom, WA 98388-0016
Tel: 253-584-4133

Sunnyside Historical Museum
704 South 4th Street
Sunnyside, WA 98944
Tel: 509-837-6010

Washington State History Museum
1911 Pacific Avenue
Tacoma, WA 98403
Tel: 253-798-5914 Fax: 253-597-4186
www.washingtonhistory.org/wshm
Hours: Tue–Sat 10–5 pm, Sun 12–5 pm

Contact: Nancy S. Jackson, Collections Manager
Institution type: History museum, state museum
Collection type: Clothing, accessories, uniforms, costumes, general textiles, quilts, flags
Description: 1851–present. More than 6,000 items. Clothing collection dates predominantly from the late nineteenth and twentieth centuries and includes everyday wear, as well as evening, wedding, and other clothing for special functions. Of importance are large collections of military uniforms and fraternal organization costumes, most notably from the Independent Order of Odd Fellows. In addition, the collection includes artifacts from a millinery shop in Tacoma.

$

Tenino Depot Museum

399 West Park
Tenino, WA 98589
Tel: 360-264-4637

Yakama Nation Cultural Heritage Center and Museum

100 Spilyi Loop
Toppenish, WA 98948
Tel: 509-865-2800

Clark County Historical Museum

1511 Main Street
Vancouver, WA 98660
Tel: 360-993-5679 Fax: 360-993-5683
Hours: Tue–Sat 11–4 pm

Contact: Curator of Collections
Institution type: County museum
Collection type: Clothing, accessories, uniforms, general textiles, quilts
Description: 1800–present. Approximately 25 quilts from 1850 to 1970; several coverlets from 1836 to 1900; Native American woven blankets; military uniforms, due to the proximity of Historic Fort Vancouver and the military barracks; clothing for women and children from circa 1840 to the 1970s as well as hats, shoes, and fine dresses of the period; and Native American buckskin and beadwork.

Wenatchee Valley Museum and Cultural Center

127 South Mission
Wenatchee, WA 98801
Tel: 509-664-3340
www.wenatcheevalleymuseum.com

Yakima Valley Museum and Historical Association

2105 Tieton Drive
Yakima, WA 98902
Tel: 509-248-0747
www.yakimavalleymuseum.org

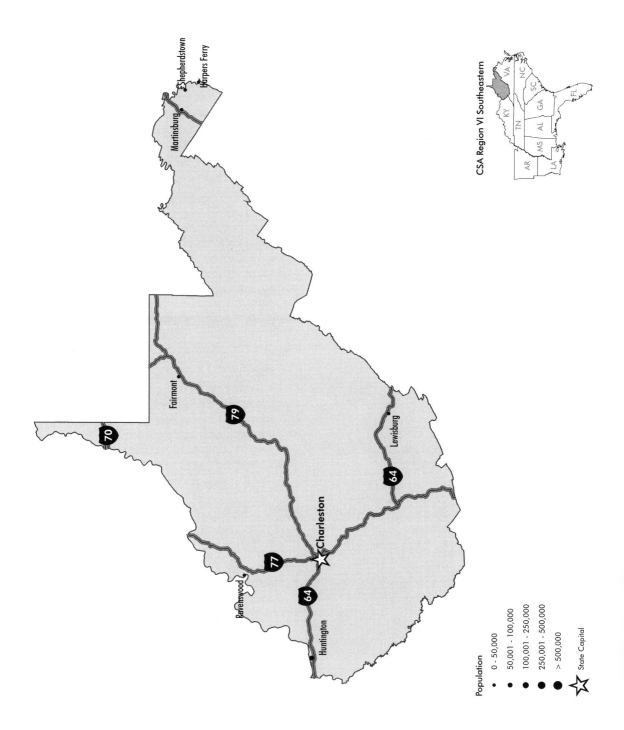

CSA Region VI Southeastern

Shepherdstown
Harpers Ferry
Martinsburg

Fairmont

79

70

Lewisburg

64

Charleston

77

Ravenswood

64

Huntington

Population

· 0 - 50,000
• 50,001 - 100,000
● 100,001 - 250,000
● 250,001 - 500,000
● > 500,000

☆ State Capital

WEST VIRGINIA

West Virginia State Museum

1900 Kanawha Boulevard East
Charleston, WV 25305
Tel: 304-558-0220
www.wvculture.org
Hours: Mon–Thu 9–8 pm, Fri 9–6 pm, Sat–Sun 10–6 pm
Contact: Charles W. Morris III, Director of Collections
Institution type: Art museum, history museum, state museum
Collection type: Clothing, accessories, uniforms, costumes, general textiles, quilts, flags
Description: 1760–present. More than 57,000 artifacts, including personal adornment, military, household treatments, tools and equipment, art, transportation, and natural history items. Textiles include flags, outerwear, undergarments, quilts, uniforms, hats, and shoes. Collection pertains to West Virginia.

Fairmont State University

1201 Locust Avenue
Fairmont, WV 26554
Tel: 304-367-4298 Fax: 304-367-4587
www.fscwv.edu
Hours: Mon–Fri 8–4 pm, call for appointment
Institution type: University collection

HISTORIC TEXTILE BAG COLLECTION
Contact: Beth Newcome

Collection type: Clothing, accessories, general textiles
Description: 1915–present. More than 1,000 artifacts of cotton bags from the original unopened chain stitched bag to a variety of handmade end uses such as clothing and household items. Known as feed sacks, the bags were used to package seeds, grain, flour, corn meal, beans, sugar, and salt. Small bags held tobacco, jacks, or marbles, while large, heavy cotton bags held cement, fertilizer, or hardware.

MASQUER'S HISTORIC COSTUME COLLECTION
Contact: Beth Newcome
Collection type: Clothing, accessories, uniforms
Description: 1800–present. Collection of apparel and accessories contains original garments dating from 1840 to 1970, including men's,

Detail, belt influenced by King Tut discovery, 1920s. Courtesy of Fairmont State University.

women's, and children's clothing and accessories. Of particular interest are 5 maternity dresses from the 1890s. The garments uniquely represent north central West Virginia.

Harpers Ferry National Historical Park

Fillmore Street
Harpers Ferry, WV 25425
Tel: 304-535-6224
www.nps.gov/hafe

Huntington Museum of Art

2033 McCoy Road
Huntington, WV 25701
Tel: 304-529-2701
www.hmoa.org

North House Museum

301 West Washington Street
Lewisburg, WV 24901
Tel: 304-645-3398
www.greenbrierhistorical.org/nhx.html

General Adam Stephen House

309 East John Street
Martinsburg, WV 25402
Tel: 304-267-4434

Washington's Lands Museum and Sayre Log House

200 Henrietta Street
Ravenswood, WV 26164
Tel: 304-273-2961
Hours: Sat–Sun 1–5 pm (May–Oct)
Contact: Ed Rauh
Institution type: History museum, historic house, county museum
Collection type: Clothing, uniforms, quilts
Description: 1800–1914. Clothing, quilts, hooked rugs from the late 1800s, and some military uniforms from the early 1900s.
✍

Historic Shepherdstown Museum

129 East German Street
Shepherdstown, WV 25443
Tel: 304-876-0910

WISCONSIN

Albion Academy Historical Museum
605 Campus Lane
Albion, WI 53534
Tel: 608-884-4809

Langlade County Historical Society Museum
MORRISSEY WEDDING DRESS COLLECTION
404 Superior Street
Antigo, WI 55409
Tel: 715-627-4464
www.langladehistory.com
Hours: Mon–Fri 9:30–3:30 pm, Sat–Sun 10–3 pm
Contact: Barb McPhail
Institution type: County museum
Collection type: Clothing, accessories
Description: 1900–1914. Anna Deleglise was the daughter of the founder of Antigo and a prominent figure in the county's history. Her memorabilia, donated to the museum, includes her wedding dress, shoes, gloves, and letters from her courtship.

🖎

Hearthstone Historic House Museum
625 West Prospect Avenue
Appleton, WI 54911
Tel: 920-730-8204 Fax: 920-730-8266
www.hearthstonemuseum.org
Hours: Tue–Fri 10–3:30 pm, Sat 11–3:30 pm
Contact: Christine Cross
Institution type: Historic house
Collection type: Clothing, accessories, general textiles
Description: 1850–1960. Hearthstone was the first home in the world lit by a hydroelectric central station. Collection focuses on early electricity and domestic life during the late nineteenth century and includes textiles, furniture, tableware, and fine and decorative art.

$ 🖎

Ashland Historical Museum
509 West Main Street
Ashland, WI 54806
Tel: 715-682-4911
www.ashlandhistory.com
Hours: Mon–Fri 10–4 pm, Sat 10–2 pm (Summer)
Contact: Sharon Manthei
Institution type: History museum
Collection type: Clothing, accessories, uniforms, costumes
Description: 1850–present. Clothing worn by residents of Ashland, Wisconsin, on an everyday basis and special occasions (weddings and baptisms); military and professional uniforms; men's, women's, and children's clothing and accessories such as underwear, hats, and shoes; and costumes made for the celebration of the Ashland Centennial in 1954.

$ 🖎

La Pointe

Ashland

Hurley

Fifield

Shell Lake

Lake Tomahawk

Laona

Antigo

Marinette

Egg Harbor

Hudson **94**

Wausau

Eau Claire

Shawano

Marshfield **39**

Oneida

Green Bay (3)

Stevens Point

Waupaca

New London

Kewaunee

King

Appleton

Black River Falls

Wild Rose

Neenah

43

Oshkosh (2)

New Holstein (2)

90

Westfield

Ripon

Greenbush

La Crosse

Mauston

Fond du Lac

Sheboygan

Viroqua

Baraboo (2)

Portage

Mayville (2)

Mazomanie

Beaver Dam

West Bend

Sun Prairie

Menomonee Falls

Oconomowoc

Delafield (2)

Milwaukee (4)

Madison (3) ☆

Waukesha

West Allis

Stoughton

New Berlin

South Milwaukee

Platteville

New Glarus

Albion

Whitewater

Milton

Janesville

Elkhorn

Monroe

Beloit (2)

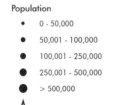

CSA Region III Midwest

ND

MN

SD

MI

NE

IA

IL

IN

OH

MO

Circus World Museum

550 Water Street
Baraboo, WI 53913
Tel: 608-356-8341
www.circusworldmuseum.com

Sauk County Historical Museum

531 4th Avenue
Baraboo, WI 53913
Tel: 608-356-1001
www.saukcounty.com/schs

Dodge County Historical Society Museum

105 Park Avenue
Beaver Dam, WI 53916
Tel: 920-887-1266

Beloit Historical Society

845 Hackett Street
Beloit, WI 53511
Tel: 608-365-7835
www.ticon.net/~beloiths

Wright Museum of Art

700 College Street
Beloit, WI 53511
Tel: 608-363-2347 Fax: 608-363-2248
www.beloit.edu/~museum/wright/index.htm
Hours: Tue–Sun 11–4 pm
Contact: Nicolette Meister, Collections Manager
Institution type: Art museum, university museum
Collection type: Clothing
Description: 1700–1914. Chinese Imperial robes, including dragon robes, 100 butterfly robes, jackets, pants, shoes, and hats.

Jackson County Historical Society

13 South 1st Street and 321 Main Street
Black River Falls, WI 54615-0037
Tel: 715-284-4927

Hawks Inn Historical Society

426 Wells Street
Delafield, WI 53018
Tel: 262-646-4794
www.hawksinn.org

St. John's Northwestern Military Academy

1101 North Genesee Street
Delafield, WI 53018

Tel: 262-646-7155
www.sjnma.org
Hours: By appointment
Contact: L. Ahlgren
Institution type: Private museum
Collection type: Clothing, uniforms, flags
Description: 1850–present. Collection represents the histories of St. John's Military Academy and Northwestern Military and Naval Academy through uniforms, caps, accessories, and athletic wear worn from 1884 to the present. Each school's flags, banners, and pennants are also housed at the museum.

Paul Bunyon Logging Camp

1110 Carson Park Drive
Eau Claire, WI 54702
Tel: 715-835-6200
www.cvmuseum.com

Cupola House

7836 Egg Harbor Road
Egg Harbor, WI 54209
Tel: 800-871-1871
www.cupolahouse.com

Webster House Museum

9 East Rockwell
Elkhorn, WI 53121
Tel: 262-273-4248
www.geocities.com/walcohistory/museum.html

Old Town Hall Museum

W7213 Pine Street
Fifield, WI 54524
Tel: 715-762-4571

Galloway House and Village

336 Old Pioneer Road
Fond du Lac, WI 54935
Tel: 920-922-0991
www.fdl.com/history
Hours: Mon–Sun 10–4 pm
Contact: Mary E. Chancellor
Institution type: Art museum, history museum, historic house, county museum
Collection type: Clothing, accessories, uniforms, costumes, general textiles, flags
Description: 1760–present. Shoes, clothing, and accessories from the Pettibone family, obtained from Paris and specifically made for the daugh-

Shoes, circa 1880s. Courtesy of Galloway House and Museum, Fond du Lac Historical Society.

ters who were friends of the Galloways. Most items are from the 1890s; oldest artifact is a pair of shoes from circa 1790, and the newest is a 1970 wedding gown. Collection kept to local significance, but because the Galloways toured extensively in Europe, there are some unusual jewelry and shoes from outside Fond du Lac.

$ ✍️

Green Bay Packer Hall of Fame
855 Lombardi Avenue
Green Bay, WI 54307
Tel: 920-499-4281

Heritage Hill State Park
2640 South Webster Avenue
Green Bay, WI 54301
Tel: 920-448-5150x10
www.heritagehillgb.org

Neville Public Museum of Brown County
210 Museum Place
Green Bay, WI 54303
Tel: 920-448-4460 Fax: 920-448-4458
www.nevillepublicmuseum.org
Hours: Vary
Contact: Louise Pfotenhauer
Institution type: Art museum, history museum, county museum
Collection type: Clothing, accessories, uniforms, costumes, general textiles, flags
Description: Pre-1700–present

$ ✍️

Wade House Stagecoach Inn and Wesley Jung Carriage Museum State Historic Site
W7747 Plank Road
Greenbush, WI 53026
Tel: 920-526-3271
www.wisconsinhistory.org/wadehouse

The Octagon House
1004 3rd Street
Hudson, WI 54016
Tel: 715-386-2654

Old Iron County Courthouse Museum
303 Iron Street
Hurley, WI 54534
Tel: 715-561-2244

Rock County Historical Society
426 North Jackson Street
Janesville, WI 53545
Tel: 608-756-4509 Fax: 608-741-9596
www.rchs.us
Hours: Mon–Fri 9–4 pm
Contact: Melissa de Bie, Collections Manager
Institution type: History museum, county museum
Collection type: Accessories, uniforms, costumes
Description: 1850–1960
✍️

Kewaunee County Historical Museum
Court House Square
Kewaunee, WI 54216
Tel: 920-388-7176
www.rootsweb.com/~wikewaun

Wisconsin Veterans Museum—King
Wisconsin Veterans Home
N2665 County Road QQ
King, WI 54946
Tel: 608-266-1009

LaCrosse County Historical Society, Hixon House
429 North 7th Street
LaCrosse, WI 54601
Tel: 608-782-1980

Northland Historical Society
7245 Kelly Drive
Lake Tomahawk, WI 54539
Tel: 715-277-3146

Camp Five Museum Foundation

5480 Connor Farm Road
Laona, WI 54541
Tel: 715-674-3414
www.camp5museum.org

Madeline Island Historical Museum

Woods Avenue and Main Street
La Pointe, WI 54850
Tel: 715-747-2415

Suffrage tunic, 1916. Courtesy of State Historical Society of Wisconsin.

State Historical Society of Wisconsin

816 State Street
Madison, WI 53706-1482
Tel: 608-264-6551
www.wisconsinhistory.org
Hours: Mon–Thu 8–9 pm, Fri–Sat 8–5 pm
Contact: Leslie Bellais
Institution type: State museum
Collection type: Clothing, accessories, uniforms, costumes, general textiles, flags
Description: 1800–present.

University of Wisconsin, School of Human Ecology

HELEN LOUISE ALLEN TEXTILE
COLLECTION
1300 Linden Drive
Madison, WI 53706
Tel: 608-262-1162
http://sohe.wisc.edu/depts/hlatc
Hours: Mon–Thu 8–9 pm, Fri–Sat 8–5 pm
Contact: Mary Ann Fitzgerald, Curator
Institution type: University museum

Collection type: Clothing, accessories, costumes, general textiles, quilts
Description: Pre-1700–present. Pre-Columbian and Coptic archeological textiles. Other major holdings are nineteenth-century American and European coverlets, quilts, and needlework, and a sub-collection of ethnographic textiles with strengths in South and Southeast Asia, Latin America, and Turkey.

Wisconsin Veterans Museum

300 West Mifflin Street
Madison, WI 53706-1482
Tel: 608-267-1799

Marinette County Historical Museum

Stephenson Island
U.S. Highway 41
Marinette, WI 54143
Tel: 715-732-0831

Upham Mansion

212 West 3rd
Marshfield, WI 54449
Tel: 715-387-3322

The Boorman House

211 North Union Street
Mauston, WI 53948
Tel: 608-462-5931

Hollenstein Wagon and Carriage Factory Museum

1 North German Street
Mayville, WI 53050
Tel: 920-387-5233
www.mayvillecity.com/organizations/historical
_society.html
Hours: 2nd and 4th Sun 1:30–4:30 pm
(May–Oct), and by appointment
Contact: Ann Guse
Institution type: History museum, city museum
Collection type: Clothing, accessories, uniforms, quilts, flags
Description: 1850–1960. Wedding dresses, 1890s–1940s; women's clothing, late 1800s–1940s; women's and men's hats; quilts; and military uniforms from the Spanish-American War to the Vietnam War.

Mayville Historical Society

1 North German Street
Mayville, WI 53050
Tel: 920-387-2420
www.mayvillecity.com

Mazomanie Historical Society

118 Brodhead Street
Mazomanie, WI 53560
Tel: 608-795-2992
Hours: 8 hours weekly (Memorial Day–Labor Day), and by appointment
Contact: Rita Frabs, Curator
Institution type: History museum
Collection type: Clothing, accessories, uniforms, costumes, general textiles, flags
Description: 1850–present. Predominately women's dress. Collection also contains underwear; accessories, including purses, hankies, hats, gloves, belts, parasols, shoes, and stockings; men's clothing, mainly circa 1900; military, school, and band uniforms; infant and children's clothing; and bed and table linens and doilies.

Old Falls Village

156 North 8480 Pilgrim Road
Menomonee Falls, WI 53051
Tel: 262-532-4775
www.oldfallsvillage.com

Milton House Museum Historic Site

18 South Janesville Street, Highways 26 and 59
Milton, WI 53563
Tel: 608-868-7772
www.miltonhouse.org

The International Clown Hall of Fame and Research Center

161 West Wisconsin Avenue, Suite LL700
Milwaukee, WI 53203
Tel: 414-319-0848

Milwaukee County Historical Society

910 North Old World 3rd Street
Milwaukee, WI 53203
Tel: 414-273-8288
www.milwaukeecountyhistsoc.org

Milwaukee Public Museum

800 West Wells Street
Milwaukee, WI 53233
Tel: 414-278-2797 Fax: 414-278-6100
www.mpm.edu
Hours: Mon–Sun 9–5 pm
Contact: Ann Horwitz
Institution type: County museum
Collection type: Clothing, uniforms, costumes, quilts
Description: 1800–present. More than 21,000 costumes and accessories with worldwide scope from 1810 to 2000. Collection also contains uniforms. Strengths are American women's wear, 1870–1920; European folk costumes; and quilts.

$ ✍

Gown by Bruyere, worn by the Incomparable Hildegarde, 1949. Courtesy of Mount Mary College Historic Costume Collection.

Mount Mary College

HISTORIC COSTUME COLLECTION
2900 North Menomonee River Parkway
Milwaukee, WI 53222
Tel: 414-256-0164
www.mtmary.edu/fashion_historic.htm
Hours: Mon–Fri 10–4 pm
Contact: Elizabeth Gaston
Institution type: University collection
Collection type: Clothing, accessories, uniforms, costumes
Description: 1750–present. 9,000 items with primary focus on women's twentieth-century garments. Accessories include hats (800), gloves, and shoes. Collection also contains personal

garments of Lynn Fontanne, an Anglo-American stage actress. The Hildegarde Collection includes performance gowns and day wear of the chanteuse Hildegarde, who was active from 1933 to 1980. The Valentina Collection contains objects from the personal wardrobe of the Russian-American designer Valentina. The Kleibacker Collection houses gowns collected by the American designer Charles Kleibacker.

Green County Historical Society
1617 9th Street
Monroe, WI 53566
Tel: 608-325-3542
Hours: By appointment
Contact: Bobette Traul
Institution type: History museum
Collection type: Clothing, accessories, uniforms, costumes
Description: 1850–1960. Items from local residents. A nice collection of "picture hats" includes wedding hats and silk, fur, beaver, and horsehair hats and is particularly strong in late-nineteenth- and early-twentieth-century styles. Collection also features women's, men's, and children's clothing, accessories, and underwear; military uniforms from World War I and World War II; and men's suits.

Hiram Smith Octagon House
343 Smith Street
Neenah, WI 54956
Tel: 920-725-4160

The New Berlin Historical Society
19765 West National Avenue
New Berlin, WI 53146
Tel: 262-542-4773

Swiss Historical Village
612 7th Avenue
New Glarus, WI 53574
Tel: 608-527-2317
www.swisshistoricalvillage.com

Calumet County Historical Society
1704 Eisenhower Street
New Holstein, WI 53061
Tel: 920-898-1333

Pioneer Corner Museum
2103 Main Street
New Holstein, WI 53061
Tel: 920-898-5258

New London Public Museum
406 South Pearl Street
New London, WI 54961
Tel: 920-982-8520
www.newlondonwi.org/museum.htm

Oconomowoc Historical Society
103 West Jefferson Street
Oconomowoc, WI 53066
Tel: 262-569-0740
www.oconomowoc.org/Library/Outreach.htm

Oneida Nations Museum
W892 County Trunk EE
Oneida, WI 54155
Tel: 920-869-2768
www.oneidanation.org/?page_id=63

Oshkosh Public Museum
1331 Algoma Boulevard
Oshkosh, WI 54901
Tel: 920-424-4733 Fax: 920-424-4738
www.publicmuseum.oshkosh.net
Hours: Tue–Sat 10–4:30 pm, Sun 12–4:30 pm, and by appointment
Contact: Debra G. Daubert
Institution type: City museum
Collection type: Clothing, accessories, uniforms, costumes, general textiles, flags
Description: 1760–present. Embroidered frock coat, horsehair bonnets, a petticoat, an eighteenth-century corset, military clothing, Native American apparel, and masons' aprons. Majority of the items have connections to the local area or the Wisconsin region.

Paine Art Center and Gardens
1410 Algoma Boulevard
Oshkosh, WI 54901
Tel: 920-235-6903
www.thepaine.org

Rollo Jamison Museum
405 East Main Street
Platteville, WI 53818
Tel: 608-348-3301
www.platteville.org

Historic Indian Agency House
Rustic Road 69
Portage, WI 53901
Tel: 608-742-6362
www.nscda.org/museums/wisconsin.htm
Hours: Mon–Sun 10–4 pm (May 15–Oct 15)
Contact: Executive Director
Institution type: History museum, historic house
Collection type: Clothing, accessories, general textiles, quilts
Description: 1800–1899. Historic house was built in 1832. Quilts and bedding, clothing and accessories, carpets, curtains circa 1833, and a few pieces from 1830 to the 1880s.

$ ✍

Little White Schoolhouse
303 Blackburn Street
Ripon, WI 54971
Tel: 920-748-6784
www.ripon-wi.com

Shawano County Historical Society
524 North Franklin Street
Shawano, WI 54166
Tel: 715-524-4981

John Michael Kohler Arts Center
608 New York Avenue
Sheboygan, WI 53801
Tel: 920-458-6144
www.jmkac.org

Washburn County Historical Society Museum
102 West 2nd Avenue
Shell Lake, WI 54871
Tel: 715-468-2982

South Milwaukee Historical Society Museum
717 Milwaukee Avenue
South Milwaukee, WI 53172
Tel: 414-762-8852
www.southmilwaukee.org/historical_society/historic.htm

Portage County Historical Society
1475 Water Street
Stevens Point, WI 54481
www.pchswi.org

Stoughton Historical Society
324 South Page Street
Stoughton, WI 53589
Tel: 608-873-3162

Sun Prairie Historical Library and Museum
115 East Main Street
Sun Prairie, WI 53590
Tel: 608-837-2511
www.sun-prairie.com

Vernon County Museum
410 South Center Street
Viroqua, WI 54665
Tel: 608-637-7396
www.frontiernet.net/~vcmuseum
Hours: Mon–Sat 12–4 pm (mid-May–mid-Sep); Tue–Thu 12–4 pm (mid-Sep–mid-May)
Contact: Judy Mathison
Institution type: History museum, county museum
Collection type: Clothing, accessories, uniforms, general textiles, flags
Description: 1850–present. Mainly women's clothing and some military uniforms, wedding dresses, and baptismal items.

✍

Waukesha County Historical Society and Museum
101 West Main Street
Waukesha, WI 53186
Tel: 262-521-2859
www.waukeshacountymuseum.org

Holly History Center and Hutchinson House Museum
321 South Main Street
Waupaca, WI 54981
Tel: 715-256-9980
www.waupacahistory.org
Hours: Holly History Center: Wed–Fri 12–3 pm, Sat 9–12 pm; Hutchinson House: Sat–Sun 1–4 pm
Contact: Julie Hintz, Director, Waupaca Historical Society

Institution type: History museum, historic house, city museum

Collection type: Clothing, accessories, uniforms, general textiles, quilts, flags

Description: 1850–1960. Civil War clothing; Victorian women's blouses and walking suits, 1875–1900; vintage wedding gowns; dresses, 1900–1920; infant and children's clothing; women's and children's mourning clothing; 1920s clothing; 1940s–1950s dresses and hats; men's and women's hats; handbags and purses; men's clothing and military uniforms; gloves, shawls, and leather shoes; laces and beadwork; and quilts and bed and table linens.

$ 🖊️

Marathon County Historical Society

410 McIndoe Street
Wausau, WI 54403
Tel: 715-842-5750
www.marathoncountyhistory.com

West Allis Historical Society Museum

8405 West National Avenue
West Allis, WI 53227
Tel: 414-541-6970

Washington County Historical Society

320 South 5th Avenue
West Bend, WI 53095-3333
Tel: 414-335-4678
www.historyisfun.com

Marquette County Historical Society

125 Lawrence Street
Westfield, WI 53964

Whitewater Historical Museum

275 North Tratt Street
Whitewater, WI 53190
Tel: 414-473-2966

Pioneer Museum

State Highway 22
Wild Rose, WI 54984
Tel: 920-622-4355

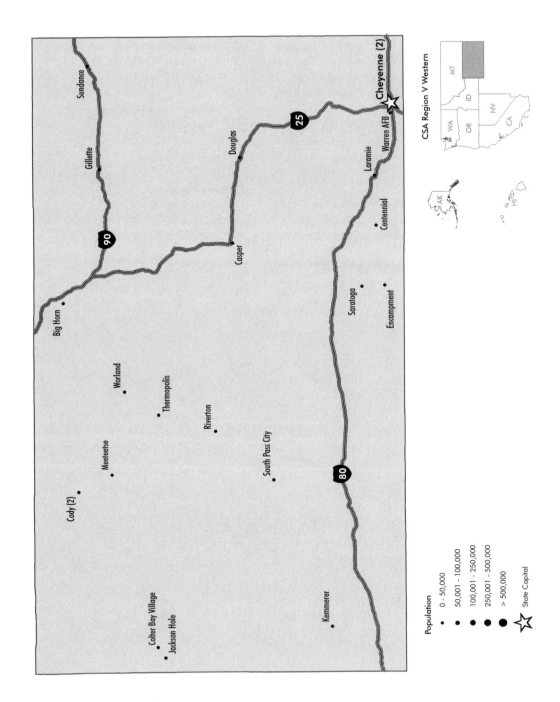

Population

. 0 - 50,000

• 50,001 - 100,000

● 100,001 - 250,000

● 250,001 - 500,000

● > 500,000

☆ State Capital

CSA Region V Western

WYOMING

Bradford Brinton Memorial and Museum

239 Brinton Road
Big Horn, WY 82833
Tel: 307-672-3173
www.bradfordbrintonmemorial.com

Fort Caspar Museum and Historic Site

4001 Fort Caspar Road
Casper, WY 82604
Tel: 307-235-8462
www.fortcasparwyoming.com

Nici Self Museum

2740 State Highway 130
Centennial, WY 82055
Tel: 307-742-7763
Hours: Fri–Mon 1–4 pm (mid-Jun–Labor Day)
Contact: Jim Chase, President
Institution type: History museum
Collection type: Clothing, accessories, uniforms
Description: 1850–1960. Museum's limited
clothing and accessories include 1 World War I
uniform, 2 dresses, coats, and a few shoes and
accessories.

✍

Cheyenne Frontier Days Old West Museum

4610 North Carey Avenue
Cheyenne, WY 82003
Tel: 307-778-7290
www.oldwestmuseum.org

Dress, circa 1910. Courtesy of the Wyoming State Museum.

Wyoming State Museum

2301 Central Avenue
Cheyenne, WY 82002
Tel: 307-777-7022 Fax: 307-777-5375
http://wyomuseum.state.wy.us
Hours: Tue–Sat 9–4:30 pm (May–Oct); Tue–Fri
9–4:30 pm, Sat 10–2 pm (Nov–Apr)
Contact: Jennifer Alexander, Jim Allison
Institution type: History museum, state museum
Collection type: Clothing, accessories, uniforms
Description: 1851–present. More than 2,000 arti-
facts, including outerwear, underwear, head-
wear, footwear, and clothing accessories.
Strengths are early-twentieth-century women's
clothing and men's military uniforms.

✍

Buffalo Bill's fringed buckskin coat, circa 1870s. Courtesy of Buffalo Bill Historical Center.

Buffalo Bill Historical Center

720 Sheridan Avenue
Cody, WY 82414
Tel: 307-587-4771
www.bbhc.org
Hours: Vary by season
Contact: Juti A. Winchester
Institution type: History museum, art museum
Collection type: Clothing, accessories, uniforms, costumes, flags
Description: 1800–present. Clothing and accoutrements that belonged to William F. Cody, his family, friends, and employees; costumes worn by Buffalo Bill's Wild West Show cast members; items connected to William F. Cody and family; and items from Cody, Wyoming, history.

$ ✍🏻

Plains Indian Museum

720 Sheridan Avenue
Cody, WY 82414
Tel: 307-587-4771
www.bbhc.org/pim
Hours: Vary by season
Contact: Emma Hansen, Curator
Institution type: History museum, art museum
Collection type: Clothing, accessories
Description: Pre-1700–present. Large collection of Plains Indian art and artifacts includes clothing of the Crow, Lakota Sioux, Cheyenne, and other Plains Indian tribes. Plains Indian

Museum tells the stories of Plains Native people as they have moved from their buffalo hunting past to the living traditions of the present.

$ ✍🏻

Colter Bay Visitor Center and Indian Arts Museum

Grand Teton National Park
Colter Bay Village, WY 83012
Tel: 307-739-3594
www.nps.gov/grte
Institution type: History museum

Wyoming Pioneer Memorial Museum

400 West Center Street
Douglas, WY 82633
Tel: 307-358-9288
www.wyshs.org/mus-wypioneer.htm

Grand Encampment Museum

807 Barnett Avenue
Encampment, WY 82325
Tel: 307-327-5308

Warren ICBM and Heritage Museum

7405 Marne Loop, Building 210
Francis E. Warren Air Force Base, WY 82005
Tel: 307-773-2980
www.pawnee.com/fewmuseum

Campbell County Rockpile Museum

900 West 2nd Street
Gillette, WY 82716
Tel: 307-682-5723 Fax: 307-686-8528
Hours: Mon–Sat 9–5 pm
Contact: Karen Barlow
Institution type: County museum
Collection type: Clothing, accessories, uniforms, general textiles, quilts, flags
Description: 1850–present. Clothing used by citizens of northeast Wyoming from the late 1800s until the present. Everyday work clothes to wedding and baptismal gowns. Also featured are handmade quilts of local interest and military uniforms from World War I and World War II.

✍🏻

Jackson Hole Historical Society and Museum

105 North Glenwood
Jackson Hole, WY 83001
Tel: 307-733-2414
www.jacksonholehistory.org

Fossil Country Frontier Museum

400 Pine Avenue
Kemmerer, WY 83101
Tel: 307-877-6551
www.hamsfork.net/~museum

Wyoming Territorial Park

975 Snowy Range Road
Laramie, WY 82070
Tel: 307-745-3733
www.wyoprisonpark.org/prisonmuseum.htm

Meeteetse Museums

1003 Park Avenue
Meeteetse, WY 82433
Tel: 307-868-2423
www.meeteetsemuseum.org

Riverton Museum

700 East Park Avenue
Riverton, WY 82501
Tel: 307-856-2665
www.wyoming.com/~rivmus

Saratoga Museum

104 Constitution Avenue
Saratoga, WY 82331
Tel: 307-326-5511

South Pass City State Historic Site

125 South Pass Main
South Pass City, WY 82520
Tel: 307-777-6323
http://wyoparks.state.wy.us/spcslide.htm

Crook County Museum and Art Gallery

309 Cleveland Street
Sundance, WY 82729
Tel: 307-283-3666
www.wyshs.org/mus-crookcty.htm

Dancing Bear Folk Center

119 South 6th
Thermopolis, WY 82443
Tel: 307-864-3391 Fax: 307-864-3582
www.dancingbear.org
Hours: Mon–Sun 9–5 pm (May 15–Sep 15);
10–4 pm (Sep 16–May 14)
Contact: Ellen Sue Blakey
Institution type: City museum
Collection type: General textiles, quilts
Description: 1800–present. Feedsack collection
includes feedsacks, bags, and usage (dolls,
clothing, linens), 1870s–1950s. Center also
holds American handwoven bedcoverings,
including jacquards, overshots, and other
weaving, as well as quilt blocks, miniature and
doll quilts, and household textiles.
$ ✍

Washakie Museum

1115 Obie Sue Avenue
Worland, WY 82401
Tel: 307-347-4102
Institution type: Art museum, history museum
Hours: Mon–Sat 10–4 pm
✍

MEET THE EDITORS

SALLY A. QUEEN is the director and founder of America's Closets, a project of her business, Sally Queen and Associates.

The mission of Sally Queen and Associates is making connections to historic cloth and clothing. Ms. Queen's specialty is eighteenth-century dress and appearance at history sites in America. Before moving to the Washington, DC, area, Ms. Queen was the manager of the Costume Design Center at Colonial Williamsburg.

Ms. Queen is the author of *Textiles for Colonial Clothing,* a workbook of swatches and information on textiles for eighteenth-century clothing. Her company publishes three additional workbooks, *Textiles for Regency Clothing, Textiles for Early Victorian Clothing,* and *Textiles for Victorian and Edwardian Clothing.* She is also the founder and editor of the Historic Fashions Calendar Series, the foundation publication for Costume Society of America's book series. Honors include selection as a Costume Society of America Fellow and Who's Who of American Professional Women.

VICKI L. BERGER is the director of the Arizona Historical Society Museum at Papago Park in Tempe and a faculty member of the American Association of State and Local History.

As director of one of the seven museums of the Arizona Historical Society, Dr. Berger oversees a museum staff of twelve who are responsible for research, exhibitions, and programming related to recent central Arizona history.

Before moving to Arizona, Dr. Berger served as Curator of Costume and Textiles and Collections Management Section Chief at the North Carolina Museum of History, where she curated exhibitions, gave presentations, and served on the senior management team. She also taught Introduction to Museology, a graduate level public history course at North Carolina State University.

Dr. Berger earned her bachelor of science degree in fashion merchandising and promotion and master of science degree in historic costume and textiles from the University of Arizona. She earned a PhD in historic costume and textiles from Florida State University. In addition to her teaching and museum experiences, Dr. Berger is active in professional societies and non-profit groups.

ABOUT CSA

FOUNDED IN 1973, the Costume Society of America (CSA) is an international organization devoted to the study of dress. The primary role of the organization is to encourage and support scholarship and its dissemination through research papers and publications. The society functions to raise the profile and credibility of studies in all aspects of dress or fashion.

Representing a broad diversity of backgrounds and professions, CSA members share an abiding appreciation for the study and interpretation of clothing, its creation, and its history. Combining the interests of educators, researchers, curators, collectors, designers, and much more, the CSA sustains vital links across the public and private sectors from museums and libraries to performing arts and the apparel industry.

CSA members enjoy participation in active regional chapters and in a national symposium. They also receive copies of Dress (a peer-reviewed journal of scholarly articles), the CSA Membership Directory, and electronic and print newsletters. The organization sponsors numerous grants and awards for students, scholars, and authors, as well as for their publications, museum exhibitions, and small collections.

CSA also promotes the publication of important information, and this guide is just one example. It may help you locate period pieces of clothing for study, exhibition, or as a source of inspiration for a new design or reproduction piece.

CSA invites you to become an active and valued member. Further details can be found at www.costumesocietyamerica.com or by calling 1-800-CSA-9447. Let us hear from you.